DEFINING DOCUMENTS
IN AMERICAN HISTORY

The Emergence of Modern America

(1874-1917)

DEFINING DOCUMENTS
IN AMERICAN HISTORY

The Emergence of Modern America (1874-1917)

Editor

Michael Shally-Jensen, PhD

SALEM PRESS
A Division of EBSCO Information Services
Ipswich, Massachusetts

GREY HOUSE PUBLISHING

Library of Congress Cataloging-in-Publication Data

The emergence of modern America (1874-1917) / editor, Michael Shally-Jensen, PhD
Jensen, PhD. -- [First edition].

   pages ; cm. -- (Defining documents in American history)

   Edition statement supplied by publisher.
   Includes bibliographical references and index.
   ISBN: 978-1-61925-489-3

   1. United States--History--1865-1921--Sources. 2. United States--Economic conditions--1865-1918--Sources. 3. United States--Social conditions--1865-1918--Sources. 4. United States--Foreign relations--1865-1921--Sources. 5. Working class--United States--History--Sources. 6. Minorities--United States--History--Sources. I. Shally-Jensen, Michael.

E661 .E447 2014
973.8

Table of Contents

The End of the Frontier and the Start of a New Era

Labor Pains

The Lives of Workers

Capital Concerns

Conflicts Farther Afield

Minorities and Mistreatments

Women, Suffrage, and Society

Reformers and Remedies

A TECHNOLOGICAL BREAKTHROUGH

APPENDIXES

Publisher's Note

Defining Documents in American History series, produced by Salem Press, consists of a collection of essays on important historical documents by a diverse range of writers on a broad range of subjects in American history. *Defining Documents in American History: The Emergence of Modern America* (1874-1917) surveys key documents produced during this period – organized under nine broad categories:

- The End of the Frontier and the Start of a New Era
- Labor Pains
- The Lives of Workers
- Capital Concerns
- Conflicts Further Afield
- Minorities and Mistreatments
- Women, Suffrage, and Society
- Reformers and Remedies
- A Technological Breakthrough

Historical documents provide a compelling view of this unique period of American history. Designed for high school and college students, the aim of the series is to advance historical document studies as an important activity in learning about history.

Essay Format

The Emergence of Modern America contains 49 primary source documents – many in their entirety. Each document is supported by a critical essay, written by historians and teachers, that includes a Summary Overview, Defining Moment, Author Biography, Document Analysis, and Essential Themes. Readers will appreciate the diversity of the collected texts, including journals, letters, speeches, political sermons, laws, government reports, and court cases, among other genres. An important feature of each essays is a close reading of the primary source that develops evidence of broader themes, such as author's rhetorical purpose, social or class position, point of view, and other relevant issues. In addition, essays are organized by section themes, listed above, highlighting major issues in the period, many of which extend across eras and continue to shape American life. Each section begins with a brief introduction that will explain the questions and problems underlying the subjects in the historical documents. A brief glossary included at the end of most documents highlights keywords important in the study of the primary source. Each essay also includes a Bibliography and Additional Reading section for further research.

Appendixes

- **Chronological List** of all documents by year.
- **Web Resources** is an annotated list of web sites that offer valuable supplemental resources.
- **Bibliography** lists helpful articles and books for further study.

Contributors

Salem Press would like to extend its appreciation to all involved in the development and production of this work. The essays have been written and signed by scholars of history, humanities, and other disciplines related to the essay's topics. Without these expert contributions, a project of this nature would not be possible. A full list of contributor's names and affiliations appears in the front matter of this volume.

Editor's Introduction

Although there are some differences of opinion among historians on the matter, most would agree that the range of years forming the core of the present work, the 1880s through the 1910s, represents not one but two identifiable historical periods: the Gilded Age and the Progressive Era. The Gilded Age, so-named because an 1873 novel by Charles Dudley Warner and Mark Twain, *The Gilded Age: A Tale of Today*, seemed to capture the spirit of the times, ran roughly from the end of Reconstruction (mid-1870s) through the decade of the 1880s. Some would include most of the 1890s, as well. The Progressive Era, on the other hand, which takes its name from the prominence of social and political reform efforts during that period, is generally regarded as extending from the early 1890s to about 1920. Again, different historians would make different adjustments on either side of the range of years comprising these eras, but it is safe to say that the two together spanned the time between Reconstruction and World War I (including, some would say, the postwar years).

Dealing with the two periods together is a useful undertaking, because there was considerable continuity between them and, besides, the notion of historical periods or eras (or "periodization," as it is called) refers not to the experience of the people living in these years but rather to a set of dynamics, problems, and solutions that researchers have identified as characteristic of the time. The years covered in this volume were years in which the world indeed saw the emergence of modern America through its creation of large-scale industrial enterprises, its welcoming of masses of immigrants, its imperialistic tendencies abroad (aimed at ensuring markets and gaining power), and its social, political, and economic reform efforts aimed at reducing poverty and inequality and making the nation a fairer and more representative place.

The Gilded Age (and After)

Much of the industrial growth that gave birth to the Gilded Age was centered on the expansion of the railroads. Not only did the railroads themselves employ huge numbers of people—more than any other industry up to that time—but various industries associated with the building of railroads did likewise. Iron and steel factories rose up to supply the hardware used in laying track and constructing locomotive engines and cars. Coal plants and oil refineries grew in response to the need for fuel. Electric power lines spread out from the main cities, often along rail lines, and were later used as a source of power for commuter trains. And, as somebody had to finance it all, banks and the banking industry grew rapidly, as well. Industrial growth occurred in other, unrelated areas, too, such as the garment industry, agriculture, construction, and machinery manufacturing. Many have referred to the technological progress that took place then as the Second Industrial Revolution.

With such massive growth came great wealth for the individuals, corporations, and family dynasties that owned these works. Men like Jay Gould, Andrew Carnegie, Henry Clay Frick, Cornelius Vanderbilt, James Hill, J. P. Morgan, John D. Rockefeller, and Leland Stanford made vast fortunes during this period. Benefitting, too, were the politicians and middlemen who lubricated the wheels of the system and facilitated the business expansion. The somewhat cynical label "Gilded Age," after all, was meant by its authors to suggest a fancy façade hiding an ugly reality beneath, one where corruption, bribes, kickbacks, and thuggish pressure techniques were commonplace. When, for example, a shady land deal was arranged to support railroad expansion, the owners of the railroad, along with their bankers and political backers, could be fairly certain that they would come out ahead, even if the deal soured and led to bankruptcy of the business because, with the proper payoffs in place, a federal bailout of one type or another would likely be forthcoming. There was more than one way to get rich during the Gilded Age.

Equally characteristic of the era was the great increase in immigrants arriving on U.S. shores. Before 1890, most of the new arrivals were from the countries of Northern and Western Europe—principally England, Ireland, Germany, and Scandinavia. The year 1882 was a peak year: about 750,000 immigrants. Even then, a portion of the new arrivals were from Southern and Eastern Europe—Italy, Greece, Portugal, Hungary, Russia, and Romania—numbers that only increased after 1890. On average some 350,000 immigrants per year arrived in the United States. During the decade between 1901 and 1910, some 8.5 million new immigrants arrived, most of them from Southern and Eastern Europe. Employers in the major urban centers of the north welcomed them.

However, there was another ugliness lurking in the

shadows in this period: the conditions faced by the immigrant workers and their families. The work week was long (50 to 60 hours), the pay was minimal, the benefits nonexistent, and there were no protections in place in the event of injuries or layoffs (both of which were fairly common). Employers hired and fired workers as they saw fit, based on the business cycle; and sometimes they adjusted workers' pay to reflect ups and downs in the same cycle. Labor unions, such as they were, were young and had yet to make any headway in building networks of union members and union shops. When necessary, business owners might hire gangs of special agents to break up workers' strikes or shield their factories against union activity.

On the home front, inside ethnic districts within the cities, life could be equally ugly. Childhood labor was prevalent, and school attendance was dismal. While older children might work in factories, younger children worked either in factories or in various "home industries." In general, the tenement buildings in which these young people and their families lived and worked embodied the idea of squalor. Most were unsafe and unsanitary. They were jam-packed with human beings—kids routinely sleeping three and four to a bunk. The psychological impact on children was troublesome, as well, as they and their parents and relatives coexisted throughout much of the day in small quarters, sleeping, eating, laboring, and so on, to make ends meet. The roots of the Progressive Era that followed were planted in the 1890s when reformers such as Jane Addams sought to address these kinds of urban social ills.

Populism

One response to the economic growth in the cities, and to the political and financial arrangements lying behind that growth, was what came to be known as the Populist movement. The Populists represented a loose coalition of farmers' alliances, labor groups, utopian idealists, and middle-class reformers who wanted a new approach to doing business. They objected to the prevailing philosophies of laissez-faire and Social Darwinism—"survival of the fittest"—and argued that more could be done to make society just and equitable. To that end they founded the People's Party, also known as the Populist Party, in 1891 in Cincinnati, Ohio. Populism was, in essence, an agrarian, Midwest protest movement, but one that found strong interest and participation elsewhere in the country.

Unlike today's Tea Party, which is sometimes compared to the Populist movement, the original members of the People's Party sought an increase, not a reduction, in government involvement in the economy. They wanted to nationalize the railroads in order to make them subject to citizen control and lessen the amount of corruption and favoritism surrounding them. They sought to put silver on par with gold as a basis for the dollar (called bimetallism), thus lowering the value of the currency, boosting inflation, and bringing more in the way of a return to commodity producers such as themselves. They also proposed a graduated income tax, tighter restrictions on immigration, the expansion of farmers' cooperatives, an eight-hour workday in industry, and the direct election of senators. One of their models of an effectively operating public institution was the U.S. Post Office. Additionally, the Populists advocated for improvements to infrastructure, the creation of a national weather service, an expanded and improved Census Bureau, and the establishment of common schools, teachers' colleges, and land-grant universities. Mostly, however, Populists sought to put capital and political control in the hands of small farmers, workers, and the middle class.

Although the Populist moment was relatively brief in duration, ending by 1908, it had a significant impact on American political culture. It awakened the populace to a shortage of egalitarianism in the existing system, and it put conservatives, in particular, on notice that the status quo could not and would not prevail. It gave people a sense that, through the intelligent use of government resources, injustice, inequality, and corruption could be banished from the land. In that respect, Populism was more a precursor to the New Deal of the 1930s than to the goals of the present-day Tea Party.

As for the People's Party itself, it fared fairly well at the congressional level, sending fifty elected representatives from sixteen states and one territory to the Capitol between 1891 and 1903. In 1896 the party joined with the Democratic Party in nominating William Jennings Bryan, a prominent "bimetal" man, for president. The election was a close one, but Bryan lost to the staunchly pro-business Republican candidate William McKinley. Thereafter, the party never quite recaptured its earlier momentum. It elected its last presidential candidate (Thomas E. Watson, congressman from Georgia) in 1908. (See Table 1.)

The Progressive Era

The reform movement that came to define the Progressive Era grew out of both the Populist impulse and the largely religious phenomenon known as the Social Gospel. The latter was a Protestant vision seeking to apply the teachings of the Bible to the social problems of modern, industrialized America. Many, but not all, of progressivism's early leaders had Protestant, and even clerical, roots. And many of them therefore sought to eradicate the "sins" of the cities through the administration of Christian moral principles. Groups such as the Women's Christian Temperance Union (WCTU) pushed not only for the prohibition of alcohol but for improved living conditions for working families, a greater role for women in society (including women's suffrage), and the abolition of child labor. The women's suffrage movement itself, though generally secular, made some alliances with religious groups (including the WCTU) and had a measurable impact beyond its narrow focus on votes for women. A lesser but still salient role was played by such organizations as the Young Men's Christian Association and the Young Women's Christian Association.

In politics, progressives fought for women's rights, the establishment of primary elections, the direct election of Senators, and the use of ballot initiatives, referendums, and recall elections. By these means they sought to have a greater say in the selection of government representatives and the establishment of government policies. They would also thereby have a way to hold government officials accountable for their actions. In economics, progressive activists supported antitrust legislation, public ownership (or regulation) of utilities, various banking industry and currency reforms, and the institution of the income tax. In education, they sought new methods of teaching as an alternative to rote memorization. John Dewey, for instance, introduced so-called "child-centered" learning, which took account of human interests and activities beyond the traditional reading, writing, and arithmetic. In journalism, "muckrakers" such as Nellie Bly, Ida Tarbell, Lincoln Steffens, and Upton Sinclair revealed the depravities and excesses of the ruling class and the questionable business operations in which members of that class sometimes were engaged.

Progressivism may have got its start with Jane Addams's Hull House experiment in Chicago in 1889, with its focus on domestic conditions, but it is primarily associated with Theodore Roosevelt and, to a lesser extent, Woodrow Wilson. In the case of these two men's presidencies, progressivism had both a domestic and an international component. Domestically, Roosevelt was in sympathy with the muckrakers and strongly supported efforts to break up corporate trusts, expand civil services (education, roads, the mail), regulate food and drugs, and protect the environment. Internationally, Roosevelt's progressivism stood in the tradition that spawned the Spanish-American war in 1898; it was a forward-leaning political attitude that sought to put the stamp of the United States on foreign affairs and steer the course of events in America's favor. Wilson, for his part, was more of an internationalist. His progressive vision was to move beyond the parochialism of national politics to the world stage, where he sought a League of Nations. Nevertheless, domestically he was able to achieve such successes as creating the Federal Reserve, establishing a corporate income tax, closing antitrust loopholes (left open by the Sherman Antitrust Act of 1890), launching the Federal Trade Commission, and a variety of others. Even so, as World War I unfolded in Europe and eventually drew in the United States, Wilsonian domestic progressivism started to draw down. The Progressive movement really ended with the war, but it is often counted as extending through the Wilson presidency, which lasted until 1921.

Bibliography and Additional Reading

Calhoun, Charles W., ed. *The Gilded Age: Essays on the Origins of Modern America*, 2d ed. Lanham, MD: Rowman & Littlefield, 2006.

Cashman, Sean Dennis. *America in the Gilded Age: From the Death of Lincoln to the Rise of Theodore Roosevelt*. New York: Oxford University Press, 1993.

Dawley, Alan. *Struggles for Justice: Social Responsibility and the Liberal State*. Cambridge, MA: Belknap Press, 1993.

Diner, Steven J. *A Very Different Age: Americans of the Progressive Era*. New York: Hill & Wang, 1998.

Kazin, Michael. *The Populist Persuasion: An American History*, rev. ed. Ithaca, NY: Cornell UP, 1998.

McGerr, Michael. *A Fierce Discontent: The Rise and Fall of the Progressive Movement in America, 1870-1920*. New York: NYU Press, 2005.

McMath, Robert C. *American Populism: A Social History, 1877-1898*. New York: Hill & Wang, 1993.

Painter, Nell Irvin. *Standing at Armageddon: A Grassroots History of the Progressive Era*. New York: W.W. Norton, 2013.

Rodgers, Daniel T. *Atlantic Crossings: Social Politics in a Progressive Era*. Cambridge, MA: Harvard UP, 1998.

Trachtenberg, Alan. *The Incorporation of America: Culture and Society in the Gilded Age*, 25th Anniversary ed. New York: Hill & Wang, 2007.

Contributors

Michael P Auerbach
Marblehead, MA

William E. Burns
George Washington University

Steven L. Danver, PhD
Mesa Verde Publishing
Washougal, Washington

Tracey DiLascio, Esq., JD
Framingham, Massachusetts

Kevin E. Grimm, PhD
Beloit College

Bethany Groff, MA
Historic New England

Mark S. Joy, PhD
Jamestown College

Lee Tunstall
Calgary, Alberta

Vanessa E. Vaughn, MA
Chicago, Illinois

Donald A. Watt, PhD
McGovern Center for Leadership
and Public Service

U.S. Presidents (and Their Opponents) 1877-1921

President	Party	Term of Office	Losing Candidate	Party
Rutherford B. Hayes	Republican	1877-1881	Samuel J. Tilden [1]	Democratic
James A. Garfield	Republican	1881-1881 [2]	Winfield Scott Hancock	Democratic
Chester A. Arthur [3]	Republican	1881-1885	N/A	N/A
Grover Cleveland	Democratic	1885-1889	James G. Blain	Republican
Benjamin Harrison	Republican	1889-1893	Grover Cleveland	Democratic
Grover Cleveland	Democratic	1893-1897	Benjamin Harrison	Republican
William McKinley [4]	Republican	1897-1901	William Jennings Bryan	Democratic/Populist
Theodore Roosevelt	Republican	1901-1909	Alton B. Parker	Democratic
William H. Taft	Republican	1909-1913	William Jennings Bryan	Democratic
Woodrow Wilson	Democratic	1913-1921	Theodore Roosevelt (1912); Charles Evans Hughes (1916)	Republican

[1] The Hayes-Tilden election of 1876 produced unclear results, but by agreement between the two parties Hayes was seated as president while Tilden and the Democrats got a pullout of federal troops in the South.

[2] Garfield was assassinated while in office.

[3] As vice-president, Arthur succeeded Garfield and served one term.

[4] McKinley won re-election in 1900, again against Bryan, but was assassinated in 1901, six months into his second term.

DEFINING DOCUMENTS
IN AMERICAN HISTORY

The Emergence of
Modern America
(1874-1917)

THE END OF THE FRONTIER AND THE START OF A NEW ERA

We open *The Emergence of Modern America* with a look at two notable documents from the late 1880s and early 1890s. The first document describes the famous—and tragic—"land rush" that opened up Oklahoma Territory to white settlers on a first-come-first-serve basis. Although, technically, the American Indian tribes that earlier had been relocated to the region retained large tracks of land, realistically they became a powerless minority overnight. Initially, whites were to inhabit only the so-called unassigned areas. But the even set the stage for widespread white settlement and control of the region. The document presented here provides an eye-witness account of the land rush and of the settlers as they seek to "stake a claim" and start a new life.

The second document here offers a statement of "The Significance of the Frontier in American History." In this landmark 1893 essay, historian Frederick Jackson Turner argues that the end of the historical development of the American nation has arrived and that that development has been marked above all by the steady westward shift of the frontier lands. What began at the Appalachians moved out to the Mississippi River and on to the Great Plains and the Pacific Ocean. By the closing years of the nineteenth century, Turner maintained, the western frontier was no more. And yet, he felt, it was the frontier and frontier life, more than anything else, that had shaped American national character. Turner's famous "frontier thesis" left a lasting impression on American thought.

■ "The Rush to Oklahoma"

Date: May 18, 1889
Author: William Willard Howard
Genre: article

Summary Overview

In the 1830s, many American Indian tribes from the eastern part of the United States were relocated to the region known as Indian Territory, comprising present-day Oklahoma and Kansas as well as part of Nebraska, under the Indian Removal Act. After the Civil War, the federal government bought some land in the middle of present-day Oklahoma from the Creek, or Muskogee, tribe and the Seminole tribe, which became known as the Unassigned Lands. Early in 1889, Congress authorized opening these lands to settlement, and President Benjamin Harrison set April 22, 1889, as the opening date. Land seekers congregated around the Unassigned Lands, and when the deadline passed, they rushed into the area to stake their claims. Journalist William Willard Howard's firsthand account of the event, the first of several Oklahoma land runs, was published in the magazine *Harper's Weekly* in May of that year.

Defining Moment

In the thirty years after the Civil War, the last great expansion of agricultural settlement in the United States took place, largely in the lands west of the Mississippi River. Westward settlement across the United States initially skipped over the Great Plains region. The open, largely treeless plains, increasingly arid the farther west one went, seemed inhospitable to American farmers, and early settlers moved on to the mountain regions and the Pacific Coast. By the 1880s, however, many would-be settlers believed that the best available lands elsewhere had already been claimed, and they began to reconsider the Great Plains, and particularly the Unassigned Lands in the center of what is now Oklahoma. Prospective settlers called for this land to be opened for homesteading and settlement, as did the Atchison, Topeka, and Santa Fe Railroad, which had built a line

through the area. Business owners and land speculators calling for settlement of these lands were often called "boomers."

Early in 1889, Representative William Springer of Illinois introduced an amendment to the Indian Appropriations Bill that would allow settlement in the Unassigned Lands. President Harrison signed the legislation, and set the official opening of the lands for noon on April 22, 1889. Immediately before that date, eager land seekers surrounded the Unassigned Lands, ready to rush in as soon as the deadline passed. People were seeking land not only for farms and ranches, but also for town sites and business locations. Howard's account captures the unbridled frenzy of the run into the land. But despite great enthusiasm among the land-hungry people who made the run, there was an unrealized irony to their eagerness. As farming was already at the dawn of a long-term transition from the small family farm to large-scale farming and agribusiness, the era of the family farmer was beginning to wane, and many of those who took out homesteads would never prosper. Nevertheless, this first land run was a significant step toward the formation of the Oklahoma Territory in May 1890.

Author Biography

William Willard Howard was born in Iowa on November 8, 1859. He had a long career as a popular journalist specializing in firsthand investigative reports, publishing widely in prominent magazines such as *Harper's Weekly*, *Scribner's*, and the *Century*. In addition to the Oklahoma land run, he covered the Detroit International Exposition and Fair of 1889 for *Harper's* and also made a trip to Colombia to report on platinum mining there. In the 1890s, Howard traveled abroad to distribute relief funds to Armenians and investigate the reports of massacres committed by the Ottoman Empire. He is perhaps best known for his book on the subject, *Horrors of Armenia: The Story of an Eyewitness*, pub-lished in 1896. Howard died in New York on December 6, 1933.

HISTORICAL DOCUMENT

The preparations for the settlement of Oklahoma had been complete, even to the slightest detail, for weeks before the opening day. The Santa Fe Railway, which runs through Oklahoma north and south, was prepared to take any number of people from its handsome station at Arkansas City, Kansas, and to deposit them in almost any part of Oklahoma as soon as the law allowed; thousands of covered wagons were gathered in camps on all sides of the new Territory waiting for the embargo to be lifted. In its picturesque aspects the rush across the border at noon on the opening day must go down in history as one of the most noteworthy events of Western civilization. At the time fixed, thousands of hungry home-seekers, who had gathered from all parts of the country, and particularly from Kansas and Missouri, were arranged in line along the border, ready to lash their horses into furious speed in the race for fertile spots in the beautiful land before them. The day was one of perfect peace. Overhead the sun shown down from a sky as fair and blue as the cloudless heights of Colorado. The whole expanse of space from zenith to horizon was spotless in its blue purity. The clear spring air, through which the rolling green billows of the promised land could be seen with unusual distinctness for many miles, was as sweet and fresh as the balmy atmosphere of June among New Hampshire's hills.

As the expectant home-seekers waited with restless patience, the clear, sweet notes of a cavalry bugle rose and hung a moment upon the startled air. It was noon. The last barrier of savagery in the United States was broken down. Moved by the same impulse, each driver lashed his horses furiously; each rider dug his spurs into his willing steed, and each man on foot caught his breath hard and darted forward. A cloud of dust rose where the home-seekers had stood in line, and when it had drifted away before the gentle breeze, the horses and wagons and men were tearing across the open country like fiends. The horsemen had the best of it from the start. It was a fine race for a few minutes, but soon the riders began to spread out like a fan, and by the time they had reached the horizon they were scattered about as far as eye could see. Even the fleetest of the horsemen found upon reaching their chosen localities that men in wagons and men on foot were there before them. As it was clearly impossible for a man on foot to outrun a horseman, the inference is plain that Oklahoma had been entered hours before the appointed time. Notwithstanding the assertions of the soldiers that every boomer had been driven out of Oklahoma, the fact remains that the woods along the streams within Oklahoma were literally full of people Sunday night. Nine-tenths of these people made settlement upon the land illegally. The other tenth would have done so had there been any desirable land left to settle upon. This action on the part of the first claim-holders will cause a great deal of land litigation in the future, as it is not to be expected that the man who ran his horse at its utmost speed for ten miles only to find a settler with an ox team in quiet possession of his chosen farm will tamely submit to this plain infringement of the law.

Some of the men who started from the line on foot were quite as successful in securing desirable claims as many who rode fleet horses. They had the advantage of knowing just where their land was located. One man left the line with the others, carrying on his back a tent, a blanket, some camp dishes, an axe, and provisions for two days. He ran down the railway track for six miles, and reached his claim in just sixty minutes. Upon arriving on his land he fell down under a tree, unable to speak or see. I am glad to be able to say that his claim is one of the best in Oklahoma. The rush from the line was so impetuous that by the time the first railway train arrived from the north at twenty-five minutes past twelve o'clock, only a few of the hundreds of boomers were anywhere to be seen. The journey of this first train was well-nigh as interesting as the rush of the men in wagons. The train left Arkansas City at 8:45 o'clock in the forenoon. It consisted of an empty baggage car, which was set apart for the use of newspaper correspondents, eight passenger coaches, and the caboose of a freight train. The coaches were so densely packed with men that not another human being could get on board. So uncomfortably crowded were they that some of the younger boomers climbed to the roofs of the cars and clung perilously to the ventilators. An adventurous person secured at great risk a seat on the forward truck of the baggage car.

In this way the train was loaded to its utmost capacity. That no one was killed or injured was due as much to the careful management of the train as to the ability of the passengers to take care of themselves. Like their friends in the wagons, the boomers on the cars were exultant with joy at the thought of at last entering into possession of the promised land. At first appearances of the land through which the train ran seemed to justify all the virtues that had been claimed for it. The rolling, grassy uplands, and the wooded river-bottoms, the trees in which were just bursting into the most beautiful foliage of early spring, seemed to give a close reality of the distant charm of green and purple forest growths, which rose from the trough of some long swell and went having away to meet the brighter hues in the far-off sky. Throughout all the landscape were clumps of trees suggesting apple orchards set in fertile meadows, and here and there were dim patches of gray and white sand that might in a less barbarous region be mistaken for farmhouses surrounded by hedges and green fields. Truly the Indians have well-named Oklahoma the "beautiful land." The landless and home-hungry people on the train might be pardoned their mental exhilaration, when the effect of this wonderfully beautiful country upon the most prosaic mind is considered. It was an eager and an exuberantly joyful crowd that rode slowly into Guthrie at twenty minutes past one o'clock on that perfect April afternoon. Men who had expected to lay out the town site were grievously disappointed at the first glimpse of their proposed scene of operations. The slope east of the railway at Guthrie station was dotted white with tents and sprinkled thick with men running about in all directions.

"We're done for," said a town-site speculator, in dismay.

"Someone has gone in ahead of us and laid out the town."

"Never mind that," shouted another town-site speculator,

"but make a rush and get what you can."

Hardly had the train slackened its speed when the impatient boomers began to leap from the cars and run up the slope. Men jumped from the roofs of the moving cars at the risk of their lives. Some were so stunned by the fall that they could not get up for some minutes. The coaches were so crowded that many men were compelled to squeeze through the windows in order to get a fair start at the head of the crowd. Almost before the train had come to a standstill the cars were emptied. In their haste and eagerness, men fell over each other in heaps, others stumbled and fell headlong, while many ran forward so blindly and impetuously that it was not until they had passed the best of the town lots that they came to a realization of their actions.

I ran with the first of the crowd to get a good point of view from which to see the rush. When I had time to look about me I found that I was standing beside a tent, near which a man was leisurely chopping holes in the sod with a new axe.

"Where did you come from, that you have already pitched your tent?" I asked.

"Oh, I was here," said he.

"How was that?"

"Why, I was a deputy United States marshal."

"Did you resign?"

"No; I'm a deputy still."

"But it is not legal for a deputy United States marshal, or any one in the employ of the government, to take up a town lot in this manner."

"That may all be, stranger; but I've got two lots here, just the same; and about fifty other deputies have got lots in the same way. In fact, the deputy-marshals laid out the town."

At intervals of fifteen minutes, other trains came from

the north loaded down with home-seekers and town-site speculators. As each succeeding crowd rushed up the slope and found that government officers had taken possession of the best part of the town, indignation became hot and outspoken; yet the marshals held to their lots and refused to move. Bloodshed was prevented only by the belief of the home-seekers that the government would set the matter right.

This course of the deputy United States marshals was one of the most outrageous pieces of imposition upon honest home-seekers ever practiced in the settlement of a new country. That fifty men could, through influence, get themselves appointed as deputy United States marshals for the sole purpose of taking advantage of their positions in this way is creditable neither to them nor to the man who made their appointment possible. This illegal seizure thus became the first matter of public discussion in the city of Guthrie.

When the passengers from the first train reached the spot where the deputy-marshals had ceased laying out lots, they seized the line of the embryo street and ran it eastward as far as their numbers would permit. The second train load of people took it where the first left off, and ran it entirely out of sight behind a swell of ground at least two miles from the station. The following car of home-seekers went north and south, so that by the time that all were in for the day a city large enough in area to hold 100,000 inhabitants had been staked off, with more or less geometrical accuracy. A few women and children were in the rush, but they had to take their chances with the rest. Disputes over the ownership of lots grew incessant, for the reason that when a man went to the river for a drink of water, or tried to get his baggage at the railway station, another man would take possession of his lot, notwithstanding the obvious presence of the first man's stakes and sometimes part of his wearing apparel. Owing to the uncertainty concerning the lines of the streets, two and sometimes more lots were staked out on the same ground, each claimant hoping that the official survey would give him the preference. Contrary to all expectations, there was no bloodshed over the disputed lots. This may be accounted for by the fact that no intoxicating liquors of any kind were allowed to be sold in Oklahoma. It is a matter of common comment among the people that the peaceful way in which Oklahoma was

settled was due entirely to its compulsory prohibition. Had whiskey been plentiful in Guthrie the disputed lots might have been watered in blood, for every man went armed with some sort of deadly weapon. If there could be a more striking temperance lesson than this, I certainly should like to see it.

When Congress gives Oklahoma some sort of government the prohibition of the sale of intoxicating liquor should be the first and foremost of her laws.

It is estimated that between six and seven thousand persons reached Guthrie by train from the north that first afternoon, and that fully three thousand came in by wagon from the north and east, and by train from Purcell on the south, thus making a total population for the first day of about ten thousand. By taking thought in the matter, three-fourths of these people had provided themselves with tents and blankets, so that even on the first night they had ample shelter from the weather. The rest of them slept the first night as best they could, with only the red earth for a pillow and the starry arch of heaven for a blanket. At dawn of Tuesday the unrefreshed home-seekers and town-site speculators arose, and began anew the location of disputed claims. The tents multiplied like mushrooms in a rain that day, and by night the building of frame houses had been begun in earnest in the new streets. The buildings were by no means elaborate, yet they were as good as the average frontier structure, and they served their purpose, which was all that was required.

On that day the trains going north were filled with returning boomers, disgusted beyond expression with the dismal outlook of the new country. Their places were taken by others who came in to see the fun, and perhaps to pick up a bargain in the way of town lots of commercial speculation.

By Wednesday the retreat from Guthrie was at its height. Two persons went home to each one that came in, yet the town seemed to be as lively and as populous as ever. The north-bound boomers asserted that there was nothing in or about Guthrie to support a city; that only a limited number of quarter sections of land on the river bottom were worth settling upon, and that the upland country was nothing but worthless red sand coated over with a film of green grass. To bear out their assertions, these disgusted men pointed to the city of Guthrie, where the red dust was ankle-deep in the main street. The red dust was an argument that could not be contradicted. It rose in clouds and hovered above the feverish city until the air was like fog at sunrise; it sifted through the provision boxes in the tents, it crept into blankets and clothing, and it stuck like wax to the faces and beards of the unhappy citizens. The heat and the dust and the phenomenal lack of food during the first three days created a burning thirst, which seemingly could not be quenched. This thirst was intensified tenfold by the knowledge that water was scarce, hard to get, and sometimes unfit to drink. The yellow Cimarron and the lukewarm Cottonwood were the only streams where water could be obtained, and on the third day he was very thirsty indeed who would drink from either. Boomers who were not engaged in holding down town lots peddled water in pails to their thirsty neighbors at five and ten cents a cupful. Once, when compelled to moisten my parched throat from one of these pails, I noticed that the water was unusually yellow and thick.

"See here," said I to the Frenchman who held the pail; "you have washed your face in this water."

"No, monsieur," he said, with grotesque earnestness; "I do not wash my face for four days!"

I did not doubt it. His face had become so thickly encrusted with red dust and perspiration that he would not have recognized himself had he chanced to look in a mirror.

In this respect he was not worse off than his neighbors, most of whom had not thought of washing their faces since entering Oklahoma. This was not due to any personal negligence, but entirely to the scarcity of water. When men spent their whole time, night and day, in the work of keeping possession of town lots, they could not be expected to go half a mile or a mile for such a trifling diversion as washing their faces.

During the first three days food was nearly as hard to get as water. Dusty ham sandwiches sold on the streets as high as twenty-five cents each, while in the restaurants a plate of pork and beans was valued at seventy-five cents. Few men were well enough provided with funds to buy themselves a hearty meal. One disgusted home-seeker

estimated that if he ate as much as he was accustomed to eat back in Missouri his board would cost him $7.75 per day. Not being able to spend that amount of money every day, he contented himself with such stray sandwiches as were within his means. In this manner he contrived to subsist until Wednesday afternoon, when he was forced to return to civilization in southern Kansas in order to keep from starving to death. A newspaper correspondent from Wichita, Kansas, who had never before known the feeling of hunger, was so far gone in the first stages of starvation that upon his return home on Friday he was hardly able to assimilate food. In appearance he was a walking spectre of famine. The only men in Guthrie who made money during the first week were the restaurant-keepers and the water-peddlers. After the first rush had subsided, however, there was no lack of food, and by the sinking of a number of wells there was a plentiful supply of water, so that the city of Guthrie in the matter of food and drink was no worse off than the ordinary frontier town. When the first well was dug, the home-seekers had an excellent opportunity of learning the exact character of the soil. The well-digger went through several feet of red sand after the sod had been cut through, and then found layers of gray and white sand so loose that the spade would sink into it upon very slight downward pressure. Believing that all of the Oklahoma country consisted of this red, gray, and white sand, thousands of home-seekers took the earliest trains back into Kansas, more than ever contented with the fertile soil of the homes that they had left in the first rush to Oklahoma. By the end of the week the crowd of returning home-seekers had lessened, so that Guthrie had what might be called a permanent population with which to being the serious business of life. Just how long this population will remain, or what size Guthrie will be in another year, is a matter of some uncertainty, for the reason that nothing definite can be decided upon until a thorough test has been made of the farming country round about. Aside from its temporary importance as a land-office centre, the size of Guthrie will be determined, not by the speculative value of town lots, but by the agricultural capacity of the surrounding country. The city has already begun business upon a larger scale than the extent and fertility of the tributary country seems to justify. It has allowed itself the luxury of two mayors and two sets of municipal officers, one set being accredited to Guthrie proper and the other to the outlying district known as East Guthrie. I fancy that when business cools down to a substantial basis it will be found that one set of municipal officers will be enough for both towns.

The first Sunday in Guthrie showed that the new citizens had determined to begin life in the right way. Instead of spending the Sabbath in gambling, drinking, and other riotous ways of living, they held religious services in different parts of the town. If the present spirit of law and order and respectable conduct is continued, as it doubtless will be, the people of Guthrie need never be ashamed of the reputation of their town.

The rush of home-seekers into Oklahoma from the southern border was more picturesque than that from the north, although in numbers it was by no means as great. The intending settlers had been gathered at Purcell, in the Chickasaw Nation, for several months, waiting for the signal to cross the Canadian River and take possession of the coveted land. As the opening day drew near, many of the boomers provided themselves with fleet saddle-horses, and made careful observations of the half-dozen fords leading across the river, their intention being to dash into the river at noon on April 22d, and ride rapidly to their chosen claims. For this purpose the very best of horses were brought into use. Just before noon on the appointed day, hundreds of the horsemen gathered at the entrance to the fords waiting for the signal. Lieutenant Adair, of Troop "L," fifth Cavalry, was stationed on the sands on the opposite side of the river. He had arranged that at noon he should order his bugler to blow the recall, while riding a white horse around in a circle. By this means those who were too far away to hear the bugle could get the signal from the circling of the white horse. The lieutenant had caused all the boomers' watches to be set by his own, in order that there might be no false start. Just as the second hand of his watch touched the hour of twelve he gave the signal, and before the stirring notes of the bugle had found an echo against the walls of Purcell, the foremost horsemen had dashed into the fords. Spurred on by yelling and wildly excited riders, the horses made a furious dash through the water, throwing sand and spray on all sides like a sudden gust of rain and hail.

After the horsemen came the wagons, as thick as they could crowd together. The Canadian River is so treacherous, even at the fords, that horses and wagons must keep moving or run a great risk of being lost in the quicksands. The fear of the quicksands, added to the desire to reach the chosen lands, made the crossing on that quiet noonday particularly lively and stirring. The leaders ran a gallant race, but one by one they fell into deep holes in the river-bed, and for a time floundered about at imminent risk of drowning. A young woman, who pluckily held her place in the lead half-way across the river, went into a pool with a mighty splash. Even in the midst of his excitement the nearest boomer, who was racing with her, checked his horse and assisted her out to dry land, thus losing his place among the leaders. A big bay horse held the lead three-quarters of the way across the river, each furious jump giving him more and more of a lead over the others. In an unlucky moment he went into a deep pool head-first, and threw his rider half stunned upon the yellow sand. While the rider was gathering himself together in a half-dazed condition, the bit horse stood and looked at him a moment, and then started on again. He soon took his place at the lead of the race, and kept it there until the whole cavalcade had passed out of sight. Lieutenant Adair, who had watched this episode with quickening pulse, galloped up to the wet and discomfited rider.

"See here," said he, "I haven't much money about me, but if you'll take $250 for that horse, here's your money." "No, lieutenant," said the man, with a weary smile; "you needn't make me an offer, because you haven't got money enough to buy him."

Most of the boomers who crossed the river at Purcell took up quarter sections of land that they had selected many weeks before; a few tried to organize a town on the flats opposite Purcell, while the others went on to Oklahoma City and Guthrie. Hundreds of boomers came into the southern part of Oklahoma from the Pottawotamie Indian country on the east and from the lands of the wild tribes on the west. As these portions of the border are not protected by soldiers, most of the boomers crossed the line long before the appointed time, and hid in the woods until Monday forenoon, when they emerged from their hiding-places and boldly took up their claims....

In this part of the country the poverty and wretched

condition of some of the older boomers who have been waiting for years for the opening of Oklahoma were painfully apparent. Men with large families settled upon land with less than a dollar in money to keep them from starvation. How they expected to live until they could get a crop from their lands was a mystery which even they could not pretend to explain. Like unreasoning children, they thought that could they but once reach the beautiful green slopes of the promised land, their poverty and trouble would be at an end. They are now awakening to the bitter realization that their real hardships have just begun.

GLOSSARY

spectre: (or specter): a ghost or spirit

speculator: one who buys land in order to re-sell it at a profit

temperance: moderation or abstinence with respect to alcohol usage

Document Analysis

The April 1889 land run into the Unassigned Lands, which Howard describes in his article for *Harper's Weekly*, was the first of several such openings of what had been tribal lands in the Indian Territory. As such, it was an important step in the creation of the Oklahoma Territory, which occurred just one year later. All or parts of what are now Canadian, Cleveland, Kingfisher, Logan, Oklahoma, and Payne counties in the state of Oklahoma were opened for settlement and homesteading in this 1889 run.

Howard capably captures the spirit of frenzy, excitement, and optimism exhibited by the people making the run. He was impressed by what he saw, but was not taken in by the overly optimistic attitudes of the boomers and settlers he encountered. He makes note of many of the problems that arose, including the poor quality of some of the land, the scarcity of water in the area, and the fraud by which various marshals and others entered the area and laid out claims before it was legal to do so. He also notes that even during the brief time he was there, some speculative ventures, such as the sale of building lots in the newly settled towns, had already begun to fail.

Howard also describes the suffering that accompanied this opening of settlement. Many men came on their own, but if they brought their families, the children often had too little to eat due to the high price of food. Many people claimed land but had little cash to pay for supplies or to buy food until they could begin to produce their own. This was a common problem during the period of western settlement—even if settlers were given land at no cost, they still had to have some resources to live on while the land was being brought into production. Howard was realistic enough to see that the future potential of the Oklahoma region would depend on the agricultural productivity of the land. If the farms and ranches prospered, the towns and cities would as well. He predicted correctly that once some land in the heart of the Indian Territory had been opened for settlement, the rest of it would inevitably be opened as well.

Essential Themes

As the first of several runs into various parts of what would become the state of Oklahoma, the April 1889 rush into the Unassigned Lands reflects the great desire for land on the part of many would-be settlers and the frenzy with which they sought to stake their claims. This land hunger is one of the central themes of this document. Howard notes the rapidity with which claims were staked and communities were established. He reports that the town of Guthrie grew to a population of ten thousand virtually overnight. One might suspect an element of exaggeration in such a figure, but even discounting the possible overstatement, it is clear that thousands rushed into the region in a very brief period.

Fraud is also a theme illustrated in Howard's report. While the law barred entry before the official opening of the lands, there were many reports of "sooners," as they came to be called, who staked out claims earlier than the legally declared time. Howard also reports that some men serving as deputy US marshals had used their positions to stake out claims before ordinary settlers were allowed into the region. In addition, some of the new arrivals in Oklahoma realized that making money by selling supplies and services to the settlers might be a more certain business venture than starting a farm or ranch. At the end of a long supply line, settlers had to pay high and at times unreasonable prices for the supplies they needed.

Above all, Howard's account of the Oklahoma land run is characterized by the twin themes of hope and disappointment. Settlers rushed into the newly open territory, certain that owning land was an important stepping stone to individual autonomy and eventual prosperity. Some would-be settlers, however, found no land because of the many who had illegally made early claims. Others were disappointed in the quality of the land still available and ultimately returned to their original homes. After the initial excitement of the boom dissipated, those who had selected homesteads and sites for businesses realized that the real work was only just beginning.

—*Mark S. Joy, PhD*

Bibliography and Additional Reading

Gibson, Arrell M. Oklahoma: *A History of Five Centuries.* 2nd ed. Norman: U of Oklahoma P, 2010. Print.

Hoig, Stan. *The Oklahoma Land Rush of 1889.* Oklahoma City: Oklahoma Hist. Soc., 1989. Print.

Prucha, Francis Paul. *The Great Father: The United States Government and the American Indians.* 2 vols. Lincoln: U of Nebraska P, 1984. Print.

■ "The Significance of the Frontier in American History"

Date: July 12, 1893
Author: Frederick Jackson Turner
Genre: essay; speech

Summary Overview

In his seminal 1893 essay "The Significance of the Frontier in American History," Frederick Jackson Turner presents his frontier thesis, a framework through which many historians would study and understand the American West and its effect on American democracy and national character for the next century. In this essay, Turner argues that the availability of free, unsettled land beyond the western edge of settlement in the United States and the accommodations that settlers needed to make once they arrived on that frontier were the factors that have made the United States distinct from Europe. This unique frontier heritage explained not only the American love of freedom, but also the freedom that characterized American political, economic, and social structures. The challenges of settling the frontier fostered a strong sense of individualism and practicality that were not found in the same form under European hierarchical class structures or traditional customs. Turner's thesis gave the identification of Americans with the West a degree of intellectual legitimacy. There were, however, historians in Turner's day—most notably Charles Beard—who disputed the idea that the frontier was the formative factor in the development of the American national character and political culture. However, even today, popular historians still reference Turner's moving frontier, where free, unsettled land acts as the principal Americanizing force.

Defining Moment

The United States was undergoing a number of significant transformations at the time that Frederick Jackson Turner presented "The Significance of the Frontier in American History" at a meeting of the American Historical Association at the World's Columbian Exposition in Chicago in 1893. The Industrial Revolution was rapidly changing the ratio of rural to urban dwellers, as well as the nature of the work that the average American performed. Large waves of immigration, mostly from southern and eastern Europe, were changing many people's perceptions of what it meant to be an American. The large-scale migration to the American West that began in earnest after the Civil War had been changing the nation in many important ways over three decades.

When Turner stepped to the podium on July 12, 1893, at the world fair held in Chicago to mark the four hundredth anniversary of Christopher Columbus's voyage to the New World, it is doubtful that many in the audience expected him to deliver an address that would become a defining paradigm for the study of US history. His was the last of five lengthy presentations given that evening, mostly on rather mundane topics. Up to that point, the so-called germ theory of politics was one common hypothesis used to explain the historical and cultural development of the United States, positing antecedents for American institutions in the ancient Teutonic tribes of central Europe. But what the germ theory could not explain was the changes that were reshaping American society in the late nineteenth century. What had made the United States unique, and why was it now becoming more like Europe (urban, industrial, and ethnically diverse)?

The answer, to Turner, lay in the 1890 US Census Bureau report. In 1890, for the first time, settlements in the West were so numerous and widely distributed that there was no "frontier line"—a line on the map to the east of which there was a population of more than two people per square mile, and to the west of which there were fewer than two people per square mile. Now that the United States no longer had an open and unsettled frontier, Turner took the opportunity to examine the role the frontier had played in US history up until that point. It was a simple idea and a simple framework for examining an entire era of American history, but Turner's frontier thesis had a profound effect, both on how historians talked about the nation and on how Americans thought of themselves, the vibrancy of American democracy, and what was going to come next for the nation.

Author Biography

Frederick Jackson Turner was born in Portage, Wisconsin, on November 14, 1861. His father was a journalist and amateur local historian, who sparked Turner's interest in history. Turner attended the University of Wisconsin, graduating in 1884, and went on to gradu-ate school under the mentorship of the well-known historian Herbert Baxter Adams at Johns Hopkins University, where Turner received his PhD in history in 1890. At that time, he was teaching at his alma mater, the University of Wisconsin.

Although the response to Turner's 1893 address was less than enthusiastic both inside and outside of the historical profession, Turner's perseverance gradually won acceptance of his ideas. His notoriety was so great that in 1910 he left the University of Wisconsin for a position at Harvard University, where he remained until 1924. He then worked as a research associate at the Huntington Library in San Marino, California, until his death on March 14, 1932.

HISTORICAL DOCUMENT

This brief official statement marks the closing of a great historic movement. Up to our own day American history has been in a large degree the history of the colonization of the Great West. The existence of an area of free land, its continuous recession, and the advance of American settlement westward explain American development. Behind institutions, behind constitutional forms and modifications lie the vital forces that call these organs into life and shape them to meet changing conditions. Now the peculiarity of American institutions is the fact that they have been compelled to adapt themselves to the changes of an expanding people—to the changes involved in crossing a continent, in winning a wilderness, and in developing at each area of this progress out of the primitive economic and political conditions of the frontier into the complexity of city life.

Said Calhoun in 1817, "We are great, and rapidly—I was about to say fearfully—growing!" So saying, he touched the distinguishing feature of American life. All peoples show development: the germ theory of politics has been sufficiently emphasized. In the case of most nations, however, the development has occurred in a limited area; and if the nation has expanded, it has met other growing peoples whom it has conquered. But in the case of the United States we have a different phenomenon.

Limiting our attention to the Atlantic Coast, we have the familiar phenomenon of the evolution of institutions in a limited area, such as the rise of representative government; the differentiation of simple colonial governments into complex organs; the progress from primitive industrial society, without division of labor, up to manufacturing civilization. But we have in addition to this a recurrence of the process of evolution in each western area reached in the process of expansion. Thus American development has exhibited not merely advance along a single line but a return to primitive conditions on a continually advancing frontier line, and a new development for that area.

American social development has been continually beginning over again on the frontier. This perennial rebirth, this fluidity of American life, this expansion westward with its new opportunities, its continuous touch with the simplicity of primitive society, furnish the forces dominating American character. The true point of view in the history of this nation is not the Atlantic Coast, it is the Great West. Even the slavery struggle, which is made so exclusive an object of attention by writers like Professor von Holst, occupies its important place in American history because of its relation to westward expansion.

In this advance, the frontier is the outer edge of the wave—the meeting point between savagery and civilization. Much has been written about the frontier from the point of view of border warfare and the chase, but as a field for the serious study of the economist and the historian it has been neglected.

What is the frontier? It is not the European frontier— a fortified boundary line running through dense populations. The most significant thing about it is that it lies at the hither edge of free land. In the census reports it is treated as the margin of that settlement which has a density of two or more to the square mile. The term is an elastic one, and for our purposes does not need sharp definition. We shall consider the whole frontier belt, including the Indian country and the outer margin of the "settled area" of the census reports. This paper will make no attempt to treat the subject exhaustively; its aim is simply to call attention to the frontier as a fertile field for investigation, and to suggest some of the problems which arise in connection with it.

But with all these similarities there are essential differences, due to the place element and the time element. It is evident that the farming frontier of the Mississippi Valley presents different conditions from the mining frontier of the Rocky Mountains. The frontier reached by the Pacific Railroad, surveyed into rectangles, guarded by the United States Army, and recruited by the daily immigrant ship, moves forward at a swifter pace and in a different way than the frontier reached by the birch canoe or the pack horse. The geologist traces patiently the shores of ancient seas, maps their areas, and compares the older and the newer. It would be a work worth the historian's labors to mark these various frontiers and in detail compare one with another. Not only would there result a more adequate conception of American development and characteristics, but invaluable additions would be made to the history of society.

Loria, the Italian economist, has urged the study of colonial life as an aid in understanding the stages of European development, affirming that colonial settlement is for economic science what the mountain is for geology, bringing to light primitive stratifications. "America," he says, "has the key to the historical enigma which Europe has sought for centuries in vain, and the land which has no history reveals luminously the course of universal history." He is right. The United States lies like a huge page in the history of society. Line by line as we read from west to east we find the record of social evolution.

It would not be possible in the limits of this paper to trace the other frontiers across the continent. Travelers of the eighteenth century found the "cowpens" among the canebrakes and pea-vine pastures of the South, and the "cow drivers" took their droves to Charleston, Philadelphia, and New York. Travelers at the close of the War of 1812 met droves of more than a thousand cattle and swine from the interior of Ohio going to Pennsylvania to fatten for the Philadelphia market. The ranges of the Great Plains, with ranch and cowboy and nomadic life, are things of yesterday and of to-day. The experience of the Carolina cowpens guided the ranchers of Texas. One element favoring the rapid extension of the rancher's frontier is the fact that in a remote country lacking transportation facilities the product must be in small bulk, or must be able to transport itself, and the cattle raiser could easily drive his product to market. The effect of these great ranches on the subsequent agrarian history of the localities in which they existed should be studied.

The maps of the census reports show an uneven advance of the farmer's frontier, with tongues of settlement pushed forward and with indentations of wilderness. In part this is due to Indian resistance, in part to the location of river valleys and passes, in part to the unequal force of the centers of frontier attraction. Among the important centers of attraction may be mentioned the following: fertile and favorably situated soils, salt springs, mines, and army posts.

The frontier army post, serving to protect the settlers from the Indians, has also acted as a wedge to open the Indian country, and has been a nucleus for settlement. In this connection, mention should also be made of the government military and exploring expeditions in determining the lines of settlement. But all the more important expeditions were greatly indebted to the earliest pathmakers, the Indian guides, the traders and trappers, and the French voyageurs, who were inevitable parts of governmental expeditions from the days of Lewis and Clark. Each expedition was an epitome of the previous factors in western advance.

In an interesting monograph, Victor Hehn has traced the effect of salt upon early European development, and has pointed out how it affected the lines of settlement and the form of administration. A similar study might be made for the salt springs of the United States. The early settlers were tied to the coast by the need of salt, without which they could not preserve their meats or live in comfort. Writing in 1752, Bishop Spangenburg says of a colony for which he was seeking lands in North Carolina,

They will require salt & other necessaries which they can neither manufacture nor raise. Either they must go to Charleston, which is 300 miles distant ...Or else they must go to Boling's Point in Va on a branch of the James & is also 300 miles from here...Or else they must go down the Roanoke—I know not how many miles—where salt is brought up from the Cape Fear. This may serve as a typical illustration.

An annual pilgrimage to the coast for salt thus became essential. Taking flocks or furs and ginseng root, the early settlers sent their pack trains after seeding time each year to the coast. This proved to be an important educational influence, since it was almost the only way in which the pioneer learned what was going on in the East. But when discovery was made of the salt springs of the Kanawha, and the Holston, and Kentucky, and central New York, the West began to be freed from dependence on the coast. It was in part the effect of finding these salt springs that enabled settlement to cross the mountains.

From the time the mountains rose between the pioneer and the seaboard, a new order of Americanism arose. The West and the East began to get out of touch of each other. The settlements from the sea to the mountains kept connection with the rear and had a certain solidarity. But the over-mountain men grew more and more independent. The East took a narrow view of American advance, and nearly lost these men. Kentucky and Tennessee history bears abundant witness to the truth of this statement. The East began to try to hedge and limit westward expansion. Though Webster could declare that there were no Alleghenies in his politics, yet in politics in general they were a very solid factor.

Good soils have been the most continuous attraction to the farmer's frontier. The land hunger of the Virginians drew them down the rivers into Carolina, in early colonial days; the search for soils took the Massachusetts men to Pennsylvania and to New York. The exploitation of the beasts took hunter and trader to the West, the exploitation of the grasses took the rancher west, and the exploitation of the virgin soil of the river valleys and prairies attracted the farmer. As the eastern lands were taken up, migration flowed across them to the west. Daniel Boone, the great backwoodsman, who combined the occupations of hunter, trader, cattle-raiser, farmer, and surveyor—learning, probably from the traders, of the fertility of the lands of the upper Yadkin, where the traders were wont to rest as they took their way to the Indians, left his Pennsylvania home with his father, and passed down the Great Valley road to that stream.

Learning from a trader whose posts were on the Red River in Kentucky of its game and rich pastures, he pioneered the way for the farmers to that region. Thence he passed to the frontier of Missouri, where his settlement was long a landmark on the frontier. Here again he helped to open the way for civilization, finding salt licks, and trails, and land. His son was among the earliest trappers in the passes of the Rocky Mountains, and his party are said to have been the first to camp on the present site of Denver. His grandson, Col. A. J. Boone, of Colorado, was a power among the Indians of the Rocky Mountains, and was appointed an agent by the government. "Kit" Carson's mother was a Boone. Thus this family epitomizes the backwoodsman's advance across the continent.

The farmer's advance came in a distinct series of waves. In Peck's *New Guide to the West*, published in Cincinnati in 1848, occurs this suggestive passage:

Generally, in all the western settlements, three classes, like the waves of the ocean, have rolled one after the other. First comes the pioneer, who depends for the subsistence of his family chiefly upon the natural growth of vegetation, called the "range," and the proceeds of hunting. His implements of agriculture are rude, chiefly of his own make, and his efforts directed mainly to a crop of corn and a "truck patch." The last is a rude garden for growing cabbage, beans, corn for roasting ears, cucumbers, and potatoes. A log cabin, and, occasionally, a stable and corn-crib, and a field of a dozen acres, the timber girdled or "deadened," and fenced, are enough for his occupancy. It is quite immaterial whether he ever becomes the owner of the soil. He is the occupant for the time being, pays no rent, and feels as independent as the "lord of the manor."

With a horse, cow, and one or two breeders of swine, he strikes into the woods with his family, and becomes the founder of a new county, or perhaps state. He builds his cabin, gathers around him a few other families of similar tastes and habits, and occupies till range is somewhat subdued, and hunting a little precarious, or, which is more frequently the case, till the neighbors crowd around, roads, bridges, and fields annoy him, and he lacks elbow room. The Preemption Law enables him to dispose of his cabin and cornfield to the next class of emigrants; and, to employ his own figures, he "breaks for the high timber, clears out for the New Purchase," or migrates to Arkansas or Texas to work the same process over.

The next class of emigrants purchase the lands, add field to field, clear out the roads, throw rough bridges over the streams, put up hewn log houses, with glass windows and brick or stone chimneys, occasionally plant orchards, build mills, school-houses, courthouses, etc., and exhibit the picture and forms of plain, frugal, civilized life.

Another wave rolls on. The men of capital and enterprise come. The settler is ready to sell out and take the advantage of the rise in property, push farther into the interior and become, himself, a man of capital and enterprise in turn. The small village rises to a spacious town or city; substantial edifices of brick, extensive fields, orchards, gardens, colleges, and churches are seen. Broad-cloths, silks, leghorns, crepes, and all the refinements, luxuries, elegancies, frivolities, and fashions are in vogue. Thus wave after wave is rolling westward—the real Eldorado is still farther on.

A portion of the two first classes remain stationary amidst the general movement, improve their habits and condition, and rise in the scale of society.

The writer has traveled much amongst the first class—the real pioneers. He has lived many years in connection with the second grade; and now the third wave is sweeping over large districts of Indiana, Illinois, and Missouri. Migration has become almost a habit in the West. Hundreds of men can be found, not over 50 years of age, who have settled for the fourth, fifth, or sixth time on a new spot. To sell out and remove only a few hundred miles makes up a portion of the variety of backwoods life and manners.

Omitting the pioneer farmer who moves from the love of adventure, the advance of the more steady farmer is easy to understand. Obviously the immigrant was attracted by the cheap lands of the frontier, and even the native farmer felt their influence strongly. Year by year the farmers who lived on soil, whose returns were diminished by unrotated crops were offered the virgin soil of the frontier at nominal prices. Their growing families demanded more lands, and these were dear. The competition of the unexhausted, cheap, and easily tilled prairie lands compelled the farmer either to go west and continue the exhaustion of the soil on a new frontier, or to adopt intensive culture. Thus the census of 1890 shows, in the Northwest, many counties in which there is an absolute or a relative decrease of population. These States have been sending farmers to advance the frontier on the Plains, and have themselves begun to turn to intensive farming and to manufacture. A decade before this, Ohio had shown the same transition stage. Thus the demand for land and the love of wilderness freedom drew the frontier ever onward.

Having now roughly outlined the various kinds of frontiers and their modes of advance, chiefly from the point of view of the frontier itself, we may next inquire what were the influences on the East and on the Old World. A rapid enumeration of some of the more noteworthy effects is all that I have time for.

First, we note that the frontier promoted the formation of a composite nationality for the American people. The coast was preponderantly English, but the later tides of continental immigration flowed across to the free lands. This was the case from the early colonial days. The Scotch-Irish and the Palatine Germans, or "Pennsylvania Dutch," furnished the dominant element in the stock of the colonial frontier. With these peoples were also the freed indented servants, or redemptioners, who at the expiration of their time of service passed to the frontier. Governor Spotswood of Virginia writes in 1717, "The inhabitants of our frontiers are composed generally of such as have been transported hither as servants, and, being out of their time, settle themselves where land is to be taken up and that will produce the necessaries of life with little labor." Very generally these redemptioners were of non-English stock.

In the crucible of the frontier the immigrants were

Americanized, liberated, and fused into a mixed race, English in neither nationality nor characteristics. The process has gone on from the early days to our own. Burke and other writers in the middle of the eighteenth century believed that Pennsylvania was "threatened with the danger of being wholly foreign in language, manners, and perhaps even inclinations." The German and Scotch-Irish elements in the frontier of the South were only less great. In the middle of the present century the German element in Wisconsin was already so considerable that leading publicists looked to the creation of a German state out of the commonwealth by concentrating their colonization. Such examples teach us to beware of misinterpreting the fact that there is a common English speech in America into a belief that the stock is also English.

In another way the advance of the frontier decreased our dependence on England. The coast, particularly of the South, lacked diversified industries, and was dependent on England for the bulk of its supplies. In the South there was even a dependence on the Northern colonies for articles of food. Governor Glenn of South Carolina writes in the middle of the eighteenth century:

> Our trade with New York and Philadelphia was of this sort, draining us of all the little money and bills we could gather from other places for their bread, flour, beer, hams, bacon, and other things of their produce; all which, except beer, our new townships begin to supply us with, which are settled with very industrious and thriving Germans. This no doubt diminishes the number of shipping and the appearance of our trade, but it is far from being a detriment to us.

Before long the frontier created a demand for merchants. As it retreated from the coast it became less and less possible for England to bring her supplies directly to the consumer's wharfs and carry away staple crops, and staple crops began to give way to diversified agriculture for a time. The effect of this phase of the frontier action upon the northern section is perceived when we realize how the advance of the frontier aroused seaboard cities like Boston, New York, and Baltimore, to engage in rivalry for what Washington called "the extensive and valuable trade of a rising empire."

The legislation which most developed the powers of the national government, and played the largest part in its activity, was conditioned on the frontier....

So long as free land exists, the opportunity for a competency exists, and economic power secures political power. But the democracy born of free land, strong in selfishness and individualism, intolerant of administrative experience and education, and pressing individual liberty beyond its proper bounds, has its dangers as well as its benefits. Individualism in America has allowed a laxity in regard to governmental affairs which has rendered possible the spoils system and all the manifest evils that follow from the lack of a highly developed civic spirit....

From the conditions of frontier life came intellectual traits of profound importance. The works of travelers along each frontier from colonial days onward describe certain common traits, and these traits have, while softening down, still persisted as survivals in the place of their origin, even when a higher social organization succeeded. The result is that, to the frontier, the American intellect owes its striking characteristics. That coarseness and strength combined with acuteness and inquisitiveness, that practical, inventive turn of mind, quick to find expedients, that masterful grasp of material things, lacking in the artistic but powerful to effect great ends, that restless, nervous energy, that dominant individualism, working for good and for evil, and withal that buoyancy and exuberance which comes with freedom—these are traits of the frontier, or traits called out elsewhere because of the existence of the frontier. ...

For a moment, at the frontier, the bonds of custom are broken and unrestraint is triumphant. There is not *tabula rasa*. The stubborn American environment is there with its imperious summons to accept its conditions; the inherited ways of doing things are also there; and yet, in spite of environment, and in spite of custom, each frontier did indeed furnish a new field of opportunity, a gate of escape from the bondage of the past; and freshness, and confidence, and scorn of older society, impatience of its restraints and its ideas, and indifference to its lessons, have accompanied the frontier.

What the Mediterranean Sea was to the Greeks, breaking the bond of custom, offering new experiences, calling out new institutions and activities, that, and more, the ever retreating frontier has been to the United States directly, and to the nations of Europe more remotely. And now, four centuries from the discovery of America, at the end of a hundred years of life under the Constitution, the frontier has gone, and with its going has closed the first period of American history.

GLOSSARY

girdled or "deadened": a process by which a tree's circumference is cut into or "ringed" in order to kill and dry the tree, thus improving its flotation qualities for river transport

salt lick: a natural surface deposit of salt or other minerals, used by animals for nutritional purposes

Webster: Daniel Webster (1782—1852), US senator from Massachusetts; the quote about "no Alleghenies" refers to Webster's view that state concerns are often national concerns—there are no barriers in that regard

Document Analysis

Frederick Jackson Turner's thesis begins with a simple statement of fact: the frontier, the line between densely populated and sparsely populated land, was gone as of 1890, according to the US Census report. In this essay, Turner seizes upon that simple fact to reflect upon and argue a whole host of points about the development and unique aspects of American society. Whereas many historians have criticized Turner's thesis, arguing against his assertions about American exceptionalism in regard to egalitarianism, many others have used Turner's thesis as the basis for their fundamental views on what defines and distinguishes the United States and Americans. In the most sweeping of statements, Turner asserted that "the existence of an area of free land, its continuous recession, and the advance of American settlement westward explain American development. . . . Now, the peculiarity of American institutions is the fact that they have been compelled to adapt themselves to the changes of an expanding people—to the changes involved in crossing a continent, in winning a wilderness, and in developing at each area of this progress out of the primitive economic and political conditions of the frontier into the complexity of city life." Turner clearly saw the frontier's influence as foundational to the development of a distinct American national character, as well American political and social institutions and customs. He contrasts the United States with most other countries, where "development has occurred in a limited area; and if the nation has expanded, it has met other growing people whom it has conquered."

What Turner describes as the frontier line was less a specific location than a process that was repeated time after time as Americans pushed ever further west. Americans, entering a new territory, had to create new institutions out of a raw, unsettled, and primitive setting. These institutions had to serve the needs of a population made up of people who typically did not own the property they tilled and were roughly equal with one another. Turner believed that the availability of free land to be tamed by American settlers was what ensured the independence of thought that many foreign commentators, such as Alexis de Tocqueville and J. Hector St. John Crèvecoeur, had written about as a distinguishing feature of the American people. That independence filtered up to the national government, and Turner argues that the central ideas about the role of the government in the United States were first created on the frontier.

In terms of the development of American society, Turner argued that "this perennial rebirth, this fluidity of American life, this expansion westward with its new opportunities, its continuous touch with the simplicity of primitive society, furnish the forces dominating American character." Whereas the East Coast was the great commercial and cultural center of the nation at the time, Turner asserts that the forces that created

American society were not furnished by immigrants from Europe but from the harsh experiences of settlers in the West. Turner argues that the West was where savagery met civilization, and the interaction between the two provided continual vitality to the progress of American society.

Turner's thesis asserts that the frontier process explains what he calls the "the first period of American history," but the unspoken corollary of Turner's thesis was that there was uncertainty at best as to what would happen during the next century, now that the availability of unsettled land in the West had been exhausted. His implicit conclusion is that, with the disappearance of the frontier, the United States could become more susceptible to the class tensions and social ills that he associated with Europe.

Essential Themes

Turner had his critics, even among his contemporaries. Another prominent historian of the time, Charles Beard, asserted that while the availability of free land was an important factor, that alone could not explain American development, but needed to be combined with the spread of agriculture and the presence of slavery, common labor, and capitalism. However, throughout the early twentieth century, it seemed that Turner's disciples outnumbered his critics. Some of Turner's most prominent adherents were Ray Allen Billington, whose book *Westward Expansion: A History of the American Frontier* (1949) relied heavily on the Turner thesis, and Walter Prescott Webb, who used the Turner thesis to explain the development of white American populations in various locations from the Great Plains to the Southwest.

Beginning in the 1960s, many historians began to turn away from Turner's triumphalist celebration of western individualism and egalitarianism. With the emergence of the field of new western history in the 1980s, Turner's frontier thesis fell further out of favor. The work of new western historians concentrate on aspects of America's frontier past that Turner and his disciples had never considered adequately in their work, arguing that factors other than the process of settling the frontier make the history of the American West distinctive. Further, new western historians have sought to illuminate the experiences of those not included in Turner's West, namely women, American Indians, and other minority groups. New western historian Patricia Nelson Limerick challenges many elements of the Turner thesis in her 1987 book *The Legacy of Conquest: The Unbroken Past of the American West*; for example, Limerick highlights the cultural diversity of the West and the competition for resources among various ethnic groups as critical to the historical development of the region.

However, Turner's ideas have not been done away with completely. Contemporary adherents of the Turner thesis have accepted the fact that the new western historians added the experiences of previously overlooked groups to the historical study of the American West but assert that the Turner thesis is still useful as a tool to explain the progressive development of the United States through the advance of the frontier line. Furthermore, Turner's ideas have had a significant influence on the field of environmental history, which emerged in the 1980s and examines the influence of the regional environment on societal development in cultures worldwide. Well over a century after its initial presentation, Frederick Jackson Turner's frontier thesis still looms large in both historical discussions as well as dialogues over whether there is an exceptional nature to the American character.

—*Steven L. Danver, PhD*

Bibliography and Additional Reading

Cronon, William. "Turner's First Stand: The Significance of Significance in American History." *Writing Western History: Essays on Major Western Historians.* Ed. R. W. Etulain. Albuquerque: U of New Mexico P, 1991. 73–101. Print.

Gressley, Gene M. "The Turner Thesis: A Problem in Historiography." *Agricultural History* 32.4 (1958): 227–49. Print.

Limerick, Patricia Nelson, Clyde A. Milner II, and Charles E. Rankin, eds. *Trails: Toward a New Western History.* Lawrence: UP of Kansas, 1991. Print.

Turner, Frederick Jackson. *The Frontier in American History.* Rev. ed. Tucson: U of Arizona P, 1994. Print

LABOR PAINS

The later decades of the nineteenth century came to be known as the Gilded Age because of the fantastic wealth that accrued to the owners of the nation's major industries, along with their financiers and principal investors. For millions of working-class Americans, however, the era was anything but golden. Unions were in their infancy, and factory owners and managers held considerable freedom in exercising their authority in order to extract the most from their workers—for the least amount of pay. The Gilded Age, in other words, is known also as a battleground between labor and capital.

The first document in this section details the famous Haymarket Riot in Chicago in 1886. What began as a peaceful anarchist gathering and workers' demonstration, the day after several workers had been killed by city police, devolved into chaos and violence when a bomb was thrown into the crowd, killing seven policemen and a number of civilians. Anarchist leaders were subsequently tried, convicted, and, in some instances, executed for their alleged involvement—even though their criminal cases were not airtight. The event became a watershed in the battle between labor and capital.

One of the most prominent radical labor leaders in these decades was Eugene Debs, an advocate of labor socialism and five-time candidate for president of the United States. In an essay by Debs included here, we read in somewhat mocking tones of his disdain for industry leaders and social reformers who seek to "help" workers raise themselves up in society. According to Debs, workers do not need any such help; they need only to be properly compensated for their work and allowed to organize on their own behalf.

In contrast, we hear from Henry Clay Frick, a captain of industry, that workers do not know what is in their own best interest. In an interview included here, Frick discusses the need to break labor strikes by any means possible (including the use of private security agents) and to reduce wages as necessary to deal with downturns in business. Managers must be allowed to run their businesses as they see fit, says Frick, and in doing so they would benefit workers too. Frick argues his case during The Homestead Strike, a strike that is covered a second time in this section by U.S. Congressman from Alabama, William C. Oates, who paints a darker picture of Frick and his hired guns.

Two other workers' strikes are also explored in this section. The first is the Pullman Sleeping Car strike of 1894. The document presented centers on the issue of tips provided to train car porters—virtually all of whom were black—and what the act of tipping means in terms of the larger economic picture. The second strike examined here is a 1902 coal miners' strike organized by the United Mine Workers (UMW). Two documents, from opposing points of view, lay out the issues involved and the different perspectives brought to bear. We learn from the workers themselves about the appalling conditions they faced in the mines. And we learn from an industry leader about the economic difficulties caused by the strike.

■ "Account of the Haymarket Riot"

Date: May 5, 1886
Author: Unknown, in the *Chicago Herald*
Genre: article

Summary Overview

Published shortly after a series of dramatic events at an anarchist gathering in Chicago's Haymarket Square left at least eleven people dead and another sixty wounded, the Chicago Herald's account of what has become known as the Haymarket Riot shows the blend of objective journalism and sensationalism that characterized the public presentation of the affair. The demonstration changed quickly from peaceful to violent, and the rapid turn of events has made unraveling them impossible even more than a century later. The effects of the confrontation between demonstrators and police, however, had a significant and lasting impact on the nation. The Haymarket Riot and the subsequent conviction and execution of four anarchist leaders connected to the events changed the tone of the radical labor movement in the United States and left an enduring legacy of controversy as Americans debated how to present the events in the public sphere.

Defining Moment

The late nineteenth century was a tumultuous time in US economic and political history. As industrialization swept much of the nation, native-born Americans and new immigrants alike swelled the populations of industrial urban centers seeking jobs at factories, warehouses, stockyards, and other places of employment. The populations of industrial cities exploded; the number of Chicagoans, for example, rose from just over 110,000 on the eve of the Civil War to nearly 300,000 by 1870 and to almost 1.1 million two decades later.

Such quick expansion, however, carried its own set of challenges. Population pressures taxed the city's infrastructure, including public safety. Social and economic tensions arose between the usually better-educated and wealthy class of native-born Americans and the expanding foreign-born or first-generation American immigrant working class. Many of these immigrant workers had roots in Ireland, Germany, or regions of Eastern Europe. The economic gap between the native-born and immigrant groups was a large one; immigrant workers often filled jobs that required relatively little skill but great physical effort in difficult working conditions for low pay. Frustrated, some activists began to develop a labor movement that sought to organize industrial workers into labor unions that could agitate for improved wages, shorter hours, and other workplace goals on the behalf of all associated employees. Labor unions, such as the Knights of Labor, organized meetings, demonstrations, and strikes to agitate for change. Business owners and, often, government resisted these efforts. At the same, some activists believed that labor unions did not go far enough. They demanded a more significant reordering of society along socialist, communist, or anarchist lines.

Among these more radical voices were some influential Chicagoans. August Spies was a German-born immigrant and anarchist who had come to Chicago during the 1870s and helped run a German-language socialist newspaper. He and Albert Parsons, a prominent native-born labor activist, were both members of the city's Socialist Labor Party along with other anarchist groups. These organizations argued that the elimination of government would bring about a more equitable and harmonious society, but they failed to agree about the best way to enact this revolutionary change. Some anarchists argued that violent resistance was necessary. Americans who viewed socialist and anarchist movements as dangerous and un-American feared that radical demonstrations and strikes would inevitably lead to violence and destruction.

By the mid-1880s, tensions over radical activity in Chicago ran high. Unions and other labor activist groups organized a series of demonstrations on May 1, 1886, that involved thousands of workers across the country. Although the Chicago demonstrations were mostly peaceful, they made Spies and Parsons, who led some of the events, notorious in the eyes of antiradicals. Two days later, Spies spoke at a labor rally that ended in a confrontation between demonstrators and police as a riot broke out at a nearby factory where workers were striking. Angered by police brutality against demonstrators, a group of anarchists decided to hold an outdoor labor rally at Haymarket the following evening, May 4.

Author Biography

Written by an unidentified journalist, this account of the events in Haymarket Square was published in one of Chicago's leading dailies of the late nineteenth century, the *Chicago Herald*. The city's other main newspapers also published extensive accounts of the riot and the later trial and executions. During this time period, local newspapers enjoyed a growing readership and provided the main source of information about the events of the day. Newspaper of this era were undergoing a shift away from the open infusion of editorial commentary directly into news stories, but they had not yet embraced the objective, factual style of reporting that modern publications typically employ. The tone of the coverage of an event or individual, therefore, had the ability to influence public perception greatly.

HISTORICAL DOCUMENT

Policeman Joe Deegan and three unknown Bohemians dead, Policemen Sheehan, Barrett, Redden, Keller, and Miller mangled and dying, thirty-five other policemen wounded more or less severely, and nobody knows how many citizens and rioters wounded is the result of an encounter between the police and an Anarchistic meeting in the old market square at the corner of Randolph and Desplaines streets. . . .

Mayor Harrison was early on the scene, but it was not until after 10 o'clock that the police determined to disperse the crowd by reading the riot act. A bomb or hand grenade thrown into their ranks wrought terrible havoc with life and limb, and then ensued a scene of wild carnage with revolvers, bludgeons, and other missiles. . . . Three thousand men and boys stood around three barrels and boxes erected as a platform on the square at 8 o'clock last evening. August Spies, the editor of the *Arbeiter Zeitung*, the Anarchist organ in this city, stood upon one of the barrels. He made a brief speech to the crowd, and then introduced A. R. Parsons, one of the prominent leaders of the Socialists of Chicago. The latter told his hearers that instead of getting ten hours' pay for eight hours' work statistics proved that workingmen to-day were only getting two hours' pay for ten hours' work, and if they worked eight hours at the same wages they would only be getting three hours' pay for eight hours' work. He warned his audience that the time would come when the brutal oppression of the capitalists would drive every one save themselves into the ranks of socialism....

Samuel Fielden, a grim-visaged Anarchist, wearing a black slouch hat, then leaped upon a barrel. He said that the newspapers of the city charged the Socialists with cowardice, saying that they would sneak away from real danger. They were there to-night to repel the lie and prove that they were willing to risk their lives in the cause. It were a glorious death to die like a hero rather than be starved to death on 60 cents a day. . . .

While the Anarchist was talking a dark cloud rolled out of the northern horizon. It swept to the zenith and had the appearance of a cyclone. A fierce, cold blast of wind roared down the street. Signs creaked violently, and bits of paper flew in the air. The great crowd of Socialists, fearing that a tornado was approaching, began to seek shelter. The Anarchist leaders urged the men to adjourn to Zepf's Hall, which is only about half a block away. The ominous cloud had now passed over the stand, and north of Lake street the stars shone out again. The vast audience was now encouraged to remain by Fielden, who said he would detain them but a few moments, as it was getting late and threatening rain. . . .

. . . South of Randolph on Desplaines street a body of men was dimly seen approaching in measured tread.

It appeared like a phalanx of Masons returning from a private assembly or drill. The stillness of their approach was ominous and appalling. The 3,000 Anarchists crept closer to the barrels, and Fielden swept the street under a roof formed by the fingers of his right hand. The silent marchers came nearer, until the gas lamps on Randolph street threw their flickering light upon them. Then a hundred stars and a thousand brass buttons flashed in horizontal and perpendicular lines at the street intersections. The silent marchers were 400 police officers arranged in platoons, and choking the street from gutter to gutter. As they crossed the car tracks on Randolph street the officers clutched their clubs with a firmer grasp and then hurried forward, thus compelling the 3,000 Anarchists still massed in the street to fall back before the measured advance. Just as the officers reached the barrels upon which Spies, Parsons, and Fielden were standing a serpentine stream of fire burst from a window or the roof of Crane Brothers' manufacturing establishment on the opposite side of the street. It burned like the fuse of a rocket and hissed as it sped through the air. The mysterious stranger sputtered over the heads of the Anarchists and fell amid the officers. There was an explosion that rattled the windows in a thousand buildings, a burst of flame lit up the street, and then a scene of frightful and indescribable consternation ensued. The mysterious meteor was the fuse of a bomb hurled from the Crane Building by an Anarchist.

The work it done when it fired the explosives stored in the shell was murderous—ghastly. Over a score of officers were stretched upon the ground. Blood gushed from a hundred wounds, and the air was filled with the agonizing cries of the dying and injured. Those who escaped the deadly missiles which flew from the boom wavered for a moment. They dashed over the mangled bodies of their comrades with drawn revolvers, the glittering barrels of which were belching fire every instant. Bullets sped into the howling Anarchists in murderous storms, strewing the street with dead and dying. No quarter was given or asked. The Anarchists dodged behind boxes and barrels, from which they poured a withering, merciless fire from revolvers and guns. Officers and Socialists fall in hand-to-hand combat, and others were brought to earth by the assassin. Bystanders who had been attracted by the roar of the battle shared no better. They were shot down where they stood, or overtaken by the leaden storm while fleeing. The street was littered with the victims. Exploding cartridges flashed like a swarm of firebugs in a thicket. They came from windows, from dark alleys, and from behind every conceivable barricade.

The officers were crazed with fury. They pressed forward into the teeth of a hurricane of bullets and stones, driving their antagonists toward Lake street. The latter fled into the stores on either side of the thoroughfare....

While the battle was at its height patrol wagons filled with officers with drawn revolvers rattled down the streets from all the outlying precincts. They leaped out of the vehicles and hurried to the assistance of their comrades, who had by this time succeeded in dispersing the mob as far north as Fulton street. The officers, nearly a thousand strong, now formed in platoons and cleared all the streets within an area of three blocks. Then they returned to their comrades, who were strewn about the sidewalks and in the roadway. As fast as they were picked up they were borne to the Desplaines Street Station in patrol wagons. Many were at the point of death; all were horribly mangled. Seven bullets had pierced one officer, the legs of another had been nearly torn off by the exploding shell, and another was bleeding from a shocking gash in the neck. All were covered with blood and dirt....

So hot was the battle and so sudden the crowd's flight that no arrests were made. On their retreat to the station the police stopped to pick up the wounded members of the mob. All the patrol wagons in the city were hurried to the spot and the wounded citizens and officers were taken to the station. The citizens were taken down stairs to the cell-room and cared for by physicians as soon as they could be procured. Thence many of them were sent to the County Hospital....

Inspector Bonfield described the scene of the explosion as follows: "There were about one hundred and thirty men in the platoon, in three companies, commanded by Lieutenants Ward, Stanton, Hubbard, and Steele. We marched from the station north to Randolph street and found the crowd gathered north of Halsted street, on the east side of Desplaines. Captain Ward's company went ahead, he and I in front of the line. When we got about one hundred feet north of Randolph street and within fifteen feet of the wagon on which Fielden was holding forth Captain Ward read the statutory command in the name of the state to disperse peaceably. Some ran away at this, but Fielden was just in the midst of a sentence exhorting the crowd that 'This was the time to arm themselves,' and the words were scarcely out of Captain Ward's mouth when someone in the crowd threw the bomb. It sizzled over the heads of Captain Ward and myself, who were somewhat in advance of the line, and struck right in the middle of the line. It exploded the minute it struck, and then immediately, as if the explosion were a preconcerted signal, the crowd began to fire. Our men pulled their weapons at once and charged northward into the crowd, firing as they went. The mob scattered in every direction, but some of them fired back as they ran."....

The result of this terrible encounter will not be known for hours. Two policemen are already dead. John Degan, shot in the region of the heart; Olaf Hanson, and twenty-one others are more or less wounded, five of them seriously. Fifty or more of the strikers must be dead and wounded. The street was strewn with them, and many escaped, dragging broken limbs behind them. One, a boy, died in a drug store at the corner of Halsted and Madison streets, and an unknown Bohemian lies dead in the Desplaines Street Station.

GLOSSARY

Bohemian: literally, one from Bohemia, a region in what is now the Czech Republic; used metaphorically to refer to a socially unconventional person or someone involved in the arts

organ: newspaper or other publication with a particular political slant; mouthpiece for a group

preconcerted: preplanned, organized

Document Analysis

Published the day after the events at Haymarket Square, the *Chicago Herald's* account shows the anti-anarchist tone that would infuse public perception of the affair for the crucial first months and overtly places the blame for the events on the anarchist organizers. It opens by listing the names of several dead or injured police officers who responded to the event, immediately suggesting that the greatest tragedy of the day was the violence inflicted upon the police; only afterward and in an anonymous and more dehumanized way were the dead or injured workers acknowledged. This division informs the entire article and subtly directs the reader to view the events from a perspective that assumes the guilt of the anarchists.

The account embellishes the bare facts of the riot with dramatic, loaded language. Anarchist speaker Samuel Fielden is described as "grim-visaged," and an injury sustained by a police officer as a "shocking gash." The police contingent sent to disperse the meeting is "ominous and appalling" in its "measured advance" as the still-speaking Fielden makes a movement that could be interpreted by the reader as a symbol to act. A great deal of description is given to the throwing of the bomb, the turning point of the meeting from gathering to riot.

That the guilt lay with the anarchists is clearly argued throughout the piece. Fielden's request that the crowd stay to listen to the remainder of the speeches despite a gathering rainstorm is transformed by the account into an ominous sign of the events to come. Of the throwing of the bomb, the *Herald* asserts that the "mysterious meteor was . . . hurled from the Crane Building by an Anarchist." The bomb is stated to immediately affect only the police, with some two dozen officers injured but no anarchists harmed. Although the article discusses the intense and violent response by the police, its language implies that the response was warranted. The anarchists are said to have "escaped," as the police overcome a period during which they are "crazed with fury" over the bomb's slaying of their men to tend to the deceased and wounded. A lengthy quotation provides the police argument that the bomb was premeditated and coordinated with an attack by the assembled anarchists. The "terrible encounter" is thus linked to the radical organizers of the demonstration rather than to the response of the police in breaking up the meeting.

Essential Themes

The contemporary sensationalist coverage of the Haymarket affair has long impeded efforts to truly understand the events of the day. Shortly after the riot, Chicago police arrested the anarchist leaders and accused them of engineering a bomb plot. Altogether, eight Chicago anarchists—five of whom had not even been at the Haymarket demonstration at the time the bomb exploded and two of whom were totally unconnected to it—were put on trial for the murder of the only police officer undisputedly killed from the bomb blast itself. At the time, Chicago's newspapers blurred the lines between editorial commentary and news reporting, condemning the events as the work of the anarchists and inflaming public opinion against the accused. All eight of the accused men were convicted; one committed suicide while awaiting execution, three were imprisoned (though later pardoned), and four, including Parsons and Spies, were hanged on November 11, 1887. The convictions, made on thin evidence by a jury containing members who admitted to being influenced by the press coverage before the trial, reflected a general distrust of immigrants and radicals that continued for many years. No one has ever definitively determined who threw the bomb that incited the riot.

The physical explosion in the square also had a less tangible but quite destructive influence on the American radicalism. Although the Haymarket leaders became martyrs for the international radical community, the larger proportion of Americans who suspected that anarchists and associated groups were crazed and violent felt that the events at Haymarket confirmed those beliefs. The hangings of the accused anarchist leaders were a severe blow to not only the anarchist movement in the United States but also less extremist labor movements. Public outcry over the event led labor leaders to distance their organizations from the notion of idealist revolutionary reform based on opposition to the capitalist economic system as a whole. The movement for the eight-hour workday, the issue over which the Haymarket demonstration had been convened, was temporarily derailed. Some local unionists abandoned their affiliation with the more radical Knights of Labor, of which Parsons had been a member, to join with the American Federation of Labor instead.

Over time, the public view on the Haymarket Riot has changed, however. An 1889 Chicago statue honoring the police killed at Haymarket was damaged so frequently that it was eventually moved from the site. Sympathy for the convicted anarchists has grown tremendously, particularly in the twentieth and twenty-first centuries, and the eight-hour workday was adopted as a national standard by the 1930s.

—*Vanessa E. Vaughn, MA*

Bibliography and Additional Reading

Avrich, Paul. *The Haymarket Tragedy*. Princeton: Princeton UP, 1984. Print.

David, Henry. *The History of the Haymarket Affair: A Study in the American Social-Revolutionary and Labor Movements*. New York: Russell, 1958. Print.

Green, James. *Death in the Haymarket: A Story of Chicago, the First Labor Movement and the Bombing that Divided Gilded Age America*. New York: Pantheon, 2006. Print.

Rushing, Kittrell. "The Case of the Haymarket Riot (1886)." *The Press on Trial: Crimes and Trials as Media Events*. Ed. Lloyd Chiasson. Westport: Greenwood, 1997. Print.

Smith, Carl. *The Dramas of Haymarket*. Chicago Historical Soc. and Northwestern U. Web. 28 Mar. 2014.

■ Eugene Debs: "What Can We Do for Working People?"

Date: April 1890
Author: Eugene V. Debs
Genre: article; editorial; essay

Summary Overview

During the so-called Gilded Age of the late nineteenth century, two competing visions of America were propagated. One, put forth by people such as industrialist Andrew Carnegie, emphasized the beneficial role of the wealthy in society. The other, which was held by union and Socialist Party leader Eugene Victor Debs, was more focused on working-class Americans whose well-being was often at the mercy of factory owners' desire for more wealth. In his essay "What Can We Do for Working People?," Debs presents the case that organizing into unions will allow working people to control their destiny and throw off the ideals of the wealthy, whose goal is to ensure that workers are employed for as little money as possible. By utilizing the power of the ballot box during elections and incorporating collective action in the workplace, working people will be better able to determine the course of their lives.

Defining Moment

Debs wrote his essay at a very difficult time for America's nascent labor movement. The prosperity of Gilded Age America was concentrated in the hands of those who owned the means of production. Men such as John D. Rockefeller, Andrew Carnegie, and John Pierpont Morgan controlled entire industries and spent as little as possible on their workers' wages and safety. The working class saw little, if any, benefit from the booming economy of the Industrial Revolution, and they exercised little power over the terms of their employment.

Though trade unions had worked to organize skilled workers for over a century, common laborers had no such protection until the rise of the Knights of Labor, which sought to bring together common workers and collectively negotiate to improve their lot. However, because of the violence that occurred during a labor rally at Chicago's Haymarket Square in 1886, many US citizens associated unions with foreign radicalism and the ideologies of anarchism and socialism.

Debs would not be deterred, however, and he continued to argue in favor of unions as the only way for working people to achieve higher wages, safe working conditions, and an eight-hour day. But the labor movement did not come together to create a united front: as trade unions such as the American Federation of Labor (AFL) organized to improve the conditions of specially skilled workers, the Knights of Labor, which represented the interests of common workers, declined in influence as they became associated with radicalism. The AFL sought to distance itself from partisan politics, whereas Debs encouraged workers to take action both in the workplace and at the polling place in order to elect pro-labor candidates who would institute the long-term goals of the labor movement. Whereas AFL leader Samuel Gompers preferred an issues-based alliance with politicians from the major parties, Debs encouraged workers to become active participants in the political organizations dedicated to the working peoples' agenda, such as the Socialist Labor Party (SLP) and the People's Party (also known as the Populist Party).

Debs's perspective was much more in line with the view espoused two years earlier by utopian novelist Edward Bellamy in *Looking Backward* (1888). A thorough critique of Gilded Age capitalism, Bellamy's view appealed to working people, with whom his ideal society, free of social divisions and conflict, resonated. But the only way to achieve a utopia such as Bellamy espoused was through voting and through organizing industrial workers to take control of their own fate.

Author Biography

Eugene V. Debs was born in Terre Haute, Indiana, on November 5, 1855. Like many young men at that time, he left school and entered the workplace at the age of fourteen. Around 1870, he became active in the railways employees union, the Brotherhood of Locomotive Firemen and Enginemen, and started a career as an advocate for working people. During the 1880s, Debs, still a member of the Democratic Party, won a seat in the Indiana state legislature. However, his true calling was with the railroad workers, and he became national secretary of the Brotherhood in 1880. It was during this period that his essay, "What Can We Do for Working People?" appeared in the union's periodical, the *Locomotive Firemen's Magazine*.

During the 1890s, Debs would expand his role nationally and found and lead the American Railway Union (ARU) in 1893. The ARU, which would soon become the largest organized union in the nation, accepted any white railway worker below the position of foreman, and Debs became instrumental in some of the union's most important labor actions before becoming a national political figure and running for president of the United States as a Socialist in 1900, 1904, 1908, and 1912.

HISTORICAL DOCUMENT

In one form or another certain persons are continually asking, "What can we do, or, What can be done for working people?" Why should such a question be asked at all in the United States? What gives rise to it? Are there circumstances and conditions warranting such an interrogatory? Who propounds it?....

Philanthropists of a certain type ask, "What can be done for working people?" and recommend soup houses, free baths, and more stringent laws against idleness and tramping, together with improved machinery in penitentiaries.

Another class devote time and investigation to diet, to show if wages decline that a man can live on ten cents a day and keep his revolting soul within his wretched body.

Another class, in answering the question, "What can we do for the working people?" reply by saying, "We will organize an Insurance Bureau which shall insure workingmen against accident, sickness, and death. We will supply them with medicine, doctors, and hospitals, taking so much from their wages to maintain the Bureau, and then, by compelling them to sign a contract which virtually reduces them to chattels, and makes them a part of our machinery, we will permit them to work for such pay as we choose to determine."

Another class answer the question, "What can we do for working people?" by telling them that unless they consent to abandon their labor organizations, absolve themselves from all obligations to such organizations, so far as they are concerned they shall have no work at all.

There are others, still, who discuss schemes for doing great and good things for working people, excepting, so far as it has come under the notice of the writer, to pay fair, honest wages.

This whole business of doing something for working people is disgusting and degrading to the last degree. It is not desirable to deny that in some quarters the question is asked honestly, but in such cases it is always in order to manifest pity for the questioner.

He is not inconvenienced by a surplus of brains. The question, "What can we do for working people?" as a general proposition, finds its resemblance in a question that might be asked by the owner of a sheep ranch, "What can I do for the sheep?" The reply would be, doubtless, "shear them." The ranch man takes care of the sheep that he may shear them, and it will be found that the men who ask with so much pharisaical solicitude, "What can we do for working men?" are the very ones who shear them the closest when the opportunity offers—strip them of everything of value that they may the more easily subjugate them by necessities of cold and hunger and nakedness, degrade and brutalize them to a degree that they become as fixed in their servitude as the wheels, cogs, cranks, and pins in the machinery they purchase and operate.

The real question to be propounded is, "What can workingmen do for themselves?" The answer is ready. They can do all things required, if they are independent, self-respecting, self-reliant men.

Workingmen can organize. Workingmen can combine, federate, unify, cooperate, harmonize, act in concert. This done, workingmen could control governmental affairs. They could elect honest men to office. They could make wise constitutions, enact just laws, and repeal vicious laws. By acting together they could overthrow monopolies and trusts. They could squeeze the water out of stocks, and decree that dividends shall be declared only upon cash investments. They could make the cornering of food products of the country a crime, and send the scoundrels guilty of the crime to the penitentiary. Such things are not vagaries. They are not Utopian dreams. They are practical. They are honest, they are things of good report.

Workingmen are in the majority. They have the most votes. In this God-favored land, where the ballot is all powerful, peaceful revolutions can be achieved. Wrongs can be crushed — sent to their native hell, and the right can be enthroned by workingmen acting together, pulling together.

What can workingmen do for themselves? They can teach capitalists that they do not want and will not accept their guardianship; that they are capable of self-management, and that they simply want fair pay for an honest day's work, and this done, "honors are easy." Fidelity to obligation is not a one-sided affair. Mutual respect is not the offspring of arrogance. There may have been a time when it was proper for the Southern slave owner to ask himself, "What can I do to better the condition of my slaves?" He owned them, they were his property; he controlled their destiny. He made them work as he did his cattle, mules, and horses, and appropriated all their earnings. Their children were his property as were the calves and colts of his cows and mares. But there never was a time beyond the dark boundary line of slavery when an employer of American workingmen could ask himself such a question without offering a degrading insult to every self-respecting workingman, and when a workingman hears it or anything like it and his cheek does not burn with righteous indignation he may know that he is on the road to subjugation, and if there exists a more humiliating spectacle within the boundaries of all the zones that belt the earth, what is it?

At every turn the question recurs, "What can workingmen do for themselves?" The question demands an answer, and unbidden a thousand are ready. We have not space for them. Let each workingman answer for himself. For one, we say the workingman can educate himself. He can read, study, and vote. He can improve his time and perfect his skill. He can see as clearly as others coming events, and prepare for their advent.

GLOSSARY

chattel: property; a slave

pharisaical: hypocritically self-righteous; condemnatory

tramping: wandering, vagabondage

Document Analysis

Having been involved in the trade union movement for over a decade, Debs was adjusting his beliefs as the labor movement began to transform. Rather than concern himself with the betterment of working conditions of a particular industry, Debs's essay reflects a growing awareness of the commonality of all industrial workers, skilled and unskilled. Debs was one of a growing number of reformers, often from the upper classes of American society, who were considering ways to appease American workers who were voicing and demonstrating their dissatisfaction with their pay, working conditions, or terms of employment.

Debs begins the essay by noting that reformers in his time sought to ensure that industrial workers were pacified enough to continue to provide the cheapest possible labor for the benefit of America's factory owners and industrialists (much as slaveholders had before them). Each group of reformers is addressed by Debs, who analyzes their proposals and notes that each refuses to consider paying "fair, honest wages," which, Debs claims, is "disgusting and degrading to the last degree."

Debs asks, "What can workingmen do for themselves?," and then answers that they can organize into unions to collectively bargain for what is in their best interests and can utilize their voting power to choose candidates who will best represent them in state and federal government.

Essential Themes

After "What Can We Do for Working People?" was published, Debs became increasingly outspoken. His speeches became dominated by the ideals of socialism and argued that the model of industrial capitalism was fundamentally flawed. Many in the middle and upper classes condemned the labor movement for promoting what they considered to be radical ideologies, but Debs and the ideas he expressed persisted.

Debs led the American Railway Union through tumultuous times, including the April 1894 strike against robber baron Jay Gould's Great Northern Railroad and the massive Pullman Strike the following month. Debs was imprisoned for six months for his role in the Pullman Strike, and when he was released he announced he was a socialist and helped to form the Social Democratic Party, which then became the Socialist Party. Debs ran as the Socialist Party candidate for US president for four consecutive elections between 1900 and 1912.

In 1905, Debs helped to found the Industrial Workers of the World (IWW), which best represented his ideas about American industrial workers and socialism. The IWW's goal was to create "one big union" of industrial workers across the nation. Debs's ideas, however, were again considered too radical, and the IWW lacked the support of the American middle and upper classes.

Though Debs and AFL leader Samuel Gompers disagreed on some aspects of unionism, they saw each other as allies, and the AFL eventually became more inclusive of workers from across the broad spectrum of American industry, though it still organized on a per-industry basis. After losing the 1912 presidential election, Debs won an Indiana congressional seat in the 1916 election, running on a pacifist platform and in opposition to America's involvement in World War I. He continued to voice his opposition when the United States entered the war in 1918, which resulted in his arrest and incarceration for sedition and violation of the Espionage Act. Nominated for the presidency by the Socialist Party in 1920, Debs ran his campaign from prison and received six percent of the popular vote. He was released upon the order of President Warren Harding on Christmas Day 1921. Debs died in 1926.

—*Steven L. Danver, PhD*

Bibliography and Additional Reading

Ginger, Ray. *The Bending Cross: A Biography of Eugene Victor Debs*. Chicago: Haymarket, 2007 Print.

Kloppenberg, James T. *Uncertain Victory: Social Democracy and Progressivism in European and American Thought, 1870–1920*. New York: Oxford UP, 1988. Print.

Lipset, Seymour Martin, and Gary Marks. *It Didn't Happen Here: Why Socialism Failed in the United States*. New York: Norton, 2000. Print.

Salvatore, Nick. *Eugene V. Debs: Citizen and Socialist*. 2nd ed. Urbana: U of Illinois P, 2007. Print.

■ Frick's Fracas—Henry Frick Makes His Case

Date: July 8, 1892
Author: Henry Clay Frick
Genre: interview; article

Summary Overview

During the 1892 strike at the Homestead Steel Works, a facility of Carnegie Steel, company chair Henry Clay Frick offered his thoughts on the tense standoff between the company and the plant's striking employees in an interview with the *Pittsburgh Post*. Frick argued for reduced wages for employees and defended Carnegie's employee policies. He also railed against the strikers' tactics, defending his use of private security agents from the Pinkerton National Detective Agency and calling upon the state of Pennsylvania to intervene in the strike.

Defining Moment

The late nineteenth century was marked by strong growth in the US economy, spurred in large part by the expansion of the American railways. Major enterprises such as the Carnegie Steel Company thrived, generating massive profits even during occasional economic downturns. This growth and prosperity was made possible by the country's working class, and a vast majority of American laborers worked long hours in often hazardous environments at low wages. In light of these inadequate working conditions, labor unions also experienced significant growth and activity during this period of economic growth, as members sought better wages and working conditions.

In late June and early July of 1892, a major confrontation between labor and corporate leadership took place at the Carnegie Steel Company's Homestead Steel Works facility in Homestead, Pennsylvania. Tensions had begun earlier in February, when the Amalgamated Association of Iron and Steel Workers, which represented a large number of Carnegie's most skilled employees, negotiated to renew the union's contract, which was set to expire on June 30, 1892. Andrew Carnegie, the owner of Carnegie Steel, had the company's chair, Frick, make a bombshell offer to the union: he proposed a wage reduction of more than eighteen percent and the removal of a number of positions from the union's collective bargaining unit. For the Homestead workers, wages were tied to the selling price of steel (a practice known as "sliding scale" wages). While there was no cap for increasing prices and wages, there was a limit at which the decline of wages relative to prices stopped, and Frick and Carnegie had proposed lowering the minimum limit of compensation even further. Based on the recent increase in the Homestead facility's output, the union had entered the negotiations under the expectation that Carnegie would offer a wage increase. The move, which many historians believe was deliberately orchestrated by Carnegie himself in an attempt to provoke a strike in order to undermine organized labor, was both bold and unexpected.

In late June, several days prior to the expiration of the union's collective bargaining agreement, Frick closed portions of the mill and barred entry to union employees. Although less than eight hundred employees were members of Amalgamated, more than three thousand employees agreed to strike in protest. Left alone to manage the strike by Carnegie (who was touring Scotland), Frick quickly completed the construction of a tall fence around the plant in order to keep out striking workers; the workers organized picket lines to surround the facility and prevent its operations from resuming.

In an effort to regain control of the Homestead plant, Frick dispatched by boat three hundred armed Pinkerton agents on the night of July 5 to enter the facility by river. Upon their arrival at the mill, the Pinkerton agents were met by the striking employees. A violent confrontation ensued as the Pinkertons and workers exchanged heavy gunfire. Nine workers and several Pinkerton agents were killed, and several hundred people suffered injuries. In light of the violence, Frick contacted the governor of Pennsylvania, Robert E. Pattison, in Harrisburg. Pattison deployed the state militia to Homestead. The presence of the militia enabled Frick to resume operations at the plant by employing strikebreakers. An assassination attempt on Frick on July 23 dissolved public support for the strike, and the strikers voted to return to work on Carnegie's terms. With the collapse of the union, Homestead workers saw their wages slashed, work hours increased, and the elimination of several hundred jobs at the facility.

Two days after the violent confrontation between Pinkerton agents and striking workers on July 6, a Pennsylvania newspaper published an interview with Frick, in which he justified his actions and unequivocally expressed his disdain for organized labor.

Author Biography

Henry Clay Frick was born in West Overton, Pennsylvania, on December 19, 1849. He briefly attended Otterbein College in Westerville, Ohio, but he did not finish his studies. Instead, he moved to Pittsburgh, where he entered the coal and coke (a fuel used in steelmaking) business with his cousins in 1871. By 1880, he bought his cousins out of their partnership and founded the H. C. Frick Coke Company. Within a decade of its founding, Frick's company was producing more than eighty percent of the Pittsburgh steel industry's coke, rapidly turning Frick into a millionaire. In 1882, Frick and industrialist Carnegie entered a major partnership, bringing together Carnegie's steel empire and Frick's growing coke industry. Later in life, Frick moved to New York, where he constructed a massive mansion to house his growing art collection. Frick died on December 2, 1919, and he bequeathed his extensive art collection to create The Frick Collection, a museum inside his New York City residence.

HISTORICAL DOCUMENT

In an interview yesterday afternoon with Mr. George N. McCain, correspondent of the Philadelphia Press, Mr. H. C. Frick, chairman of the Carnegie Steel Company, Limited, said:

The question at issue is a very grave one. It is whether the Carnegie Company or the Amalgamated Association shall have absolute control of our plant and business at Homestead. We have decided, after numerous fruitless conferences with the Amalgamated officials in the attempt to amicably adjust the existing difficulties, to operate the plant ourselves. I can say with the greatest emphasis that under no circumstances will we have any further dealings with the Amalgamated Association as an organization. This is final. The Edgar Thomson Works and our establishment at Duquesne are both operated by workmen who are not members of the Amalgamated Association with the greatest satisfaction to ourselves and to the unquestioned advantage of our employees. At both of these plants the work in every department; goes on uninterrupted; the men are not harassed by the interference of trade union officials, and the best evidence

that their wages are satisfactory is shown in the fact that we have never had a strike there since they began working under our system of management.

What was the basis of the differences existing at present between the Carnegie company and their men, Mr. Frick?

FIRST POINT AT ISSUE.

There, were three points upon which we differed. The skilled workmen in the Amalgamated Association work under what is known as a sliding scale. As the price of steel advances the earnings of the men advance; as the prices fall their earnings decrease in proportion. While there is no limit to an advance of earnings on the scale, there is a limit at which the decline stops. It is known as the minimum, and the figure heretofore has been $25 per ton for 4 by 4 Bessemer billets. We believe that if earnings based on the selling price of steel can advance without limit the workmen should be willing to follow the selling price down to a reasonable minimum, and so this figure was finally fixed by the Carnegie Company at the rate of $23 instead of $25. The reason for asking this upon our part was that the Carnegie Company has spent large sums of money in the introduction of new machinery in its Homestead plant, by means of which the workmen were enabled to increase their daily output, thereby increasing the amount of their own earnings. We had originally asked a reduction to $22, but subsequently agreed to compromise the rate at $23. The Amalgamated Association was unwilling to consider a reduction below $24 on steel billets, notwithstanding the fact that the improved machinery would enable their members, even at $23, to earn more than is paid in other Amalgamated mills. This was the first point at issue.

OTHER STUMBLING BLOCKS.

Under the present Amalgamated system the date of the expiration of the sliding scale is June 30, annually. We asked that this date be changed to December 31 (same as at Edgar Thomson), for the reason that the change would permit us to take our estimate upon the wages that we must pay during the year, beginning on January 1, so that we would be enabled to make contracts for the year accordingly. This point the Amalgamated Association refused to accede, and demanded the old date. The third proposition was the reduction in tonnage rates in those departments in the mills where the improvements I have spoken of have been made and which enable the workingmen to increase the output and consequently their earnings. Where no such improvements had been made there was no request on our part for a reduction in tonnage rate. In other words, we asked no reduction in any department of which the output had not been greatly increased by reason of our expensive improvements since the scale of 1889 went into effect.

As a rule, the men who were making the largest wages in the mill were the ones who most bitterly denounced the proposed revision of the scale, for out of the 3,800 men employed in every department only 325 were directly affected by this reduction.

WORKMEN HELD SWAY.

Finding that it was impossible to arrive at any agreement with the Amalgamated Association we decided to close our works at Homestead. Immediately the town was taken possession of by the workmen. An advisory committee of 50 took upon itself the direction of the affairs of the place; the streets were patrolled by men appointed by this committee, and every stranger entering the town became an object of surveillance, was closely questioned, and if there was the slightest reason to suspect him he was ordered to leave the place instantly under the threat of bodily harm. Guards were stationed at every approach to Homestead by the self-organized local government. Our employees were prohibited from going to the mills, and we, as the owners of the property, were compelled to stand by powerless to conduct the affairs of our business or direct its management. This condition of affairs lasted until Tuesday, when I appealed to the sheriff of Allegheny County, stating the facts as I have outlined them. The sheriff visited Homestead and talked with the advisory committee. Its members asked that they be permitted to appoint men from their own number to act as deputy sheriffs; in other words, the men who were interfering with the exercise of our corporate rights, preventing us from conducting our business affairs, requested that they be clothed with the authority of deputy sheriffs to take charge of our plant. The sheriff declined their proposition, and the advisory committee disbanded. The rest of the story is a familiar one; the handful of deputies sent up by the Sheriff McCleary were surrounded by the mob and forced to leave the town, and then the watchmen were sent up to be landed on our own property for the protection of our plant.

Why did the Carnegie Company call upon the Pinkertons for watchmen to protect their property?

We did not see how else we would have protection. We only wanted them for watchmen to protect our property and see that workmen we would take to Homestead—and we have had applications from many men to go there to—were not interfered with.

DOUBTED THE SHERIFF'S POWER.

Did you doubt the ability of the sheriff to enforce order at Homestead and protect your property?

Yes sir; with local deputies.

Why?

For the reason that three years ago our concern had an experience similar to this. We felt the necessity of a change at the works; that a scale should be adopted based on the sliding price of billets, and we asked the county authorities for protection. The workmen began tactics similar to those employed in the present troubles. The sheriff assured the members of the firm that there would be no difficulty, that he would give them ample protection and see that men who were willing to work were not interfered with. What was the result? The posse taken up by the sheriff—something over 100 men—were not permitted to land on our property; were driven off with threats of bodily harm, and it looked as if there was going to be great destruction of life and property. That frightened our people. Mr. Abbott was then in charge of the Carnegie, Phipps & Co. business, and was asked by the Amalgamated officials for a conference, which he agreed to, fearful if he did not do so there might be loss of life and destruction of property. Under that stress, in fear of the Amalgamated Association, an agreement was made and work was resumed. We did not propose this time to be placed in that position.

The Pinkerton men, as generally understood, had been summoned and all arrangements made with them to be on hand in case of failure by the sheriff to afford protection. Is that a fact or not?

The facts concerning the engagement of the Pinkerton men are these: From past experience, not only with the present sheriff but with all others, we have found that he has been unable to furnish us with a sufficient number of deputies to guard our property and protect the men who were anxious to work on our terms. As the Amalgamated men from the 1st of July had surrounded our works placed guards at all the entrances, and at all avenues or roads leading to our establishment and for miles distant therefrom, we felt that for the safety of our property, and in order to protect our workmen, it was necessary for us to secure our own watchmen to assist the sheriff, and we knew of no other source from which to obtain them than from Pinkerton agencies, and to them we applied.

TRIED TO AVOID TROUBLE.

We brought the watchmen here as quietly as possible;

had them taken to Homestead at an hour of the night when we hoped to have them enter our works without any interference whatever and without meeting anybody. We proposed to land them on our own property, and all our efforts were to prevent the possibilities of a collision between our former workmen and our watchmen. We are to-day barred out of our property at Homestead, and have been since the 1st of July. There is nobody in the mills up there now; they are standing a silent mass of machinery with nobody to look after them. They are in the hands of our former workmen.

Have the men made overtures for a settlement of the difficulties since this trouble commenced?

Yes, sir. A leading ex-official in the Amalgamated Association yesterday, when this rioting was going on, called on the sheriff and I am informed asked him to come down to see me, stating that if he could get a promise that we would confer with the representatives of the Amalgamated Association looking toward an adjustment of this trouble, that he would go to Homestead and try to stop the rioting.

Did you consider his proposal?

No, sir. I told the gentleman who called that we could not confer with Amalgamated Association officials. That it was their followers who were rioting and destroying our property, and we would not accept his proposition. At the same time this representative of our former workmen said that they were willing to accept the terms offered, and concede everything we asked except the date of the scale, which they insisted should be June 30 in place of December 31.

FUTURE OF IT ALL.

What of the future of this difficulty?

It is in the hands of the authorities of Allegheny County. If they are unable to cope with it, it is certainly the duty of the governor of the State to see that we are permitted to operate our establishment unmolested. The men engaged by us through the Pinkerton agencies were sent up to Homestead with the full knowledge sheriff and by him placed in charge of his chief deputy, Col. Gray, and, as we know, with instructions to deputize them in case it became necessary. We have made an impartial investigation and are satisfied beyond doubt that the watchmen employed by us were fired upon by our former workmen and their friends for twenty-five minutes before they reached our property, and were fired upon after they had reached our property. That they did not return the fire until after the boats had touched the shore, and after three of the watchmen had been wounded, one fatally. After a number of the watchmen were wounded, and Capt. Rodgers, in charge of the tow-boat, at their request, had taken the injured away, leaving the barges at our works unprotected, our former workmen refused to allow Capt. Rodgers to return to the barges that he might remove them from our property, but fired at him and fatally wounded one of the crew.

You doubtless are aware, Mr. Frick, that the troubles at the Homestead mill invited widespread attention, and as a result Congress proposes to investigate the trouble, as well as the employment of Pinkerton detectives?

I am aware of the fact, sir. While nobody could regret the occurrences of the last few days more than myself, yet it is my duty, as the executive head of the Carnegie Company, to protect the interests of the association. We desire to, and will protect our property at all hazards. So far as Congressional investigation is concerned, I can say with the utmost candor that we welcome the investigation proposed. We are prepared to submit facts and figures which will convince unprejudiced men of the equity of our position. More than this, I believe that when all of the facts are known revelations will be made which will emphasize the justice of all our claims.

AS TO POLITICS.

How do you regard the present troubles at Homestead from a political standpoint. What effect will it have as a tariff issue in the political campaign of the coming fall?

We have never given a thought as to what effect our affairs might have on either of the political parties. We cannot afford to run our business and run politics at the same time. It would prove very unprofitable if we were to trim our sails to meet political issues. At the same time I may say that it is not a matter in which the protective tariff is involved, and every intelligent man, whether he be a manufacturer or employee, is aware of the fact. It is, however, a question as to whether or not the proprietors or its workmen will manage the works.

We did not propose to reduce the earnings of our employees below those of Amalgamated men in other mills. As I have said, we have put in improved machinery which other mills do not possess; increased our output and increased the earnings of our men. We asked that a reduction be made in these departments so that the earnings of our employee's would be on a par with other workmen in other Amalgamated mills. It is not a question of starvation wages, for you will please bear in mind the fact that the proposed equalization of earnings affects only about 325 men out of 3,800, and they are the ones who earn the most money in our establishment. It has no effect upon the wages of more the 15,000 other employees engaged in our establishment at Duquesne, Braddock, Pittsburg, Beaver Falls, and in the coke region.

GLOSSARY

billet: a small bar of metal used in metals manufacturing

concern: a firm or company

sliding scale: a wage scale that varies with the selling price of goods produced, the cost of living, or profits

Document Analysis

Despite his stated willingness to negotiate in good faith with the union members, Frick was an outspoken opponent of organized labor. His comments to the *Pittsburgh Post* reflected this attitude: in his interview, Frick accuses the Amalgamated Association of Iron and Steel Workers of attempting to take over Carnegie Steel and of inciting the violence and destruction that occurred during the standoff with Pinkerton agents. He also places responsibility for keeping the peace in the hands of the local, regional, and state law enforcement authorities.

When asked about the events leading up to the strike, Frick declares that the Amalgamated Association is an unwelcome organization. Other Carnegie Steel Company plants, he argues, operate without the presence of Amalgamated personnel "with the greatest satisfaction to ourselves and to the unquestioned advantage of our employees." He adds that Amalgamated members have simply refused to hear Carnegie's side of the issue and were being intransigent in their demands. On the issue of sliding scale wages, for example, Frick argues that linking wages to the selling price of steel (and putting in place a minimum to prevent bottoming out) balances the interests of the corporation and its employees. Frick further argues that Carnegie initially requested a reduction in wages in order to purchase far more efficient machines and equipment that had boosted the daily output of Homestead workers, thereby increasing their earnings. Even the number of employees affected by wage reductions was relatively small (about 325 of 3,800 workers), he claims.

Frick claims that because Amalgamated and the striking workers refused to negotiate in good faith with Carnegie, it was necessary to cut ties with the union and close the plant to the striking workers. He accuses the union of essentially laying siege to the town and states that he appealed directly to the sheriff of Allegheny County, where Homestead was located. However, when the sheriff's deputies arrived, they too were intimidated by the large numbers of hostile striking workers. No local force could counter the union mob, Frick suggests, necessitating the arrival of the Pinkerton agents and the state militia. When asked whether he believed the strike had political implications, Frick responds that his job is to operate a business, regardless of how either political party views his company.

Essential Themes

Frick's comments to the media following the end of the Homestead Strike were defiant and accusatory, assigning responsibility for the strike and the violence that ensued entirely to the Amalgamated members. He remained adamant in his belief that Amalgamated had grossly misinterpreted the company's wage policies and was unnecessarily stubborn in their demands. He argued that the principal issue of the strike was the "question as to whether or not the proprietors or its workmen will manage the works." He further pointed at the union as the instigator of a violent situation so difficult to contain that Frick had to call in private contractors to ensure security. Frick's company, he stated, was well within its legal rights to make operational changes, while Amalgamated was engaged in blatantly illegal activities.

The aftermath of the Homestead Strike saw a significant diminishment in the power and influence of unions, not only in the Pittsburgh steel industry but also nationwide. Throughout the United States, many employers became reluctant to enter into contracts with unions. The violent confrontation at Homestead is illustrative of the tensions between organized labor and management that were playing out across the country at the end of the nineteenth century and the beginning of the twentieth.

—*Michael P. Auerbach, MA*

Bibliography and Additional Reading

MacKay, James. *Andrew Carnegie: Little Boss*. New York: Random, 2012. Print.

Skrabec, Quentin R., Jr. *Henry Clay Frick: The Life of the Perfect Capitalist*. Jefferson: McFarland, 2010. Print.

Standiford, Les. *Meet You in Hell: Andrew Carnegie, Henry Clay Frick, and the Bitter Partnership that Changed America*. New York: Broadway, 2006. Print.

■ The Homestead Strike: A Congressional View

Date: September 1892
Author: William C. Oates
Genre: essay; report

Summary Overview

The circumstances that led to the Homestead Strike did not happen overnight. The skilled laborers in the mill had been engaged in a contest of wills with their employer, Carnegie Steel, for over a decade before the lid blew off and resulted in what came to be known as the "Battle of Homestead," in which ten workers were killed. The issues underlying the Homestead Strike had to do with the rights of workers to organize into unions and collectively bargain for better wages pitted against the need for increasing profits by company owner Andrew Carnegie and his business partner who ran the Homestead Mill, Henry Clay Frick. However, the implications of what happened at Homestead would have ramifications far beyond Carnegie's considerable steel empire, as the supremacy of the corporations over the workers and their unions—and even the local, state, and federal governments—would hold for many years.

Defining Moment

By 1892, Andrew Carnegie had been in the steel business for seventeen years and was the owner of the largest manufacturing company in the United States, producing over a quarter of the nation's steel. Nine years earlier, in 1883, Carnegie had acquired a massive new mill near Pittsburgh, the Homestead Steel Works, which was only two years old at the time of purchase, and Carnegie made it the centerpiece in his steel empire. Though Carnegie had often been viewed as one of the more enlightened of the "robber barons," the episode that occurred at Homestead would show him to be just as ruthless as his contemporaries when it came to the competition between workers' rights and corporate profits.

As late as 1886, Carnegie had written a piece in a national periodical defending the workers' right to form unions, though his business partner, Henry Clay Frick, disagreed. In 1889, the nearly four thousand workers at Homestead went on strike, and to end the unrest, Carnegie signed a three-year agreement with the Amalgamated Association of Iron and Steel Workers, recognizing the union and guaranteeing very favorable working conditions and wages to the workers. The contract had a three-year term, which was set to expire June 30, 1892. In those three years, Carnegie and Frick became increasingly convinced that the only way to increase the profits at Homestead was to decrease workers' wages—and the only way to do that was to break the union.

Labor strife at Homestead was not an isolated event. In 1886, a strike against the McCormick Harvesting Machine Company had led to the violent explosions at Chicago's Haymarket Square, which dealt a crippling blow to the first national union, the Knights of Labor. During 1892, coal miners went on strike in Tennessee, rail workers in New York, copper miners in Idaho, and nearly all workers in New Orleans. However, Carnegie was determined that a strike at Homestead would result in the breaking of the union.

In the months leading up to the end of the contract, Carnegie, preferring to watch the action from his family home in Dunfermline, Scotland, instructed Frick to increase production and stockpile steel plates in order to withstand a prolonged labor stoppage. His communication with his partner was very clear that he supported Frick, who had a well-earned reputation for ruthlessness, in his efforts to completely destroy the union. Carnegie assumed that the workers would capitulate and give up the union in order to keep their jobs. The more realistic Frick prepared by constructing an eleven-foot fence around the Homestead Mill to keep the workers out after the contract ran out, and he arranged for the Pinkerton Detective Agency to serve as a private police force that would enforce the lockout. With negotiations ending between the union and Frick on June 24, 1892, the stage was set for what would become a touchstone moment in the history of business and organized labor.

Author Biography

William C. Oates was elected to the Unites States House of Representatives from his home state of Alabama in 1880. He served in Congress until 1894, when he was elected governor of Alabama. The Confederate Civil War veteran and member of the Democratic Party sat on the House's Judiciary Committee and was given the chairmanship of the subcommittee conducting the investigation into the violence and bloodshed that had taken place at Homestead. Specifically concentrating on the role that the hiring of the Pinkerton agents had in fomenting the violence that ensued, Oates interviewed nearly everyone involved in the Homestead affair, including Henry Clay Frick, mill superintendent John A. Potter, Pinkerton Detective Agency owners William and Robert Pinkerton, and a number of the mill workers. His report would do much to expose the events that happened before and during the strike.

HISTORICAL DOCUMENT

THE HOMESTEAD STRIKE. A CONGRESSIONAL VIEW.

BY THE HON. WILLIAM C. OATES, CHAIRMAN OF THE CONGRESSIONAL INVESTIGATING COMMITTEE.

Homestead is a very comfortable-looking, neat little town of 10,000 to 12,000 inhabitants, situated on the left bank of the Monongahela River, seven miles east of the city of Pittsburg. Its inhabitants are chiefly laborers and mechanics of various degrees of skill, from the highest down to the ordinary laborer, with a competent number of small merchants and tradespeople. About one-half of the population are of foreign birth and represent various European nationalities.

About one mile up the river from the heart of the town are located the Homestead Works of Carnegie, Phipps & Co., the cost of which, exclusive of the ground, is near $6,000,000. At these works they manufacture structural materials used largely in fireproof buildings, such as beams, channels, etc. They also manufacture steel armor plates for use in the construction of war vessels. The 119-inch mill at which these plates are finished is one of the best of its kind in the world. The armor plate for the new Cruisers 9 and 10 now being constructed is manufactured here. The Navy Department has a contract with this company for 6,000 tons of armor plate to be used in the construction of our new war vessels. They also manufacture at Homestead all kinds of plate and do a general miscellaneous business.

Up to the last of June there were employed in these works about 3,800 men, including a number of boys. The pay-roll showed a disbursement for the month of May alone of something over $200,000. Wages have been from 14 cents per hour to the common laborer, that being the lowest, up to $280 per month (which was the highest paid in the month of May), a majority of the skilled laborers receiving $200 and less.

While the Carnegie company under its present management has been exacting, it has also performed many acts of liberality and kindness to its employees. It has at times loaned money to some of them to purchase lots and build their homes, for the use of which it has charged them but 6 per cent, interest. It receives from them deposits upon which it pays them 6 per cent, interest, the aggregate amount of which the last of June was $140,000.

On July 1, 1889, the company through its officers made a contract with a number of skilled workmen, through the Amalgamated Association of Iron and Steel Workers, to run for three years, or until the 30th of June, 1892.

The basis of that contract was a certain sum per ton of the products in different mills, and $25 per ton as the minimum price for 4x4 Bessemer steel billets, with a sliding scale so that if the market price of billets went above that figure the workmen would get the benefit of the rise; if the market price fell below $25 per ton, the compensation of the workmen would not be less than the minimum. When this contract was about to expire, the company, through its President and chief manager, Mr. Frick, and its chief superintendent, Mr. Potter, submitted a proposition to the workmen, which proposed a reduction of the minimum to $22 per ton of steel billets; also a reduction in some of the departments of the amount of tonnage rate paid; also to change the time of the year when the contract should expire, from the 30th of June to the last day of December.

After considerable negotiation the company proposed to raise the minimum to $23 per ton, and the workmen offered to take $24—which was refused. The workmen also refused to accede to the proposed change in the time of the expiration of the contract, on the ground that the company would have them at a disadvantage in any renewal of contract which would expire in mid-winter. The negotiations were broken off on the 24th of June.

Mr. Frick, who is a very intelligent and shrewd business man, gives as his chief reasons for the proposition to reduce the wages of his employees:

First, That the price of steel billets, blooms, slabs, etc., has fallen to such a figure in the market that, in justice to his company, the minimum should be reduced (or abolished, as there was no maximum); and,

Secondly, That the improved machinery put in some of the mills since the contract of 1889 doubles the output of the finished product with no increase in the number of laborers, which very greatly increases their tonnage compensation. This latter point is contested by the workmen and explained in several ways, so it would require an expert to pass a perfectly intelligent and just judgment upon the point. Mr. Frick testified before the Congressional Committee that his company has lost money this year, and he thinks the greater part of last year, on every ton of slabs, billets and blooms produced and sold by them. He claims

that the McKinley law has nothing to do with this question; that it reduced the duties on all products, the like of which he manufactures, and still these are practically prohibitory, as the diminished amounts of importations clearly proves. He attributes the fall in price to increased domestic production.

In 1874 there were produced in the United States but 91,000 tons of steel ingots, whereas in 1890 the total production was 4,131,000 tons.

Our protective tariff laws, which destroy foreign competition, it is claimed, are enacted for the benefit of the skilled laborers employed by the manufacturers. The advocates of the McKinley tariff law during its consideration proclaimed its purpose to be to give the American market to the American manufacturer, and thereby to enable him pay his laborers higher wages. These promises have not been faithfully kept. Wages have in no case been increased, but in many instances they have been reduced. The promises made to the operatives have been disappointing. Mr. Frick claims that over-production has caused a most remarkable decline in prices within the last three years, and that this makes it necessary for the Carnegie company to reduce expenses.

The high protection extended by Congress to manufacturers, principally on such articles as this company has been manufacturing, has induced the investment of capital in the manufacture of iron and steel, until by this unnatural stimulus over-production has resulted. It disturbs the laws of trade — of supply and demand — and by thus producing more than there is a demand for, prices are driven down and a necessity is created for cutting down the expenses of the manufacturer, and it may be the wages of labor included. In this way the protective tariff disappoints the laboring man and becomes the parent of trusts, combines, strikes and lockouts. The manufacturer, no more than the laborer, can help it, though he is largely responsible for it. He asks Congress for the protection he receives and must bear the consequences. It disturbs and disappoints labor, while professing to protect and foster it. After the breaking off of negotiations on the 24th of June a feeling of estrangement rapidly developed between the employees at Homestead and the officers of the Carnegie company. Messrs. Frick and Potter were hanged in effigy within the works. On the 30th of June the works were closed. On July 1st the striking workmen congregated about the gates and stopped and persuaded the foremen and employees who came to enter to go away. An advisory committee of fifty was raised from the Amalgamated Association. The watchmen of the company were turned away from the works; guards were placed at all the entrances thereto, the river, streets and roads entering the town were patrolled by guards, and a rigid surveillance exercised over those who entered the town or approached the works.

When the sheriff came on the 4th of July and demanded to put deputies of his own selection in possession of the works, to guard them for the company, his request was declined, the striking workmen proposing to place guards of their own and give indemnity for the safety of the property, but this the sheriff declined because it would enable them to keep non-union men whom the company might employ from taking the places lately held by the strikers. On the 5th of July, when the sheriff sent twelve deputies to take possession of the works, they were not allowed to do so and were driven away.

As early as about the 20th of June Mr. Frick began negotiations with Robert A. Pinkerton, of New York, for the employment of 300 watchmen to be placed in the works at Homestead. On the 25th he wrote a letter to Pinkerton giving instructions as to the movements of the guards, who were to rendezvous at Ashtabula, Ohio, and from thence to be transported by rail to Youngstown, and from thence to be transported by boat up the river and landed in the works at Homestead.

Arms and ammunition for the men were sent in goods boxes from Chicago by William A. Pinkerton, according to the direction of Mr. Frick, and placed on Captain Rodgers's boats at Allegheny. On the evening of the 5th of July Captain Rodgers' boats, with Deputy Sheriff Gray, Superintendent Potter and some of his assistants on board, dropped down the river with two barges in tow, until they met the Pinkerton men, who were embarked on the barges. The boats took the barges in tow, and on the way up one of the steamers became disabled, while the other took both barges, endeavoring to land at Homestead before day, when the people would be asleep and the strikers would likely know nothing of it until after the Pinkerton men were safely within the picket fence surrounding the works. They did not violate any law of Pennsylvania, but they knew that the hostility to the Pinkerton men upon the part of all labor organizations was calculated to produce a breach of the peace.

The greatest mistake made by Mr. Frick was that he did not appeal to the State and county authorities for protection in the first instance. He began to negotiate for the employment of the Pinkerton forces before the negotiations for the re-employment of the workmen were broken off. His company had a legal right to put Pinkerton men or any other employees into the works at Homestead as guards or otherwise, provided in doing so it did not trespass upon the rights of person or property of others. It is but fair to say that this he tried to avoid. The Pinkertons are professional detectives, and guards or watchmen, and in the latter capacity may properly be characterized as a sort of private police or semi-military force.

Mr. Frick should have first appealed to the sheriff of his county for protection. He gave as a reason why he did not, his want of confidence in the efficiency of the sheriff and the deputies he would likely have employed. The sheriff may be a very inefficient officer and lacking in that pluck and energy that is so essential at times to be exercised by an executive officer, but had Mr. Frick and his learned attorneys urged the sheriff and aided him by their counsel, although his efforts in the discharge of his duty were but puerile and futile, if the officers of the Carnegie company had joined him in the appeal to the Governor, and Mr. Frick had gone to him in person and laid the facts before him, there is no doubt that Governor Pattison would, as he finally did do in obedience to a sense of official duty, have supplied a sufficient force to enable the sheriff to take possession and deliver the works to the officers of the company, to the end that they might operate them in whatever way they saw proper.

Men of wealth and capital, as well as the poor mechanics and laborers in this country, must learn to respect the law and the legally constituted authorities, and have recourse to these to redress their wrongs and obtain their rights in preference to undertaking to do these things by private or personal instrumentalities. If men of wealth and corporations may with impunity hire guards in great numbers to perform the functions of the county and State officials in protecting property and preserving the peace, its inevitable effect will be to bring local government and civil authority into contempt.

When Capt. Rodgers's boat with the barges in tow was approaching Homestead, just as day was breaking, a small steamer used by the strikers for patrol purposes set up a whistle, which was responded to by all the engines in town under their control. This caused a crowd to at once assemble along the bank of the river, where it kept pace with the boat, discharging firearms. When the crowd on shore reached the fence around the works they were temporarily halted, but tearing down a part of it they rushed through. A part of the crowd on the shore came down near to the boat when the gang-plank was pushed out. A short war of words was followed by firing on each side, which resulted ultimately in the death of three of the Pinkerton men and seven of the workmen, and the wounding of many on each side. After a brief fusillade those on shore fled in various directions, and the Pinkerton men retreated into their barges. An hour or two later, after having made the barges fast to the wharf, Capt. Rodgers took the wounded upon his boat, and with Superintendent Potter and Deputy Sheriff Gray steamed up the river to take the wounded to a hospital. About 11 o'clock the boat returned, the deputy sheriff still on board. He said that it was his intention to tow the barges and the Pinkerton men away, but the boat received a heavy fire from the striking workmen with small arms and artillery from both sides of the river. One or two of her crew were either killed or severely wounded, and at one time the pilot for safety abandoned his post and let the steamer drift, so that it became impossible for her to take the barges in tow, and with great difficulty it ran the gauntlet of the fire and escaped to Pittsburg.

At this time the strikers on shore were endeavoring to use a piece of artillery upon the barges, but they could not depress h. sufficiently and consequently fired over them. They also poured oil into the river above the barges and set it on fire, but this failed of its purpose, because the water in the river is slack at this point and the wind was blowing up instead of down the river. About five o'clock in the afternoon the Pinkertons displayed a white flag, and negotiated terms of surrender, by which they were allowed to take out their clothing, but their

arms and everything else fell into the possession of the Homestead people. The barges were immediately set on fire and burned, and in their burning the pump-house belonging to the Carnegie company was also destroyed. The Pinkerton men now being practically prisoners of war, were marched up town to the skating rink for temporary imprisonment, and on their way, instead of receiving that protection which Mr. Hugh O'Donnell, the chairman of the Advisory Committee, in negotiating the terms of surrender had promised, they were brutally and outrageously maltreated. The injuries inflicted upon them, in some cases, were indecent as well as brutal. Whether these men were of good or bad character, the offence which they had committed against the feelings of the people of Homestead could in no degree justify the indignities with which they were treated.

The sheriff was notified and that night came down and took the prisoners away, informed Governor Pattison of what had transpired, and called upon him again for troops to enforce law and order, to which the Governor responded, as his duty under the law required.

I think that Mr. Frick, like many other manufacturers, is not infatuated with labor organizations, and hence is opposed to the Amalgamated Association and its methods, and had no very great desire to contract with his workmen through that organization. This was the true reason why he appeared to them as autocratic and uncompromising in his demands. They claim that he was too stern, brusque and autocratic to reason with them and hear their arguments. If the business of his company, on account of a fall in the market price of the products of the works, required a reduction of the wages of the employees, he should have appealed to their reason and shown them the true state of the company"s affairs. I am persuaded that if he had done so an agreement would have been reached and all the troubles which followed would thus have been avoided.

Secret political organizations are inconsistent with our American republican system of government, because the public at large has the right of participation in all matters pertaining to government. Laborers, farmers, and men engaged in any business, have the right to organize for their mutual benefit and protection, and even though their organization be secret that constitutes no objection if it is non-political. But no organization of laborers or others has the right of enforcing its wishes or the decrees of its councils by strong hand, setting at defiance the rights of others, or by violations of the law.

I have no doubt that the Amalgamated Association, which is, as I understand it, non-political, may be very useful to its members in many ways if properly limited and directed. While I do not assume it as to this association, there is such a thing as over-organization, to the extent of making the members thereof zealots, and then its unreasonable demands, like a boomerang in its rebound, injure its devotees more than the blow injures the supposed enemy at whom it is aimed, and in this way its usefulness is greatly impaired or destroyed.

The right of any man to labor, upon whatever terms he and his employer agree, whether he belong to a labor organization or not, and the right of a person or corporation (which in law is also a person) to employ any one to labor in a lawful business is secured by the laws of the land.

In this free country these rights must not be denied or abridged. To do so would destroy that personal freedom which has ever been the just pride and boast of American citizens. Even the "moral suasion" which the members of labor organizations may use to prevent non-union men from accepting employment must not be carried too far or it may become intimidation and coercion, and hence be unlawful. We must recognize the fact that in this country every man is the architect of his own fortune. A denial or obstruction of this right should not be tolerated, palliated, or excused. Our entire system of government, State and Federal, is based upon the idea of the individual right of every citizen to life, liberty, and the pursuit of happiness. It is not the business of government to aid anyone in the acquisition of property, but it is the business of governments and their duty, each acting within its sphere, to protect the citizen, the humblest as well as the most autocratic, in the enjoyment of the right to his life, his liberty, and the pursuit of happiness. Not to make property for him, nor to furnish him the opportunity of making it, but to amply protect him in his lawful efforts to make it and to enjoy the fruits of his labor.

Congress has, from time to time, arrogated to itself the right to legislate in a manner and upon subjects of which it can properly have no jurisdiction, until the people have become educated to the idea that its powers to legislate are unlimited, and hence, whatever occurs that is deemed an evil, Congress is at once appealed to by thousands for a legislative remedy or relief. It is a familiar principle enunciated by every respectable commentator upon the constitution, and decided many times by the Supreme Court of the United States, that the powers of Congress must be sought alone in some express grant in the constitution, or be found necessary to carry into effect such powers as are therein granted; and that the states have exclusive jurisdiction of all local matters.

Congress, therefore, has no power to interfere by legislation in the labor troubles at Homestead, nor in any similar ones which may subsequently occur there or elsewhere. A voluntary arbitration law was passed by Congress, applicable to railroad strikes, and there is also one in Pennsylvania applicable to her own affairs, but neither of them is of any practical utility. Parties will not have recourse to that method of settlement, and there is no way to enforce the award when rendered.

Nor is a compulsory arbitration law practicable. Such a law could only be enacted by the State, and compulsory arbitration would be no arbitration at all, since it would at once be the exercise of judicial power.

Courts can afford remedy for violated contracts, but in a case like that at Homestead, where the parties fail to agree,—where they fail to make a contract,—if the State could invest a tribunal with authority to step in and say that the proposition of the Carnegie Company was reasonable and that the striking workmen should accept it and go to work, thus making for them a contract which they refused to make, and the workmen did not choose to obey the award, how could it be enforced ?

No legislative authority can deprive any man of the right to contract in respect to his own private property or labor and without his consent confer that power upon another person or tribunal His discretion and personal right cannot be thus taken from him, for that would at once destroy his freedom.

The rights of property and personal liberty are secured by the fundamental laws of the state and nation, just as they were by the English common law and Magna Charta, which the old barons, sword in hand, wrested from King John, at Runnymede.

The legislature of every state should be diligent in enacting wise, conservative and just laws for the protection of both labor and capital, so that demagogues may have a narrower field for agitation. Unless something of this kind be done, within the next decade we may reasonably expect a revolution and bloodshed which may work a change in the form of our government. Laboring men and poor people generally are much more interested in preventing this calamity than are the rich. The poor man derives but little benefit from a strong government, which would be the probable outcome of revolution.

Congress can contribute much towards allaying agitation by repealing all class legislation and greatly restricting foreign immigration.

Wm. C. Oates.

GLOSSARY

billet: a small rectangular bar of steel or iron used in manufacturing

fusillade: a discharge from several firearms at once; a rapid firing

moral suasion: an appeal to one's sense of right and wrong; here, suggesting a forcible appeal or threat

Document Analysis

Congressman William C. Oates, who was placed in charge of the congressional investigation into the Homestead incident, sought to accomplish two important things in his report. First, he recounted, as accurately as possible, the events that transpired and what led to them. Second, and more importantly, he made recommendations as to what actions Congress should or should not take in response to the events at Homestead. In an ancillary way, Oates also made some evaluative comments as to who was to blame for what transpired, and in this, he was fairly evenhanded, assigning guilt to both sides in various degrees.

Oates begins by describing the factory at Homestead as well as the importance of Carnegie Steel both to the nation's growing urban centers and to the US Navy, which demonstrates that although strikes were common throughout the period, this strike in particular stood to cripple an industrial hub that Oates thought was vital to national interests. He then moves to a discussion of the negotiations between the Amalgamated Association of Iron and Steel Workers and Carnegie Steel's president, Henry Clay Frick. Oates notes the offers of both sides without showing bias as to which side he believed to have the more reasonable position. Understanding both Frick's desire to cut labor costs and the union's resistance to the cuts, Oates blames Congress through its passage of the McKinley Tariff two years earlier in 1890 for creating the circumstances that led to the impasse and resulting violence.

Where Oates does take Frick to task is in his decision not to let the local authorities enforce the law but rather to hire three hundred private Pinkerton agents, which Oates describes as "a sort of private police or semi-military force," to protect the mill. When guns arrived to arm the agents, violence ensued. Oates saw that Frick was spoiling for a fight, noting that he had negotiated for the Pinkerton agents before negotiations with the union had failed. For this, Oates condemns Frick, stating, "If men of wealth and corporations may with impunity hire guards in great numbers to perform the functions of the county and State officials in protecting property and preserving the peace, its inevitable effect will be to bring local government and civil authority into contempt." Whereas he blamed the workers for their poor treatment of the Pinkerton agents they captured, the fact that the Pinkerton agents were there at all was both provocative and demonstrated a lack of respect for local authorities.

Essential Themes

The Battle of Homestead, as it has come to be known, came to an end when some eight thousand Pennsylvania state militia arrived on July 12, restoring order and protecting the plant for Carnegie Steel. Though the strikers did not return to work, Carnegie Steel was able to resume production using scab labor, workers willing to replace the strikers, despite local and national opinion favoring the strikers and viewing Carnegie Steel as greedy and at fault for the violence. However, just as the violence at Chicago's Haymarket Square six years earlier seriously damaged the Knights of Labor's credibility in public opinion, an attempt on Frick's life by an anarchist less than two weeks later colored the public view of the strikers at Homestead. By November, the strike was over and the Amalgamated Association left, and Carnegie Steel was able to implement the lower wages and longer hours that it had initially sought.

For the workers at Homestead, their wages decreased by twenty percent between 1892 and 1907, while their work days increased from eight hours to twelve. The persistent pressure of the corporations caused membership in labor unions to decrease dramatically during the 1890s as a nationwide economic depression made good factory jobs more difficult to come by. For the next forty years, Frick and Carnegie's goal was realized, with Carnegie Steel remaining defiantly nonunion. Many other mills and other industries followed suit by refusing to sign agreements with labor unions and weathering the strikes to achieve their goal of reducing the amount paid for labor.

Regardless of the party deemed to be at fault, violent events at places like Homestead caused labor unions to become associated with violence in the minds of much of the American public. Combined with the increasing power of corporations like Carnegie Steel to influence the actions of the local, state, and federal governments, it became increasingly difficult for unions to prevail in any sort of labor disagreements against the corporations. Despite Oates's assigning much of the blame for the violence to Frick and Carnegie, the federal government, when it did anything about labor unrest, typically acted in the interests of the corporations rather than the workers until well into the twentieth century.

—*Steven L. Danver, PhD*

Bibliography and Additional Reading

Brody, David. *Steelworkers in America: The Nonunion Era*. New York: Harper, 1969, Print.

Burgoyne, Arthur G. *The Homestead Strike of 1892*. Pittsburgh: U of Pittsburgh P, 1979. Print.

Demarest, David. *"The River Ran Red"*: *Homestead 1892*. Pittsburgh: U of Pittsburgh P, 1992. Print.

Kahan, Paul. *The Homestead Strike: Labor, Violence, and American Industry*. New York: Routledge, 2014. Print.

Krause, Paul. *The Battle for Homestead, 1880–1892: Politics, Culture, and Steel*. Pittsburgh: U of Pittsburgh P, 1992. Print.

Nasaw, David. *Andrew Carnegie*. New York: Penguin, 2007. Print.

■ Senator Sherman on the Pullman Strike

Date: July 7, 1894
Authors: John Sherman; *Cleveland Gazette*
Genre: article; interview

Summary Overview

In June of 1894, a strike at the Pullman Palace Car Company threatened to bring the American railroad industry to a halt. The strike was initiated in response to widespread layoffs of skilled workers, reduced wages, and the high cost of living. President Grover Cleveland secured an injunction that hastened the end of the strike, but the issue regarding worker compensation in an economy in the midst of a depression persisted. In an interview with the *Cleveland Gazette*, US senator John Sherman, a Republican from Ohio, commented on worker wages, arguing against tipping when employee pay remained too low.

Defining Moment

In the late nineteenth century, the United States experienced a number of major industrial changes. The railway industry continued to boom during the post-Civil War years, providing consistent work to skilled and unskilled workers alike across the country. The rail boom allowed George Pullman—who popularized the luxury sleeping car—to construct a town (Pullman, Illinois) in which his twelve thousand employees would live and work at his facilities.

However, in 1893, another industrial shift occurred—a major economic depression that would last five years. Industrialists like Pullman were forced to cut back on staff and wages in order to weather the economic storm. In the railroad industry, a large number of skilled workers who enjoyed considerable autonomy with regard to on-site practices were released from their jobs. Those who remained employed saw wage cuts, more regulations, and reductions in hours. Even wage structures were dramatically altered—Pullman's company changed from paying employees by the day to compensating them for each completed task ("piece rate" wages), which Pullman's managers believed would incentivize workers to increase production.

In Pullman, Illinois, wages and hours changed but the cost of living did not. Even the depression could not sway Pullman to lower rents or other expenses in his working community. This trend, coupled with the company's wage and policy changes, led workers to walk off the job in 1894. Although Pullman's managers did engage and negotiate with the striking workers, the two sides saw little common ground. Adding to the issue was the fact that Pullman was considered by the public to be a model employer. Therefore, the striking employees turned to the founder of the American Railway Union (ARU), Eugene V. Debs, to assist them in their efforts. During the strike, more than one-third of Pullman's workers were members of the ARU.

Debs and the ARU brought nationwide support to the strikers. Although many (including Debs) were concerned that a boycott of the rails would foster a backlash, the ARU proceeded to call for one. To the surprise of many, the public's response to the boycott was positive. Although public support was strong, political leadership was more concerned about the virtual shutdown of the railroads. Many mayors, governors, and legislators held their tongues on the Pullman strike, hoping to avoid garnering a negative reaction from organized labor, which was continuing to build strength in the latter nineteenth century. Violence and large-scale confrontations between the railroad managers and the ARU led President Grover Cleveland to dispatch the National Guard to intervene in Chicago.

Despite the sentiment in favor of the workers, Pullman's company held fast in its refusal to work with the ARU and the striking employees. Even as Debs—who recognized the high improbability of success—called for arbitration, the company would not negotiate. Ultimately, the strike was put down, Debs was arrested for interfering with the US mail system, and the Pullman Company welcomed back workers who renounced Debs and the ARU.

Author Biography

John Sherman was born in Lancaster, Ohio, on May 10, 1823. His father, an attorney, died when Sherman was six years old. Self-described as "troublesome," Sherman attended public school before studying law under his brother, Charles, and his uncle, a judge. Sherman, then a Whig, was elected to the US House of Representatives in 1854. When the Republican Party formed, Sherman joined and rose through party ranks. He was elected to the US Senate, serving as Ohio's senator from 1861 to 1877. He left the Senate to become secretary of the treasury, but returned to the Senate in 1881, holding the post until 1896. Among his accomplishments were the Sherman Antitrust Act (1890) and the Sherman Silver Purchase Act (1890). After a year-long stint as President William McKinley's secretary of state, Sherman retired in 1898. He died on October 22, 1900.

The Cleveland Gazette, a weekly newspaper published in Cleveland, Ohio, between 1883 and 1945, was that relatively rare thing at the time of the Pullman strike: an African American newspaper. It was founded and run by Harry C. Smith (1863–1941), a strong advocate of civil rights and later (1926, 1928) Republican contender for governor. At the time of Smith's death, the *Cleveland Gazette* was the longest-running African American newspaper in existence.

HISTORICAL DOCUMENT

Senator Sherman, in speaking on the "Pullman" strike, made the following pertinent comment:

> Then, too, I think the system of tipping employees should be discontinued. It is a small matter to the individual case, but it is extortion to pay the porter each trip you take. The trouble is that men are not paid enough by the company. If they were paid adequate salaries the passengers would not be obliged to come forward to help them.

The senator might have as truly stated that the money paid those ornaments, the sleeping car conductors, ought to be paid the hard-working porters, and their offices abolished. That is the proper way of doing away with the necessity for tipping. The porter can, and in many cases does, perform his own and also the conductor's duties. Some years ago the sleeping car conductor was unknown. Nowadays such a useless ornament is paid $75 and $100 a month while the porter receives from the company anywhere from $10 to $12 dollars a month and orders to do nine-tenth the work. The patrons of sleeping cars are expected by the company to liberally tip the poorly paid porter to secure him living wages. In plainer words, every sleeping car company indirectly extracts tips from its patrons (for its porters) as well as the usual price of berths, etc. They compel their porters to do the mendicant business Senator Sherman complains of that they may save the difference between a decent salary and the pittance paid the porters.

Document Analysis

Senator Sherman was known as an advocate for labor as well as an opponent of anticompetitive business practices. Four years before the Pullman strike took place, he had sponsored a landmark bill—the aforementioned Sherman Antitrust Act—which targeted monopolistic or otherwise anticompetitive corporate policies. Such policies, Sherman believed, resulted in cutthroat competition among the largest corporations, which frequently caused employee reductions, lower wages, and longer hours for workers.

Among the myriad issues involved in the Pullman strike was what Sherman sees as an imbalance in work and wages among the conductors and porters aboard a Pullman car. Porters (most of whom were black), Sherman says, earned wages that were barely enough to sustain themselves. Pullman customers would feel obligated to give a tip to the porters, given their knowledge of the relatively meager wages they earned.

When approached by the *Cleveland Gazette* in July of 1894, Sherman offered his thoughts regarding tips for porters. An occasional tip for good service, he says, was not the problem. Rather, the concern was the fact that tips were an integral part of the porter's salary. Porters needed tips in order to simply attain a living wage, Sherman argues. The fact that they had to earn tips on every trip amounted to what he dubbed "extortion" by the railroad companies. If porters were paid a reasonable wage, Sherman said, passengers would not feel the need to supplement the porters' income.

The *Gazette* article adds the suggestion that Sherman would also take issue with the wide disparity in wages paid to porters and conductors, particularly when porters seemed to perform the lion's share of the work in the Pullman cars. Porters earned on average $10 to $25 per month. Those holding the position of conductor (which the article states was nonexistent only a few years earlier), on the other hand, were earning between $75 and $100 monthly. The article argues that the position of conductor should be abolished, as porters often performed the overwhelming majority of the conductors' daily duties in conjunction with their own assigned tasks.

Such a change in policy would accomplish three goals. First, it would make possible an increase in wages for the woefully underpaid—in the eyes of Sherman—porters. Second, it would save the Pullman Company significantly by doing away with a largely redundant and expensive position. Third, it would eliminate the expectation that Pullman's patrons should be responsible for paying a large percentage of porters' salary by generously tipping these underpaid employees.

Essential Themes

Senator Sherman was one of a number of key political figures who were unafraid to speak out in favor of the workers embroiled in the Pullman strike. The author of the Sherman Antitrust Act, Sherman offered a brief statement to the *Cleveland Gazette* that focused on but one area of the broad range of pay and work environment issues that were at the center of the strike. Still, his comments could have been applied to any number of industries experiencing massive growth and prosperity (even during the 1893 depression) with regard to low-wage workers.

While Sherman was not averse to the idea of tipping, he viewed with disdain the fact that tips were seen by the Pullman Company as a major part of porters' wages. Pullman car patrons—not the employer—were expected to bring the porters' salaries to a living-wage level. Such a policy meant that porters should receive a salary that kept them out of poverty only if they performed well enough on the job to receive adequate tips from the passengers. In his comments to the newspaper, Sherman said that the burden of paying a living wage to porters should fall on the employer and not the patrons.

According to the *Cleveland Gazette*, Sherman, took issue with the fact that porters were grossly underpaid. The *Cleveland Gazette* compared the pay of porters to that of sleeping car conductors (whom the paper called "ornaments"). The position of conductor was relatively new, and even when conductors —who earned $65 to $75 more per month than did porters—became part of Pullman's workforce, porters still performed a great many of their tasks.

Unstated but implicit in the article was an irony: Pullman (like many other industry giants) was so concerned with the ongoing depression that it was willing to cut wages and workers. However, he was still willing to make room and provided good compensation for conductors, even if the work they were expected to perform had been done by less expensive porters. By abolishing conductors and the practice of tipping for porters, the article suggested, Pullman could pay porters what they deserved without a strain on the company's budgets.

—*Michael P. Auerbach, MA*

Bibliography and Additional Reading

Burgan, Michael. *The Pullman Strike of 1894*. North Mankato: Compass Point, 2007. Print.

"John Sherman's Life and Career (1823–1900)." *Shermanhouse.org*. John Sherman House, n.d. PDF file.

Lindsey, Almont. *The Pullman Strike: The Story of a Unique Experiment and of a Great Labor Upheaval*. Chicago: U of Chicago P, 1964. Print.

Papke, David Ray. *The Pullman Case: The Clash of Labor and Capital in Industrial America*. Lawrence: UP of Kansas, 1999. Print.

Schneirov, Richard, Shelton Stromquist, and Nick Salvatore, eds. *The Pullman Strike and the Crisis of the 1890s: Essays on Labor and Politics*. Champaign: U of Illinois P, 1999. Print.

"Sherman, John, (1823–1900)." *Biographical Directory of the United States Congress*. Office of the Hist., n.d. Web. 24 Apr. 2014.

■ Coal Strike Hearings: The Miners Testify

Date: December 18, 1902
Author: Unknown
Genre: article

Summary Overview

The anthracite coal strike of 1902 came on the heels of significant labor agitation in the preceding years. In 1897, the United Mine Workers of America (UMWA)—working in bituminous, or soft coal, mines— won both wage increases and improved conditions, and miners' union membership grew significantly. Workers in anthracite, or hard coal, mines in eastern Pennsylvania went on strike in May 1902, demanding a reduction in hours, an increase in pay, and an end to unsafe working conditions. The strike continued through the summer, but by October, when it seemed that the strike would interfere with the winter's heating supply, President Theodore Roosevelt intervened, calling a meeting of the UMWA, the mine owners, and government arbitrators. Though the union initially refused to end the strike, following the establishment of an arbitration commission, the strike was called off on October 23, 1902, after 163 days. An article on the testimony taken by the commission was published in the newspaper *Public Opinion* in December 1902.

Defining Moment

When anthracite coal miners in eastern Pennsylvania went on strike in 1902, it was with the knowledge that their fellow coal miners in the Midwest had made significant gains in their strike of 1897 and that in the following five years, both anthracite and bituminous coal miners had been able to gain small concessions through union activity. In 1900, a general strike had been called, and under pressure from a looming election, Republican senator Mark Hanna persuaded the mine owners to make wage and arbitration concessions. The strike was called off, without the UMWA or any other union being recognized by the mine owners.

By 1902, many of the same issues that arose in 1900 were pressing again. Wages were low, conditions in the mines were dangerous, and hours were long. On May 12, 1902, union miners went on strike, and in June, maintenance employees, such as firemen and engineers, did so. In total, nearly 150,000 workers participated in the strike.

Resentful of governmental interference in the 1900 strike, the mine owners were not interested initially in any federal involvement. During the summer, strikers clashed with strikebreakers, police, private security personnel hired by the mine owners, and even the Pennsylvania National Guard. As the situation escalated and became the focus of national attention, President Roosevelt sought to protect the nation's winter heating supply and return the miners to work. Though Attorney General Philander Knox counseled against Roosevelt's involvement, as the strike continued and neither side seemed willing to negotiate, the president decided to call a meeting of labor, management, and government representatives on October 3. Roosevelt found the mine owners stubborn and rigid, while John Mitchell, the president of the UMWA, saw the meeting as a de facto recognition of the union and so was eager for it to be a success. However, the workers voted to continue the strike three days after the meeting, as they were unwilling to trust the word of the mine owners.

Despite the overall failure of the meeting, the federal government did not end its attempt to resolve the strike peacefully. At the behest of the White House, Secretary of War Elihu Root and businessman J. P. Morgan used Morgan's influence with mine owners to propose the creation of a five-member commission composed of two engineers, a judge, a coal expert, and a sociologist, which would hear testimony from the mine workers and seek to address their grievances. The workers and mine owners agreed, and a Catholic bishop and the commissioner of labor, Carroll D. Wright, were soon added to the commission. After 163 days, the coal strike ended on October 23.

The commission toured the area immediately after the strike ended and heard testimony from more than five hundred witnesses over the next several months. The commission determined that there were grounds to demand improvements in working conditions and wages, but it also confirmed that striking miners had harmed and in some cases killed nonstriking workers and destroyed property. In the end, the strikers won a 10 percent wage increase and a reduction of work hours from ten to nine hours, and though the UMWA was not officially recognized, an arbitration board was set up to address labor disputes. Miller and the UMWA considered the strike an important victory not only for Pennsylvania mine workers but also for labor unions nationwide.

HISTORICAL DOCUMENT

Since the anthracite coal strike commission resumed its sessions, on December 3, some very interesting testimony has been given by mine-workers relative to the conditions of their employment. The operators have already announced that they will rebut many of the statements made, and, if this is done, their side of the case will be given a hearing at a later date.

James Gallagher, who has worked for Markle & Co. for twenty-one years, stated that in all the time he worked for the company he only once had received any money, and that was $50. "We traded at the company store and got credit," he explained. "We had to buy provisions there, though the prices are from 10 to 12 per cent higher than at other stores; but clothing, which is 20 per cent higher, we could buy elsewhere. I made an average of $1.25 a day every day of the years I've been working, I guess, but I was never out of debt. Sometimes I've owed the company a big amount—as high as $211 once. Every time I worked hard and reduced the debt until I was nearly clear, the company would take me out of the place where I was making $60 or $70 a month and put me in a place where I could not make $25, and then back into debt I'd be again."

Andrew Chippa, a breaker boy, employed by the same company, started to work last spring to wipe out a debt of $54 owed the company by his father when he was killed in the company's mines. The lad has not received any money for his work, but his earnings have been credited against the company's bill. As he has a mother and three brothers and sisters, his earnings have not been enough to reduce the bill. Instead it has grown to $88.17.

The first description of the work of a fireman was given when Jacob Ansbach, a Coxe employee, took the stand. He said that he worked one week from 6 A.M. to 4:30 P.M., and the next reversed these hours. His pay was $1.57 a day. Every other Sunday he worked twenty-four hours at a stretch. In the six years he had had his place, he paid between $700 and $800 on a house which he had bought for $900.

The most pathetic story yet told to the commission was that of Henry Call, a Markle employee. The old miner, decrepit from many injuries, told under the examination how the evictions were carried on. The wife was sick and her 100-year-old mother was blind and unable to walk. The day on which they were "thrown out" was rainy. He took them the best way he could to Hazelton, seven miles away, and placed them in a cold, damp, empty house. This was last month, when the atmosphere on the Hazelton mountain was quite cold. His wife became worse. Medical aid was kindly furnished free by a Hazelton doctor, but it did not help her much. "We were greatly worried because of our having been turned out of our house, and, one night," the witness said, between sobs, "she died."

W. H. Dettry, president of a local union, employed as a miner by Coxe Bros., said that company men are paid an average of $7.20 a week, and all contractors are required to stay in the mines from 7 A.M. until 3 P.M., regardless of whether they have enough cars to fill with coal they had mined. He said a black-list exists at the Coxe mines, and that he was on it for nine months, because he refused to work a breast which netted him only three dollars a week. He also complained of the docking system.

James McMonigle, a miner formerly employed by Markle & Co., said the breast he was working in was so dangerous that he complained to the company officials that he might be killed. He was told if he worked any other breast he would not be given any cars. He went out on strike, and after the suspension he was refused work and evicted from his house.

John Early, a check weighman, employed at the Gypsy Grove colliery of the Erie company, who was president of the Gypsy Grove "local," told, on stand, of an alleged attempt made by a former mine foreman named Grimes to bribe two presidents of local unions of the miners to have ten men in each local use their influence to have a resolution passed sending the men to work, thus making a serious break in solid ranks of the strikers. Each of the president was to receive $2,500 and a good position as mine foreman, and each of the ten men was to get from $100 to $200 each. Early refused the money and told Grimes he would see him later. Early reported the matter to District President Nichols, of the union, who gave out a public statement, in which he intimated bribery was being resorted to in order break the strike, and the whole thing fell through.

The Delaware and Hudson company presented figures to the commission December 10, they being the first certified statistics to be handed in. They show the average earnings of the miner in 1901 to have been $622.63, and his laborer $449.47. Mr. Mitchell, on the stand, said that $600 should be the minimum wage.

Father J. V. Hussie, pastor of St. Gabriel's church of Hazelton who has been a close friend of the miners, said, of the living conditions: "There has been much change in the last six years. The condition in and about Hazelton is deplorable. I say it without any coloring. The people are barely able to exist. The deplorable condition is most strikingly evident in cases of sickness, the sick being unable to secure bare necessities. Markle & Co. have a burial fund, because their people cannot save enough money to insure them burial. The foreigners have burial societies. It is impossible to keep families together. The children have to leave their homes and get work. The average age when the miners' children leave school is little over eleven years."

GLOSSARY

breaker boy: a child worker in a coal-breaking plant who removes impurities (e.g., slate) from broken clumps of coal

breast: the face being worked at the end of a tunnel

check weighman: a worker who weighs and records other workers' loads

Document Analysis

Published on December 18, 1902, in the Pennsylvania newspaper *Public Opinion*, the article on the coal strike hearings documents some of the miners' testimony taken by the strike commission and a Catholic priest who was familiar with the workers' living conditions. The article states that the mine operators intended to call this testimony regarding working and living conditions into question and that the paper would report their side of the case as well. Throughout the strike of 1902, *Public Opinion* sought not only to present a balanced view of the strike and the activities of the commission, but also to record the varying opinions set forth in other newspapers. In this case, however, the newspaper records the testimony of miners who described a system that kept them in a state of virtual slavery and forced them to work in dangerous conditions.

Several of the workers testify that the mine stores, where workers were forced to purchase food at inflated prices, consumed their wages and left them in debt to the company. One miner, James Gallagher, testifies that each time he had repaid nearly all of his debt, he was transferred to a lower-paying position, ensuring that he would never be debt-free. A worker's debt to the company did not disappear when he died; rather, it was passed on to his family, as a young man working to pay off his deceased father's debt explains to the commission. Workers who were unable to pay their debt were forced from company-owned houses or houses on which the company held the note. One elderly miner testifies that his family was evicted during a particularly rainy and cold period, resulting in the death of his already-ill wife, while another miner tells the commission that he was evicted after refusing to work in a particularly dangerous area of the mine.

In addition to testimony concerning the financial peril of working in the mines, testimony is given about the mine owners' attempts to intimidate workers and infiltrate the union. One worker testifies that he was placed on a blacklist when he refused to work in a low-paying position. Another reports that the mine owners attempted to bribe the miners into voting against the strike. They refused and reported the attempted bribery to union officials.

The article concludes by documenting the testimony of a local priest, Father J. V. Hussie, who testifies that living conditions for miners and their families were "deplorable," particularly for those whose family members fell ill or died. In some cases, families could not afford to bury their dead and were forced to rely on charity. Hussie also reports that children were often forced to leave their homes around age eleven to look for work.

Essential Themes

"The Coal Strike Hearings" illustrates the hardships faced by workers in the anthracite mines, shedding light on the union's justification for the strike. UMWA hoped that the union was seen by the commission and the American people not as the instigator of the coal shortage that would result from the strike but as a champion of working people who had been driven to extreme measures by unjust and inhumane treatment. Since the commission would determine any concessions to be made, testimony was given that supported that argument—firsthand accounts of men who were evicted from their homes when they fell ill, young men falling deeper into debt with no chance to get ahead, and companies that resorted to bribery and intimidation to keep their workers impoverished, indebted, and unable to advocate for themselves without penalty. The mine owners' testimony illustrated the darker side of the strike, including the violence dealt to workers who refused to strike and acts of arson and sabotage against company property. Still, the testimony of the workers made a powerful impression on the commission, whose findings were generally in favor of the strikers.

—*Bethany Groff, MA*

Bibliography and Additional Reading

Cornell, Robert J. *The Anthracite Coal Strike of 1902.* Washington: Catholic U of Amer., 1957. Print.

Dublin, Thomas, and Walter Light. *The Face of Decline: The Pennsylvania Anthracite Region in the Twentieth Century.* Ithaca: Cornell UP, 2005. Print.

Grossman, Jonathan. "The Coal Strike of 1902—Turning Point in U.S. Policy." *U.S. Dept. of Labor.* U.S. Dept. of Labor, n.d. Web. 15 Apr. 2014.

"Public Opinion: Part of Life in the Cumberland Valley." *Public Opinion.* Chambersburg Public Opinion, 2014. Web. 15 Apr. 2014.

■ "Echoes from the Recent Pennsylvania Coal Strike"

Date: February 12, 1903
Author: George F. Baer
Genre: testimony; speech

Summary Overview

In a series of hearings on the conditions of American coal mines that lasted from October 1902 to February 1903, Philadelphia and Reading Railroad president George F. Baer testified that the 163-day anthracite coal strike conducted by the United Mine Workers (UMW) union was illegal and that the "lawlessness" and reckless conditions in the mines were created not by mine owners but by the workers and the unions themselves. Baer also argued that any reduction in "exertion" by workers would result in lower production and, therefore, less pay for the workers. His testimony was later published in the April 1903 issue of *Cassier's Magazine*, a monthly engineering journal.

Defining Moment

By the turn of the twentieth century, the United States was heavily dependent on coal for virtually every aspect of life, including transportation, home heating, factory operation, and many other elements of industrialized society. Demand for coal was high, and miners worked arduously, in dangerous conditions and for little pay. In 1900, John Mitchell, president of the UMW, successfully led a strike against bituminous coal field owners. Although he succeeded in securing improved wages—aided by the fact that President William McKinley, in an election year, intervened to end the strike—Mitchell and the UMW union could not gain recognition as the mines' representative in labor negotiations.

In May of 1902, anthracite coal miners, seeking higher pay, eight-hour workdays, and recognition of the UMW as their union, walked out of the mines in Pennsylvania. Anthracite coal was a cleaner and more efficient form of coal and was, therefore, in very high demand on the heavily populated Eastern Seaboard. As a result, this strike would have major implications for the American economy. Coal operators refused to negotiate with the UMW, and the strike continued well into the fall. The operators brought in thousands of security officers to keep striking workers away from the mines, but more workers walked off their jobs. There were a number of incidents of violence and vandalism, and eventually the Pennsylvania National Guard was deployed to maintain order in the region.

As winter approached, President Theodore Roosevelt pushed for a resolution, convening meetings in Washington between the UMW and the operators. Unfortunately, the meetings proved fruitless, and workers continued their strike. Roosevelt and the government understood the implications of failure to resolve this strike and moved toward a more heavy-handed approach. Roosevelt's next step was to threaten military intervention, an action that would benefit neither side. The two parties agreed to end the strike while a government-appointed commission was established to review the issues. The commission was taken on tours of the mines and given a firsthand view of the industry. After completing the tours, the commission returned to Washington and began three months of hearings.

The hearings would become a major spectacle, with a high-profile set of closing arguments between George F. Baer, a prominent attorney and president of the Philadelphia and Reading Railroad, and outspoken trial lawyer Clarence Darrow. After hours of Baer's and Darrow's arguments, the commission began its review of thousands of pages of findings and rendered its decision. The workers were granted a 10-percent wage increase and an eight-hour workday, but the UMW did not receive recognition as the official negotiator for the workers.

Author Biography

George Frederick Baer was born on September 26, 1842, in Somerset County in southwestern Pennsylvania. At the age of thirteen, he left school and began working in the printing office of a local newspaper, the *Somerset Democrat*, which he would later purchase in partnership with his brother. Baer entered Franklin and Marshall College in 1860 but left a year later, after the Civil War broke out, to serve as a captain in the 133rd Pennsylvania Volunteers. Following the war, Baer was admitted to the bar in Berks County, Pennsylvania, and became local counsel to the Philadelphia and Reading Railroad. In 1896, after thirty-three years of service, he was elevated to the post of president of the railway. Baer would later become president of Franklin and Marshall College. A Social Darwinist, he continued his legal career until his death in Philadelphia in April 1914.

HISTORICAL DOCUMENT

I think there is, from lack of thought, much confusion in the minds of many people as to the rights, powers and duties which properly belong to industrial organisations, including both capital and labor organisations. In general, no one denies the right of men to organise for any lawful purpose; but the right to organise, and the power of the organisation when organized, must still be governed and controlled by the general law of the land under which individual and property rights are protected.

We constantly hear the phrase: "Capital organises. Why may not labor organise?" As if this settled the problem. But capital cannot organise for an illegal purpose. Organised capital is subjected to sharper scrutiny than any other kind of organisation. A possible violation of individual rights is at once seized upon by the public as requiring some new and drastic law, if existing laws are not sufficient to meet public expectations. For example, may capital organise in such a way that one manufacturer may employ pickets to surround the establishment of another competing manufacturer to prevent ingress or egress to the works, or interfere with the sale of its commodities by intercepting its customers, or interfere with the transportation of its products and the orderly conduct of the rival business? We concede to organised labor the same rights that we claim for organised capital. Each must keep, within the law. There cannot be one law for citizens and corporations and another law for labor organizations.

The lawlessness in the coal regions was the direct result of mistaken theories of the rights of the Mine Workers. It will not do to say that the leaders have not encouraged violence and crime. It is true, no doubt, that they did not directly advise it. They at times counseled against it and issued paper proclamations calling for peace, and at other times they have expressed regrets for it. Nevertheless, they are legally and morally responsible for the situation they created, and from which this violence and crime resulted.

They complain bitterly of the decisions of the legally constituted courts whereby riotous conduct, unlawful destruction of property and interference with legal rights of citizens are simply restrained. They even demand of their political supporters the passage of laws which will place trades unions above and beyond the customary and the ordinary jurisdiction of the courts. They blindly refuse to see that the peace and prosperity of the community and the rights of the citizen can be maintained only through the supremacy of the law and its just and equal administration. The overthrow of the civil power, whereby whole communities are at the mercy of the mob, so delights them that they cry out lustily against the soldiers who are sent to protect life and property. Why this denunciation of courts, of police, and of soldiers, if the measures to support a strike are to be only peaceful and persuasive? The law is a terror only to evil doers. In the exercise of lawful acts we need fear neither courts, police, nor soldiers.

We have been told time and again how boys to the number of over twenty or thirty thousand in the coal regions have been admitted to membership in the Mine Workers' organization; how foreigners, without reference to the fact as to whether they are or are not American citi¬zens—foreigners of many nationalities and speaking diverse tongues—with the boys, compose a majority of this organization. These boys, like most boys, have not been disciplined to reverence law and order, and we do not expect boys to behave very well unless they are under strong restraint. The foreigners, many of them, have been governed in their old homes by stringent police regulations. The law, in the person of a policeman or a gendarme, confronted them everywhere. They have come to this country with confused ideas of what free government means. The distinction between liberty regulated by law, and license, is practically unknown to them. Therefore, when a powerful organization of which they are members, led by men who are upheld and encouraged in a respectable community, tells them that. Force may be used to compel men to join their union, that scabs should be ostracised, that they are given power to suspend operations at a colliery where the employees do not join the union, is it not a direct invitation,—nay, more,—a command to commit the violence and crime that characterised the reign of terror in the mining regions?

Men who teach these false doctrines, pose as they may, are inciting to riot. Every day they saw the results of their work in outrages against persons and property. They made no reasonable effort to restrain the violence. They even ease their conscience with the fallacy that until a man is convicted in the courts he is guilty of no crime, and, therefore, they can shut their eyes to what is going on around them.

The legal responsibility they incur gives them little concern. They assume that juries selected from among their own members or sympathizers will not find them guilty. They will not become incorporated for fear of civil suits resulting in heavy damages. Still, the moral and legal responsibility exists, even though there is at times no adequate remedy for its enforcement.

We do not object to our employees joining labor organizations. This is their privilege. But we will not agree to turn over the management of our business to a labor organization because some of our employees belong to it. Our employees, union and non union, must respect our discipline. It is essential to the successful conduct of our business, and is peculiarly necessary in mining operations to prevent accidents. We must be left free to employ and discharge men as we please. If any of our officers abuse this privilege, then it is our duty to hear the case and review the action so that substantial

justice may be reached. But we do not admit the right of an organization, the moment we exercise the power of discipline, to coerce us, before inquiry, by strike, or interference with our management.

The employer ought, I think, to meet his employees personally or a representative of such employees, provided such representative acts only for the particular employees and does not act in the interests of persons who are not employees of the particular colliery. To illustrate—in a controversy as to conditions existing at one colliery, the employees of that colliery must limit their demands to the particular conditions affecting that colliery, and if they see fit to be represented by someone acting as their attorney—we do not care what name they give him, he may be president, or a vice president, or anything else—he must be limited in the same way, he must not inject a theory as to what would be fair towards employees of another company a hundred or a thousand miles away.

It is on this account that we have objected to the interference of the president of the United Mine Workers in our business. If he simply represented our own employees and was acting exclusively for them, there could be no objection to dealing with him. But he represents an organization having for its object some Utopian scheme of uniformity of wages and conditions in the mining of coal all over the United States. And instead, therefore, of considering only the questions at issue between our employees and ourselves he is considering a general proposition which relates to all the coal miners dwelling under the sun. The fact that the miners' organization does restrict the quantity of coal a man may mine is clearly proven. It is not only proven, but it is defended as a right. Restriction on production, limiting the quantity a man may produce, seems to be based on the theory that this is essential to give employment to the many. The illustration given by one of the miners' attorneys was this: that if there is only a loaf to divide, you must divide it equally and give no one man more than his just proportion. The illustration is fallacious in this, that it is not germane to the subject. Labor is not a division of an existing thing. It is a power which produces things. Labor is not the loaf, but that by which in various forms the loaf is produced. Any restriction, therefore, on labor must necessarily reduce the number of loaves which are essential to feed the hungry.

To limit the right of exertion, of work, is to limit production. It is not only a wrong done to the individual, but it is a violation of sound economic principles, and, therefore, an injury to society. The ultimate effect of restricting production so as to divide employment and increase wages, must be to keep on dividing the wage fund as often as new men seek employment. There must be a limit to an increase of wages, but there can be no limit to the increase of workmen. The process must inevitably lead to the destruction of the industry or the reduction of the wages of every man to a sum barely sufficient to sustain life. Wages can increase only when each individual is left free to exert himself to his fullest capacity, thereby creating which, in turn, gives new employment—creates demand for commodities and demand for workmen to produce them. Only in this way can the wage fund be increased.

The country is agitated over the possible dangers to the common welfare by combinations of capital. These combinations, or rather consolidations of many interests into one common company, are all based on the theory that they will result in greater economy, that the cost of production will be decreased, and that the public will be benefited in many ways, especially by regularity in production, stability of employment, and reduction in cost to the consumer.

The criticisms as to over valuation and capitalization are financial questions, and only indirectly affect the public economic questions. If men see fit to invest their money in watered securities, that is their business, and the public is not responsible for ultimate losses. Economic laws will in the final windup work out the financial problem. But the public are rightly anxious as to the effect on the consumer.

All free men oppose monopoly. It is instinctive, and the possibilities of it alarm us. The mere fear of it suggests all manner of devices to prevent it. It is unquestionably true that if the recent combinations of capital, instead of proving a benefit to the public, as their organisers honestly believe, shall prove detrimental and result in creating monopolies guilty of extortion and oppression, legal and peaceful remedies will surely be found to curb their rapacity and oppression. But these large industrial combinations produce only things which are desirable, not absolutely necessary to sustain life. If the price of steel or any other like commodity is too high, or its production is stopped by striking workmen, for the time being, because of low wages, or by owners because of low profits, the public will be put to temporary inconvenience, but it can cause no general suffering.

But if we are over anxious as to the probable effect of these mere possibilities of monopoly (I say possibilities, because it is not probable that in a rich, energetic country like ours any such industrial monopolies can be either created or maintained) what must be the measure of anxiety: as to placing the control of the fuel of the country in one organization, and that, too, an organization without capital or responsibility?

Fuel is the life's blood of our age. It is as essential as food. Food production can never be monopolized. However low the wages and small the reward of the tillers of the soil, the labor reformer has not succeeded in controlling farming. The farmers know no restriction in hours of labor.

But what of fuel? Without a dollar invested in property, the fuel of the country has been absolutely monopolized. Not a ton of coal could be mined in the United States without the consent of the United Mine Workers of America unless it was mined protected by guns and at the risk of destruction of life and property. Is this a serious situation? The dangers from combinations of capital are mere possibilities, but the results of the fuel monopoly are actual.

We are not left to conjecture. The facts are before us. The United Mine Workers have created a monster monopoly. They did shut up the anthracite mines for more than five months. They taxed the bituminous laborers and all laborers over whom organised labor had control to support the strike. The owners of bituminous mines, some in self defense, others in the hope of gain, contributed freely to the strike fund. The public contributed freely. More than three million dollars were raised to carry on what they called the industrial war. With what result? The price of both anthracite and bituminous coal more than doubled. The supply was inadequate. The public was suffering not only from the high price, but from the scarcity of coal. Industrial operations closed down and men were thrown out of employment. All over the land, except in the districts that could be supplied by the great anthracite coal companies, the poor, the honest workman and the well to do suffered for want of fuel. In the middle of winter, in a land of plenty, this gigantic monopoly had the power to create a scarcity of fuel and bring distress upon a whole nation.

It is seldom that the violation of sound economic business rules so quickly brings with it such a series of disasters. How far the public will take to heart the lesson that has been taught is, of course, as it always is, an unknown problem. But this Commission represents the dignity which ever must uphold law and order, the justice that is inherent in righteous judgment, and the wisdom that can respect the progress and mighty achievements of our social and business conditions which have produced such marvelous prosperity. And, holding fast to that which is good, it will be slow to recommend a new order of things that may lead to the dire results which a six months' trial has already produced.

But someone will say, "Oh, all these direful results might have been averted by you operators." How? By a surrender to unjust demands. Yes; the evil day could have been postponed.

Let us not deceive ourselves. Men charged with the management of property, conscious of no wrong doing, believing they are dealing justly with their employees, ought not to surrender at the dictation of labor leaders whose reputation and subsistence depend upon their success in formulating impractical demands, and thereby stirring up strife. The record shows that an honest effort was made to convince the United Mine Workers that their demands were unjust.

The anthracite coal trade has for fifty years been a most perplexing problem. It has, perhaps, aroused greater expectations and caused more disappointments than any large business enterprise in the country. To the untutored mind it seems so easy to dig coal and to sell it at a profit. But to the men who have given their best thoughts and years to the problem it becomes one of the most complex of all industrial problems. Indeed, when I look back over more than thirty years of my own connection with the Reading system and recall the struggles of the system and the able men who have gone before me, it seems that their labors were like those of Sisyphus.

You know that coal cannot be well stored. Bituminous coal cannot be stored in very large quantities because it is apt to ignite. Anthracite coal can be stored, but the cost of storing it is very great. We have made some experiments as to storing coal and picking it up again. The cost, with the breakage and the lowering of the grade of the coal, amounts, as near as we can get at it, to twenty six cents a ton. We have found that we cannot store coal and must not overlook the fact that if wages go up, then materials and supplies necessarily participate in the increase, and the general cost of mining coal is increased. The proportion of wages on a ton of coal is about $1.45 to $1.50 This represents the average cost under the present conditions of producing a ton of coal—that is, the wage labor of producing a ton of coal—and from 40 to 45 cents represent the supplies that go into the cost of the coal. Our coal roundly costs us about $2 to put on the car, and $1.45 to $1.50 represent wages.

The production of coal is one of the few industries in which there are three parties to be considered: first, the operator, because he controls the business—for the present at least; second, the workmen; and third, the consumer. In most industrial operations the consumer is only indirectly interested. He need not purchase the things if their cost is too great; but coal he must purchase. If he is a manufacturer, he requires it for power, and everyone needs it to cook his breakfast and warm his home. The price cannot be arbitrarily fixed. It is undoubtedly true that the mine workers must receive an adequate compensation, measured by like wages under similar conditions in other industries, and, I take it—with some hesitation—that the operator may be permitted, under a normal condition of society, to have a little profit on the capital and work lie bestows in the business. If the anthracite mine operator fixes the price on anthracite coal so high that the manufacturer cannot use it, the manufacturer will do one of two things—purchase bituminous coal, or, if in the locality of his manufactory that cannot be had to advantage, he will abandon the site of his manufactory and go to a more favored locality where fuel is cheap and plentiful. In this problem of manufacturing, fuel is the foundation of everything. It, therefore, becomes a business duty and a business necessity to see that manufacturers are given coal at a reasonable price. If they cannot get it, they will be driven out of business. And if they are driven out of business, then the sources of trade for the railroads fail.

These are problems that captains of industry in these days must consider, and must daily consider—how to increase the wealth of the community they are serving by increasing its prosperity—because only in that way can they add to their revenues; how to return to their stockholders a just payment for the money they have invested, and how to give honest wages, fair and full wages, to the men they employ. These are burdens. You may think they are light; but to a man who is charged with responsibility they become terrible realities.

What, then, can be done practically? If you increase wages, what will you accomplish? If they are too low, increase them; it will pass on to the consumer, and that consumer will be the rich and the poor. If they are just, then let them alone.

What evidence have you that they are unjust? We were led to believe, when an attack was made upon the horrible conditions in the anthracite fields, that a condition existed whereby men were being oppressed. Attention, however, has been called to the fact that on the basis of wages supposedly being paid in the anthracite regions, the advance claimed makes less than the wages that have actually been paid.

Now, that the wages are fair we demonstrated by a number of things to which I want to call your attention. You will remember that it has been said that one of the evils in the coal region is that there is too much labor there. What does that indicate? Why, that labor there is attractive. There is plenty of work in the United States, and those men could get employment elsewhere. Are you going to increase the rate of wages, and attract still more people there to sit down and wait in the hope of getting enough money in a day to support them for a week? Will you improve the congested labor condition in the anthracite fields by raising the price of wages so as to attract all unemployed labor into that field and bring on a worse condition of things?

Remember how easily the trade of anthracite mining is acquired. There is no apprenticeship, such as in ordinary trades; no such conditions as many of us went through when, as boys, we served as apprentices, working night and day to acquire a trade, with little or no remuneration.

Under the mining laws of Pennsylvania a man, of course, must be a certified miner. But each year hordes of strong men come from over the sea. They come as laborers and obtain work in the mines. They are paid larger wages than they ever dreamed of in their own countries—from $1.50 up to $1.75 or $2 a day. They work as laborers for two years in the mines receiving this pay, and at the end of two years they can become certified miners. This is the only apprenticeship they serve. After that they can go into the mine early in the morning and drill their hole and blast their coal, and at eleven o'clock walk out to smoke their pipe and enjoy leisure.

It is no skilled trade. There is no apprenticeship such as prevails in the arts—with the carpenter and the mason and the bricklayer and all artisans, and, above all, the machinist, who has to devote years to acquiring great skill. Are these men who work five and six hours a day, and earn the sums of money we have shown you that they do earn, to become public pensioners at the expense of every honest workingman in this city and in all the cities of the seaboard? Shall he be made to buy coal to keep himself warm and to cook his meals at an unfair price?

If there is any sociological question involved here it requires you to consider most carefully whether, in trying to do some favor to the coal miners in the anthracite regions you are not only going to work injustice to the operators, but you are going to do a wrong to every consumer of coal.

I have heretofore called attention to the sliding scale. I intended to discuss the question of eight hours a day; but I will let that go. Enough has been said upon that subject. I do not believe in the theory. There are some trades where eight hours are enough, but there ought to be no limitation on work in the collieries. If the breaker time is reduced to eight hours per day, the output of coal would be so restricted that the cost of coal would be increased enormously. Of course, the answer would be, "Build new breakers and sink new shafts." That is easily said. Expend another half million dollars at each colliery, and then the public would have to pay the cost. It is one of the things that you cannot help. If you are oppressed in one direction, and the price has to go up, the public is the forgotten man; but there is where it falls all the time. The consumer pays for it. And those of us who stand up to protect the consumer, who represents the average man in the community, are always to be treated as merciless, tyrannical men.

That brings me to say one word in defense of our own companies. I submit that the companies I represent, the Philadelphia & Reading Coal and Iron Company and Lehigh & Wilkesbarre Coal Company, have suffered the most at the hands of these people, in that a number of our collieries are destroyed. Where is the evidence of our wrong doing? What have we done? Have we ill treated our men? Have we wronged them in any way? Is there any testimony here to cast a shadow of doubt on the integrity and the honesty and the fairness of these companies in dealing with their men? Who is there that will dare to say, or has said, that the humblest man in our employment has been refused redress or consideration of any complaint?

Superintendents tell you that they hear every complaint and treat it justly. Such is their instruction. This company is too big to be dishonest. It means to deal fairly with all men. It means it because its management is honest and its policy is honest. And I protest that nothing has been more unfair than to drag us here into a controversy of this kind, without showing that there was any wrong done, or that anything in our system needed to be corrected.

Now, then, what is the practical suggestion that I have to make? I would gladly see a return to the sliding scale. For some reason or other the sliding scale meets with little favor among, labor leaders. You are asked to fix the price of coal practically for three years. I am not a prophet. I do not know what the business conditions of the next three years will be.

I can hope that the general prosperity of the country will continue so that wages can be even increased. But I know, as a business man, that I am not willing to commit myself to the payment of wages for three years based upon the existing condition of things. I do not know the day nor the hour when a break may come, and, as a cautious man of the world, charged with grave responsibilities, I want some system adopted that will work like the governor on an engine and regulate the speed at which we go.

I want to say that, while it is entirely true that some of the men have not been as prompt as we wished them in working on holidays, and some of them have shut

down the breakers at one colliery and another to go to a funeral, and sometimes in times of great distress they would not work when we thought they ought to work, I will say that, taking the whole situation through, the behaviour of men in our companies since the strike is over has been admirable. They have rendered efficient work, and produced all the coal which, under the circumstances, could be produced, unless they had worked on these exceptional holidays, and while that would have been desirable, you cannot ignore the conditions and the traditions of people. These foreigners come here with many holidays. They have been accustomed to observe all their holidays. I am not going to find fault with a man who keeps his native holiday, even though it does deprive us of a little coal. There are some things that must be allowed to individual freedom, and this is one of them.

Now, what is my proposition? That the rate of wages now paid shall be the minimum basis for the next three years.

That from the first of November to the first of April, 1903, all employees, other than contract miners, shall be paid an additional five per cent.

That on and after April, 1903, for each five cents in excess of $4.50 per ton on the average price realized for white ash coal in the harbour of New York, on all sizes above pea, wages shall be advanced one per cent.; the wages to rise or fall one per cent. for each five cents increase or decrease in prices; but they shall never fall during the next three years below the present basis.

Now, before I give the result, let me just explain what that means. We will take the risk of guaranteeing for three years the present basis of wages. I say risk. We take a great risk in doing that. It means that the price of coal must be kept in New York harbour $4.50, or otherwise we are carrying on operations at a loss. We are willing to take that risk, and to pay, in addition, one per cent. increase in wages for each five cents increase on coal, taking the prices at New York harbour, which eliminates all calculations, as a basis.

The average price for each region to be ascertained by a competent accountant, to be appointed by judge Gray, chairman of the Commission, or by one of the United States Circuit judges holding courts in the City of Philadelphia, the compensation of the accountant to be fixed by the judge making the appointment, and to be paid by the operators in proportion to the tonnage of each mine; each operator to submit a full statement each month to said accountant of all the sales of white ash coal, and the prices realized therefrom, f. o. b. New York, with the right of the accountant to have access to the books to verify the statement.

Document Analysis

Baer's testimony makes an effort to undermine the UMW's position as well as assert the perceived rights of the owners and operators. He claims that there are limits to the mineworkers' perceived "right to organise," taking into consideration what he deems the "lawlessness" of the workers and the unions that attempted to organize them. Baer also argues that employers should retain the right to directly engage their employees with regard to grievances and business operations instead of working through union negotiators. He further calls into question the legitimacy of the United Mine Workers, accusing the union of taking monopolistic steps while undercutting one of the economy's most vital natural resource industries. The result of acceding to the workers' demands, he argues, would be lower wages for workers, higher prices for coal, and a negative overall trend in American industrial development.

Baer's first point is that he and his fellow operators do not object to the right of workers to join a union; rather, the problem at hand is one specific union, the UMW. Mitchell's group, Baer argues, organized under dubious and illegal means, including, he alleges, forcing foreigners and others to join their cause. The purpose of the UMW is not to protect the workers, he says, but to "incit[e them] to riot." He claims that the union made no effort to address the violence that occurred during the strike, preferring instead to teach members to simply push on with lawlessness. Baer insists that UMW's record speaks for itself: in 1900, they shut down countless bituminous mines "for more than five months," and now they encouraged similar closures in anthracite mines.

Baer also argues that the owners and operators should have the right to address employee issues directly with those workers rather than rely on an intermediary such as the UMW. An external party such as UMW operates without knowledge of the issues specific to each mine and instead attempts to address each issue using "some Utopian scheme of uniformity of wages and conditions." As an example, he criticizes the idea of limiting the amount of coal produced by each miner as an attempt to create work for additional workers, arguing that such ideals in fact only reduce production.

Baer uses economics to argue against the notion of raising wages for workers. Such a raise, he says, would directly impact the price of coal production, a cost that would then be passed along to the consumer. Rather, he suggests, wages for non-contract employees should be raised by five percent and maintained at that level until April 1903, after which pay would be tied to market prices for three years; though wages might decrease as well as increase under this scheme, he stipulates that they would never fall below the present level.

The anthracite coal strike had already had an impact, driving up the price of bituminous coal. Despite the best efforts of the operators to negotiate, Baer claims, the union refused to halt the strike. He alleges that the UMW is a monopolistic organization that seeks to perpetuate the strike despite the risks to the marketplace, the workers, and the American economy.

Essential Themes

George Baer's closing argument at the hearing in February 1903, delivered to a hostile audience that included labor activists, workers, and the famous civil libertarian Clarence Darrow, was greeted with considerable animosity. His expectation that employers should have the right to deal with their respective employees' issues in the manner of their choosing was perceived by many as reminiscent of the presumed "divine right" of monarchs to rule over their subjects. Nevertheless, Baer's comments represented the perspective of many mine owners and operators on the issue.

Baer did address the plight of the workers, touching on the issues of wages and working conditions, but he did so within the context of a broader argument: that workers performed their respective tasks as a result of the forces dictated by the marketplace. The exertion that workers experienced was necessary, he said, because Americans needed coal production, and any changes in hours or wages would impact coal prices and ultimately adversely impact workers. In order to avoid such conditions, Baer proposed a wage increase tied to market prices rather than one that he deemed arbitrary and imposed by external political entities.

As he argued for the right of owners to address wage and labor issues, Baer discounted the UMW as an illegal organization. Labor had the right to organize, he said, but the UMW, which he deemed a "monopoly" because of its singularity as a mineworkers union, could never serve as a legitimate advocate in negotiations simply because it was not knowledgeable of the specific interests and operations of each mine. Furthermore, according to Baer, UMW had a reputation for forcing workers to join and engage in illegal activity in strike situations. Given UMW's uneducated and illegal activity, Baer argued, it could not represent the workers at the negotiating table. On this point, the government agreed; while it allowed for a wage increase and permitted a fact-finding tour of the mines, the special commission still refused to identify UMW as the workers' representative.

—Michael P. Auerbach, MA

Bibliography and Additional Reading

Bechtel, Ali. "Building Is Tribute to Prominent Berks Attorney Who Once Battled Clarence Darrow." *Berks Barrister* (Spring 2013): 10–13. Web. 17 Feb. 2014.

Blatz, Perry K. *Democratic Miners: Work and Labor Relations in the Anthracite Coal Industry, 1875–1925.* Albany: State U of New York P, 1994. Print.

Connelly, Scott. "The Greatest Strike Ever." *Pennsylvania Center for the Book.* Pennsylvania State U, Spring 2010. Web. 17 Feb. 2014.

Lindermuth, John R. *Digging Dusky Diamonds: A History of the Pennsylvania Coal Region.* Mechanicsburg: Sunbury, 2013. Print.

McDonough, Jack. *The Fire Down Below: The Great Anthracite Strike of 1902 and the People Who Made the Decisions.* Scranton: Avocado, 2002. Print.

Painter, Nell Irvin. *Standing at Armageddon: A Grassroots History of the Progressive Era.* New York: Norton, 1987. Print.

United States Anthracite Coal Strike Commission. *Report to the President on the Anthracite Coal Strike of May–October, 1902.* Washington: GPO, 1903. Print.

THE LIVES OF WORKERS

The masses of immigrants landing in the United States in the late nineteenth and early twentieth centuries often moved beyond their initial port of entry, New York City, to inhabit other parts of the country. However, New York was, without a doubt, ground zero in the experiment of populating the nation with waves of European arrivals. Another great experiment going on at the time—the reason why most of the immigrants came—was the large-scale industrialization of the nation's major cities. Never before had so many people lived and worked in such close proximity and under such harrowing conditions. Long hours, poor working conditions, unsafe practices, unsanitary living quarters, and child labor were commonplace.

In this section, we look at the conditions workers endured at work and at home. There are three accounts of child labor and the home and work environments; indeed, home and work were often indistinguishable, since small items for sale, such as artificial flowers, would be manufactured at home under the strict direction of a parent, guardian, or self-proclaimed entrepreneur. Thus, we present documents from two well-known figures, Jacob Riis (author of *How the Other Half Lives*) and Jane Addams (social worker and pro-

ponent of "settlement houses"), that take child labor as their main subject. Complementing these is a comprehensive report by an activist and philanthropist, Mary Van Kleeck.

We also look at conditions that adult workers faced in the factories. One account, by a young Jewish girl from Poland named Sadie Frowne, provides a glimpse into the world of an immigrant garment worker laboring in the sweatshops by day and trying to have fun and find a marriage partner by night. The piece is short, lively, entertaining, and informative at the same time. Another account, written by the noted writer and activist Upton Sinclair and taken from his famous novel The Jungle, supplies insight into the grim meatpacking industry in Chicago at the dawn of the twentieth century. Sinclair's descriptions were so effective that they led to reforms in that industry.

We end the section with a document examining fire hazards in New York City factories. Prepared in response to the devastating 1911 Triangle Shirtwaist Factory fire that killed 146 workers, the problems identified in the report could be found in many other urban centers at the time.

From *How the Other Half Lives*

Date: 1890
Author: Jacob Riis
Genre: essay

Summary Overview

In 1890, *New York Evening Sun* reporter Jacob Riis published an extensive book on life in the slums of the East Side of Manhattan. Riis's book, which served as the inspiration for social reformers in New York, graphically depicted the life of squalor in which the residents—particularly the children—of this area lived. This excerpt describes how a number of children lived in these conditions, avoiding school, the reformatory, and the dangers of life on the street. Riis calls upon readers to combat poverty in New York by focusing on improving the lives of children, such as the ones he describes in the book.

Defining Moment

The American Industrial Revolution represented a great set of opportunities for those seeking employment, not only for Americans but also for countless immigrants. German Jews fleeing the 1848 revolution, Irish men and women escaping the 1846–51 potato famine, and many other groups of laborers unable to find work in their homelands all braved harsh travel conditions and long delays in New York Harbor to arrive in what they thought would be a better way of life. According to the census data, New York's population just prior to the Civil War was 805,658; by 1890, the population had exceeded 1.5 million.

The tremendous influx of immigrants in New York City occurred without corresponding development. To be sure, New York City had been constructing tenement houses, but immigrants simply packed into them in numbers far too great to make any space hospitable. Apartments were tiny, overpriced, poorly ventilated and lit, and dilapidated. Many tenements were not fit properly for sewage and water, resulting in widespread public health dangers and the spilling of waste into alleys and roads. In the streets, the situation was no better: according to an 1866 report, tons of garbage and other waste littered the streets and blocked sewers, and cattle marched through crowded streets, endangering anyone in their paths.

The issue was not lost on the government, but it could do little to address the problems. In 1867, the New York City Council of Hygiene, for example, passed regulations that required tenements to be built with such features as proper ventilation, fire escapes, bathrooms, and sewer linkage. While such laws were largely ineffective (enforcement was extremely difficult), they did at least generate awareness about this issue. In fact, these laws laid the groundwork for later local, state, and federal laws.

In 1890, Riis, who at the time was a police reporter whose work occasionally appeared in the New York media, launched a personal investigation into the conditions in New York City's slums. Riis had the benefit of using a new piece of technology: a flash camera, capable of illuminating dark tenement apartments, alleys, basements, and other places where immigrants lived and took shelter. A social reformer, Riis was himself an immigrant who had arrived in 1870. He used this experience and motivation to pen an in-depth book on life in the slums of New York's East Side, complete with stark photos of the most vulnerable of the slums' residents: the children.

Author Biography

Jacob Riis was born on May 3, 1849, in Ribe, Denmark. In 1870, at the age of twenty-one, he immigrated to the United States in search of work. However, he found little success and resorted to begging and taking shelter in police barracks. Riis performed a wide range of odd jobs before he found employment as a police reporter.

63

Committed to correcting the social ills that he had experienced, he continued to take tours of the slums and tenements in New York after the success of *How the Other Half Lives*. He was befriended by New York City police commissioner Theodore Roosevelt and was later offered a chance to serve in Roosevelt's presidential administration but declined. Riis continued to advocate for open space and parks in New York until his death on March 26, 1914.

HISTORICAL DOCUMENT

The problem of the children becomes, in these swarms, to the last degree perplexing. Their very number makes one stand aghast. I have already given instances of the packing of the child population in East Side tenements. They might be continued indefinitely until the array would be enough to startle any community. For, be it remembered, these children with the training they receive—or do not receive—with the instincts they inherit and absorb in their growing up, are to be our future rulers, if our theory of government is worth anything. More than a working majority of our voters now register from the tenements. I counted the other day the little ones, up to ten years or so, in a Bayard Street tenement that for a yard has a triangular space in the centre with sides fourteen or fifteen feet long, just room enough for a row of ill-smelling closets at the base of the triangle and a hydrant at the apex. There was about as much light in this "yard" as in the average cellar. I gave up my self-imposed task in despair when I had counted one hundred and twenty-eight in forty families. Thirteen I had missed, or not found in. Applying the average for the forty to the whole fifty-three, the house contained one hundred and seventy children. It is not the only time I have had to give up such census work. I have in mind an alley—an inlet rather to a row of rear tenements—that is either two or four feet wide according as the wall of the crazy old building that gives on it bulges out or in. I tried to count the children that swarmed there, but could not. Sometimes I have doubted that anybody knows just how many there are about. Bodies of drowned children turn up in the rivers right along in summer whom no one seems to know anything about. When last spring some workmen, while moving a pile of lumber on a North River pier, found under the last plank the body of a little lad crushed to death, no one had missed a boy, though his parents afterward turned up. The truant officer assuredly does not know, though he spends his life trying to find out, somewhat illogically, perhaps, since the department that employs him admits that thousands of poor children are crowded out of the schools year by year for want of room. There was a big tenement in the Sixth Ward, now happily appropriated by the beneficent spirit of business that blots out so many foul spots in New York—it figured not long ago in the official reports as "an out-and-out hog-pen"—that had a record of one hundred and two arrests in four years among its four hundred and seventy-eight tenants, fifty-seven of them for drunken and disorderly conduct. I do not know how many children there were in it, but the inspector reported that he found only seven in the whole house who owned that they went to school. The rest gathered all the instruction they received running for beer for their elders. Some of them claimed the "flat" as their home as a mere matter of form. They slept in the streets at night. The official came upon a little party of four drinking beer out of the cover of a milk-can in the hallway. They were of the seven good boys and proved their claim to the title by offering him some.

The old question, what to do with the boy, assumes a new and serious phase in the tenements. Under the best conditions found there, it is not easily answered. In nine cases out of ten he would make an excellent mechanic, if trained early to work at a trade, for he is neither dull nor slow, but the short-sighted despotism of the trades unions has practically closed that avenue to him. Trade-schools, however excellent, cannot supply the opportunity thus denied him, and at the outset the boy stands condemned by his own to low and ill-paid drudgery, held down by the hand that of all should labor to raise him. Home, the greatest factor of all in the training of the young, means nothing to him but a pigeon-hole in a coop along with so many other human animals. Its influence is scarcely of the elevating kind, if it have any. The very games at which he takes a band in the street become polluting in its atmosphere. With no steady hand to guide him, the boy takes naturally to idle ways. Caught in the street by the truant officer, or by the agents of the Children's Societies, peddling, perhaps, or begging, to help out the family resources, he runs the risk of being sent to a reformatory, where contact with vicious boys older than himself soon develop the latent possibilities for evil that lie hidden in him. The city has no Truant Home in which to keep him, and all efforts of the children's friends to enforce school attendance are paralyzed by this want. The risk of the reformatory is too great. What is done in the end is to let him take chances—with the chances all against him. The result is the rough young savage, familiar from the street. Rough as he is, if anyone doubt that this child of common clay have in him the instinct of beauty, of love for the ideal of which his life has no embodiment, let him put the matter to the test. Let him take into a tenement block a handful of flowers from the fields and watch the brightened faces, the sudden abandonment of play and fight that go ever hand in hand where there is no elbow-room, the wild entreaty for "posies," the eager love with which the little messengers of peace are shielded, once possessed; then let him change his mind. I have seen an armful of daisies keep the peace of a block better than a policeman and his club, seen instincts awaken under their gentle appeal, whose very existence the soil in which they grew made seem a mockery. I have not forgotten the deputation of ragamuffins from a Mulberry Street alley that knocked at my office door one morning on a mysterious expedition for flowers, not for themselves, but for "a lady," and having obtained what they wanted, trooped off to bestow them, a ragged and dirty little band, with a solemnity that was quite unusual. It was not until an old man called the next day to thank me for the flowers that I found out they had decked the bier of a pauper, in the dark rear room where she lay waiting in her pine-board coffin for the city's hearse. Yet, as I knew, that dismal alley with its bare brick walls, between which no sun ever rose or set, was the world of those children. It filled their young lives. Probably not one of them had ever been out of the sight of it. They were too dirty, too ragged, and too generally disreputable, too well hidden in their slum besides, to come into line with the Fresh Air summer boarders. With such human instincts and cravings, forever unsatisfied, turned into a haunting curse; with appetite ground to keenest edge by a hunger that is never fed, the children of the poor grow up in joyless homes to lives of wearisome toil that claims them at an age when the play of their happier fellows has but just begun. Has a yard of turf been laid and a vine been coaxed to grow within their reach, they are banished and barred out from it as from a heaven that is not for such as they. I came upon a couple of youngsters in a Mulberry Street yard a while ago that were chalking on the fence their first lesson in "writin'." And this is what they wrote: "Keeb of te Grass." They had it by heart, for there was not, I verily believe, a green sod within a quarter of a mile. Home to them is an empty name. Pleasure? A gentleman once catechized a ragged class in a down-town public school on this point, and recorded the result: Out of forty-eight boys twenty had never seen the Brooklyn Bridge that was scarcely five minutes' walk away, three only had been in Central Park, fifteen had known the joy of a ride in a horse-car. The street, with its ash-barrels and its dirt, the river that runs foul with mud, are their domain. What training they receive is picked up there. And they are apt pupils. If the mud and the dirt are easily reflected in their lives, what wonder? Scarce half-grown, such lads as these confront the world with the challenge to give them their due, too long withheld, or—. Our jails supply the answer to the alternative.

A little fellow who seemed clad in but a single rag was among the flotsam and jetsam stranded at Police Headquarters one day last summer. No one knew where he came from or where he belonged. The boy himself knew as little about it as anybody, and was the least anxious to have light shed on the subject after he had spent a night in the matron's nursery. The discovery that beds were provided for boys to sleep in there, and that he could have "a whole egg" and three slices of bread for breakfast put him on the best of terms with the world in general, and he decided that Headquarters was "a bully place." He sang "McGinty" all through, with Tenth Avenue variations, for the police, and then settled down to the serious business of giving an account of himself. The examination went on after this fashion:

"Where do you go to church, my boy?"

"We don't have no clothes to go to church." And indeed his appearance, as he was, in the door of any New York church would have caused a sensation.

"Well, where do you go to school, then?"

"I don't go to school," with a snort of contempt.

"Where do you buy your bread?"

"We don't buy no bread; we buy beer," said the boy, and it was eventually the saloon that led the police as a landmark to his "home." It was worthy of the boy. As he had said, his only bed was a heap of dirty straw on the floor, his daily diet a crust in the morning, nothing else.

Into the rooms of the Children's Aid Society were led two little girls whose father had "busted up the house" and put them on the street after their mother died. Another, who was turned out by her step-mother "because she had five of her own and could not afford to keep her," could not remember ever having been in church or Sunday-school, and only knew the name of Jesus through hearing people swear by it. She had no idea what they meant. These were specimens of the overflow from the tenements of our home-heathen that are growing up in New York's streets to-day, while tender-hearted men and women are busying themselves with the socks and the hereafter of well-fed little Hottentots thousands of miles away. According to Canon Taylor, of York, one hundred and nine missionaries in the four fields of Persia, Palestine, Arabia, and Egypt spent one year and sixty thousand dollars in converting one little heathen girl. If there is nothing the matter with those missionaries, they might come to New York with a good deal better prospect of success.

By those who lay flattering unction to their souls in the knowledge that to-day New York has, at all events, no brood of the gutters of tender years that can be homeless long unheeded, let it be remembered well through what effort this judgment has been averted. In thirty-seven years the Children's Aid Society, that came into existence as an emphatic protest against the tenement corruption of the young, has sheltered quite three hundred thousand outcast, homeless, and orphaned children in its lodging-houses, and has found homes in the West for seventy thousand that had none. Doubtless, as a mere stroke of finance, the five millions and a half thus spent were a wiser investment than to have let them grow up thieves and thugs. In the last fifteen years of this tireless battle for the safety of the State the intervention of the Society for the Prevention of Cruelty to Children has been invoked for 138,891 little ones; it has thrown its protection around more than twenty-five thousand helpless children, and has convicted nearly sixteen thousand wretches of child-beating and abuse. Add to this the standing army of fifteen thousand dependent children in New York's asylums and institutions, and some idea is gained of the crop that is garnered day by day in the tenements, of the enormous force employed to check their inroads on our social life, and of the cause for apprehension that would exist did their efforts flag for ever so brief a time.

Nothing is now better understood than that the rescue of the children is the key to the problem of city poverty, as presented for our solution to-day; that character may be formed where to reform it would be a hopeless task. The concurrent testimony of all who have to undertake it at a later stage: that the young are naturally neither vicious nor hardened, simply weak and undeveloped, except by the bad influences of the street, makes this duty all the more urgent as well as hopeful. Helping hands are held out on every side. To private charity the municipality leaves the entire care of its proletariat of tender years, lulling its conscience to sleep with liberal appropriations of money to foot the bills. Indeed, it is held by those whose opinions are entitled to weight that it is far too liberal a paymaster for its own best interests and those of its wards. It deals with the evil in the seed to a limited extent in gathering in the outcast babies from the streets. To the ripe fruit the gates of its prisons, its reformatories, and its workhouses are opened wide the year round. What the showing would be at this end of the line were it not for the barriers wise charity has thrown across the broad highway to ruin—is building day by day—may be measured by such results as those quoted above in the span of a single life.

GLOSSARY

bier: a coffin on its stand

catechize: instruct or teach

deputation: a delegation representing or acting on another's behalf

proletariat: working class; wage earners

ragamuffin: a ragged, unkempt child

tenement: an apartment building or similar living unit—typically a run-down one

Document Analysis

Although considered one of the nation's first "investigative reporters," Riis, in *How the Other Half Lives*, does not shy away from showing his own emotion when he reports the sights and stories encountered in the tenements, alleys, and streets of the East Side. In this excerpt, Riis puts particular focus on the children living in this environment, reminding readers of the fact that the "future rulers" of the nation are living in abject squalor and in near-constant danger.

Riis takes the reader on a tour of a tenement in which so many people reside that it is nearly impossible to count them all. In one house, Riis takes an informal census but, acknowledging that there were more than a dozen children missing, instead makes a rough estimate of exactly how many children were living in the small, dark enclosures in each apartment. Riis is hardly alone in his inability to count all of the children living in these houses; he says that truant officers are similarly handicapped, knowing that there could be thousands of children who should be in school but go missing. Bodies wash up in the river, he reports, with no one coming forth to identify them.

Without formal schooling and even a stable home in which to rest and eat, the children of the East Side slums were largely left to their own devices, Riis reports. Many may actually have serviceable skills worthy of gaining them good-paying jobs, but strict restrictions imposed by labor unions have kept these children from honing their skills in trade schools. A large number of these children would, therefore, find unskilled positions at meager wages with long hours.

Those children who do not find employment, Riis says, fall victim to their idleness. They spend their days hiding from truant officers and other officials because if they are caught, they could be sent to a reformatory. There, life does not necessarily improve, as they encounter other delinquent children, who could force and/or influence them into a life of crime. A child in such conditions becomes a "rough young savage," Riis says.

These young savages, however, are still children, Riis states. They still have a willingness to make the world a better place, citing an example of children gathering flowers for a deceased woman, whose coffin was in the street. These children need school, he argues, as well as clothes and attention. Riis provides a number of case studies as evidence: a young boy who does not attend church because he fears he has no decent clothes; a young girl who only knows of Jesus Christ because she has heard people using his name when swearing; and still another girl whose stepmother has turned her out on the streets because the woman "could not afford to keep her."

Riis states that the protection and nurturing of New York's children is central to successfully combating urban decay and poverty. Adults should change their views of the children on the streets, looking past their "savagery" and at their innocence and potential, Riis writes. In doing so, society can relieve children of the burdens of poverty and crime and help them reach their full potential.

Essential Themes

Riis was himself an immigrant, living much in the same conditions as those he documented and photographed when developing *How the Other Half Lives*. As a result, his book both enlightens the reader and serves as an imperative for the social reform Riis advocated throughout his career. New Yorkers were likely aware of the city's slums as well as the plight of the immigrants who crowded into the city's tenements and streets. However, his book painted an in-depth portrait of the dangers and horrors of life in the slums of New York.

Riis had the benefit of using a camera and flash powder during his investigation. Flash technology, newly developed in the 1880s, enabled him to photograph the faces of the children and others living in the alleys and basements as well as the overcrowded and dark apartments in the tenement houses. He also documented the countless images he saw in the streets: the children who spent their days either working in low-skilled, low-wage jobs or evading truant officers in order to keep away from the even worse criminal behavior found in the reformatories and social service centers. This use of photographic equipment made Riis a pioneer in the field of photojournalism.

As shown in this excerpt, Riis uses the images and experiences of the children he encountered to create a social and moral imperative for others to follow. Riis unflinchingly details the extent to which slum dwellers suffered—the sewage in the streets, the bodies in the river, and the people packed in small, dark quarters. Riis challenges his readers to use this information to influence the future of New York. According to Riis, the rest of the population had an obligation to ensure that these children had every opportunity to become educated and upstanding members of society.

—Michael P. Auerbach, MA

Bibliography and Additional Reading

"About Jacob Riis." *Victorian Richmond Hill*. New York: Richmond Hill Chapter, Queens Hist. Soc., 1980. Web. 8 Apr. 2014.

Anbinder, Tyler. Five Points: *The Nineteenth Century New York City Neighborhood that Invented Tap Dance, Stole Elections, and Became the World's Most Notorious Slum*. New York: Simon, 2001. Print.

Baba, Mary. "Irish Immigrant Families in Mid-Late Nineteenth Century America." *Yale-New Haven Teachers Institute*. Yale-New Haven Teachers Inst., 1990. Web. 8 Apr. 2014.

Lubove, Roy. *The Progressives and the Slums: Tenement House Reform in New York City, 1890–1917*. Pittsburgh: U of Pittsburgh P, 1963. Print.

Markel, Howard. *Quarantine! East European Jewish Immigrants and the New York City Epidemics of 1892*. Baltimore: Johns Hopkins UP, 1999. Print.

An Immigrant Garment Worker's "Days and Dreams"

Date: September 25, 1902
Author: Sadie Frowne
Genre: autobiography; article

Summary Overview

In 1898, a young Polish girl named Sadie Frowne and her mother immigrated to the United States in search of greater economic opportunities. Their journey was arduous: they traveled in steerage, crowded into dark and damp conditions along with many other immigrants. Less than a year after arriving in New York City, her mother died, leaving Frowne to fend for herself. Frowne found employment at one of New York's many sweatshops, working long hours in dangerous conditions. In 1902, she gave an interview to the New York *Independent*, a reform-minded newspaper, in which she describes her experiences immigrating to and living in America.

Defining Moment

Beginning in the late nineteenth century, immigrants began arriving in the United States at an unprecedented rate. Between 1881 and 1920, more than twenty-three million immigrants settled in the United States, and the country's population more than doubled in that time, increasing from fifty million in 1880 to more than one hundred million by 1920. On the East Coast, large numbers of eastern and southern European immigrants came to major city centers such as New York in search of better financial opportunities or to escape political or religious persecution in their homelands. According to data from the 1860 US Census, New York City's population just prior to the outbreak of the Civil War was about 814,000; by 1890, the population of New York City exceeded 1.5 million. Immigrants often settled in ethnic neighborhoods, where they were crowded into dark and poorly made tenement houses. Most immigrants, particularly those who did not speak English well, earned meager wages at factories, dockyards, and sweatshops throughout the city.

Young Sadie Frowne was among a wave of eastern European Jewish immigrants arriving in New York just prior to the turn of the twentieth century. Frowne's parents had owned a small grocery business in their small village in eastern Poland. However, Frowne's father died when she was ten years old, and her mother struggled to maintain their business following his death. Like many immigrants, Frowne's mother reached out for assistance to a relative who had already immigrated to the United States. Frowne's Aunt Fanny, who was living in New York City, encouraged the Frownes to come join her in New York and even gave them the financial assistance needed to make the trip. After a long and dangerous transatlantic voyage in the ship's overcrowded steerage section, Frowne (who was now thirteen) and her mother arrived in New York.

Not long after their arrival, Frowne's mother died of tuberculosis, an infectious disease that spread quickly in the crowded tenement buildings of New York City's immigrant neighborhoods. Following the death of her mother, Frowne found work in one of the city's garment factories (also known as sweatshops). The substandard working conditions at these sweatshops are infamous—long hours, poor lighting and ventilation, a lack of emergency exits and other safety procedures, frequent injuries, and low pay were the norm for Frowne and her coworkers. She also experienced the sexual harassment of her male coworkers and other forms of workplace abuse.

Frowne was eager to assimilate into American society. She moved from the Lower East Side to Brownsville, a predominantly Jewish community in Brooklyn, and began attending night classes at a nearby public school. She also became involved with the local unions, paying a monthly union membership fee and taking part in several strikes to demand better pay and shorter workdays. At the age of seventeen, she agreed to be interviewed by a New York–based newspaper called the *Independent*, which was compiling a story about sweatshops and the experiences of the immigrants who worked therein.

Author Biography

Not much is known about Sadie Frowne beyond the information that she provided to the *Independent*. She was born in 1885 in a small village in eastern Poland. Her mother was a well-educated, multilingual owner of a grocery business, and her father was a farmer. After her father died, expenses became too great for Frowne and her mother to support themselves, and they moved to New York City in 1898. Her mother died of tuberculosis shortly after their arrival, leaving Frowne to fend for herself. She worked long hours in a sweatshop during the day and pursued her education at night. In 1902, she was interviewed by the *Independent*, which included her brief autobiography in an article that depicted the life of sweatshop workers.

HISTORICAL DOCUMENT

We came by steerage on a steamship in a very dark place that smelt dreadfully. There were hundreds of other people packed in with us, men, women and children, and almost all of them were sick. It took us twelve days to cross the sea, and we thought we should die, but at last the voyage was over, and we came up and saw the beautiful bay and the big woman with the spikes on her head and the lamp that is lighted at night in her hand.

Aunt Fanny and her husband met us at the gate of this country and were very good to us, and soon I had a place to live out while my mother got work in a factory making white goods.

I was only a little over thirteen years of age and a greenhorn, so I received $9 a month and board and lodging, which I thought was doing well. Mother, who, as I have said, was very clever, made $9 a week on white goods, which means all sorts of underclothing, and is high class work.

But mother had a very gay disposition. She liked to go around and see everything, and friends took her about New York at night and she caught a bad cold and coughed and coughed. She really had hasty consumption, but she didn't know it, and I didn't know it, and she tried to keep on working, but it was no use. She had not the strength. Two doctors attended her, but they could do nothing, and at last she died and I was left alone. I had saved money while out at service, but mother's sickness and funeral swept it all away and now I had to begin all over again.

I got a room in the house of some friends who lived near the factory. I pay $1 a week for the room and am allowed to do light housekeeping—that is, cook my meals in it. I get my own breakfast in the morning, just a cup of coffee and a roll, and at noon time I come home to dinner and take a plate of soup and a slice of bread with the lady of the house. My food for a week costs a dollar, just as it did in Allen Street, and I have the rest of my money to do as I like with. I am earning $5.50 a week now, and will probably get another increase soon.

It isn't piecework in our factory, but one is paid by the amount of work done just the same. So it is like piecework. All the hands get different amounts, some as low as $3.50 and some of the men as high as $16 a week. The factory is in the third story of a brick building. It is in a room twenty feet long and fourteen broad. There are fourteen machines in it. I and the daughter of the people with whom I live work two of these machines. The other operators are all men, some young and some old.

Henry has seen me home every night for a long time and makes love to me. He wants me to marry him, but I am not seventeen yet, and I think that is too young. He is only nineteen, so we can wait.

I have been to the fortune teller's three or four times, and she always tells me that though I have had such a lot of trouble I am to be very rich and happy. I believe her because she has told me so many things that have come true.

So I will keep on working in the factory for a time. Of course it is hard, but I would have to work hard even if I was married.

I get up at half-past five o'clock every morning and make myself a cup of coffee on the oil stove. I eat a bit of bread and perhaps some fruit and then go to work. Often I get there soon after six o'clock so as to be in good time, though the factory does not open till seven. I have heard that there is a sort of clock that calls you at the very time you want to get up, but I can't believe that because I don't see how the clock would know.

At seven o'clock we all sit down to our machines and the boss brings to each one the pile of work that he or she is to finish during the day, what they call in English their 'stint.' This pile is put down beside the machine and as soon as a skirt is done it is laid on the other side of the machine. Sometimes the work is not all finished by six o'clock and then the one who is behind must work overtime. Sometimes one is finished ahead of time and gets away at four or five o'clock, but generally we are not done till six o'clock.

The machines go like mad all day, because the faster you work the more money you get. Sometimes in my haste I get my finger caught and the needle goes right through it. It goes so quick, though, that it does not hurt much. I bind the finger up with a piece of cotton and go on working. We all have accidents like that. Where the needle goes through the nail it makes a sore finger, or where it splinters a bone it does much harm. Sometimes a finger has to come off. Generally, though, one can be cured by a salve.

All the time we are working the boss walks about examining the finished garments and making us do them over again if they are not just right. So we have to be careful as well as swift. But I am getting so good at the work that within a year I will be making $7 a week, and then I can save at least $3.50 a week. I have over $200 saved now.

The machines are all run by foot-power, and at the end of the day one feels so weak that there is a great temptation to lie right down and sleep. But you must go out and get air, and have some pleasure. So instead of lying down I go out, generally with Henry. Sometimes we go to Coney Island, where there are good dancing places, and sometimes we go to Ulmer Park to picnics...

For the last two winters I have been going to night school. I have learned reading, writing and arithmetic. I can read quite well in English now and I look at the newspapers every day. I read English books, too, sometimes.

GLOSSARY

hasty consumption: incurable tuberculosis

piecework: payment based on the number of pieces completed

steerage: the section of a passenger ship, originally amid or near the steering equipment, having the cheapest seats

Document Analysis

Prior to her arrival in the United States, Sadie Frowne lived with her parents in a small apartment behind their store in eastern Poland, while her father's farming income supported their grocery business. When he died, however, Frowne and her mother entered a period of great tumult—they fell behind on their rent and ultimately closed the store. On the advice of Frowne's Aunt Fanny, they traveled across the Atlantic to settle in New York City, where they had heard it was easier to earn a living.

The trip aboard the steamer was, as Frowne recalls, extremely trying. Steerage—the cheapest section—was packed with fellow immigrants, many of whom were ill with various ailments. The accommodations thus smelled "dreadfully," as she describes, and both Frowne and her mother worried that they too would fall ill and never make it to the "beautiful bay and the big woman with the spikes on her head" (the Statue of Liberty). They did arrive safely, however, and were greeted by Aunt Fanny and her husband, with whom they lived until they obtained lodging for themselves.

Frowne first found work as a household servant, while her mother worked at a garment factory. However, her mother quickly succumbed to tuberculosis, and the cost of her care and funeral wiped away all of their meager savings. Frowne, then sixteen years old, began working at a sweatshop on Allen Street in Manhattan.

She had sewing skills but needed to quickly learn how to sew dresses and other complex clothes at a fast pace. Frowne accounts how she wakes up each day at 5:30 in the morning, eats a light breakfast, and gets to work an hour before the sweatshop opens. When the facility opens its doors at 7:00, Frowne and her coworkers immediately sit down at their respective machines, while the foreman brings around a large pile of materials—called a "stint"—that had to be completed by the end of the day, some eleven hours later. Frowne faced a daunting task daily: she needed to perform consistently high-quality work yet complete it within a strict time limit. She already worked long hours during a typical day—any mistakes she made resulted in a much longer day toiling at her machine.

Frowne's story illustrates the physically draining work performed at sweatshops. The machines "go like mad all day," she explains, with each worker's feet operating it. Sometimes, her finger would get caught under the needle, an injury that would occur so frequently she eventually would think nothing of it, even when it resulted in bone fractures. Meanwhile, the foreman would walk up and down the cramped aisles to review the workers' stints—if the project was not done to standards, the worker was verbally harangued and forced to remain at work after hours until the stint was completed in a satisfactory manner.

Frowne refused to allow the physical and psychological challenges of the sweatshop to overcome her. She was savvy with her money, carefully budgeting her limited pay in such a way that she could afford groceries and other living expenses and still pay for new clothes and outings with her boyfriend, Henry. While many of her coworkers spent their time off resting up from their long and arduous shifts, Frowne insists that one "must go out and get air, and have some pleasure." Frowne frequently used a portion of her earnings to go to the theater or go out dancing. She even used some of her savings to attend night school, learning English and obtaining a basic education so that she could better assimilate into American society.

Essential Themes
Frowne's story provides an illustration of the nineteenth-century immigrant experience in New York City.

Frowne's account describes the frightening conditions aboard the transatlantic steamships that brought millions of European immigrants to New York Harbor. It also illustrates the daily challenges facing American laborers at the turn of the century, before the introduction of stringent labor laws, and Frowne's working experience illustrates the lack of safety regulations, the long hours, and inadequate pay that characterized the work lives of many American laborers at the time. Her enthusiasm for her local union and willingness to strike for better working conditions and pay reflects the nascent labor movement of the time.

Frowne's account is also illustrative of the increasing independence experienced by young working women of the time. These working women of the early twentieth century were often the first women in their families to experience some measure of independence—living outside of the family, often unmarried, and financially supporting themselves. Frowne's remarks regarding her boyfriend Henry's desire to get married and her decision to wait reflect the increasing financial and social independence of working women of the time.

—*Michael P. Auerbach, MA*

Bibliography and Additional Reading
Anbinder, Tyler. *Five Points: The 19th-Century New York City Neighborhood That Invented Tap Dance, Stole Elections, and Became the World's Most Notorious Slum*. New York: Simon, 2001. Print.
Katzman, David M., and William M. Tuttle, Jr. *Plain Folk: The Life Stories of Undistinguished Americans*. Champaign: U of Illinois P, 1982. Print.
Lubove, Roy. *The Progressives and the Slums: Tenement House Reform in New York City, 1890–1917*. Pittsburgh: U of Pittsburgh P, 1963. Print.
Markel, Howard. *Quarantine! East European Jewish Immigrants and the New York City Epidemics of 1892*. Baltimore: Johns Hopkins UP, 1999. Print.
Wenger, Beth S. *The Jewish Americans: Three Centuries of Jewish Voices in America*. New York: Random, 2007. Print.

■ Jane Addams: "Child Labor and Other Dangers of Childhood"

Date: December 1906
Author: Jane Addams
Genre: speech; address

Summary Overview

In 1906, social activist and feminist Jane Addams addressed a convention of the American Humane Association on the issue of child labor. She argued that putting children to work in the growing American industrial complex denied them the ability to develop in a healthy manner. Child labor, she said, contributed to crime and societal ills. She called for new laws that kept children of a certain age from working. She also urged Americans to take notice of this issue and to take action to halt child-labor practices.

Defining Moment

During the latter half of the nineteenth century, the Industrial Revolution took hold in the United States. Across the spectrum of industries, the country saw unparalleled growth and prosperity. However, while this success strengthened the upper and middle classes, the American Industrial Revolution hinged upon the hard work of the country's poorest citizens. The manufacturing industry, for example, offered jobs, but those jobs commonly required extremely long hours, dangerous and unhealthy working conditions, and low wages.

As a result of these employment options, families who moved to US cities (including a high volume of immigrants) in search of opportunities had little choice—parents and children alike needed to work in order to support themselves. While the parents were physically able to endure the harsh conditions prevalent at manufacturing "sweatshops," children were far less physically and mentally fit for this type of work, according child-labor opposition groups. Even if children could handle the work, there remained a question about the effects of labor on children's long-term development and health.

In light of these concerns, the call for reform of the nation's child endangerment and labor laws increased steadily among child advocates and social reformers. One such reformer was Addams, who, with her friend Ellen Starr, founded the social settlement known as Hull House in Chicago in 1889. Hull House was dedicated to combating society's ills through better understanding and volunteerism. In light of her work with Chicago's neediest children, Addams was particularly well-suited to see and appreciate the gravity of the child-labor issue.

Addams was not alone in her observations of the impacts of child labor. In 1904, the National Child Labor Committee (NCLC) was formed at a conference of Americans concerned about this issue. In 1911, Addams joined the NCLC's board of directors. In 1906, Lewis Hine, working for the NCLC, started taking photographs of children at work. He captured haunting images of children working arduously for little pay in cotton mills, mines, and other industrial complexes. These images further fueled public pressure for the reform of child-labor laws. To be sure, most states had passed laws regarding child labor, but, with lax enforcement, those laws were only effective if businesses chose to adhere to them. Activists, such as Addams, and members of the NCLC therefore advocated for stricter laws, passed at the federal level and enforced uniformly in each state.

Author Biography

One of nine children, Laura Jane Addams was born on September 6, 1860, in Cedarville, Illinois. Her father, John, was a prominent Illinois state legislator and friend to President Abraham Lincoln. Her mother, Sarah, died while giving birth to a stillborn child. Addams attended Rockford Female Seminary (later Rockford College, and as of 2013, Rockford University). She started medical school in Philadelphia in 1881, but health problems forced her to stop; she instead traveled throughout Europe. She became a prominent Chicago city leader and an internationally renowned feminist, labor leader, and activist. A founder of the ACLU and a member of the executive board of the NCLC, Addams was awarded the Nobel Peace Prize in 1931, but was admitted to a Baltimore hospital with heart problems on the day she was to receive it. She died on May 21, 1935, from cancer.

HISTORICAL DOCUMENT

The whole problem of life is involved in that subject. It may be said that if a child is starving or neglected, society takes care of it and under the law it is the duty of the inspectors to investigate every case of that kind and relieve it, and in addition to that it is their duty to search around and find out such cases, and when such cases are discovered, it only needs to be brought to public notice to be remedied. But that is not the only or chief evil which threatens childhood in our city, and indeed in every city throughout this country. To my mind, much of the evil which threatens and surrounds childhood is due to the vast enterprises which are now being pushed forward with such vigor and are connected intimately with the industrial situation. I refer to the employment of children in industrial centers, in short, to child labor which we know exists to an alarming extent, and which it is the duty of every thinking man and woman to limit as far as possible, if it cannot be abolished. I think we all agree that the child is entitled to the advantages which result from an opportunity to play and develop, and the doctors put more stress on the child's advantages to play, as being the very basis of a healthy development of the mind and body; and if we assume, as we must, that the child is entitled to those advantages, then we must admit that putting him or her to work prematurely deprives the child of those advantages which by right it is entitled to.

There is no need to discuss that proposition, for it is too self-evident to need discussion. If we want to go into child labor as England goes into it, then it is easy to say that children should be put to work at 12 years of age, at which age child labor is legal in England; that is, the child may work half a day and attend school half a day, if the parents consent to it, but with such a law it has been proven that the child has been deprived of the advantages to which it is entitled, and that its development, both mentally and physically, is impaired and undermined thereby. It has been found by repeated examinations and tests, that if a child who has been put to work thus early is measured and weighed and the result compared with that of children who go to school all day and are afforded the opportunities for play and development which is natural, the first child was an inch and a half shorter, weighed considerably less, and was stunted in other directions. Those are facts, and cannot be controverted.

I quite agree with what was said by a probation officer in this room that an examination of the children brought in by their officers in every instance disclosed that they were abnormal, due solely to their being deprived of the advantages which as children they are entitled to. In cases where they have had children who were brought in there, most of them were found to be abnormal from a medical standpoint, and it has been stated that sixty-three per cent of the boys brought there are poorly nourished, and suffering from mal-nutrition and want of sleep. That is my experience, and the experience of everyone who is engaged in this work. That applied to children who are compelled to go to work. They do not have their meals properly and do not have sufficient food to stand the physical strain, and the result is their minds and nerves become overstrained, and the next result is, many of them become at an early age mental and physical wrecks.

We know one thing, too, that the requirements of the working man are that he shall be at his post early in the morning, and apply all his energies to his work during the day, and walk home soberly at night. All his working hours are required for his maintenance and that of his family, and his physical development enables him to do that. But that does not apply to a boy. There is one thing he will not do unless compelled to, and that is, work for his maintenance; but the very thing that is not demanded of him he will do the next moment, if opportunity is afforded him, and that is play, because that is his prerogative. Now, if we insist that the boy shall throw over all the natural tendencies of play, and the needs of his moral nature and his opportunity to go to school and receive mental and moral training, and yet expect him to walk along in moral paths, we are demanding of him that which he will not perform, and if he does it will be at the expense of his mental and physical development.

I remember in early years one of the mistakes we made in Hull House was in not having sufficient rooms at command to meet the wants of roomers, and particularly of those who were the victims of that pernicious system of child labor. I remember we had one little fellow there who had tried to support his mother and grandmother, and he got along very well and brought home to his mother his wages regularly and was the man of the house at twelve; and that continued for some years; but when he got to be eighteen he fell in with other boys, and exhibited a strange moral perversion, and finally became a tramp and threw the whole burden which he had carried for years on society. Why? Because we had put on him a man's burden when he was but twelve years of age. He was not old enough, had not the development physically, mentally and morally to assume the burden of life at that age and became a wreck at nineteen, whereas, if he had been kept at school and had had the advantages of natural development until the time he would naturally have quit school he would have taken to a man's duties the same as anyone else.

Over and over again we take children and put them into a position where they have no opportunity for development, compel them to work and leave them to acquire an education as best they may, and the inevitable result is, we break them down mentally and physically; they lose the mental vigor they would have acquired by play and education, and it is easy to understand that their mental standard is lowered at the same time.

Now it seems to me that this body, this society, deeply interested as it is in all humane measures, should take every possible step to remedy this evil and to remove the

cause of it, and to look at it from every standpoint and see that humane laws are enacted where they are so much needed, for to my mind it is the most important question of the day.

I have told a story of a little child I once saw in a cotton mill who worked all night, although only five years old, and I spoke to the foreman of the mill about her. He said it was perfectly wonderful the way that child worked night after night, and spent her nights with other children in the same factory. This little child would walk around and join the threads on the cotton mill with little knots and entered into the work fully with others who were there. When she was tired she would lie down in a corner on some rags and rest a little while, and her place would be temporarily filled by one of the other children. The foreman did not enter into the situation at first, but when we called his attention to it, he became very much alarmed when the matter was shown to him in its proper light; but we did not dare to express ourselves very empathetically, because we were there only by courtesy. He did not see what he had to do with it, but permitted her to lie down at night in a corner when she became tired. Of course he said he would not make a rule of doing that with the others, but it was what we said to him went home.

Now that same thing is occurring all about us, and people do not see it, and if they can only be made to do so, their human instincts will at once be brought into play to put a stop to those things. Philanthropists do not stop to consider that this child labor causes the child to grow into an old young man, and there is no excuse for it, and it is up to this society to make clear that the demands for child labor in those large commercial industries, and in this commercial generation shall cease, and it should apply itself to securing the enactment of laws which will abolish this child suffering.

Take the sister states in the United States, and we have here the worst possible child legislation, a very great deal worse than it is in England, because there the child cannot commence work until it is twelve years old; and, as a whole, the laws relating to child labor in the United States are worse than can be found anywhere in Europe. Why is it we are willing to shirk our duty to the children? It is largely because we have directed our philanthropy in another direction, but I repeat it is the duty of this humane society to actively work along the line of saving children from brutal treatment, notwithstanding it means a long and bitter fight; and in this connection I urge upon you the necessity of having careful examinations made of children who are put out of work, and note the results. I know there are many who think it is all right to put boys to work, because they have made themselves obnoxious to society by getting into mischief; but I unhesitatingly assert that if an examination were made into the cases of the worn-out men we see so often around us, it would be found that in the large number of instances their condition was the result of being put to work too young. We once made an examination of men who came to us in Chicago, who were completely worn out and prematurely old, most of whom were Americans, and it was surprising to find how many of them were under thirty-five years of age, and their condition was brought about by their having been put to work too young. They have become disgusted with the whole business, and we know that in our own cases if we liked certain dishes of food but were compelled to eat them all the time we would revolt at them, so these young-old men have revolted at those burdens which were prematurely placed upon them, and finally developed into tramps.

I would subject to this society the proposition that it will be doing the most valuable work it can engage in by addressing itself to this question of the premature labor of children which prevails in every large city, and it is one of the things which sooner or later must be taken up with vigor. At times, when I see things around me, I am so ashamed that I sometimes wonder if we are civilized. It is one of those things that will be laid upon against us, and a hundred years hence people will ask if we could possibly have been civilized, and yet have permitted these things to continue. I do not favor idleness for children, but every child ought to have the advantage of industrial training, and it ought to have a chance for mental training, and to adjust its strength and development to the burdens it will have to bear.

Document Analysis

Addams reminds the conference participants of her primary concern: child welfare. In a society, Addams says, people are driven to action whenever a child is hungry, neglected, or otherwise mistreated. However, she identifies a particular danger to children looming at the turn of the century: that of industrial enterprises consistently using—and endangering—children in their pursuit of productivity.

For a child to work in a sweatshop instead of attending school or playing with other children, Addams argues, is to jeopardize that child's physical and mental development. She cites studies performed in England (which resulted in legal limitations on work hours and conditions for children there) showing that children who worked on assembly lines instead of attending school were shorter and otherwise physically stunted in comparison with their schoolyard counterparts. Americans need to take heed of such studies, the results of which she argues are undeniable fact, and implement similar child-labor laws.

Addams further comments on the social implications of child labor. Here, she cites her own personal experience at Hull House as well as her encounters with fellow child-protection advocates. Hull House has had a large number of clients who were working children, she says. These boys and girls were subjected to high levels of stress when they worked to support their families. In addition to the physical impacts of such stress—weight loss and chronic illness among them—many of the working children she encountered also suffered socially, demonstrating antisocial and criminal behavior. Addams adds that law-enforcement officers with whom she has interacted (including a probation officer she met at the conference where she spoke) revealed that children who worked at sweatshops and other industrial sites were more likely to commit crime.

Addams continues by underscoring the fact that adults who worked in such conditions could barely handle the stress of their work. In comparison, children are especially ill-equipped to take on such roles when they should instead be in the classroom, Addams argues. If they continue to be forced into the workforce at a young age, Addams says, child laborers will be so stunted and "worn out" that even when they reach an adult age, they would likely know and be able to handle menial tasks only.

Americans have long been blind to the issue of child

labor and its impacts on young workers (as well as society as whole), Addams says. Congress and the rest of the federal government should enact the strictest child-labor laws, she argues, adding that government was acting far too slowly on the issue, allowing for working children to grow into maladjusted adult laborers with behavioral issues. Addams emphasizes that this trend was not based on speculation: she saw the effects of child labor on the adults with whom she worked daily at Hull House. It is time, she argues, for the federal government to act quickly and pass laws strictly regulating child labor in the United States. If no such laws are enacted, she states, American society can hardly consider itself "civilized" in the future.

Essential Themes

When Addams addressed the American Humane Association in 1906, she offered two perspectives to support her claims with regard to the nation's child-labor issue. First, she cited statistics and other trend information that revealed the short- and long-term ill effects of child labor on the Americans. Second, she offered her own experience with both child workers and adult former child laborers. The information revealed from both sources, she said, made enacting strict child-labor laws at the federal level not just a necessary legal step but a moral imperative that had implications on future American society.

Children were working long hours in sweatshops and other industrial complexes, Addams said, instead of going to school and learning a wide range of social skills. This trend meant that American laborers were increasingly maladjusted and unable to perform work beyond the menial tasks to which they were exposed as children. The education children received at school far exceeded the lessons learned on an assembly line. After all, she said, normal child development was the product of school and childhood social interaction: children who were denied these experiences were highly likely to have psychological problems (and even criminal tendencies) that would keep them from contributing meaningfully to society.

Addams also relied on her own experiences at Hull House to support her position. Far too many children, she said, were coming to Hull House with social and behavioral issues resulting from having to work. Some came back to Hull House as adults, suffering from a "moral perversion" that would ultimately cause harm to society.

Addams concluded that it was time for Congress to enact strict regulations on child labor. When children were old enough to handle the stress of the workplace, she said, they should be allowed to do so. However, she argued, in the meantime, children should be sent to school to prepare them for the adult world.

—Michael P. Auerbach, MA

Bibliography and Additional Reading

Addams, Jane. *Twenty Years at Hull House*. London: Penguin, 1910. Print.

"Childhood Lost: Child Labor during the Industrial Revolution." *Eastern Illinois University*. Eastern Illinois University, n.d. Web. 16 Apr. 2014.

Hindman, Hugh D. *Child Labor: An American History*. Armonk: Sharpe, 2002. Print.

Linn, James Weber. *Jane Addams: A Biography*. Champaign: U of Illinois P, 1935. Print.

Rosenberg, Chaim M. *Child Labor in America: A History*. Jefferson: McFarland, 2013. Print.

■ From *The Jungle*

Date: 1906
Author: Upton Sinclair
Genre: excerpt

Summary Overview

In the 1906 novel *The Jungle*, novelist and journalist Upton Sinclair describes the success of Chicago's meatpacking industry in hiding unsanitary factory conditions, as well as the dangers of working in such facilities. Sinclair also comments on the political forces at play, telling the story of a Chicago meatpacker's union that helps decrease the political influence of the factory owners by voting sympathetic candidates into power. The novel was based on Sinclair's own experiences investigating Chicago's meatpacking industry, and his findings would inspire the passage of new food safety laws in the United States.

Defining Moment

Throughout the nineteenth century, the meatpacking industry was one of the largest employers in the Midwest. In the years leading up to the Civil War, this industry employed thousands of Americans, most of whom were located in Cincinnati, Ohio, and other parts of the Ohio River Valley. During and after the Civil War, the meatpacking industry shifted to Chicago, Illinois, a hub of the nation's growing railway system.

In 1865, the establishment of the Union Stock Yards, a meatpacking district just south of Chicago, bolstered Chicago's position as the nation's leader in meatpacking. The stockyards were tremendous, using fifteen miles of railway track to deliver livestock to the slaughterhouses and transport the final products throughout the nation. They also relied on the Chicago River for water, using 500,000 gallons per day, and sent contaminated wastewater back into a river fork. By the beginning of the twentieth century, the Union Stock Yards covered 475 acres, with fifty miles of roads and 130 miles of railway track servicing them.

The industry was highly lucrative, with a growing service area. During the Civil War era, the Cincinnati- and Chicago-based industries were focused on servicing the Midwest. However, the advent of the refrigerated boxcar made it possible to send fresh meat throughout the country, and even around the world. By 1900, the Union Stock Yards employed more than 25,000 people. The meatpacking companies wielded tremendous political and financial influence over the areas in which they operated, and government oversight was limited.

In light of the high degree of economic prosperity the Union Stock Yards brought to the Chicago area, as well as the insular manner in which the meatpacking industry managed itself, few people outside of the industry knew the realities of working at that massive complex. The thousands of workers there, mainly Eastern European immigrants, worked exceptionally long hours in unsanitary and highly dangerous conditions. It was not until the beginning of the twentieth century, when novelist and social activist Upton Sinclair published his novel *The Jungle*, that the nation as a whole began to pay attention to the harsh and unsanitary environment that was the meatpacking industry. The novel inspired the passage of the Federal Food and Drugs Act of 1906, which regulated the manufacture and sale of various foods and medicinal products.

Author Biography

Upton Beall Sinclair was born on September 20, 1878, in Baltimore, Maryland. He and his parents moved to New York City when he was ten. At the age of eighteen, he graduated from what is now the City University of New York and continued his education at Columbia University. Having developed an interest in writing as a teenager, Sinclair published short stories and dime novels throughout his time in college and continued to publish fiction after completing his education. He also became a socialist, and in 1904, embarked on an investigation of the meatpacking industry for the socialist newspaper *Appeal to Reason*. Sinclair traveled to Chicago and remained there for several weeks, observing the life of meatpacking workers and the conditions that surrounded them. These observations became the basis for *The Jungle*, serialized in *Appeal to Reason* in 1905 and published in book form in 1906. Sinclair wrote numerous novels after *The Jungle*, some of which, including the 1927 novel *Oil!*, also proved influential. In 1934, Sinclair unsuccessfully ran for governor of California. Afterward he returned to the private sector, writing a number of historical novels. He died on November 25, 1968, at the age of ninety.

HISTORICAL DOCUMENT

...And then there was the condemned meat industry, with its endless horrors. The people of Chicago saw the government inspectors in Packingtown, and they all took that to mean that they were protected from diseased meat; they did not understand that these hundred and sixty-three inspectors had been appointed at the request of the packers, and that they were paid by the United States government to certify that all the diseased meat was kept in the state. They had no authority beyond that; for the inspection of meat to be sold in the city and state the whole force in Packingtown consisted of three henchmen of the local political machine!...

And then there was "potted game" and "potted grouse," "potted ham," and "deviled ham"—devyled, as the men called it. "De-vyled" ham was made out of the waste ends of smoked beef that were too small to be sliced by the machines; and also tripe, dyed with chemicals so that it would not show white, and trimmings of hams and corned beef, and potatoes, skins and all, and finally the hard cartilaginous gullets of beef, after the tongues had been cut out. All this ingenious mixture was ground up and flavored with spices to make it taste like something. Anybody who could invent a new imitation had been sure of a fortune from old Durham, said Jurgis's informant, but it was hard to think of anything new in a place where so many sharp wits had been at work for so long; where men welcomed tuberculosis in the cattle they were feeding, because it made them fatten more quickly; and where they bought up all the old rancid butter left over in the grocery stores of a continent, and "oxidized" it by a forced-air process, to take away the odor, rechurned it with skim milk, and sold it in bricks in the cities! . . .

There were the men in the pickle rooms, for instance, where old Antanas had gotten his death; scarce a one of these that had not some spot of horror on his person. Let a man so much as scrape his finger pushing a truck in the pickle rooms, and he might have a sore that would put him out of the world; all the joints of his fingers might be eaten by the acid, one by one. Of the butchers and floorsmen, the beef boners and trimmers, and all those who used knives, you could scarcely find a person who had the use of his thumb; time and time again the base of it had been slashed, till it was a mere lump of flesh against which the man pressed the knife to hold it. The hands of these men would be criss-crossed with cuts, until you could no longer pretend to count them or to trace them. They would have no nails,—they had worn them off pulling hides; their knuckles were swollen so that their fingers spread out like a fan. There were men who worked in the cooking rooms, in the midst of steam and sickening odors, by artificial light; in these rooms the germs of tuberculosis might live for two years, but the supply was renewed every hour. There were the beef luggers, who carried two-hundred-pound quarters into the refrigerator cars, a fearful kind of work, that began at four o'clock in the morning, and that wore out the most powerful men in a few years. There were those who worked in the chilling rooms, and whose special disease was rheumatism; the time limit that a man could work in the chilling rooms was said to be five years. There were the wool pluckers, whose hands went to pieces even sooner than the hands of the pickle men; for the pelts of the sheep had to be painted with acid to loosen the wool, and then the pluckers had to pull out this wool with their bare hands, till the acid had eaten their fingers off. There were those who made the tins for the canned meat, and their hands, too, were a maze of cuts, and each cut represented a chance for blood poisoning. Some worked at the stamping machines, and it was very seldom that one could work long there at the pace that was set, and not give out and forget himself, and have a part of his hand chopped off. There were the "hoisters," as they were called, whose task it was to press the lever which lifted the dead cattle off the floor. They ran along upon a rafter, peering down through the damp and the steam, and as old Durham's architects had not built the killing room for the convenience of the hoisters, at every few feet they would have to stoop under a beam, say four feet above the one they ran on, which got them into the habit of stooping, so that in a few years they would be walking like chimpanzees. Worst of any, however, were the fertilizer men, and those who served in the cooking rooms. These people could not be shown to the visitor—for the odor of a fertilizer man would scare away any ordinary visitor at a hundred yards, and as for the other men, who worked in tank rooms full of steam, and in some of which there were open vats near the level of the floor, their peculiar trouble was that they fell into the vats; and when they were fished out, there was never enough of them left to be worth exhibiting—sometimes they would be overlooked for days, till all but the bones of them had gone out to the world as Durham's Pure Leaf Lard!...

There was never the least attention paid to what was cut up for sausage; there would come all the way back from Europe old sausage that had been rejected, and that was mouldy and white—it would be dosed with borax and glycerine, and dumped into the hoppers, and made over again for home consumption. There would be meat that had tumbled out on the floor, in the dirt and sawdust, where the workers had tramped and spit uncounted billions of consumption germs. There would be meat stored in great piles in rooms; and the water from leaky roofs would drip over it, and thousands of rats would race about on it. It was too dark in these storage places to see well, but a man could run his hand over these piles of meat and sweep off handfuls of the dried dung of rats. These rats were nuisances, and the packers would put poisoned bread out for them, they would die, and then rats, bread, and meat would go into the hoppers together. This is no fairy story and no joke; the meat would be shovelled into carts, and the man who did the shoveling would not trouble to lift out a rat even when he saw one—there were things that went into the sausage in comparison with which a poisoned rat was a tidbit. There

was no place for the men to wash their hands before they ate their dinner, and so they made a practice of washing them in the water that was to be ladled into the sausage. There were the butt-ends of smoked meat, and the scraps of corned beef, and all the odds and ends of the waste of the plants, that would be dumped into old barrels in the cellar and left there. Under the system of rigid economy which the packers enforced, there were some jobs that it only paid to do once in a long time, and among these was the cleaning out of the waste barrels. Every spring they did it; and in the barrels would be dirt and rust and old nails and stale water—and cart load after cart load of it would be taken up and dumped into the hoppers with fresh meat, and sent out to the public's breakfast. Some of it they would make into "smoked" sausage—but as the smoking took time, and was therefore expensive, they would call upon their chemistry department, and preserve it with borax and color it with gelatine to make it brown. All of their sausage came out of the same bowl, but when they came to wrap it they would stamp some of it "special," and for this they would charge two cents more a pound....

And then the editor wanted to know upon what ground Dr. Schliemann asserted that it might be possible for a society to exist upon an hour's toil by each of its members. "Just what," answered the other, "would be the productive capacity of society if the present resources of science were utilized, we have no means of ascertaining; but we may be sure it would exceed anything that would sound reasonable to minds inured to the ferocious barbarities of Capitalism. After the triumph of the international proletariat, war would of course be inconceivable; and who can figure the cost of war to humanity—not merely the value of the lives and the material that it destroys, not merely the cost of keeping millions of men in idleness, of arming and equipping them for battle and parade, but the drain upon the vital energies of society by the war-attitude and the war-terror, the brutality and ignorance, the drunkenness, prostitution, and crime it entails, the industrial impotence and the moral deadness? Do you think that it would be too much to say that two hours of the working time of every efficient member of a community goes to feed the red fiend of war?"

And then Schliemann went on to outline some of the wastes of competition: the losses of industrial warfare; the ceaseless worry and friction; the vices—such as drink, for instance, the use of which had nearly doubled in twenty years, as a consequence of the intensification of the economic struggle; the idle and unproductive members of the community, the frivolous rich and the pauperized poor; the law and the whole machinery of repression; the wastes of social ostentation, the milliners and tailors, the hairdressers, dancing masters, chefs and lackeys. "You understand," he said, "that in a society dominated by the fact of commercial competition, money is necessarily the test of prowess, and wastefulness the sole criterion of power. So we have, at the present moment, a society with, say, thirty per cent of the population occupied in producing useless articles, and one per cent occupied in destroying them…"

And then there were official returns from the various precincts and wards of the city itself! Whether it was a factory district or one of the "silk-stocking" wards seemed to make no particular difference in the increase; but one of the things which surprised the [Socialist] party leaders most was the tremendous vote that came rolling in from the stockyards. Packingtown comprised three wards of the city, and the vote in the spring of 1903 had been five hundred, and in the fall of the same year, sixteen hundred. Now, only a year later, it was over sixty-three hundred—and the Democratic vote only eighty-eight hundred! There were other wards in which the Democratic vote had been actually surpassed, and in two districts, members of the state legislature had been elected. Thus Chicago now led the country; it had set a new standard for the party, it had shown the workingmen the way!

—So spoke an orator upon the platform; and two thousand pairs of eyes were fixed upon him, and two thousand voices were cheering his every sentence. The orator had been the head of the city's relief bureau in the stockyards, until the sight of misery and corruption had made him sick. He was young, hungry-looking, full of fire; and as he swung his long arms and beat up the crowd, to Jurgis he seemed the very spirit of the revolution. "Organize! Organize! Organize!"—that was his cry. He was afraid of this tremendous vote, which his party had not expected, and which it had not earned. "These men are not Socialists!" he cried. "This election will pass, and the excitement will die, and people will forget about it; and if you forget about it, too, if you sink back and rest upon your oars, we shall lose this vote that we have polled today, and our enemies will laugh us to scorn! It rests with you to take your resolution—now, in the flush of victory, to find these men who have voted for us, and bring them to our meetings, and organize them and bind them to us! We shall not find all our campaigns as easy as this one. Everywhere in the country tonight the old party politicians are studying this vote, and setting their sails by it; and nowhere will they be quicker or more cunning than here in our own city. Fifty thousand Socialist votes in Chicago means a municipal-ownership Democracy in the spring! And then they will fool the voters once more, and all the powers of plunder and corruption will be swept into office again! But whatever they may do when they get in, there is one thing they will not do, and that will be the thing for which they were elected! They will not give the people of our city municipal ownership—they will not mean to do it, they will not try to do it; all that they will do is give our party in Chicago the greatest opportunity that has ever come to Socialism in America! We shall have the sham reformers self-stultified and self-convicted; we shall have the radical Democracy left without a lie with which to cover its nakedness! And then will begin the rush that will never be checked, the tide that will never turn till it has reached its flood—that will be irresistible, overwhelming—the rallying of the outraged workingmen of Chicago to our standard! And we shall organize them, we shall drill them, we shall marshal them for the victory! We shall bear down the opposition, we shall sweep it before us—and Chicago will be ours! Chicago will be ours! CHICAGO WILL BE OURS!"

GLOSSARY

borax: a white, crystalline powder (hydrated sodium borate) used as a cleaning agent

tripe: the stomach lining of a cow or ox, used as food

Document Analysis

The Jungle tells the story of a Lithuanian immigrant, Jurgis Rudkus, who arrives in Chicago in search of work. He and his family settle in an area known as Packingtown, where they experience a wide range of hardships. Jurgis finds work in the meatpacking industry but continues to struggle with poverty and crime in addition to the physical dangers of his work environment. He eventually becomes interested in socialism and labor unions, seeing them as a possible solution to the rampant corruption of the meatpacking industry. Though *The Jungle* is a work of fiction, the novel is a thinly veiled commentary on life at the Union Stock Yards and expresses Sinclair's positive views of unionization and socialist ideals.

Throughout *The Jungle*, Jurgis witnesses firsthand many of the unsanitary conditions and unhealthy products being assembled in Packingtown. Some departments within the facility in which he works use dye and other chemicals, parts of older and unused meat segments, and even diseased animal corpses in the creation of household food products. The production of sausage continues even after rat droppings as well as cleaning chemicals, dirt, and sawdust have fallen into the openly stored piles of meat. Sinclair's descriptions of these unhygienic conditions are graphic and clearly demonstrate that meat products produced in such conditions are unfit for human consumption.

Sinclair likewise uses the novel to draw attention to the corruption of the meatpacking industry as well as its human cost. Government inspectors visit Packingtown but accomplish little, as the companies pay or otherwise influence the inspectors to sign off on their unsanitary practices. Workers, such as Jurgis, are unable to improve the sanitary conditions of their work environment; in fact, the plants of Packingtown are even said to lack hand-washing facilities. Workers returning home carry germs and harmful substances on their hands and clothes, exposing their families to those environmental conditions as well. Furthermore, Sinclair, through Jurgis, emphasizes the extreme dangers associated with working in Packingtown. Picklers, boners, butchers, and other workers are said to be at constant risk of injury, and thanks to the unsanitary working conditions and numerous hazardous substances around them, even the smallest cut has the potential to develop a terrible infection. Other workers, such as those responsible for operating hoisting machinery, spend so much time bent over that they walk around "like chimpanzees."

After experiencing the hardships of meatpacking work, Jurgis eventually meets Dr. Nicholas Schliemann, a Swiss native whose socialist views appear to provide a solution. Schliemann convinces Jurgis of the value of unions, which could allow the meatpackers to unite and speak with one voice. Jurgis realizes that unionization could empower the people of Packingtown and give them the ability to take control of Chicago politics and put an end to the harmful and exploitative practices of the meatpacking industry.

Essential Themes

In *The Jungle*, Jurgis Rudkus arrives in the United States in search of opportunity, but he instead encounters hardship, crime, corruption, and danger in a large system of slaughterhouses known as Packingtown. The story is fictional, but Sinclair's novel is heavily based on his experiences and observations at the very real Union Stock Yards outside of Chicago. Sinclair believed that the secrets of the meatpacking industry—then hidden from the prying eyes of critics, activists, and the public at large—needed to be revealed to all Americans, and the novel form allowed him to do so in an accessible manner, presenting a depiction of the meatpacking industry that resonated with readers on several levels.

In the novel, it is common for workers to be injured, maimed, or even killed while working in Packingtown. Death can be immediate, Jurgis learns, or it can be long and painful due to infection. Sinclair calls attention to the terrible human cost of the meatpacking industry, presenting in unflinching detail the amputations, mutilations, and deaths that commonly occur in a work environment that favors production over worker safety. In addition, the meatpacking industry is shown to use extremely unsanitary and unhealthy practices in the production of its products. Chemicals, animal waste, and other foreign substances are commonly dumped into the meat, and expired and even rancid byproducts are packaged and sold to customers. The government is shown to monitor these practices, but, as Jurgis learns, government inspectors are on site as a service to the companies themselves rather than the public. By describing the unsanitary production of food products in detail, Sinclair made it clear to his readers that poor working conditions in meatpacking facilities affected not only the people who worked there, but also the unsuspecting consumers who ate the contaminated products—perhaps including the readers themselves.

—*Michael P. Auerbach, MA*

Bibliography and Additional Reading

Barrett, James R. *Work and Community in the Jungle: Chicago's Packinghouse Workers, 1894–1922*. Champaign: U of Illinois P, 1990. Print.

Halpern, Rick. *Down on the Killing Floor: Black and White Workers in Chicago's Packinghouses, 1904–1954*. Urbana: U of Illinois P, 1997. Print.

Stromquist, Shelton, and Marvin Bergman. *Unionizing the Jungles: Labor and Community in the Twentieth-Century Meatpacking Industry*. Iowa City: U of Iowa P, 1997. Print.

Warren, Wilson J. *Tied to the Great Packing Machine: The Midwest and Meatpacking*. Iowa City: U of Iowa P, 2007. Print.

■ Child Labor in the New York City Tenements

Date: January 18, 1908
Author: Mary Van Kleeck
Genre: report

Summary Overview

As the Industrial Revolution unfolded in the United States, many poor urban children left school to work in factories and stores to help support their families. As new federal and state laws required school attendance for children of certain ages and restricted labor outside the home during the academic year, child labor shifted to home manufacturing—a practice where goods manufacturers provided finishing work on a piecemeal basis to anyone who could complete it. Since child-labor laws did not prohibit this practice, many children who left factory work were forced into long hours of after-school labor helping their parents finish goods at home. In conjunction with several reform organizations and government agencies, Mary Van Kleeck authored the report "Child Labor in New York City Tenements" to uncover the truths behind this practice, hoping to protect children from unfair labor practices and improve their chances of obtaining a proper education.

Defining Moment

In the late nineteenth and early twentieth centuries, the Industrial Revolution was in full swing in the United States. Across the country—although primarily in eastern cities—manufacturing replaced agriculture as the driving force behind economic growth. As large corporations sought ever-larger profits, workers found themselves in increasingly dire positions. Workers commonly engaged in ten- to fourteen-hour shifts surrounded by fast-moving heavy machinery, leading to extremely dangerous working conditions.

With stiff competition for unskilled labor employment in the crowded cities, wages were often so low that working families could not afford to house, feed, and clothe their children. Eventually, the children needed to leave school and work to help support the family. Unfortunately, this perpetuated the cycle of poverty, since these children lost the opportunity to obtain the education necessary to find employment outside of the factories.

After significant efforts, state and federal governments passed laws to restrict child labor in factories and stores, particularly during the school year. Combined with compulsory school attendance laws, children in cities such as New York left the factory floor and returned to the classroom. However, no laws prevented the use of child labor in "sweating system" work—a system whereby laborers of any age could perform manufacturing work at home. Although New York state law required homes to be both inspected for sanitation and safety and licensed before permitting such work, doing so proved difficult to regulate and enforce. Additionally, the sweating system provided immense financial benefits to companies, as it allowed them to skirt many labor rules. As such, corporate interests lobbied hard to ensure the practice could continue.

In 1908, child-labor activist Van Kleeck authored a report on child labor in New York City tenements. Van Kleeck worked with the National Consumers' League and the Consumers' League of New York City, the National and New York Child Labor Committees, and the College Settlements Association to prepare the report. Using both statistics and personal stories obtained by interviewing families and children engaged in home manufacturing, Van Kleeck's report brought attention to the sweating system and the role children occupied within it. She acknowledged the difficulties in both passing and enforcing effective laws but strongly advocated for regulations that might help protect children from exploitative labor practices.

Author Biography

Mary Abby Van Kleeck was born in Glenham, New York, on June 26, 1883. After her father's death in 1892, she moved with her family from their upstate home to the Flushing, Queens, neighborhood of New York. She received her AB from Smith College in 1904, then moved back to New York City to study sociology at Columbia University and work with employment-related organizations including the College Settlement Association and the Alliance Employment Bureau.

Van Kleeck's primary academic and philanthropic interests included factory women and child labor. Her work led to sponsorship by the Russell Sage Foundation, as well as several teaching positions in social work and labor rights. During World War I, she helped establish legal standards for women's employment in war industries and served on several boards, including the War Labor Policies Board and the US Department of Labor's Women in Industry Service.

After officially retiring in 1948, Van Kleeck ran for the New York State senate as a member of the American Labor Party, but was not elected. In 1953, she was summoned before US senator Joseph McCarthy's committee for investigation because of her affiliation with organizations declared "subversive" to the government. She remained mostly out of the public eye until her death in Kingston, New York, in 1972.

HISTORICAL DOCUMENT

The following brief report gives the results of a joint investigation made during the months from October, 1906, to April, 1907, into the labor of children in manufacture in tenement houses in New York City. The National Consumers' League and the Consumers' League of New York City, the National and New York Child Labor Committees, and the College Settlements Association co-operated in the undertaking.

In the most thickly populated districts of New York City, especially south of Fourteenth street, little children are often seen on the streets carrying large bundles of unfinished garments, or boxes containing materials for making artificial flowers. This work is given out by manufacturers or contractors to be finished in tenement homes, where the labor of children of any age may be utilized. For the laws of New York state, prohibiting the employment of children under fourteen years of age in factories, stores, or other specified work-places, have never been extended to home workrooms. In this fact is presented a child labor problem—as yet scarcely touched—namely: How to prevent employment of young children in home work in manufacture?

So difficult has been the problem of regulating by law the conditions of employment in home workrooms, that advance in measures to protect children against premature toil in factories has had no parallel in provisions designed to regulate manufacture in tenement homes. Between these two systems of manufacture—one carried on in factories and the other in the homes of the workers—there are, therefore, some striking contrasts in the law. No maker of artificial flowers can employ in his factory any child under fourteen years of age, but he may give out work to an Italian family, in whose tenement rooms flowers are made by six children, aged two and one-half, five, eight, ten, fourteen and sixteen years. In another family Angelo, aged fourteen years, cannot work legally in a factory until he reaches a higher grade in school, nor can he work at home during hours when school is in session, but his little sister Maria, aged three years, because she is not old enough to go to school and because the home work law contains no prohibition of child labor, may help her mother pull bastings and sew on buttons. A public school teacher notices that Eva and Mary R., aged eleven and ten years, are pale and undernourished, but although the compulsory education law supports her in requiring their attendance in school during school hours, she cannot prevent their making flowers at home from three o'clock until nine or ten at night. Many good citizens would demand the prosecution of a manufacturer who employed in his factory Tony aged four years, Maria aged nine, Rose aged ten, Louisa aged eleven, and Josephine aged thirteen years. For such an offense the employer might be fined $100 for each child under fourteen years of age found at work in his factory. Yet public has not raised an effective protest against the same employer when he turns these children's home into a branch of his factory and gives them work in which even the smallest child in the family joins through long hours under a necessity as imperious in its demand for the constant work and attention of the child as would be the commands of a foreman in a factory.

In brief, the law which regulates home work manufacture in New York City, contains no provisions to prevent the employment of children nor to restrict the working hours of minors or women. It provides merely that work on certain specified articles (forty-one in number) given out by manufacturers or contractors, nay not be carried on in a tenement living room, unless the owner of the house has first obtained a license from the New York State Department of Labor. Any articles not named in the law may legally be manufactured in unlicensed houses.

That the law in New York state does not protect more effectively these child workers in tenement homes, is due not to a lack of opposition to premature employment of children, but to the impossibility of dealing with the problem merely as a child labor question apart from deep-rooted evils essential to the "sweating system," of which home work is an important part. The evils of the system—intense competition among unskilled workers in a crowded district, low wages, unrestricted hours of work, irregularity of employment, and utilization of child labor—are the very conditions which make the system possible and profitable to the employer. Any effective attempt to improve conditions must therefore be an attack upon the sweating system. The manufacturer or contractor, whose employees work in their home, escapes responsibility entailed by the presence of workers in his factory. He saves costs of rent, heat, and light; avoids the necessity of keeping the force together and giving them regular employment when work is slack. And by turning the workers' homes into branches of the factory, he escapes in them the necessity of observing the factory laws. Instead of the manifold restrictions which apply to employees working in the factory, he is here responsible only for keeping a list of his home workers and he may not send any goods, which are named in the home work law into a tenement which has not been licensed.

SOME TYPICAL CASES

The salient features of child labor in home work in New York City may best be illustrated by describing conditions of work of a few of the children so employed, indicating the baffling nature of the problem and at the same time disclosing the serious defect in the present law already described—its failure to prevent child labor.

If fifty of these children could be gathered together to tell their stories, they would be found to illustrate very distinct conditions under which work is carried on in tenement homes. There is the child of the very poor family who, for various reasons, has fallen below the level of economic independence, and is receiving partial support from a relief society. Another child belongs to a family whose earnings from employment outside the home are entirely adequate for support, but who because of the custom of the neighborhood and a desire to earn a little extra money, take work from a factory to be done at home by members who would otherwise be non-wage earners, the mother and the younger children. In other cases supplementary income derived from home work enables wage earners in outside employments to work with less regularity or to underbid their competitors.

Aside from differences in family circumstances, the children's employment varies greatly in regularity. One child goes every day to school and works only when school is not in session. Another, although of school age, has been kept at home more or less regularly throughout the day, to make flowers or pull bastings. Others, ever since their arrival in the United States, have succeeded in escaping the truant officer, to add their daily earnings to the family income. And although living in the most crowded districts of New York City have never learned to speak or write the English language. Finally there are those who, although they take little part in work brought from the factories, nevertheless bear the burden of the home work system by being compelled to care for younger children or do house work while the mother sews or makes flowers or engages in some other of the numerous varieties of work carried on in tenement homes.

The children are found to illustrate also various phases of the law's application, according to their relation to compulsory education on the one hand and the attempted regulation of home work on the other. This relation of the child to the law demands especial emphasis as illustrating concretely the scope of present regulations.

WORK IN LICENSED HOUSES

To a casual visitor, the brightest side of home work would appear in the tenements on Sullivan, Thompson, Macdougal, Houston, and neighboring streets, among makers of artificial flowers. Many houses are "new law" tenements, in which provision has been made for light and air. In many of them there is full compliance with the provisions of the home work law. It is therefore a neighborhood which illustrates well the limitations of the licensing system.

So general is the custom of home work in this district that as one mounts the stairs in any one of these houses one finds on every floor, and in almost every apartment, families of flower-makers.

On the top floor of a licensed house on Sullivan street two children, Angelina aged eleven years, and Katharine aged eight years, were at work helping an older sister make roses at eight cents a gross. The apartment was clean and light and the family prosperous, with an income of at least $20 a week from sources other than home work—the wages of the father and two brothers. The older sister aged eighteen years, worked at home rather than in a factory so that she might help her mother with housework. So small was the pay for flowers that she forced her two younger sisters to work steadily after school hours until eight o'clock at night, in order that together they might earn eighty cents a day, the wages paid for making, counting and bunching 1,440 small roses. At the neighboring school it was found that both Angelina and Katherine attended regularly, but that their marks in "proficiency" were lower than their marks in "effort and deportment." Of Katharine, the younger, the teacher said, "The child is very sleepy during school hours." Yet the children were obeying the compulsory education law, and their work was done in a clean house where the required framed license hung in the hallway. No statute was therefore violated by their employment.

On the same floor where Katharine and Angelina lived, four other children, Vito, aged fourteen years, Karie aged twelve, Jennie nine, and Antoinette seven, were at work making "June buds" at eight cents a gross. Their total earnings combined with the wages of their mother and older sister were between fifty and sixty cents a day. On the next floor below, Michael aged thirteen years, and his mother were making paper flowers. Across the hall, Maggie aged sixteen years, Angelina aged fourteen, Josephine aged eight, Tony aged six, and Frank aged four, were at work on a more complicated kind of rose for which the employer paid twenty-five cents a gross. But this work brought no higher wages than cheaper grades of flowers, since to make three and one-half gross in a day the family must work until 9 p.m. One child, Josephine who was often kept at home to help in flower making, had been absent from school one day in three through the autumn when the flower season was at its height. Nearby was a family who made black violets at five cents a gross—Antoinette, aged eight years, and Mary aged thirteen, helping after school. When the materials come from the factory the petals stick together and must be separated before they are pasted on the stems. This work was done by Lucy aged six years who, a visitor reported, "is not very well, so the mother does not send her to kindergarten. She works almost all day or else cares for the baby."

In the same house were several other children who made roses or violets or other flowers, of cheap grade: John B. aged thirteen years; Jennie V. aged thirteen; Jasmine aged fourteen, and James D. aged six, who lived in the rear apartment of the first floor, where high buildings nearby shut out the light so that it is necessary to keep gas burning in the rooms where work is done. Also Celia aged fourteen years, Julia aged ten, and Josie aged six, who lived in the front apartment on the first floor, were helping their mother make violets at three and one-half cents a gross. They worked until 9 p.m. to finish between 1,440 and 1,700 flowers in a day, for which they were paid thirty-five or forty cents.

In no case was the manufacturing violating the labor law in employing these children. Not only were these cases of child labor quite permissible under the present attempted legal regulation of home work, but even an increased stringency in those sanitary requirements which are the essential feature of the present law would probably not affect in any way this house or the work of these children, since sanitary conditions were satisfactory.

The licensing system does not re-enforce the compulsory education law. If Farah M., an Italian child aged ten years had not lived in a licensed tenement it would not have been so difficult for the school authorities to compel her parents to send her to school. After sixty days' absence and four fruitless visits from a truant officer she was found still working at home, sewing buttons on corduroy trousers. The framed certificate in the hall showed that the house was licensed, and for this reason it was not possible to re-enforce the compulsory education law by preventing the child's employment at home. The family was very poor, there were four children younger than Sarah, and the father, an unskilled day laborer, was out of work. The possibility of working at home without any interference by the inspectors of the Labor Department, placed a premium upon the child's truancy. The aid of a relief society was finally secured on the ground that a family who were obliged to depend upon the work of a child of ten years, were evidently not self-supporting and should be aided on condition that the child be sent to school as the law requires. But even after this, the society reported that it would be necessary to watch the family. For it was the busy season in the clothing trade, the time when every member of the homeworkers' households is pressed into service to fill the contractors' orders.

WORK WHERE THERE IS DISEASE

Although the present provisions of the home work law are intended to prevent manufacture in apartments where there is disease, by requiring immediate action by the State Department of Labor and the city Department of Health, the licensing system does not guard sufficiently against work where disease exists. After a house has been properly licensed, some member of a family of workers may be afflicted with tuberculosis, and the fact may not be reported either to the Board of Health or the Department of Labor. To guard against the danger of manufacturing articles under such conditions, would require constant watching of the shifting population of a New York City tenement. It is hardly to be expected that among the great crowds of possible home workers peopling a city block, each family can be watched by the over- burdened Labor Department upon which devolves, besides the work of factory inspection, the task of examining regularly more than 5,000 licensed tenements in Greater New York, and of detecting any work carried

on illegally among the far greater number of unlicensed houses.

The possibility of homework in an apartment where there is disease, and the employment of children under these unhealthy conditions, is illustrated by an Italian family referred to a relief society in the autumn of 1906. The house had been licensed in the preceding year, when the sanitary conditions presumably were satisfactory to the Department of Health, the Tenement House Department, and the Department of Labor, and there must have been no evidence of disease among the tenants. Yet in 1906 it was found that for weeks a family living in the house had been finishing clothing in the room where the oldest daughter, Vincenza, aged sixteen years, lay dying of tuberculosis.

A visitor of the relief society found Rosina aged thirteen years, helping her mother and father in the work of finishing trousers. Since the arrival of the family in the United States seven years before, neither Rosina nor Vincenza had attended school, and neither could read or write. With the father ill of tuberculosis, Vincenza no longer able to work, and four younger children, aged eleven, seven, five and two years, to be cared for. Rosina, who had helped to support the family since she was six years old, was now the chief wage earner. Her brother, Giuseppe, aged eleven years helped in the sewing after school hours. But at the price of four cents a pair, for "felling" seams, finishing linings, and sewing buttons on trousers, all the workers in the family—father, mother and two children, by united effort, could not earn more than four or five dollars a week.

When the relief society aided the family, Vincenza was sent to a hospital, and Rosina for the first time in her life began to go to school. But she continued to sew at home after school hours. A later entry in the society"s records reports that "Rosina and Giuseppe were busy at work finishing. Rosina said that she went to school regularly all day sessions, and that she and her brother helped at finishing after school."

All that the law could do for Rosina was to add school work to the ceaseless toil in which she had spent her days since early childhood. In her work at home from the time she was six years old for a manufacturer of clothing no provision of the labor law was violated. After her eighth birthday, her work at home, in that it prevented her attending school, caused a violation of the compulsory education law. But the work in itself, so long as the family lived in a licensed tenement, was never at any time illegal until Vincenza developed tuberculosis. Nor was this and the danger to the public health from the presence of a communicable disease in the home workroom prevented by the Department of Labor or the Board of Health.

Where, however, disease is detected in the homes of workers, the action of these two departments is swift and as effective as possible under present conditions.

A widow and four children were living in a rear tenement on Chrystie street where they rented two rooms at nine dollars a month. The house is an old one, with old fashioned worn-out wooden stairs and sinks from which water frequently overflows on the stair landings. Three of the children in the family referred to—Messina aged eleven years, Mary aged nine, and Ida aged six, helped their mother in finishing overcoats of good quality well lined with black satin. The children were undernourished and undeveloped, entirely unfit physically for any work, especially sewing heavy cloth overcoats. The rooms in which they lived were very dirty, and the family owned only one bed. At night they used the cloth overcoats for covering.

The case was brought to the notice of the Department of Labor, by a relief society, who aided the family for some years. Angelo, the oldest boy, had been examined by a physician, who reported that he had scabies (itch), a disease liable to attack all the members of the family at any time. The physician recommended that all the clothing be burned and the rooms thoroughly cleaned.

When the State Department of Labor was notified inspectors "tagged" all goods in process of manufacture throughout the house, refused a license and forbade further work until sanitary conditions should be improved and the disease cured. Ten days later the mother tried to bring home more work, but the landlord (who in case any tenant disobeyed the orders of the Department of Labor would have been liable to prosecutions as though he himself had been engaged in this unlawful manufacture), refused to allow her to do any more sewing in her home, and shortly afterwards told her that she must move, in order that the house might be licensed. After their dispossession, the landlord succeeded in obtain-

ing the license permitting work in the house. When last they were heard from, some months later, they were still engaged in home work in another house to which they had moved, described by the Department of Labor as old ramshackle building in a most dilapidated and dirty condition.

All that can now be done is to report the conditions there to the Health Department. All that we could do in the matter of the former dwelling was to delay issuing the license until the objectionable family moved, which we did.

The presence of a contagious, infectious, or communicable disease, or the existence of unclean or unsanitary conditions is sufficient ground for forbidding home work. But if no such unhealthy or unsanitary conditions exist, and if the tenement is properly licensed, the fact that three sickly children, aged eleven, nine and six years, are at work, is the concern of no official department, a violation of no law.

WORK IN UNLICENSED HOUSES

Since it is the theory of the licensing system that no home work is to be permitted in any tenement until the Department of Labor is convinced that the premises are sanitary, it is clear that the existence of work in unlicensed tenements is evidence of failure in the law's enforcement. The day after Christmas, 1906, three child workers, Vito aged thirteen years, Maggie aged eleven, and Billy aged nine, were visited in a tenement on James street. Vito had just brought from a nearby shop ten dozen pairs of boys' trousers to be finished for the wage of four cents a dozen. The father, a plasterer, who can earn $1.75 a day, was idle, depending for a while on the earnings of his wife and children, whose wages were higher during holidays than when school attendance interrupted their work. The family, consisting of father, mother and six children, of whom the youngest were aged six years, three and one, lived in two rooms for which they paid $11 a month. Home work was a regular means of supplementing the father's irregular earnings, and it was the habit of the family to take work as often as possible from the contractor, whose shop was within a block of their home. Yet the house in which they lived had never been licensed by the Department of Labor, and landlord, contractor, and worker were all breaking the labor law. That any possibility of prosecution was remote from the minds of the workers was indicated by the fact that although the visitors were strangers, the family made no attempt to conceal the work.

Just across the street from Sarah M., whose work at home during school hours has been described, lived another child who had been a truant from the same school. On September 16, 1903, she had been admitted to the 3-A grade, but she was kept at home so often to help her mother "finish" clothing, that on April 27, 1905, she was still enrolled in the same grade which she had entered nearly two school years before. The truant officer was sent to visit the family and his report, entered in the school records, read: "Kept at home by mother." When the child had been absent a year and six months, a private organization made further efforts to compel her parents to send her to school, but after searching for the passport to prove her age, it was found that she had just passed her fourteenth birthday and was beyond the jurisdiction of the compulsory education law.

During this time, no one had attempted to compel the child's return to school, by preventing effectively the work which was the most important cause of her absence. In this case the labor law might have re-enforced the compulsory education law, because the house in which the child lived had not been licensed. Owing, however, to the fact that compliance with the legal provision requiring the display of a license in a conspicuous place in the hall, has not been demanded, private individuals and organizations cannot co-operate effectively in enforcing the law, without consulting the records of the Department of Labor. It is therefore difficult for anyone who is not an inspector of the department to detect violations.

Moreover, in the case of this child, the aid of the labor law would have been only temporary for the permit was withheld merely pending application by the owner of the house. An official "notice to apply" had been sent to him, and the speedy possession of a license would allow tenants, including their children, to engage in home-work.

The lack of private co-operation in reporting to the Labor Department the addresses of unlicensed houses where home work is found, is illustrated in the story of two families whose children were truants because of home work. The fact that the Labor Department had refused to license the house in which they were working, was not used by anyone as a means of preventing the children's employment. Nor was this fact known until investigators who were especially interested in the operation of the home work law visited the family and afterwards consulted the records of the Labor Department.

In the meantime, it had required the combined efforts of a settlement, a relief society, and school officers, to keep these children in school even for a few days. Nellie aged six years, Josephine aged eleven, and Josie aged nine, worked all day long, often until 10 o'clock at night "finishing" coats at four to six cents apiece. The two families who lived together numbered eleven, Giuseppina, Nellie and their father and mother and four younger children. The two men worked only at rare intervals, and depended upon the women and children to support the families. They refused therefore to let the children go to school, even long enough to learn to read and write. Compliance with the law was finally secured by means of court summons against the parents for truancy of their children. But after this had been accomplished, the children were still compelled to work at home continuously during hours when school was not in session.

One other phase of home work needs illustration: namely, the kinds of manufacture which are legal even though carried on in unlicensed houses. In a tenement which the Department of Labor had refused to license, two Italian boys, Mario aged twelve years, and Louis aged nine, were found sewing by hand the small tapes under the buttons and buttonholes for fine kid gloves. The mother was a widow with four children, aged fourteen, twelve, nine and five years. They lived in one small room, for which they paid a rent of $7.00. Their combined earnings from home work were not more than sixty cents a day, and they were aided necessarily by a relief society. Since the Department of Labor had found the house unworthy of a license, the tenants could not legally make flowers or finish clothing, or produce thirty-nine other articles specified in the statute; but because gloves are not named in the home work law their manufacture in tenement homes is neither prevented nor regulated.

In the same way, Bessie S. aged seven and one-half years, who helped to make silk tassels; Harry, Elise and Charles R., aged thirteen, eight and six years, who carded buttons at five cents a gross; and Mary and Jennie M. aged eleven and nine years, who fastened cords to pencils for souvenir cards at forty cents a thousand, were all legally employed at home out of school hours, although no one of them lived in a licensed tenement.

In these descriptions of children's employment, the twofold aspect of home work in its relation to child labor is illustrated. In one group are the children whose work at home is legal because they live in licensed houses or because they are at work on articles not named in the home work law; in the other are those whose employment is illegal, not because they are children, but because the tenements in which they live do not fulfill the sanitary requirements necessary for a license. The problem is complicated by the vast extent of the home work system in New York City.

EXTENT OF EMPLOYMENT

To count the number of homeworkers has proved as baffling a task as to attempt to regulate their conditions of employment. There are no official figures showing the number of children employed in homework in New York City, nor has it been known in recent years how many adults are at work in licensed houses. There are, however, certain data by which the extent of the system is indicated. Between 1899 when the provision for issuing licenses to families went into force, and 1904, when the law was amended to provide for licensing houses rather than individual apartments, the records of the Department of Labor showed each year the total number of licenses in force and the number of persons thus autho-

rized to work. Since 1904, the official reports state the number of tenement houses which have been licensed by the department, but the number of workers must be inferred from records in previous years.

With these figures as a basis it is illuminating to combine the results of special investigation, such as the report on home work of the New York Bureau of Labor Statistics in 1902; the Department of Labor's special inquiry into the employment of children in licensed houses on certain specified streets in March, 1907, and the present investigation.

The facts contained in the annual report of the New York Department of Labor, 1902, when the Bureau of Labor Statistics made a special investigation of more than 1,000 home workers in New York City indicate the wide extent of the system at the time when the licensing provision had been in force three years. Says the report:

It appears that in New York City 16,068 family workrooms were licensed in 1901, and that 27,019 persons were authorized to work therein. These numbers have since been slightly increased (1902) but may still be regarded as sufficiently representative for use in this connection. The important fact to be noted is that seven-ninths of all the licensed homeworkers in New York City are women, and that six-sevenths of these women work on clothing, nearly all of whom are "home finishers." There were also among the female home-workers somewhat more than one thousand makers of neckwear and nearly a thousand makers of artificial flowers.

GLOSSARY

gross: a dozen dozen, or 144

fell: to finish a seam

scabies: a contagious skin disease caused by a parasitic mite

Document Analysis

Van Kleeck's report opens by identifying a key gap in New York State child-labor laws—while children under the age of fourteen are prohibited from working outside the home in factories and stores, no regulations prevent them from finishing manufactured goods at home. She acknowledges the difficulty in regulating the practice referred to as the "sweating system," and provides il-

lustrations of the practical effects of this conflict: For example, a fourteen-year-old boy cannot work during school hours because of compulsory attendance laws, but his three-year-old sister can legally work all day and night because she is not of school age.

Van Kleeck notes that many circumstances under which children's work at home does not violate labor laws. She describes scenarios in which children live in clean, well-lit tenements that are properly licensed for home labor, and they attend school as required during daytime hours. However, from the end of the school day until late at night, the children work at home making artificial flowers or finishing garments. As a result, their academic performance suffers, casting doubt on the usefulness of compulsory attendance laws in light of the seemingly ineffective child-labor laws.

The report also addresses the difficulty in assuring that licensed homes are free of contagious, infectious, and communicable diseases, as required by the Labor and Health Departments. While initial licensing requires an inspection of health and sanitation conditions inside the home, there is little ongoing protection against diseases that may be introduced into the environments later. For example, Van Kleeck recalls visiting a family that was finishing garments in the same room where their daughter was dying of tuberculosis, a highly communicable respiratory disease. The entire family lived in a single room, so there was no place else to complete the work.

Additionally, some families work in unlicensed homes, as the immediate need for food, shelter, and clothing takes precedence over any possible legal repercussions. Sometimes, a license can be obtained quickly if an investigation is imminent; more often, however, no one bothers to check. Furthermore, only certain articles are covered by the licensing requirement: Van Kleeck reports on several young children employed sewing gloves and carding buttons, neither of which requires a home license, so the homes are not subject to inspection.

Van Kleeck concludes by observing that New York City cannot accurately count the number of children employed in home manufacturing, whether licensed or not. Following an investigation of more than 1,000 home workers in New York City by the US Bureau of Labor Statistics, the New York Department of Labor published a report stating that 16,068 homes were licensed in 1901, with 27,019 individuals authorized to work in them. However, the statistics do not break down the number of children employed at home.

Essential Themes

Van Kleeck's report highlights the unfortunate result of incomplete child-labor laws at the turn of the twentieth century in New York City. In this report, she explains how employers benefit from using the "sweating system" to circumvent child-labor laws. Because of the high concentration of poor, unskilled laborers in New York City, intense competition for low-skill jobs meant companies could pay workers extremely low wages. Under this system, companies save money by contracting labor and not needing to provide factory space, heating, and lighting. Van Kleeck notes that attempts at reform would be resisted by companies that profit under the system because of the financial benefits.

In an effort to maintain some order and safety to the practice, Health and Labor Departments established certain criteria for the approval of a home manufacturing license. However, some of these criteria—such as the requirement that homes be kept free of contagious, infectious, or communicable disease—presented complications. By government regulation, any home manufacturing location where disease was discovered had to be shut down immediately and its license revoked until the situation was resolved and conditions improved. Furthermore, any landlord who permitted work to be done in his building in violation of a Health Department order could have been prosecuted for illegal manufacturing, even if he was not doing the manufacturing himself. Since many tenements housed numerous families, and many of these families were involved in home manufacturing, landlords were highly motivated to quickly evict any family whose health conditions interfered with the building's license.

The report uncovered a wide variety of family circumstances for children who worked at home. Some attended school regularly and only worked when school was not in session. Others attended school, but worked at home every night or cared for younger siblings while their parents were working. Still others were kept out of school altogether to work all hours of the day. Van Kleeck observes that compulsory school attendance only further burdened the already-exhausted children without providing much educational benefit. She identifies the need for further reform and better enforcement to ensure that child-labor laws cover a wider variety of realistic scenarios and actually provide the intended benefit to children they are meant to protect.

—*Tracey M. DiLascio, JD*

Bibliography and Additional Reading

"Childhood Lost: Child Labor during the Industrial Revolution." *Teaching with Primary Sources*. Eastern Illinois University, n.d. Web. 10 Apr. 2014.

"Mary van Kleeck Papers, 1849–1998: Biographical Note." *Sophia Smith Collection*. Smith College, n.d. Web. 10 Apr. 2014.

Nardinelli, Clark. *Child Labor and the Industrial Revolution*. Bloomington: Indiana UP, 1990. Print.

Zinn, Howard. *A People's History of the United States: 1492 to Present*. New York: Harper, 2005. Print.

■ Fire Hazards in New York City Factories

Date: 1912
Author: New York Factory Investigating Commission
Genre: report

Summary Overview

In 1911, a fire destroyed a garment factory in New York City, killing 146 workers. Community activists and political leaders called upon the New York General Assembly and the governor to investigate the conditions that started the fire, in the hope that other workplace disasters could be avoided. The Commission's findings and recommendations resulted in major revisions to the state's (and later the country's) occupational safety laws and regulations.

Defining Moment

On March 25, 1911, a fire broke out in a crowded workroom at the Triangle Waist Company, an apparel factory occupying the top three floors of a ten-story building in Manhattan. (A "waist" was an article of women's clothing in the nineteenth and early twentieth centuries, sometimes also called a "shirtwaist," and this disaster has become known to history as the Triangle Shirtwaist Factory fire.) The fire spread quickly throughout the factory, aided by the overabundance of flammable waste in the factory. Employees of the factory (and the rest of the building) were unable to escape the smoke and flame, as emergency exits were blocked by piles of fabric or otherwise locked, and the sole fire escape collapsed. When the fire department arrived, it could not elevate its ladders above the sixth floor and even their innovative high-pressure hoses were unequal to the task, leaving the upper floors vulnerable to the fire. Workers, unable to descend via fire escapes or stairs, dove from windows to their deaths on the street below. One hundred forty-six people, most of whom were women and teenagers, perished in the fire.

In the minds of those who worked for Triangle, the fire and massive loss of life were both foreseeable and avoidable. Two years earlier, the International Ladies Garment Workers' Union, representing many of Triangle's 900 employees, launched a strike to protest working conditions—including the illegal locking of exit doors and the lack of sufficient fire escapes. However, Triangle locked out its striking employees and hired replacements to continue working at the Washington Place factory. Ultimately, the strikers gained some concessions on wages and hours, and though management agreed to safety improvements, those were never undertaken, and conditions deteriorated.

The Triangle disaster sent shockwaves through New York City. Community, religious, and political leaders as well as citizens packed into the Metropolitan Opera House to discuss fire safety at the city's workplaces, and more than one hundred thousand mourners marched up Fifth Avenue to honor the dead. Shortly after the mass meeting, the march, and the funerals, the call went up to the state capitol in Albany: the government needed to intervene and examine the conditions that led to the deaths of 146 New Yorkers.

From the Metropolitan Opera House meeting, a special committee was established to lead the charge on the seat of state government. The New York Committee on Safety arrived to find a captive audience, as legislators only days before had seen a fire take place in the State House. Led by Senate majority leader Robert F. Wagner and Senator Alfred E. Smith, the New York General Assembly quickly established the Factory Investigating Commission. The commission was the first of its kind in the United States: it was granted the power to investigate all manner of working conditions at manufacturing facilities in every city in the state. It could assess inspection practices, review construction plans, compel testimony under oath, and enter any manufacturing facility for inspection.

The assembly had initially given the commission a

one-year mandate but quickly extended that framework to three years. The commission's investigative work, however, was complete within two years, and was comprehensive and voluminous. Between 1911 and 1912, the commission had visited fifty plants across the state and investigated more than 3,300 others, interviewed nearly 500 witnesses, and conducted fifty-nine public hearings, generating more than 7,000 pages of testimony. Upon completion of its investigation of every major manufacturing industry in New York, the commission issued its findings and recommendations to the assembly, on which the burden to issue new workplace safety and health laws and regulations would next fall.

HISTORICAL DOCUMENT

CREATION OF COMMISSION.

On Saturday afternoon, March 25, 1911, a fire took place in the business establishment of the Triangle Waist Company, at No. 23–29 Washington Place, in the Borough of Manhattan, City of New York, in which 145 employees, mainly women and girls lost their lives.

This shocking loss of life aroused the community to a full sense of its responsibility. A superficial examination revealed conditions in factories and manufacturing establishments that constituted a daily menace to the lives of the thousands of working men, women and children. Lack of precautions to prevent fire, inadequate fire-escape facilities, insanitary conditions that were insidiously undermining the health of the workers were found existing everywhere. The need of a thorough and extensive investigation into the general conditions of factory life was clearly recognized.

THE EXISTING FIRE PROBLEM IN NEW YORK CITY.

Five kinds of buildings are used for factory purposes in the City of New York.

THE CONVERTED DWELLING OR TENEMENT.

Owing to the increase in land values and change in the residence localities, a number of buildings formerly used for living purposes have been made over into factories. The buildings are from four to six stories in height, usually 25 feet wide by about 60 to 85 feet deep. The exterior walls are brick or stone, the floors, interior trim, stairways, beams and doors are of wood. The stairways are usually from two to three feet in width, the doors often open inward; there are no automatic sprinkler systems, no fire prevention or extinguishing appliances except fire pails, which are not always preserved for fire purposes; the workrooms are divided by wooden partitions and crowded with employees, while the machines are placed as close together as space will permit, without regard to means of exit. There are exterior fire-escapes with balconies on each floor, connected by vertical ladders (those of late construction by inclined stairways), which usually lead to a yard in the rear of the premises, or to some blind alley from which there is no means of escape. There is ordinarily a ladder from the lowest balcony to the ground, but it is generally not in place, or very difficult to use in case of fire because of its weight. There is usually but one door leading from the street.

Here we have a type of building constructed for dwelling purposes only, in which the number of occupants is multiplied any number of times without any change in the exit facilities provided.

THE LOFT BUILDING

The loft building marks an evolution in the construction of factory buildings in the City of New York.

The first lofts were built about twenty-five years ago, for the storing and sale of merchandise, but the manufacturer soon found it desirable to have his goods manufactured in workrooms adjacent to his salesroom and directly under his supervision.

Increase in land values, moreover, forced the manufacturers to extend upwards instead of spreading out horizontally. The availability of the loft for manufacturing purposes was soon appreciated, and to-day this type of building is generally used for factory purposes.

THE NON-FIREPROOF LOFT BUILDING

The non-fireproof loft building is usually six or seven stories in height, 25 feet wide by 80 feet in depth, with brick, stone or iron fronts and rears, brick side walls, wooden floors and wooden trim. There is usually one unenclosed wooden stairway, varying in width from two to three and one-half feet, and often winding around the elevator shaft. Wooden doors lead to the stairways; very often the doors open inwardly.

These buildings, as a rule, possess exterior fire-escapes similar to those found on the converted tenement described above. Usually every floor in these buildings is occupied by a different tenant, in some cases there being two or more tenants on each floor. The tenant uses the floor, or his portion of it, as sales-room, office and factory, dividing one from the other by wooden partitions. In the manufacturing part there are usually a number of machines placed as close together as possible with little aisle space between. These buildings are to be found in numbers on the lower east and west side. The number of people permitted to work on a floor is restricted only by a provision of the Labor Law which provides a minimum of 250 cubic feet of air space per person and entirely disregards the floor area. As the distance between floor and ceiling is at least ten feet, and often more, this cubic air space is easily obtained without any appreciable prevention of overcrowding and congestion. The present law does not require the posting of the number of people allowed even by this standard, and so prosecutions for violations of this law are practically unknown. These buildings usually do not contain any automatic sprinklers. They have fire pails, which are rarely kept for the proper purpose. A few of them have standpipes, with hose which is often useless.

THE FIREPROOF LOFT BUILDING LESS THAN 150 FEET HIGH

The fireproof loft building less than 150 feet in height, that is about 12 stories or under, has brick, stone or metal exterior walls, wooden floors and trim, stairways of metal or stone and elevators. Stairways are generally about three feet wide, enclosed by fireproof walls. These buildings are either 25, 50, 75 or 100 feet wide by 80 to 200 feet in depth, the usual size being 50 by 80 or 90 feet. The conditions of occupancy as to tenants are similar to those in the non-fireproof loft buildings just described. The Triangle Waist Company occupied a building of this type at 23–29 Washington Place. That building, in its

construction and interior is typical of the so-called fire-proof loft buildings, and indeed much better than hundreds of buildings used for similar purposes in New York city (sic) to-day. Some of these buildings have automatic sprinkler systems. They are usually provided with stand pipes, connected with the city water supply, and have on each floor a hose of required length, and some are provided with exterior fire-escapes. It is to be noted that in these buildings the elevators are used to go from the street to the upper floors not only by the employers but by the employees. In most cases the latter are absolutely unaware of the location of the stairways. Auxiliary fire appliances are present in most cases, but their existence is unknown to the workers and no care is given to their preservation. The interior arrangements are similar to those existing in the non-fireproof loft building, the same wooden partitions, the same congestion and doors opening inwardly.

Testimony shows that the danger in these so-called fireproof buildings results from the use of wood for floors, doors and trim. The buildings are usually of such a height that the Fire Department ladders and extensions, and even the water towers, do not reach the upper stories. Fire occurring in these places under conditions of manufacture which are hereafter described usually results in the destruction of the entire contents of the building while walls and floors remain substantially intact.

THE FIREPROOF LOFT BUILDING MORE THAN 150 FEET HIGH

This building is more than twelve stories in height. The walls are of brick, stone or metal, the floors are of cement or stone, the trim and doors are of metal or fire-resisting material, the stairways are of stone or metal, and enclosed by fireproof walls. There are usually several stairways and elevators. The buildings are sometimes supplied with automatic sprinkler systems and have standpipes to which hose is connected on each floor, and other appliances for extinguishing fires. In addition, these buildings sometimes have exterior stairways leading either to the street or to the ground in the rear. The buildings are usually 50, 75 or 100 feet or more in width and are from 75 to 200 feet deep. They are occupied for manufacturing and other purposes, and sometimes one tenant is found to occupy more than one floor. In these buildings, if a fire occurs, it is usually confined to the floor on which it starts since it cannot burn up or down except through the windows.

Above the sixth floor these buildings are open to the same objections as are fireproof buildings less than 150 feet high, namely the upper floors cannot be reached by the firemen. The exit facilities are usually well constructed, but the number of people who occupy these buildings is not determined by either exits, width of stairways, or floor space. The only restriction is, as in all other buildings, the 250 cubic feet of air space provision. The distance between the floors is usually 10 to 15 feet, so the cubic air space may fulfill the legal requirement while the floor presents a congested condition.

DANGER TO LIFE IN FIREPROOF BUILDINGS

Particular reference is made to the fireproof building which is believed on account of its construction to be safer for the occupants than the non-fireproof building and to require few if any precautions, either to prevent fire or to preserve the safety of the occupants in case of fire. The testimony discloses the weakness of these suppositions. While fireproof building itself will not burn, the merchandise, wooden partitions and other inflammable material burn as readily in a fireproof building as in any other. It is assumed by all fire insurance experts that when a fire occurs on any one floor, the contents of that entire floor will be destroyed. It is like placing paper in a fireproof box—it confines the fire to that locality, but the fire is just as hot and just as destructive within its bounds. Therefore, unless means are provided for automatically extinguishing fires and for the rapid escape of the occupants, loss of life may occur even in fireproof buildings.

The Triangle Waist Company fire is illustrative of this fact. There the building was practically left intact, yet the fire was severe enough to cause the death of a large number of the occupants. In the fireproof building the fire is confined to a limited area and is therefore more easily controlled. The occupants of floors over eighty feet from the ground cannot, however, be reached by the Fire Department's ladders, and must trust for escape to the stairways or exterior fire-escapes.

In many of these buildings the occupants manufac-ture garments and other inflammable articles. The floors are littered with a quantity of cuttings, waste material and rubbish, and are often soaked with oil or grease. No regular effort is made to clear the floors. No fireproof receptacles are provided for the accumulated waste, which in some cases is not removed from the floors for many days. Many of the workmen, foremen and employers smoke during business hours and at meal times. Lighted gas jets are unprotected by globes or wire netting, and are placed near to the inflammable material. Very often quantities of made-up garments and inflammable raw material are stored in those lofts. Fire drills are not held, save in rare instances, exits are unmarked and the location of the stairways and exterior fire-escapes is often unknown. Access to the stairway and outside fire-escapes is obstructed by machinery, wooden partitions and piled-up merchandise, while in some cases the fire-escape balcony is at such a distance from the floor as to make it almost impossible for women employees to reach it without assistance. Wired glass is not used in the windows facing the balconies of the fire-escapes except in fireproof buildings over 150 feet high. In some cases the window leading to fire-escapes are not large enough to permit the passage of grown persons readily. Automatic or manual fire-alarms are hardly ever provided, except in the larger fireproof buildings.

RECOMMENDATIONS OF THE COMMISSION

1. PREVENTION OF FIRE

Testimony was given that at least 50 per cent of the fires occurring to-day could be prevented by taking certain simple and inexpensive precautions. Some experts placed the percentage of preventable fires as high as 75 per cent. Fire extinguishment has received careful attention in the past, and to-day the means supplied for extinguishing fires are many. But little attention until recently, has been given to the subject of fire prevention. An ounce of prevention in the case of fires, as in any other case, is worth a pound of cure.

The principal causes of fires in the city of New York during the past few years have been rubbish heaps, lighted matches, cigars and cigarettes, and exposed gas jets. It is believed by the Commission that the prohibition of smoking in manufacturing establishments, and the cleaning up or removal of rubbish, cutting and waste from the floors, and providing fireproof receptacles therefor, will be most effective in the prevention of fires.

The fire in the Triangle Waist Company building was caused by a lighted cigarette thrown upon a pile of cuttings. Smoking should be strictly prohibited to both employees and employers. The Commission in its investigation visited among other establishments, a cigar factory in a converted tenement house when there were several hundred employees at work. The foreman was asked whether smoking was allowed. He stated that smoking was prohibited—although at that moment he was busily engaged in smoking his own cigar.

A number of witnesses testified that while smoking ought to be prohibited, its prevention was a hopeless task. Such an attitude surprises the Commission, as it believes from its investigation that a little education upon the subject will convince both employee and employer of the wisdom and necessity of this law. Smoking in a factory is a constant menace to all employed therein.

2. NOTICE TO AUTHORITIES IN CASE OF FIRE

No matter what care and what precautions may be taken, fire will occur, and attempts are frequently made by employees to extinguish them before calling upon the public authorities. In almost every case this is a serious mistake. In the Triangle Waist Company and Equitable Building fires, lives would have been saved and the fire would not have been nearly so severe, the Fire Department had been promptly notified. In this regard the Commission can do no more than lay before the public the facts disclosed. It had been the intention of the Commission after examining into the matter, to recommend the installation of automatic or manual fire alarms in certain factories.

3. NOTICE TO OCCUPANTS IN CASE OF FIRE

The Commission gave much thought and attention to means of notifying the occupants of a building in case of fire. After consideration of the facts before it, the Commission is of the opinion that the dangers from panic and excitement caused by any alarm, such as the ringing of a bell indicating on which floor the fire had occurred, when the alarm might be false or the fire slight and readily controlled, outweighed the advantage to be gained. Therefore the Commission does not at this time recommend any automatic fire-alarm system, save as may become necessary in connection with the operation of a fire drill hereinafter provided for.

4. FIRE DRILLS

The Commission personally witnessed fire drills in factory buildings, and some testimony was taken upon this subject. The Commission believes that in factory buildings where more than twenty-five persons are regularly employed above the second story, a fire drill should be conducted. One of the purposes of the fire drill should be to indicate to the occupants where the stairways are, and the means of reaching them. It has been found in many of the larger buildings where the occupants use the elevators to go to and from their work, that the location of the stairs or exterior fire-escapes is unknown. The Commission is of the opinion that the drill should be supervised by the local Fire Departments. A fire drill is also extremely useful in preventing panic. While of course not so effective in the case of occupants of a loft or factory building as in the case of school children, it undoubtedly would go far in preventing a mad rush towards the exits. If the fire drill accomplishes nothing more than to acquaint the occupants of a building with the different exits, to compel them to use those exits at stated intervals, and to keep them clear and unobstructed, it will have served its purpose. The periodical fire drill will constantly bring to the minds of employee and employer alike the possibility of fire and the necessity for using every proper means to prevent the same.

5. PREVENTION OF SPREAD OF FIRE

The installation of the automatic sprinkler system has been recommended by Fire Chiefs throughout the State, and by nearly all of the experts on the fire problem. The Commission does not desire to make any drastic recommendation on this subject, but it is convinced that in buildings over seven stories or 90 feet in height, in which wooden floors or wooden trim are used, and more than 200 people are employed above the seventh floor, the only safe means to prevent the spread of fire and the loss of life incidental thereto would be the installation of an automatic sprinkler system.

Chief Kenlon of the New York Fire Department testified that had an automatic sprinkler system been installed in the Triangle Waist Company building, he believed that not a single life would have been lost. If manufacturing is carried on above the seventh story of a building, or 90 feet above the ground, the manufacturer should be required to furnish every possible device to safeguard the lives of his employees in case of fire.

6. ESCAPE FROM WORKROOMS

The Commission ascertained by investigation and testimony, that exits to outside fire-escapes and to interior stairways, especially when they lead through other portions of the loft, were often unknown to many of the operatives. It certainly is necessary to indicate clearly the location of these exits.

A contributing cause to the loss of life in the Triangle Waist Company fire was the lack of clear passageways leading to the fire-escapes and stairways. The employees were so crowded together, seated at tables containing machines, with chairs back to back, that when a great number of them attempted to leave at the same time there was panic and confusion. The following is a diagram showing the arrangement of the sewing machines, and the congestion prevailing on the ninth floor of this building, where most of the deaths occurred.

In the report made by the Superintendent of the New York Board of Fire Underwriters, it was stated that 20 dead bodies were found near the machines "apparently overcome before they could extricate themselves from the crowded aisles." The condition which prevailed in this building obtains in many similar buildings. The necessity for clear and unobstructed passageways to exits should be absolutely insisted upon, otherwise with the slightest panic, even without a fire, severe injuries, if not loss of life, would occur.

The Commission has already commented on the width of doors and windows leading to outside fire-escapes. It has also found that the doors leading to stairways are too narrow. This is especially so in the old converted tenements where these narrow doors are a source of danger in case of panic or fire. The first rush is always for the doors. The attempt upon the part of a number of persons to pass through at one time leads to a jam, and if the doors are dangerously narrow, many would lose their

lives. When there are only a few persons employed upon a floor a narrow door is not a serious objection, but where a number of persons are employed, regard for their safety requires that such dangerous conditions be remedied.

7. HUMAN FACTORS
Results of the Data Obtained by the Investigation

NEGLECT OF THE HUMAN FACTOR
Brief as was the period devoted to the investigation, limited as was the number of industries and establishments inspected, and incomplete as was necessarily all our data, the conclusion that forcibly impressed itself, after the completion of the preliminary investigation, was that the human factor is practically neglected in our industrial system.

Many of our industries were found housed in palatial loft buildings, and employing the most improved machinery and mechanical processes, but at the same time greatly neglecting the care, health and safety of their employees.

Our system of industrial production has taken gigantic strides in the progressive utilization of natural resources and the exploitation of the inventive genius of the human mind, but has at the same time shown a terrible waste of human resources, of human health and life.

It is because of this neglect of the human factor that we have found so many preventable defects in industrial establishments, such a large number of workshops with inadequate light and illumination, with no provision for ventilation, without proper care for cleanliness, and without ordinary indispensable comforts such as washing facilities, water supply, toilet accommodations, dressing-rooms, etc. It is because of utter neglect on the part of many employers that so many dangerous elements are found in certain trades. These elements are not always necessary for the successful pursuit of the trade, and their elimination would mean a great improvement in the health of the workers, and would stop much of the misery caused by the occupational diseases incident to certain industries.

The construction of tenement houses in New York City is under the strict supervision of the Tenement House Department. There is no reason why the interests of the greater number of persons inhabiting factory buildings should not be conserved as much as the interests of the tenement house dwellers.

8. IGNORANCE OF THE NUMBER AND OF THE LOCATION OF INDUSTRIAL ESTABLISHMENTS

In the course the investigation, much difficulty was found in locating all the establishments in an industry or a district. At present there is no method by which every manufacturing establishment may be located, and its existence brought to the attention of the authorities. At present, any person who has the necessary capital or credit may build, lease, or hire any ramshackle building, engage as many workers as he can crowd into his premises, and work them under any conditions. The very existence of this establishment may not be known to the Labor Department, until it is discovered by accident.

In the investigation of the Cloak and Suit Industry, made during the last year, by the Joint Board of Sanitary Control, about 30 per cent of the shops were found unrecorded, and in our own investigation, our inspectors found the utmost difficulty in tracing many establishments which were never recorded by the Labor Department in the list sent by them to us.

9. LACK OF STANDARDS

The worker spends the greater part of his waking hours in the workshop and factory. The proper sanitation of the workplace is therefore of paramount importance to the worker, both to his health and to the security of his life.

It is only lately that intelligent employers have awakened to the fact that factory sanitation is very closely related to industrial efficiency, and that neglect of this subject by factory owners is detrimental to their own interests as well as extremely injurious to their workers.

It is also but lately that the workers themselves have realized the value of proper sanitation of factories, and have added this to the economic demands of their labor organizations.

Unfortunately, there is hardly a field of science where there is such a complete lack of standards as in industrial hygiene.

It is on account of this deplorable lack of standardization that many provisions of the labor laws are so vague and indefinite, and that large employers, willing to introduce modern safety devices and sanitary conveniences in their factories, are unable to do so with complete success. It is also this lack of standards that makes the enforcement of the sanitary clauses of the labor laws so unsatisfactory, for it is a most difficult matter for the inspector to exactly determine what is meant by "sufficient" fire protection, "proper light," "adequate" ventilation, "fit" toilet accommodations, etc.

The standardization of factory sanitation is one of the most important matters which the Commission has considered during its brief preliminary investigation, and we intend to devote much attention to it if our activities are continued.

Document Analysis

The Factory Investigating Commission was established to review existing manufacturing facilities in New York and to ascertain areas in which fire prevention and occupational health might be improved. The central point of reference, understandably, was the Triangle Waist Company fire. However, the commission's recommendations spoke to a wide range of other potential disasters that loomed in New York's manufacturing facilities.

Among the commission's observations were that certain buildings that were believed to be "fireproof" were just as likely to experience a deadly fire as the former tenements and other, older buildings that contained flammable building products (such as wood) in their walls and floors. Factories, the commission reports, were found in a number of structures, including former residential buildings. Builders were increasingly building high-rise lofts to accommodate expanded manufacturing needs, and although these structures were made with cement and other flame-retardant materials (as opposed to wood), they still posed a danger. This risk was not associated with the building materials; instead, it was the prevalence of flammable materials such as cloth, paper, and lubricating oils. The fact that so many workstations were close to each other in such facilities meant that fire could start and spread rapidly even in a flame-resistant structure. The commission cites the fact that the Triangle fire left the building largely intact even when the interior was completely devastated by fire.

Another important finding in the report is the fact that many fires may be prevented by simply demonstrating sensible workplace behavior and practices. For example, the commission believed that the Triangle fire was caused by a lit cigarette. The commission, in its countless interviews, learned that although smoking in manufacturing facilities was considered dangerous, far too many workers continued to smoke on the job.

The commission cites the existence of guidelines for installing automatic sprinklers in certain buildings, but stops short of reiterating those rules. Rather, it focuses on other practices that could prevent another Triangle tragedy. For example, the commission cites the chaos in the Triangle facility when fire spread. Such conditions, the members recommend, could be mitigated by informing the workers of emergency escape protocols and even conducting fire drills. Such practices, the commission argues, could reduce panic and save lives.

Employers and building owners, the commission adds, had a role to play in ensuring the safety of the employees working in New York's factories. Unblocked exits, adequate fire escapes, and wider stairwells, for example, could have saved the lives of many Triangle employees during that fire. Better lighting and ventilation were also necessary for a healthy workplace, the commission recommends. Furthermore, the commission argues, there was a need for improved industrial hygiene and sanitary standards.

The commission acknowledges that economic development in New York (and the rest of the country) at times moved faster than employee safety regulations. In fact, the commission estimates the number of industrial and manufacturing facilities in the state to be upward of 44,000—its investigation was therefore limited—which meant that it was likely that far more facilities demonstrated subpar worker safety and hygiene issues. Still, the commission recommends that the assembly enact comprehensive standards and rules that would apply to all of the state's factories, with the goal of protecting the health and safety of employees.

Essential Themes

The Factory Investigating Commission was created in the wake of one of the worst industrial accidents in US history. The commission's task was not just to ascertain the causes of the Triangle Waist Company fire but also to investigate the entire state's manufacturing sector to assess the risks of future, similar disasters. The city of Pittsburgh, Pennsylvania, had conducted a similar review of its manufacturing facilities. However, the Factory Investigating Commission was distinguished by both its extensive scope and its goal of reviewing every facility in every manufacturing industry New York contained within its borders. What it found and recommended could be reviewed in two general categories.

The first category is that of a disregard for rules and regulations already in place. The Asch Building, in which the Triangle Waist Company was housed, was what the commission deems a "fireproof" building, but a lit cigarette, overcrowded workspaces, and unkempt flammable waste helped the fire spread quickly. A lack of emergency exits and automatic sprinklers, and employee ignorance of fire-escape procedures, contributed to the massive casualty rate. Each of these practices and issues were not new concepts but had apparently been disregarded at Triangle.

The second category is the need for changes in the workplace. The Triangle plant's employees, like countless other facilities' workers, did not know what to do in the event of a fire because fire drills were not practiced consistently. Additionally, too many facilities in New York state had inadequate lighting and ventilation, insufficient waste management practices, and other issues that negatively affected worker health and safety. The commission's recommendations were extensive, moving far beyond fire prevention issues to include adequate dressing rooms, water supplies, toilets, and other necessary workplace resources. Attention to these matters would greatly improve workplace environments across the state, the commission's members concluded.

It was critical, the commission argued, that the state enact new laws that would impose new rules and protections for workers. The assembly did take this recommendation seriously, passing more than a dozen workplace safety laws in the two years that followed the commission's conclusion. The federal government, taking this commission's findings to heart, later followed suit when Frances Perkins, who had assisted with its investigation, became labor secretary in the administration of President Franklin D. Roosevelt.

—Michael P. Auerbach, MA

Bibliography and Additional Reading

Gentzinger, Donna. *The Triangle Shirtwaist Factory Fire*. Greensboro: Reynolds, 2008. Print.

"The New York Factory Investigating Commission." United States Department of Labor, 2014. Web. 28 Feb. 2014.

New York (State) Factory Investigating Commission. *Preliminary Report of the Factory Investigating Commission*. 3 vols. Albany: Argus, 1912. Print.

Stein, Leon. *The Triangle Fire. Centennial* ed. Ithaca: Cornell UP, 2011. Print.

Von Drehle, David. *Triangle: The Fire That Changed America*. New York: Grove, 2004. Print.

CAPITAL CONCERNS

In this section we explore a few key economic issues along with the rise of the Populist Party, which emerged in response to them. The section begins with a resounding cry of frustration, "Wall Street Owns the Country," by a Populist leader. The piece offers a view into the partly anti-capitalist attitude underpinning this short-lived but influential American political party. In point of fact, it was not capitalism per se that the Populists objected to but rather the arrangement of the capitalist system. The system seemed to favor bankers and speculators and looked askance at the likes of food producers—farmers—and their business needs. The United States during this period, despite its urban industrialization, was a predominantly rural, agricultural nation. And yet the capitalists in the cities, the Populists complained, reaped most of the benefits of economic growth. One can discover what the Populists desired by examining the party's 1892 political platform, which is included here.

Monetary issues were also significant at this time, and were central to the Populists' support of the "Free Silver" movement, which called for the free and unlimited coinage of silver as a means of addressing deflation and bolstering food prices to benefit farmers. An act of Congress toward that end, the Sherman Silver Purchase Act, was passed in 1890; but many felt that the law did not go far enough. Conservatives, however, worried that it went too far. Thus, in 1893, President Grover Cleveland, a conservative, pro-business Democrat, put his weight behind an effort to repeal of the act in light of a financial panic—the Panic of 1893—that was then unfolding. We include here both Cleveland's argument before Congress and an assessment of the "political causes" of the panic.

Finally, we hear from one of the top industrialists at the turn of the century, Andrew Carnegie. Carnegie, in an essay called "The Gospel of Wealth," lays out the virtues of being blessed with wealth, particularly when it has come through hard work and individual effort. At the same time, he notes, wealthy individuals owe a debt to society and should, therefore, pursue philanthropic endeavors to benefit all.

■ Wall Street Owns the Country

Date: ca. 1890
Author: Mary Elizabeth Lease
Genre: speech

Summary Overview

The late nineteenth century marked a significant point in US history. Following the Civil War, the United States expanded its reach, reincorporating the Southern states into the Union, as well as adding many new ones, especially in the West. The economies of these regions depended heavily on agriculture, but food prices and various policies that significantly affected farmers were not set by the farmers themselves. Instead, they were set by corporate and political interests that largely resided in the East. As farmers felt the burden of these policies, they banded together to form organizations such as the Farmers' Alliance and the Populist Party—officially known as the People's Party—in hopes of bringing their interests to the national stage and motivating significant change. Mary Elizabeth Lease was heavily involved in this movement in the early 1890s, and her speech "Wall Street Owns the Country" succinctly captures many of the issues and frustrations faced by farmers during this time.

Defining Moment

In the wake of the Civil War, many regions of the United States faced serious economic depression, especially in the West and South, where the economy relied heavily on agriculture. As droughts damaged crops and cotton prices plummeted, many farmers—especially tenant farmers, who rented the land on which they grew their crops—were severely in debt. Even once crop yield improved, farmers found their livelihoods dependent upon prices, taxes, availability of transportation and storage, and myriad other regulations established by corporate and political powers mainly located in the East.

These hardships paved the way for the rise of a new political party, focused primarily in the Western and Southern states. The People's Party focused on strengthening farmers' rights, as well as asserting economic and political independence from the manufacturing- and industry-dominated East Coast. Populists fought for fair crop pricing, improved and expanded options for transportation and storage, and freedom from regulations on implements, such as grain elevators, that had a serious negative impact on the economic viability of farming.

In 1890, the Populists won control of the Kansas state legislature and successfully elected their first US senator. With these successes, the party set its sights on increasing its presence on the national stage, a role that speakers such as Lease undertook. They traveled the country sharing their ideals and ideas with voters in areas similar to their own, in hopes of gaining enough support to win national elections.

Unfortunately, there was disagreement within the party over how to best accomplish this goal. Some believed teaming up with a mainstream political party such as the Democrats, who already had a strong following in the South, would help build national credibility and provide the channels necessary to reach a larger audience. Others believed this would dilute the Populist message by trying to appeal to moderates and that it was not worth the risk. By the time the Populist Convention took place in St. Louis, Missouri, in July of 1896, tension within the party ran high. Loyalties split between "fusion" Populists who favored a merger with the Democratic Party, and "mid-roaders" who believed such a merger would only help the Democrats suppress the third-party influence they had already gained. The rift proved to be too great, and the People's Party soon fell out of favor in both national and state politics.

Author Biography

Mary Elizabeth Lease was born Mary Clyens in Ridgway, Pennsylvania, in either 1850 or 1853. Her parents immigrated to the United States from Ireland during the Irish Famine; her father and brother died fighting for the Union Army in the Civil War. In the early 1870s, she moved to Kansas to teach at a Catholic missionary school, and shortly thereafter married pharmacist Charles L. Lease. The couple lost everything in the financial panic of 1873 and relocated to Texas, where Lease became active in several causes, including prohibition and women's suffrage. She and her husband had several children during this time.

When the family moved back to Kansas, Lease became involved with the labor movement, joining the Farmers' Alliance and People's Party. Between 1890 and 1896, she toured the United States, speaking at campaign rallies and political conventions. Lease eventually divorced her husband and moved to New York City with her children, where she continued her career as a lecturer and activist until her death in 1933.

HISTORICAL DOCUMENT

This is a nation of inconsistencies. The Puritans fleeing from oppression became oppressors. We fought England for our liberty and put chains on four million of blacks. We wiped out slavery and our tariff laws, and national banks began a system of white wage slavery worse than the first. Wall Street owns the country. It is no longer a government of the people, by the people, and for the people, but a government of Wall Street, by Wall Street, and for Wall Street. The great common people of this country are slaves, and monopoly is the master. The West and South are bound and prostrate before the manufacturing East. Money rules, and our Vice-President is a London banker. Our laws are the output of a system which clothes rascals in robes and honesty in rags. The [political] parties lie to us and the political speakers mislead us. We were told two years ago to go to work and raise a big crop, that was all we needed. We went to work and plowed and planted; the rains fell, the sun shone, nature smiled, and we raised the big crop that they told us to; and what came of it? Eight-cent corn, ten-cent oats, two-cent beef and no price at all for butter and eggs—that's what came of it. The politicians said we suffered from overproduction. Overproduction, when 10,000 little children, so statistics tell us, starve to death every year in the United States, and over 100,000 shopgirls in New York are forced to sell their virtue for the bread their niggardly wages deny them... We want money, land and transportation. We want the abolition of the National Banks, and we want the power to make loans direct from the government. We want the foreclosure system wiped out... We will stand by our homes and stay by our fireside by force if necessary, and we will not pay our debts to the loan-shark companies until the government pays its debts to us. The people are at bay; let the bloodhounds of money who dogged us thus far beware.

GLOSSARY

niggardly: scanty or meager

sell ... virtue: a euphemism for engaging in sex work, or prostitution

shopgirl: a woman employed in a retail store or shop

Document Analysis

Lease begins her speech by noting that the United States is a "nation of inconsistencies." She observes that the United States was founded by individuals who sought freedom from the control of England during the seventeenth and eighteenth centuries, but then used that freedom to enslave Africans and black Americans. Once slavery was technically abolished, she says, Congress passed tax laws and established national banks that enabled rich people to remain wealthy, while trapping the "common people" into a life that Lease describes as "wage slavery."

Lease then calls attention to the sharp regional divide in economic prosperity within the United States: She notes that the West and South—regions heavily dependent on agriculture—are subject to the financial whims of eastern business and political interests. She clearly expresses her personal feelings about the individuals in charge, saying that "the [political] parties lie to us and the political speakers mislead us."

To illustrate her point, Lease describes a scenario where, two years prior to her speech, politicians and corporate leaders encouraged farmers in the South and West to raise a large yield to ensure their future prosperity. With some help from good weather, the farmers' work proved quite effective, and food was plentiful that year. However, when the time came to sell the crops, the farmers found that the purchase price offered for the crops had dropped dramatically—to the point, she claims, where no one would even pay at all for butter or eggs. The same politicians claimed that prices had fallen because the farmers had "overproduced," but Lease observes that in that same year, an estimated ten thousand children starved to death in the United States, and a hundred thousand young girls in cities engaged in prostitution just to afford food.

Finally, Lease lays out the demands she and her supporters have for future policy reform. Specifically, they want money, land, and transportation, as well as the power to obtain loans directly from the government rather than through private loan sharks. She also wants to end the foreclosure system. She concludes her speech with a warning to the "bloodhounds of money": The people who have been harmed by these corporations are ready to take action, and reform is on its way.

Essential Themes

At the time of her speech, Lease and her family were living in Kansas, surrounded by farmers and oth-

ers whose livelihoods relied upon agriculture. As the United States admitted new western states following the Civil War, many felt disconnected from the money-controlling corporate powers in the East and struggled to make ends meet despite the importance of their role in producing food for the country.

Lease's speech expressed the frustration felt by many farmers in the West and South at the control these economic powers had over their livelihood, particularly with respect to setting crop prices. Many felt duped by politicians who had assured farmers that they would be able to provide for themselves and their families by producing a large amount of high-quality crops. Yet when the time came for harvest, those same powers used their influence to suppress prices to satisfy their own self-interest; the set prices were often too low for the farmers to recoup their expenses and keep up with payments on their land. Many were forced to borrow money at exorbitant rates to keep their land, repay debts incurred during the farming and harvest seasons, or move their product to market.

Some farmers who could not keep up with mortgage or debt payments lost their land to foreclosure. They wound up as tenant farmers, renting land from wealthier owners to continue making a living. Lease and others argued to end the foreclosure system hoping to protect farmers and other working poor from being forced from their homes.

Lease's anecdote about plummeting crop prices illustrates yet another "inconsistency" in the U.S. approach. Politicians claimed that overproduction caused the low prices, since the amount of supply exceeded the demand. But Lease points out that many people in the United States literally starved to death that year, so she cannot accept the argument that there is simply too much food available in the country to demand a fair price. Overall, her speech captures the frustrations and hardships faced by farmers in the United States during a time when manufacturing, corporate interests, and other hallmarks of industrialization dominated policy and political concerns. Lease's speech is sometimes quoted today to draw parallels between the Gilded Age and now.

—Tracey M. DiLascio, JD

Bibliography and Additional Reading

Edwards, Rebecca. "Mary E. Lease." 1896: *The Presidential Campaign*. Vassar College, 2000. Web. 24 Apr. 2014.

Edwards, Rebecca. "The Populist Party." 1896: *The Presidential Campaign*. Vassar College, 2000. Web. 24 Apr. 2014.

Goodwyn, Lawrence. The Populist Moment: *A Short History of the Agrarian Revolt in America*. New York: Oxford UP, 1978. Print.

Nugent, Walter. *The Tolerant Populists: Kansas Populism and Nativism*. 2d ed. Chicago: The U of Chicago P, 2013. Print.

Woestman, Kelly A. "Mary Elizabeth Lease: Populist Reformer." *Gilder Lehrman Institute of American History*: History by Era. Gilder Lehrman Institute of American History, 2014. Web. 12 Apr. 2014.

Zinn, Howard. *A People's History of the United States: 1492 to Present*. New York: Harper, 2005. Print.

Populist Party Platform, 1892

Date: July 4, 1892
Authors: Ignatius Donnelly; People's Party
Genre: political tract

Summary Overview

The People's Party—widely known as the Populist Party—grew out of the agrarian crisis of the late nineteenth century. Many American farmers faced serious problems resulting from declining commodity prices, rising debt, and transportation issues. The People's Party stemmed from the Granger movement and the regional Farmers' Alliance. In February 1892, leaders from various reform organizations met in St. Louis, Missouri, to discuss forming a new party. They issued a call for a national convention, held in July 1892, in Omaha, Nebraska, to create the party. While the party's platform addressed some of the concerns of the urban poor and the labor movement, most of its planks dealt with agrarian issues, including monetary and banking issues; government land policies; and transportation and farm-commodities storage issues.

Defining Moment

The People's Party had only a brief moment on the national political scene, but the movement encapsulated the problems facing rural Americans (and some urban workers) in the late nineteenth century. Farmers struggling with mortgage debt, falling commodity prices, and transportation issues came to believe both that they were at the mercy of social and economic forces beyond their control and that the American economy was controlled by a conspiracy of the wealthy and the powerful, who had little incentive to change the status quo. These issues, as well as the perception that neither the Democratic nor the Republican parties cared about the concerns of farmers, led to a sense of crisis. The Populists sought to address these issues by creating a new political party. Farmers had first tried to address some of their concerns through the Granger movement. The Grange began primarily as a social organiza-tion, but turned to politics when economic conditions for farmers deteriorated in the 1870s. Rather than form a third party, they backed Democratic or Republican candidates who promised to address farmers' concerns, and in many farm states, Grange backing was integral to candidates' election to local or state offices. The People's Party also had roots in the Farmers' Alliance. Like the Grange, the alliances initially had little to do with politics; they simply aimed at creating cooperative purchasing and marketing associations for farmers. But like the Grange, the Alliances eventually began to back candidates who seemed sympathetic to farmers' needs. When the People's Party announced its platform at the Omaha Convention in July 1892, outsiders considered many of the group's proposals radical. In 1896, when the Populists "fused" with the Democratic Party by endorsing William Jennings Bryan, whom the Democrats had already nominated for president, many of the Populist's other goals were eclipsed by the issue of "free silver," the focus of Bryan's campaign against the Republican candidate William McKinley. Bryan's defeat in that election marked the beginning of the Populists' decline on the national scene. While the Populists never succeeded as a national party and never elected anyone to national office, many of the reforms for which they advocated were enacted during the Progressive Era.

Author Biography

At the preliminary meeting in St. Louis in February 1892, the group appointed a committee on resolutions to draft planks for a potential party platform. The preamble to the platform, the most-often quoted portion of the document, was largely the work of Ignatius Donnelly, a journalist and political activist with a long career in third-party politics promoting reform causes. He was born on November 3, 1831, in Philadelphia,

Pennsylvania, and in 1857 moved to Minnesota, where he held several elected offices, including lieutenant governor and a seat in the US House of Representatives from 1863 to 1869. He was a candidate for the Populist presidential nomination in 1892, but his many idiosyncrasies made him too great a risk. He died on January 1, 1901.

HISTORICAL DOCUMENT

Assembled upon the 116th anniversary of the Declaration of Independence, the People's Party of America, in their first national convention, invoking upon their action the blessing of Almighty God, put forth in the name and on behalf of the people of this country, the following preamble and declaration of principles:

Preamble

The conditions which surround us best justify our cooperation; we meet in the midst of a nation brought to the verge of moral, political, and material ruin. Corruption dominates the ballot-box, the Legislatures, the Congress, and touches even the ermine of the bench.

The people are demoralized; most of the States have been compelled to isolate the voters at the polling places to prevent universal intimidation and bribery. The newspapers are largely subsidized or muzzled, public opinion silenced, business prostrated, homes covered with mortgages, labor impoverished, and the land concentrating in the hands of capitalists. The urban workmen are denied the right to organize for self-protection, imported pauperized labor beats down their wages, a hireling standing army, unrecognized by our laws, is established to shoot them down, and they are rapidly degenerating into European conditions. The fruits of the toil of millions are badly stolen to build up colossal fortunes for a few, unprecedented in the history of mankind; and the possessors of these, in turn, despise the Republic and endanger liberty. From the same prolific womb of governmental injustice we breed the two great classes—tramps and millionaires. The national power to create money is appropriated to enrich bond-holders; a vast public debt payable in legal-tender currency has been funded into gold-bearing bonds, thereby adding millions to the burdens of the people.

Silver, which has been accepted as coin since the dawn of history, has been demonetized to add to the purchasing power of gold by decreasing the value of all forms of property as well as human labor, and the supply of currency is purposely abridged to fatten usurers, bankrupt enterprise, and enslave industry. A vast conspiracy against mankind has been organized on two continents, and it is rapidly taking possession of the world. If not met and overthrown at once it forebodes terrible social convulsions, the destruction of civilization, or the establishment of an absolute despotism.

We have witnessed for more than a quarter of a century the struggles of the two great political parties for power and plunder, while grievous wrongs have been inflicted upon the suffering people. We charge that the controlling influences dominating both these parties have permitted the existing dreadful conditions to develop without serious effort to prevent or restrain them. Neither do they now promise us any substantial reform. They have agreed together to ignore, in the coming campaign, ever issue but one. They propose to drown the outcries of a plundered people with the uproar of a sham battle over the tariff, so that capitalists, corporations, national banks, rings, trusts, watered stock, the demonetization of silver and the oppressions of the usurers may all be lost sight of. They propose to sacrifice our homes, lives, and children on the altar of mammon; to destroy the multitude in order to secure corruption funds from the millionaires.

Assembled on the anniversary of the birthday of the nation, and filled with the spirit of the grand general and chief who established our independence, we seek to restore the government of the Republic to the hands of the "'plain people,'" with which class it originated. We assert our purposes to be identical with the purposes of the National Constitution; to form a more perfect union and establish justice, insure domestic tranquility, provide for the common defense, promote the general welfare, and secure the blessings of liberty for ourselves and our posterity. . . .

Our country finds itself confronted by conditions for

which there is not precedent in the history of the world; our annual agricultural productions amount to billions of dollars in value, which must, within a few weeks or months, be exchanged for billions of dollars' worth of commodities consumed in their production; the existing currency supply is wholly inadequate to make this exchange; the results are falling prices, the formation of combines and rings, the impoverishment of the producing class. We pledge ourselves that if given power we will labor to correct these evils by wise and reasonable legislation, in accordance with the terms of our platform. We believe that the power of government—in other words, of the people—should be expanded (as in the case of the postal service) as rapidly and as far as the good sense of an intelligent people and the teaching of experience shall justify, to the end that oppression, injustice, and poverty shall eventually cease in the land. . . .

Platform

We declare, therefore—

First.—That the union of the labor forces of the United States this day consummated shall be permanent and perpetual; may its spirit enter into all hearts for the salvation of the republic and the uplifting of mankind.

Second.—Wealth belongs to him who creates it, and every dollar taken from industry without an equivalent is robbery. "If any will not work, neither shall he eat." The interests of rural and civil labor are the same; their enemies are identical.

Third.—We believe that the time has come when the railroad corporations will either own the people or the people must own the railroads; and should the government enter upon the work of owning and managing all railroads, we should favor an amendment to the constitution by which all persons engaged in the government service shall be placed under a civil-service regulation of the most rigid character, so as to prevent the increase of the power of the national administration by the use of such additional government employees.

FINANCE.—We demand a national currency, safe, sound, and flexible issued by the general government only, a full legal tender for all debts, public and private, and that without the use of banking corporations; a just, equitable, and efficient means of distribution direct to the people, at a tax not to exceed 2 per cent, per annum, to be provided as set forth in the sub-treasury plan of the Farmers' Alliance, or a better system; also by payments in discharge of its obligations for public improvements.

1. We demand free and unlimited coinage of silver and gold at the present legal ratio of 16 to 1.
2. We demand that the amount of circulating medium be speedily increased to not less than $50 per capita.
3. We demand a graduated income tax.
4. We believe that the money of the country should be kept as much as possible in the hands of the people, and hence we demand that all State and national revenues shall be limited to the necessary expenses of the government, economically and honestly administered. We demand that postal savings banks be established by the government for the safe deposit of the earnings of the people and to facilitate exchange.

TRANSPORTATION—Transportation being a means of exchange and a public necessity, the government should own and operate the railroads in the interest of the people. The telegraph and telephone, like the post-office system, being a necessity for the transmission of news, should be owned and operated by the government in the interest of the people.

LAND—The land, including all the natural sources of wealth, is the heritage of the people, and should not be monopolized for speculative purposes, and alien ownership of land should be prohibited. All land now held by railroads and other corporations in excess of their actual needs, and all lands now owned by aliens should be reclaimed by the government and held for actual settlers only.

Expressions of Sentiments

Your Committee on Platform and Resolutions beg leave unanimously to report the following: Whereas, Other questions have been presented for our consideration, we hereby submit the following, not as a part of the Platform of the People's Party, but as resolutions expressive of the sentiment of this Convention.

1. RESOLVED, That we demand a free ballot and a fair count in all elections and pledge ourselves to secure it to every legal voter without Federal Intervention, through the adoption by the States of the unperverted Australian or secret ballot system.
2. RESOLVED, That the revenue derived from a graduated income tax should be applied to the reduction of the burden of taxation now levied upon the domestic industries of this country.
3. RESOLVED, That we pledge our support to fair and liberal pensions to ex-Union soldiers and sailors.
4. RESOLVED, That we condemn the fallacy of protecting American labor under the present system, which opens our ports to the pauper and criminal classes of the world and crowds out our wage-earners; and we denounce the present ineffective laws against contract labor, and demand the further restriction of undesirable emigration.
5. RESOLVED, That we cordially sympathize with the efforts of organized workingmen to shorten the hours of labor, and demand a rigid enforcement of the existing eight-hour law on Government work, and ask that a penalty clause be added to the said law.
6. RESOLVED, That we regard the maintenance of a large standing army of mercenaries, known as the Pinkerton system, as a menace to our liberties, and we demand its abolition. . . .
7. RESOLVED, That we commend to the favorable consideration of the people and the reform press the legislative system known as the initiative and referendum.
8. RESOLVED, That we favor a constitutional provision limiting the office of President and Vice-President to one term, and providing for the election of Senators of the United States by a direct vote of the people.
9. RESOLVED, That we oppose any subsidy or national aid to any private corporation for any purpose.
10. RESOLVED, That this convention sympathizes with the Knights of Labor and their righteous contest with the tyrannical combine of clothing manufacturers of Rochester, and declare it to be a duty of all who hate tyranny and oppression to refuse to purchase the goods made by the said manufacturers, or to patronize any merchants who sell such goods.

GLOSSARY

circulating medium: currency or coin

ermine of the bench: a reference to the white fur trim adorning some judge's robes

Pinkerton: a private detective agency that was used by business owners to put down workers' strikes

usurer: an exploitative moneylender

Document Analysis

The Populists had three major concerns: currency and monetary policy, transportation issues, and federal land policies. In this political tract, they call for the "free and unlimited coinage of silver and gold at the present legal ratio of 16 to 1, a policy often dubbed "free silver." Congress had ended the production of silver dollars in 1873, but the Populists wanted the government to resume coining silver dollars and to return to an 1830s policy that had pegged the value of silver at one-sixteenth that of gold. They believed that resuming silver coinage would increase the money supply, benefitting debtors. In the 1890s, the market price of silver was far lower than one-sixteenth the price of gold, so this policy would have increased the price of silver, appealing to people in mining states where silver production was important, as well as to debtors; however, its inflationary underpinning frightened middle-class and wealthy people with assets.

The Populists also call for a graduated (progressive) income tax, meaning that tax rates should increase with the level of income. No federal income tax existed at this time, and on the state and local level, real estate taxes were often a major component of government revenues; thus, the tax burden fell heavily on farmers.

Transportation costs and service issues also presented problems for farmers. The Populists advocate government ownership of the railroads, arguing that "the railroad corporations will either own the people or the people must own the railroads." Since communication services also had great impact on all the people, the Populists argue that the government should also operate telephone and telegraph services.

Land issues were also of major importance to the Populists. The federal government had given huge land grants to western railroads; the Populists want the remnants of these grants returned to the government. They also call for an end to absentee "alien ownership" of land—foreigners should not be allowed to own land in the United States unless they actually became residents.

In the section of the document entitled "Expressions of Sentiments," the Populists list items not formally part of the party platform but "expressive of the sentiment of this Convention." Some deal with direct democracy issues such as initiative and recall and electing US senators by a direct vote of the people (rather than by the legislatures of the states, as provided for in the Constitution prior to ratification of the Seventeenth Amendment in 1913). Populists express support for the concerns of urban workers and demand "further restriction of undesirable emigration." The secondary status of these issues in the platform underlines one of the problems the Populists faced: while they exhibited some concern for the needs of urban workers, they were not able to attract large numbers of the laboring class to support their party. The Populists advocated primarily rural, agrarian issues in an urbanizing nation in which the cities were increasingly the center of power and influence.

Essential Themes

Scholars consider the 1892 *Populist* platform one of the most comprehensive reform agendas in American history. The central theme evident in the preamble is the sense of crisis, connected to which is the notion of a suspected conspiracy among the wealthy, big business, and corrupt politicians that greatly endangered the American economic system, according to the Populists. "The fruits of the toil of millions are badly stolen to build up colossal fortunes for a few," the preamble asserts. A key element of this "vast conspiracy against mankind," according to the preamble, was the federal government's refusal to coin silver dollars.

In this document, the Populists also stress that the will of the people had been ignored. Republicans and Democrats had not addressed many of the issues that concerned the average worker, focusing instead on a fight over the protective tariff. To give real political power to the people, the Populists called for several "direct democracy" reforms.

In many ways, the Populists were ahead of their time, although scholars have often framed their movement as seeking to restore a lost agrarian ideal. On the national scene, the Populists failed and faded into obscurity. But as historian Richard Hofstadter has pointed out, third parties are not necessarily failures, even if they lose at the ballot box. If sound, their policies will be adopted by one of the major parties, and eventually reforms may result. Indeed, many of the reforms the Populists called for in 1892 came to fruition within the following two or three decades in the Progressive Era.

—*Mark S. Joy, PhD*

Bibliography and Additional Reading

Goodwyn, Lawrence. *Democratic Promise: The Populist Moment in America*. New York: Oxford UP, 1976. Print.

Hofstadter, Richard. *The Age of Reform: From Bryan to F.D.R.* New York: Vintage, 1955. Print.

Kazin, Michael. *The Populist Persuasion: An American History*. Rev. ed. Ithaca: Cornell UP, 1998. Print.

Stock, Catherine McNicol. *Rural Radicals: Righteous Rage in the American Grain*. Ithaca: Cornell UP, 1996. Print.

■ President Grover Cleveland on Repeal of the Sherman Silver Purchase Act

Date: August 8, 1893
Authors: Grover Cleveland
Genre: speech

Summary Overview

During the Panic of 1893, President Grover Cleveland attempted to protect dwindling US gold reserves by making the unpopular decision to repeal the Sherman Silver Purchase Act of 1890. Cleveland called for a special session of Congress and on August 8, 1893, delivered a message arguing that the law was contributing heavily to the depletion of the US gold supply. Cleveland called upon Congress to enact gold and silver standards that were reflective of the policies of other countries, thereby stabilizing gold and silver sales on the international stage.

Defining Moment

During the late 1880s, concerns arose about the sustainability of the explosive economic growth the United States had experienced following the Civil War. Farmers sought debt relief, calling for cheaper paper currency to pay their bills, especially when droughts wiped out much of their crops. By this period, the nation had gained more states, many of which were in mineral-rich areas of the Midwest and mountain regions. The increased number of silver mines from those states was flooding the market with their product, thus lowering the price of silver both in the United States and worldwide.

In 1890, the so-called Free Silver movement spurred a push in Congress for a solution to the country's rampant deflation. Ohio senator John Sherman, along with fellow Ohio senator and future president William McKinley, produced a bill known as the Sherman Silver Purchase Act, which was signed into law in June of that year. The bill required the government to purchase millions of ounces of silver using paper money that would be redeemable for either silver or gold coins. The government's purchases would, in theory, drive up the price of silver and spur inflation, thereby serving the interests of both mine owners and farmers. The government had already been required to purchase millions of ounces of silver by the 1878 Bland-Allison Act, which had been passed in a similar attempt to reinvigorate the American economy, and advocates of the act saw the need to expand greatly upon this premise.

By 1893, however, it had become clear to many that the Sherman Silver Purchase Act was not as effective as its proponents had hoped. Most notably, Americans preferred to redeem their paper money for gold rather than silver, thus drawing heavily on American gold reserves. Meanwhile, a crisis was brewing in the American economy. Railroads, which had been built throughout the country, were by that point overextended. Some fell to bankruptcy and receivership, and many banks, whose gold supplies had dwindled, also closed their doors. The Panic of 1893, as it was known, spurred a depression that would last until 1897.

President Cleveland and others believed that the Sherman Silver Purchase Act was one of the major causes of the panic. During the summer of 1893, he called a special session of Congress to debate the law's repeal. The move would be widely unpopular, as the law had the support of some of the most powerful industries in the United States, so Cleveland needed to tread lightly but deliberately. With the aid of his advisers, particularly Attorney General Richard Olney, Cleveland issued a carefully worded message to the members of Congress, calling for repeal but attempting to avoid offending the law's many supporters.

Author Biography

Stephen Grover Cleveland was born in Caldwell, New Jersey, on March 18, 1837. His father died when Cleveland was sixteen, so he opted not to attend college and instead worked to support his large family. After working as a law clerk in Buffalo, New York, Cleveland was admitted to the bar at twenty-two, despite having no college education. During the Civil War, he served as assistant district attorney in Erie County, New York. In 1870, he was elected sheriff of that county, and he was later elected mayor of Buffalo. In light of his success as a reformer, the Democratic Party nominated him for governor of New York, a position he assumed in 1883. The following year, Democrats and reform Republicans (known as Mugwumps) collectively helped Cleveland win the presidency. He was defeated by Republican challenger Benjamin Harrison in the presidential election of 1888 but returned to office in 1893, becoming the only US president to serve two nonconsecutive terms. Despite winning a second term, his hard stance with organized labor and the ongoing economic depression cost him favor in his own party. He left the White House in 1897 and retired in Princeton, New Jersey, where he died on June 24, 1908.

HISTORICAL DOCUMENT

The existence of an alarming and extraordinary business situation, involving the welfare and prosperity of all our people, has constrained me to call together in extra session the people's representatives in Congress, to the end that through a wise and patriotic exercise of the legislative duty, with which they solely are charged, present evils may be mitigated and dangers threatening the future may be averted.

Our unfortunate financial plight is not the result of untoward events nor of conditions related to our natural resources, nor is it traceable to any of the afflictions which frequently check national growth and prosperity. With plenteous crops, with abundant promise of remunerative production and manufacture, with unusual invitation to safe investment, and with satisfactory assurance to business enterprise, suddenly financial distrust and fear have sprung up on every side. . . . Values supposed to be fixed are fast becoming conjectural, and loss and failure have invaded every branch of business.

I believe these things are principally chargeable to Congressional legislation touching the purchase and coinage of silver by the General Government.

This legislation is embodied in a statute passed on the 14th day of July, 1890, which was the culmination of much agitation on the subject involved, and which may be considered a truce, after a long struggle, between the advocates of free silver coinage and those intending to be more conservative. . . .

This law provides that in payment for the 4,500,000 ounces of silver bullion which the Secretary of the Treasury is commanded to purchase monthly there shall be issued Treasury notes redeemable on demand in gold or silver coin, at the discretion of the Secretary of the Treasury, and that said notes may be reissued. It is, however, declared in the act to be "the established policy of the United States to maintain the two metals on a parity with each other upon the present legal ratio or such ratio as may be provided by law."

This declaration so controls the action of the Secretary of the Treasury as to prevent his exercising the discretion nominally vested in him if by such action the parity between gold and silver may be disturbed. Manifestly a refusal by the Secretary to pay these Treasury notes in gold if demanded would necessarily result in their discredit and depreciation as obligations payable only in silver, and would destroy the parity between the two metals by establishing a discrimination in favor of gold.

The policy necessarily adopted of paying these notes in gold has not spared the gold reserve of $100,000,000 long ago set aside by the Government for the redemption of other notes, for this fund has already been subjected to the payment of new obligations amounting to about $150,000,000 on account of silver purchases, and has as a consequence for the first time since its creation been encroached upon.

We have thus made the depletion of our gold easy and have tempted other and more appreciative nations to add it to their stock. . . .

Unless Government bonds are to be constantly issued and sold to replenish our exhausted gold, only to be again exhausted, it is apparent that the operation of the silver-purchase law now in force leads in the direction of the entire substitution of silver for the gold in the Government Treasury, and that this must be followed by the payment of all Government obligations in depreciated silver.

At this stage gold and silver must part company and the Government must fail in its established policy to maintain the two metals on a parity with each other. Given over to the exclusive use of a currency greatly depreciated according to the standard of the commercial world, we could no longer claim a place among nations of the first class, nor could our Government claim a performance of its obligation, so far as such an obligation has been imposed upon it, to provide for the use of the people the best and safest money.

If, as many of its friends claim, silver ought to occupy a larger place in our currency and the currency of the world through general international cooperation and agreement, it is obvious that the United States will not be in a position to gain a hearing in favor of such an arrangement so long as we are willing to continue our attempt to accomplish the result single-handed. . . .

The people of the United States are entitled to a sound and stable currency and to money recognized as such on every exchange and in every market of the world. Their Government has no right to injure them by financial experiments opposed to the policy and practice of other civilized states, nor is it justified in permitting an exaggerated and unreasonable reliance on our national strength and ability to jeopardize the soundness of the people's money.

This matter rises above the plane of party politics. It vitally concerns every business and calling and enters every household in the land. There is one important aspect of the subject which especially should never be overlooked. At times like the present, when the evils of unsound finance threaten us, the speculator may anticipate a harvest gathered from the misfortune of others, the capitalist may protect himself by hoarding or may even find profit in the fluctuations of values; but the wage earner-the first to be injured by a depreciated currency and the last to receive the benefit of its correction-is practically defenseless. He relies for work upon the ventures of confident and contented capital. This fail-

ing him, his condition is without alleviation, for he can neither prey on the misfortunes of others nor hoard his labor....

It is of the utmost importance that such relief as Congress can afford in the existing situation be afforded at once. The maxim "He gives twice who gives quickly" is directly applicable. It may be true that the embarrassments from which the business of the country is suffering arise as much from evils apprehended as from those actually existing. We may hope, too, that calm counsels will prevail, and that neither the capitalists nor the wage earners will give way to unreasoning panic and sacrifice their property or their interests under the influence of exaggerated fears. Nevertheless, every day's delay in removing one of the plain and principal causes of the present state of things enlarges the mischief already done and increases the responsibility of the Government for its existence. Whatever else the people have a right to expect from Congress, they may certainly demand that legislation condemned by the ordeal of three years' disastrous experience shall be removed from the statute books as soon as their representatives can legitimately deal with it.

It was my purpose to summon Congress in special session early in the coming September, that we might enter promptly upon the work of tariff reform, which the true interests of the country clearly demand, which so large a majority of the people, as shown by their suffrages, desire and expect, and to the accomplishment of which every effort of the present Administration is pledged. But while tariff reform has lost nothing of its immediate and permanent importance and must in the near future engage the attention of Congress, it has seemed to me that the financial condition of the country should at once and before all other subjects be considered by your honorable body.

I earnestly recommend the prompt repeal of the provisions of the act passed July 14, 1890, authorizing the purchase of silver bullion, and that other legislative action may put beyond all doubt or mistake the intention and the ability of the Government to fulfill its pecuniary obligations in money universally recognized by all civilized countries.

GLOSSARY

depreciation: a decrease in value because of age or market conditions

parity: equality; equivalence

pecuniary: pertaining to money

remunerative: providing a profit or compensation

tariff: a tax on imports

Document Analysis

Cleveland's message to Congress, delivered in August 1893, was designed to identify the economic crisis and its causes as well as prompt Congress to react appropriately. He begins his message by explaining that the special session was called to enact true reform and not what he dubs "unsound" fiscal policies, such as the Sherman Silver Purchase Act. The act, in Cleveland's opinion, had done more damage than good. Cleveland therefore urges Congress to take bipartisan action to repeal the 1890 law.

Through his message, Cleveland reminds senators and representatives of the ongoing fiscal crisis. Banking institutions and business enterprises once considered juggernauts on the open markets were closing their doors. Unemployment was spiking, and gold reserves were depleted. However, this crisis was, according to Cleveland, not the product of some catastrophic event, nor was it some natural retraction that would be expected after a long period of explosive growth. Rather, Cleveland argues, the panic was the result of the Sherman Silver Purchase Act of 1890. This law was creating unnecessary parity between gold and silver, rapidly draining gold reserves and fostering a general sense of fear among investors and business enterprises. The law, he explains, was introduced to settle the "long struggle" between Free Silver advocates and conservatives. However, the act's provisions had major implications for the Treasury Department, on whose discretion (which the law hampered, according to Cleveland) the country relied to guard against fiscal instability.

The main problem with the act, according to the president, was the shortage of gold it caused. Because people were redeeming the newly issued paper money for gold, the country's gold reserves were being deplet-ed at an alarming rate. Even if substantial investment in gold returned the reserves to their previous levels, the act would only continue to drain these reserves. The only course of action, he states, was to repeal the Sherman Silver Purchase Act.

Cleveland also uses the message to criticize lawmakers for putting the United States at a disadvantage in comparison to the rest of the world. The US government, he urges, should eschew "financial experiments" such as the Sherman Silver Purchase Act and instead enact "sound and stable" currency reform. Repealing the law would likely prove unpopular, he notes, as some business owners and speculators profited during the years it was in force. Despite this, Cleveland argues that Congress must act quickly to prevent the act from causing any further harm to the American economy.

Essential Themes

In his message to Congress, Cleveland focuses on identifying the crisis at hand and establishing the Sherman Silver Purchase Act of 1890 as its cause. He understood that its repeal would not be a popular move, but in his estimation, the depletion of the nation's gold reserves and the continuation of the developing fiscal depression required immediate action, regardless of the political consequences.

Cleveland's original message allegedly contained much more pointed and critical language, but he reportedly toned down that verbiage in order to appeal to both sides of the political aisle. Still, his address to Congress nevertheless refers to the law as an "experiment" and notes that no other nation in the world shared the view that such an experimental move should be taken. Indeed, he suggests, this experiment was ill-conceived, removing the Treasury's typical discretion over gold and silver prices. The perceived benefits were never realized, he argues, but the risks were clear.

In admitting to Congress that there would be many influential parties who would oppose the repeal of the law, Cleveland revealed that he had a clear understanding of the multifaceted nature of the issue. At the same time, he was solidly in favor of repealing the Silver Purchase Act, having weighed the benefits of the law against their harmful effects on the nation and found them lacking. He was ultimately successful in convincing Congress of the law's dangerous financial consequences, and the Sherman Silver Purchase Act was repealed in October of 1893.

—*Michael P. Auerbach, MA*

Bibliography and Additional Reading

Pafford, John M. *The Forgotten Conservative: Rediscovering Grover Cleveland.* Washington: Regenery History, 2013. Print.

Reed, Lawrence W. *A Lesson from the Past: The Silver Panic of 1893.* Irvington: Foundation for Economic Education, 1993. Print.

Steeples, Douglas W., and David O. Whitten. *Democracy in Desperation: The Depression of 1893.* Westport: Praeger, 1998. Print.

Wells, Merle W. *Gold Camps and Silver Cities.* Moscow: U of Idaho P, 2002. Print.

■ "Political Causes of the Business Depression"

Date: December 1893
Authors: William E. Russell
Genre: article

Summary Overview

Massachusetts governor William E. Russell, in a December 1893 article published in *North American Review*, attempts to identify the political underpinnings of the Panic of 1893 and the subsequent depression. The Democratic governor places blame for the crisis on the Republican Party, which he says forced through Congress the Sherman Silver Purchase Act and enacted other laws that entrenched poor economic policies before the Democrats could undo them.

Defining Moment

Although the national elections of the latter 1880s were considered by many to be less substantive and contested than other campaign seasons, there were some concerns about the sustainability of the explosive economic growth the United States experienced following the Civil War. Farmers sought debt relief, calling for cheaper paper currency to pay their bills, especially when droughts wiped out much of their crops. Silver mines in new Midwestern and mountain states were flooding the market with their product—the value of silver (not just in the United States, but around the world) dropped as a result.

In 1890, the so-called free silver movement spurred a push in Congress for a solution. In a bipartisan compromise that guaranteed the passing of tariff legislation, Republicans put their support behind a bill known as the Sherman Silver Purchase Act (the Sherman Act), which would require that the government purchase millions of ounces of silver using paper money. The paper notes would be redeemable for either silver or gold coins. In theory, the government's purchases would drive up the price of silver and inflation and, therefore, satisfy the interests of the mines and farmers, respectively. The government had already been required to

purchase millions of ounces of silver in the 1878 Bland-Allison Act—advocates such as Sherman saw the need to expand greatly upon this premise, and the bill was pushed through Congress.

In 1893, however, it became clear to many that the Sherman Silver Purchase Act was not as effective as its proponents had hoped. It did increase the price of silver somewhat, for example, but the fact that silver was so prevalent in the world markets meant that the price increase would not be significant. Additionally, Americans preferred to redeem their silver with gold, in essence making the two metals interchangeable in investors' eyes and drawing heavily on American gold reserves.

Meanwhile, a crisis was brewing in the American economy. Railroads, which had been built throughout the country, were overextended. The Philadelphia and Reading Railroad, for example, filed for bankruptcy shortly before Grover Cleveland began his second term as president. Other railroads fell to bankruptcy and receivership, and many banks (whose gold supplies had dwindled during this period) also closed their doors. A series of tariffs on imports also contributed to the crisis, experts argued—the protections put in place on American goods were in fact having an ill effect on revenues as well as manufacturing. The Panic of 1893, as it was known, would spur a depression that lasted until 1897.

Whether to repeal the Sherman Act and laws that increased tariffs on imports became a major issue during what was supposed to be a low-key congressional session. However, many experts and leaders pointed at the Sherman Silver Purchase Act as the main culprit. One such leader was Massachusetts governor William E. Russell, who offered his thoughts in an article published in the December 1893 edition of *North American Review*.

Author Biography

William Eustis Russell was born on January 6, 1857, in Cambridge, Massachusetts. He graduated from Harvard University in 1877 and, in 1879, graduated from Boston University Law School. He worked at his father's law firm before deciding to enter politics, gaining a seat on the Cambridge Board of Aldermen in 1883. In 1884, he was elected mayor of Cambridge, Massachu- setts, a post he held until 1887. After two unsuccessful campaigns for governor, he won his third attempt in 1890, winning as a Democrat in the heavily Republican state. He remained in office until 1894, when he decided not to run for a fourth one-year term. He remained active in Massachusetts politics until his death on July 14, 1896.

HISTORICAL DOCUMENT

That business depression exists and has existed since mid-summer no one doubts. Much as we deplore this fact, the painful proof of it is manifest; confident as we are that the worst is over and the country is now on the road to recovery, it is certainly true that a general depression, starting with stringency of money and a financial panic, has extended through all branches of business and has brought suffering and misery. It is equally true that this condition has not been limited to our country, but has been world-wide in extent, and is in part due to world-wide causes which it is quite beyond the power of legislation here, past or future, to control.

The fact remains, however, that legislation cannot escape its share of responsibility. Unwise laws can impair confidence, shake credit and disturb industrial stability, until the people, under the stress of suffering, demand and get remedial legislation by repeal or otherwise. Political action in this country can and does to a large extent affect our industrial interests. How far this connection of business with politics is wise or proper, it is not my purpose now to discuss.

Because it exists, economic and financial questions have, especially in late years, received prominent attention in political campaigns. Carefully, thoughtfully, the people have considered these matters in the firm belief that political action would affect their own material welfare. Since 1888 the political issues have been largely on these lines, and while other and sometimes local questions have also been considered, the attention of the country has been directed most to important matters of national and economic policy.

It is not strange then that again this year the old questions should have arisen. While it is an "off year," with only a few State elections, and those involving largely local issues, yet business depression and popular belief that its cause and remedy are to be found in legislation have brought both parties sharply to face the issue of responsibility for present conditions.

Unfortunately the issue is complicated by the political situation. The Democratic Party is in power, but Republican laws and policy are still in force. There has not been time yet to change or repeal these with the exception of a single measure, and that one only by a special session of a Democratic Congress convened by a Democratic President.

All other laws remain. The Republican policy upon tariff and finance, with this exception, is still the law of the land. Our revenue is still raised under Republican taxation, and our money spent under Republican appropriations. If mills are closed and men idle, it is well to remember that the McKinley Bill and high protection are still in full force; if the cause of sound money is threatened, that the Sherman law has only just been repealed; if there is an increasing deficit in the Treasury approaching fifty million dollars a year, that the Democratic Party left in March, 1889, a surplus of over one hundred millions, and that our income and expenses since have been determined by Republican laws.

There has been a change only of the Party in power with no fair chance yet to make the people's will and Democratic policy the law of the land. As measures are more important than men, so the acts and laws of a Party have the larger share of responsibility for results dependent upon political control. A Democratic administration with Republican laws to enforce is not responsible for those laws, nor for their evil results, until at least it has had opportunity to change them.

No doubt a suffering people are apt to lay their ills

to the Party in power. It is easy to say to an idle working-man: "Your Party has won a national victory, and now you are out of a job," and to ask him to believe that the one fact has caused the other. However untrue this conclusion, it is hard to reach him, and to show him the real facts and the true causes of his idleness, especially in the haste and excitement of a short campaign. No doubt this Republican appeal to idle men, and this tendency to attribute hard times to the governing Party, were important factors in the recent elections, and the Democratic Party had to suffer for causes it did not create and over which it had little control. Now that the election is over the people will more carefully and fairly consider the situation and measure Party responsibility for it.

Realizing its responsibility for present laws, the Republican Party seeks to escape from it by claiming that not these laws but the fear of laws which are to be enacted has shaken confidence and brought adversity. This then is the issue? Is our admitted distress due to existing Republican legislation which the country has condemned and ordered to be repealed, or to impending Democratic legislation which is to carry out the people's will?

Let us see what the situation is: We find the country suffering from a diminished revenue, increased expenditures, a reduced gold reserve and a flood of useless silver. The Republican Party through its McKinley Bill declared its purpose to shut off imports and so reduce revenue. Then it set the precedent of a billion-dollar Congress, and by its laws fastened this expenditure on the future. Then for partisan purposes, and with the aid of Territories which it created States, protection and silver through the Republican Party made their coalition for a double burden on the people and passed the Silver Bill against the unanimous protest of the Democratic Party. Four years of reckless, extravagant legislation had to be paid for by impaired confidence, with the inevitable result of panic and distress. Although the evil of the Sherman Bill was continually becoming more clear and burdensome, its authors in their State and National conventions either openly indorsed it or uttered no word of protest against it, until at last a financial crisis, due principally to it, broke their silence and forced them to lend their aid in undoing their own mischief. Then they claimed that the bill was passed to prevent the free coin-age of silver. But at the time of its passage the House had already defeated free coinage, and it was known that the President would veto it. Their excuse means that over a Presidential veto a Republican Senate and a Republican House by a two-thirds vote would have supported free coinage though a majority of the House had just voted the other way. The country does not credit this excuse. It believes that the Sherman Bill was passed less from a patriotic purpose to avert danger than from a political purpose to risk a danger in order to save the silver-mining States to the Republican Party and to facilitate the passage of the McKinley Bill. So Republicans themselves have declared. Senator Teller, in the recent debate upon the repeal of the Sherman Bill, said:

I want to refer to the statement made by the Senator from Ohio (Mr. Sherman) that the Sherman law was passed to save the country from a free coinage act. The Senator from Ohio was the Chairman of the Conference Committee which framed that act; and on the floor of the Senate, when he made the report, he stated in the most emphatic manner that the House of Representatives had determined in a very positive way that no free coinage bill could pass that body. Mr. President, I say here now with all due deference to the honorable Senator, and trying to keep as closely within the rules of senatorial decency and courtesy as the circumstances will admit, that his present statement was an afterthought. The records will not support it. The matter was brought here in that shape for the reason that it was supposed it would quiet the agitation and would maintain intact in the Northwest the Republican column of States. We were told in plain, unmistakable language that this might be a sop to our people which would save us and save our political organization in that great section of the country and that we could get nothing better. I repeat, Mr. President, there was not a man in this body nor anywhere else, who gave attention to this subject,—who did not know we had reached a point where it was absolutely impossible to pass a free coinage bill.

Another Republican, Senator Jones, of Nevada, is quoted in the *Boston Daily Advertiser* of September 6, 1893, as having said to his associates in the Conference Committee, which framed the Sherman Bill, these words:

> Now I want to tell you, gentlemen, that the McKinley Bill will be over in the Senate in a very short time. If you reject our ultimatum on the silver proposition the silver men in the Senate will move the free coinage bill as an amendment to the McKinley Bill, and there are enough Democrats who will vote with us to carry it. Now after that amendment is adopted in the Senate, all the Democrats will vote against the McKinley Bill because it is a protective measure, and the Eastern protectionists will vote against it because it contains free silver. The free silver Republicans in the Senate will be the only men who will vote for it; and being protectionists they will be the only consistent men in the Senate, being for protection and for the free coinage of silver. When I got through they were listening to me, and before the conference broke up the silver purchase law known as the Sherman Act was agreed to. If there are many more misrepresentations on the floor of the Senate as to the reasons why the act of 1890 was agreed to and came about, I will take the floor and explain what occurred and how it came to be adopted.

And again, but a few days ago, in the closing debate on the repeal of the Sherman Bill, at least one other Republican Senator in effect repeated the charge and served notice that the coalition of silver and protection was ended because the Republican Party had not kept faith with silver.

It is true that neither Party is united upon this question, but the difference between them is that at the critical moment the Republican Party yields to financial heresy in its ranks and the Democratic Party conquers it. This was strikingly shown by the Democratic administration from 1884 to 1888. Its unflinching stand for sound money was met by the criticism and opposition of the Republican Party, expressed in the Republican national convention of 1888, later by Republican leaders, notably by Mr. McKinley, who said in his speech at Toledo, February, 1891:

During all of his (Cleveland's) years as the head of the Government he was dishonoring one of our precious metals, one of our great products, discrediting silver and enhancing the price of gold. He endeavored even before his inauguration to stop the coinage of silver dollars, and afterwards and to the end of his administration persistently used his power to that end. He was determined to contract the circulating medium and demonetize one of the coins of commerce, limit the volume of money among the people, make money scarce and therefore dear. He would have increased the value of money and diminished the value of everything else; money the master, everything else the servant.

This was followed by Republican acts in admitting the silver Territories and in the passage of the Sherman Bill. Always the spirit of compromise was dominating that Party and giving new life and vigor to its financial unsoundness. Contrast with this the action of the Democratic Party not only from 1884 to 1888, but later in meeting division within its ranks upon this question. With an overwhelming majority in the House of Representatives in 1892 it fought and conquered the demand for the passage of silver legislation, believed by the country to be unsound and unsafe. It faced the issue again in its national convention, and settled it not by compromise, but by argument and the triumphant assertion of a sound principle and policy; and then, as its pledge for the future, it nominated as its candidate the one man most conspicuous before the country for consistent, steadfast devotion to such policy. Again, within a few weeks, when a general demand arose for the repeal of so much of the Sherman Bill as business men believed had been the great cause of depression, and the Democratic Party properly was called upon to face this responsibility, it found united action impossible and the only course open concession or a fight. It chose the latter, although the fatal spirit of compromise was in the air. Such compromise was suggested by Republican precedents, but Democratic precedents and pledges prevailed, and unconditional repeal, through a fight, obtained a great and deserved victory. Ex-Speaker Reed has recently said that this was a victory of the Democratic President over his Party. A Democratic President was indeed at the helm, but a Democratic crew was aboard the ship, and, while he "kept the rudder true," together they sailed the ship out of financial shoals into safe waters. The President stood for right and led his Party, instead of following the precedent set by his predecessor, who yielded to wrong because led by his Party. Democratic State conventions have, almost without exception, declared this leadership to be the expression and enforcement of true Democratic principles. I believe that Republican action on the silver question, marked as it has been by bargains, concessions and compromises culminating in the Sherman Bill, has been the chief cause of business depression. That bill cannot escape responsibility, as Republicans contend, on the ground that the panic did not come until three years after its passage. It took time for it to make its evil fully felt, and it will take time to recover from that evil now that the cause has ceased.

Through these three years the Sherman Bill has steadily been doing its mischievous work, heaping up silver, driving out gold and impairing the public confidence that our increasing currency could be kept at par with gold. During the [administration of President Harrison, from March, 1889, to March, 1893, the treasury gold, outside of the reserve of $100,000,000, fell from $96,000,000 to $3,000,000, while our paper currency, outside of the $346,000,000 of legal tenders, rose from $246,000,000 to $448,000,000. The proportion of free gold to this currency fell from thirty-nine to less than one per cent. Time was constantly making matters worse. The crisis had got to come. The man who fell from the third story window to the sidewalk declared that it was not the fall that hurt him, but bringing up so suddenly on the ground. Under the Sherman Bill the country had been steadily falling and was certain to bring up with a round turn at the end. The best proof that this was the cause of the business depression comes from business

itself. In the midst of its distress it knew and stated the cause of it and the remedy. From boards of trade and business centres all over the country there came a unanimous demand. For what? To let the tariff alone? No, but to repeal the Sherman Bill. Impatient of delay, as if its very life depended upon this action, business watched the movement for repeal. Every step in that movement it felt and indicated as keenly as the barometer does a change of weather. It said emphatically through its representative boards that the one predominant cause of its trouble was the financial legislation of a Republican Congress and the one remedy was its repeal. As this remedy was delayed by weeks and months of discussion and obstruction, the business depression became more serious and so deep rooted that now the repeal itself cannot produce an immediate cure.

But the Republican Party, anxious to escape its responsibility, insists that the crisis was due, not to its laws, but to impending Democratic laws; that we have not been reaping the whirlwind Republicans have sown, but are suffering because the country, by a large majority, has thrust them from power and condemned their financial and tariff policy. Let us examine their claim. What is or was the impending Democratic legislation at the time of the crisis? First, the repeal of the mischievous provisions of the Republican Sherman Bill. To that the Democratic Party was pledged; for that a Democratic President had called together a Democratic Congress in special session, which now has redeemed the pledge and met the responsibility that rested upon it. Undoubtedly this impending legislation was not feared as a cause of trouble, but hoped for as a necessary remedy. Next is the repeal of the McKinley Bill. It is true the Democratic Party has, by the deliberate, repeated judgment of the people, been charged with this duty, which it means faithfully to meet, and so obey the people's mandate to reduce the tariff. But we emphatically assert that the promise of such reduction has not caused present depression; but on the contrary that the reduction, when accomplished, will be only a blessing to the people and their industries. We know that the Republicans tell the laborer out of work that a Democratic victory which condemned unjust taxation, and promised that the power of the people's government would be used not for selfish interests but for the equal benefit of all, that this has brought him idleness and poverty.

They neglect to tell him that he is still living under high protection and the McKinley Bill, or that after three years of trial it has failed to give him its promised benefits of work, high wages and prosperity. If called upon to meet this fact, they excuse the failure of that law by asserting in the words of Mr. Reed that "The McKinley Bill is in prison under sentence of death," and they ask with him, "How can it help you or me?" No doubt that is its condition. It was charged with the crime of robbery, tried before the people fairly and fully, with proof of the influences by which it was produced, its purposes and effect, it was found guilty, sentenced and is in prison awaiting execution.

But this was last November. And even before that it had been tried and condemned. It is an old offender. It was first tried in 1890, when the facts in the case were fresh in the public mind, and was then found guilty. True, a Republican Senate and President could for a while stay proceedings. A little time might be given it for repentance and to prepare for death. But it was in prison then and has been for three years with the condemnation of the country upon it and with the certainty that it must go. Timid manufacturers who really believed that their prosperity was dependent upon it ought to have been shortening sail since 1890.

Let us look a little into the past and see how far the promise or fear of tariff reduction has injured business or caused depression. There has scarcely been a year from the close of the war until 1888 when there has not been promised and impending tariff reduction. The war tariff itself was passed with the pledge that it should be reduced when the necessity for a war revenue was over. Presidents Grant and Arthur and their Secretaries of the Treasury repeatedly recommended such reduction. Some measures in that direction, like the removal of the duty on hides in 1872, were passed. Then the tariff commission of 1882 took up the subject, and after a thorough examination recommended a reduction of duties of from twenty to twenty-five per cent; and later, in 1884, the Republican Party became very largely in favor of some reduction. Then followed the earnest recommendation of President Cleveland in 1887, and the introduction of the Mills Bill. In all these years there were promise and hope of tariff reduction through both the Republi-

can and Democratic parties, and though these efforts failed, some of them unexpectedly, nowhere did the anticipation of tariff reduction cause panic or business distress. Then came the tariff reform victories of 1890 and 1892, and not for many months after the last was there a panic or business depression. Not until our revenue fell off, and gold was exported, and the gold reserve impaired, and silver purchase enormously increased, all acts directly chargeable to Republican Legislation, not until then was confidence destroyed. After that business became stagnant and mills idle. That these were the true causes of the trouble Republicans and Protectionists have admitted. In a recent interview Mr. Thomas Dolan, the well-known protectionist of Philadelphia and of its Manufacturers' Club, said:

> I believe that the depression is almost wholly due to the silver policy. If the alarm was due to the victory of the Democrats, why was it not manifested last November? The people knew then as well as they know now that it was within the power of the new administration to repeal the tariff laws, yet no uneasiness was felt. In fact, in the woollen business everything went along swimmingly until the first of July.

The American Wool Reporter, a standard authority, corroborates this statement. It says:

> For those who believe the tariff has been and is the paramount factor in the present depression in the industrial and business world, it may be of interest to note that certain descriptions of wools actually advanced in prices in the spring months clothing wools were fully one cent per pound higher in March than in January, and some wools two cents per pound higher. If the tariff was a factor it had not made itself manifest in prices during these months. As we have shown in previous issues, the goods market was in good shape, the manufacturers with large orders in hand right through the spring months. The

depression is due to a lack of confidence in the stability of our currency.

And no less an authority than Senator Sherman, in the debate in the Senate on October 17, 1893, said:

> If we would try it (repeal of the Sherman act) to-morrow, after all the long debate that has been had, and dispose of this question as we think best for the people of the United States, while you are assuming your responsibility, we would gladden the hearts of millions of laboring men who are now being turned out of employment; we would relieve the business cares of thousands of men whose whole fortunes are embarked in trade; we would relieve the farmer and his product for free transportation to foreign countries now clogged for the want of money. In the present condition of affairs there is no money to bay cotton or corn and wheat for foreign consumption. Break down the barrier now maintained by the Senate of the United States, check this viper called obstruction to the will of the majority, give the Senate free power and play, and in ten days from this time the skies will brighten, business will resume its ordinary course, and "the clouds that lower upon our house will be in the deep bosom of the ocean buried."

Let us go a step further and see what the Democratic tariff policy is, and whether it can be an injury or cause of alarm to our industries. Its policy, as often stated, is a revenue tariff with reduction of duties to cheapen the necessaries of life, and give free raw materials to our industries. This it has declared in National and State platforms, formulated into bills and voted for in Congress. This it is pledged to give in its new bill. It means free wool, coal, iron ore and other raw materials, with fair and proper reduction on finished products.

It is something in favor of such a policy that since 1890 it has, after thorough consideration, been twice indorsed by a large majority of our people; that great manufacturing States like New York, New Jersey and Connecticut have constantly supported it, and even Massachusetts voted for it in 1890; that it has been the policy of our nation through most of its life; that, after thorough trial of the low tariff of 1846, manufacturing New England joined with the rest of the country in demanding the lower tariff of 1857,and under these low tariffs many of our great manufacturing cities were founded, and their industries established and prospered. Can such a policy now, after a generation more of active industrial life, with our industries older, with our labor more efficient, with our progress in inventions and greater aptitude for manufacturing, can it, with its assured benefit of free raw material, be a just cause for alarm?

Let us consider some pertinent facts upon this point gathered from the industries themselves, and, first, a bit of evidence from New England. In February, 1889, its iron and steel industries prepared a statement and petition, setting forth their condition and asking Congress for free coal, iron ore and reduced duties on pig and scrap iron. That statement declared that the tendency of these duties had been "to wipe out the iron and steel industries, large and small, of New England." It gives the facts to support this claim. Again, it says: "It is then clearly the duty on coal and crude iron that is strangling in New England one of the largest of all the wonderful industries of our modern days." It adds: "There is no necessity for letting it die; that it is only the existing duties on coal, ore and crude iron that are strangling it; and that the abolition of those duties will not only keep it alive, but will insure it a tremendous vitality and large increase."

This statement and petition were signed by 598 iron and steel industries of New England, including almost without exception every one of importance, and by men of both political parties, including the then Republican Governor of Massachusetts. Certainly to that industry there is hope of new life and growth when a Democratic tariff bill takes the place of the McKinley law.

Turn next to the woollen industry. The burden today of a duty upon wool is clearly shown by the fact that this industry asks and gets an additional duty on its finished products called compensatory, because given to offset this burden. The industry itself asked Congress in 1866 for free wool, and said that with it a duty of twenty-five per cent, on its finished products was sufficient, and recently over 700 woollen manufacturers and dealers, including some of the largest in the country, have again asked for this benefit. They have no fear that free wool, which in all other civilized countries has been a help to this industry, will here work it harm; and they remember that since 1888 the Democratic Party has twice formulated its policy into bills which gave free wool, still leaving a duty on its product larger than the labor cost of the product and much larger than the twenty-five percent, asked by the woollen industry in 1866.

Turn next to the boot and shoe and leather industries. What better proof could be given of the benefit of the Democratic policy of free raw materials than the growth and prosperity of those industries after the duty on hides was removed in 1872, and their unanimous protest against the proposition to reimpose that duty by the McKinley Bill? With their principal raw material free, they export annually over thirteen million dollars worth of goods, competing in the markets of the world with the labor of the world. Mr. McKinley said there was no reason for a duty on wool which did not equally apply to hides. He was right, but he did not put back the duty against this protest. The Democratic Party says that every reason which made hides free demands that wool be free, and it proposes to act upon this belief. The great advantage of free silk to the silk industry, of free rags to the paper industry, of free hides to the boot and shoe and leather industries, can and ought to be extended to other industries as a benefit not only to all the people as consumers, but to the industries themselves, giving them a larger market here and a better chance to send their products into foreign markets.

This is the policy of the Democratic Party as declared in its platforms, formulated in its measures and supported by its votes. It advocates a revenue tariff, remembering that revenue has been the basis of every tariff, even our war tariff, until 1888, when another principle, controlling the Republican Party, supplanted it and found expression in the McKinley Bill. It believes that a tariff, which gives free raw materials and cheaper necessaries of life and which is required to raise a revenue of nearly two hundred million dollars, is a conservative measure, and a benefit to industries as well as to the people. It does not believe in tariff taxation which has for its purpose and result taking from one to give to another, or burdening all to enrich the few. It opposes the principle of the McKinley Bill that taxation can be laid not for revenue, a public purpose, but solely for private interests, to kill competition, encourage trusts and cut off revenue.

The country deliberately, emphatically said in 1890 and 1892 that the Democratic policy was right in principle and would be beneficial in its results. It is hardly conceivable that its mature judgment, twice expressed, was wholly wrong. It certainly is no proof of this that a great business depression has come under another tariff policy, which by the same judgment the country condemned and ordered to be repealed.

Document Analysis

Governor Russell's comments recognize that the United States and the rest of the world, as a result of the Panic of 1893, were entering a severe economic depression, one that would impact every industrial sector. Some of the causes of this depression went beyond the scope of any legislative action, he wrote. However, some of the causes could have been avoided altogether if "unwise" legislation had not been passed into law, he adds.

Russell acknowledged that it was difficult to legislate on matters of business. Striking a balance between passing laws that protect the American economy and interfering in business matters was a vexing endeavor, he writes. Nevertheless, legislators frequently made attempts on this front. The Democratic governor says that the Republican Congress was culpable for the ongoing fiscal crisis, as these leaders—before the elections of 1892—were responsible for passing legislation that negatively affected the business and economic interests of the country. Among these missteps, he claims, were protectionist and monetary policies enacted by the Republican-controlled legislature. Even though Congress returned to Democratic control, it would take time, he writes, to undo the Republican-passed laws that were to blame for the crisis.

Russell cites two major Republican-passed laws that he said contributed to the crisis. The first was a series of bills that increased tariffs and applied taxes on other items. Democrats had criticized such measures (including one filed by Senator William McKinley) on the grounds that, by raising tariff rates, the laws were dramatically impacting revenues, generating fewer imports.

The second law—the Sherman Act—was even more impactful, Russell says. There was a great deal of political posturing when the Senate took up the act's passage, Russell states. "Silver men" strong-armed both Democrats and Republicans alike into ensuring its passage as well as the admission into the Union of silver-rich states. The debate over the act's merits and risks, Russell says, was certainly not evenly split along party lines. However, Russell points at the Republicans for their uncompromising approach to passage.

When the aforementioned taxation and silver laws began to have ill effects on the American economy, Russell says, Republicans were quick to place blame not on the Sherman Act but on the laws passed later by Democrats. Russell argues that, while the Republicans sought to escape their culpability, the Democrats were unified in undoing these two measures (the Sherman Act and the McKinley tariff law). Russell cites the testimony of a number of key industry leaders, organizations, and officials (including Sherman himself) who, when these laws were being passed, argued in favor, only to reverse their positions when the economy went sour.

Russell then turns to several industries in his home state as evidence of the need to follow the Democratic course. The wool industry, he said, would benefit greatly from a reduction in tariffs, as would the shoe and leather industries. The oil, coal, and iron industries, he adds, all stood in favor of repealing McKinley's tariffs. The Democrats, Russell concludes, offered sound policies that included the repeal of both Sherman and McKinley's respective laws.

Essential Themes

Russell was elected governor in a state that was predominantly Republican, and although he had a reputation for attaining bipartisan support on a number of issues in Massachusetts, his experience working in the political minority brought out a sense of defiance. His defiance is evident in this article, wherein he offered his opinions on the causes of the Panic of 1893 and the subsequent depression. He assigned blame for the crisis to the Republicans, whom he said had forced onerous tariff increases and the Sherman Act through Congress and into law.

After the Civil War, Russell argued, the Republicans had introduced a series of tariffs that many (Russell included) believed became too prohibitive for US industries to maintain international business. Meanwhile, the so-called silver men (leaders who strongly advocated for the Sherman Act's passage on behalf of the silver mines and farmers) refused to compromise on the silver issue, and Republicans simply acquiesced, Russell said. Some Democrats were willing to work with Republicans to establish sound policy, Russell insisted, but the Democrats were in the minority. Even now, he added, with the Democrats finally back in power in Congress, it would take a long time to undo those laws, especially when the Republicans shied away from taking responsibility for them.

Russell's article is not just replete with political rhetoric. It includes a careful analysis of the depreciation of gold as a result of the Sherman Act. It also includes commentary from a number of leaders of key industries (such as the wool, steel, and coal sectors), all of whom argue that the McKinley tariffs and other tax laws were adversely impacting their businesses. Perhaps most integral to his argument is the inclusion of testimony from industry and political leaders who had originally advocated for Sherman and McKinley's initiatives and who, when the crisis began, immediately recognized that the Sherman Act and the tariff increases were the main culprits. Russell's politically charged comments aside, statements such as these were highly influential in bringing about both measures' repeal as the depression took hold.

—Michael P. Auerbach, MA

Bibliography and Additional Reading

Hogarty, Richard A. *Massachusetts Political and Public Policy: Studies in Power and Leadership.* Amherst: U of Massachusetts P, 2002. Print.

"Massachusetts Governor William Eustis Russell." *Former Governors' Bios.* National Governors Assoc., 2014. Web. 25 Apr. 2014.

Morgan, Howard Wayne. *William McKinley and His America.* Rev. ed. Kent: Kent State UP, 2003. Print.

"Panic of 1893." *The Life and Times of Florence Kelley in Chicago 1891–1899.* Northwestern Univ. School of Law, 2008. Web. 25 Apr. 2014.

Reed, Lawrence W. *A Lesson from the Past: The Silver Panic of 1893.* Irvington: Foundation for Economic Educ., 1993. Print.

Steeples, Douglas, and David O. Whitten. *Democracy*

in Desperation: The Depression of 1893. Westport: Greenwood, 1998. Print.

"William Eustis Russell." *Mass.gov.* Commonwealth of Massachusetts, 2014. Web. 25 Apr. 2014.

Andrew Carnegie: "The Gospel of Wealth"

Date: June 1889
Author: Andrew Carnegie
Genre: article; editorial; essay

Summary Overview

For the extremely wealthy, the Gilded Age of the late nineteenth century was a time of excess. Many of the so-called robber barons amassed huge fortunes while spending extravagantly on themselves and giving little thought to the morality of what they did with their wealth. However, one of the wealthiest men in the world, who also happened to grow up in poverty, would speak to and define the responsibility of the wealthy toward society at large and the poor in particular. Andrew Carnegie, owner of the largest steel company in the world, was certainly a product of his time, and the way he treated his employees was not much different than the way many of his contemporaries treated theirs. But after selling his company, Carnegie put his words into action by using his vast fortune to improve society and offer the poor an opportunity to change their futures themselves.

Defining Moment

The term "Gilded Age" may imply a sense of glamour, but when Mark Twain wrote his 1873 novel *The Gilded Age: A Tale of Today*, he had something else in mind, satirizing the wealthy and powerful, who gave the illusion of glitter and shine but instead were hollow and corrupt. "Robber barons" is a derogatory term popularized in the nineteenth century. It was used to refer to wealthy businessmen who amassed even more wealth through dishonest or unscrupulous means, particularly when dealing with one another, smaller business owners, or with the workers they employed.

In some ways, Carnegie agreed with Twain's assessment of Gilded Age business practices and social relations, and in some ways he embodied them; more significantly, however, he viewed the accumulation of wealth by the robber barons as beneficial. Indeed, these businessmen were instrumental in transforming the United States from a predominantly agricultural, rural nation to an urbanized, industrialized world power. Carnegie believed that the actions of the robber barons were the engine of the American economy, which, in turn, led to an increase in industrial jobs, the start of the American Industrial Revolution, and ultimately the creation of the middle class.

Carnegie was as ruthless as other businessmen of the era in stifling dissent and minimizing the strength of unions among his workers. Though his partner, Henry Clay Frick, did the dirty work, Carnegie gave Frick a free hand, making him chairman of Carnegie Steel. In 1892, Frick shut down Carnegie's massive Homestead mill rather than accede to union demands that he not cut wages. He hired Pinkerton detectives to act as the company's army, waging a gun battle with strikers that resulted in ten deaths. After the National Guard arrived to establish order, Homestead reopened as a nonunion mill.

Carnegie saw no benefit in giving workers wages higher than the market would force him to pay, and he viewed giving money to the poor as morally bankrupting the recipients. His goal was to give common people the chance to succeed in the same way he had: by pulling themselves up from poverty through determination, hard work, and force of will. His "Gospel of Wealth" embodied this ethos. Carnegie was willing to use the bulk of his massive fortune to provide the tools for those people who had the kind of determination to achieve through their own efforts.

Author Biography

Andrew Carnegie was born the son of a linen weaver in the town of Dunfermline, Scotland, in 1835. When the burgeoning Industrial Revolution in Britain put his father out of work, the Carnegies moved to the United States when Andrew was thirteen. He then began work as a bobbin boy in a cotton factory, but his drive for knowledge and self-improvement enabled him to move up. After making a good living at the Pennsylvania Railroad, he left to take over the Keystone Bridge Company, and there, he saw that the future of the nation's prosperity lay in steel. Investing in the new Bessemer steel-

making process, he quickly outstripped his competitors' profits by producing steel at a lower cost. Wanting to use his fortune to pursue his vision of social uplift, he sold Carnegie Steel to financier J. P. Morgan in 1903, becoming the wealthiest man in the world. He devoted the rest of his life to philanthropy, building libraries and supporting cultural and higher educational institutions.

HISTORICAL DOCUMENT

The problem of our age is the proper administration of wealth, so that the ties of brotherhood may still bind together the rich and poor in harmonious relationship. The conditions of human life have not only been changed, but revolutionized, within the past few hundred years. In former days there was little difference between the dwelling, dress, food, and environment of the chief and those of his retainers. The Indians are to-day where civilized man then was. When visiting the Sioux, I was led to the wigwam of the chief. It was just like the others in external appearance, and even within the difference was trifling between it and those of the poorest of his braves. The contrast between the palace of the millionaire and the cottage of the laborer with us to-day measures the change which has come with civilization.

This change, however, is not to be deplored, but welcomed as highly beneficial. It is well, nay, essential for the progress of the race, that the houses of some should be homes for all that is highest and best in literature and the arts, and for all the refinements of civilization, rather than that none should be so. Much better this great irregularity than universal squalor. Without wealth there can be no Maecenas. The "good old times" were not good old times. Neither master nor servant was as well situated then as to-day. A relapse to old conditions would be disastrous to both—not the least so to him who serves— and would sweep away civilization with it. But whether the change be for good or ill, it is upon us, beyond our power to alter, and therefore to be accepted and made the best of. It is a waste of time to criticise the inevitable.

Objections to the foundations upon which society is based are not in order, because the condition of the race is better with these than it has been with any others which have been tried. Of the effect of any new

substitutes proposed we cannot be sure. The Socialist or Anarchist who seeks to overturn present conditions is to be regarded as attacking the foundation upon which civilization itself rests, for civilization took its start from the day that the capable, industrious workman said to his incompetent and lazy fellow, "If thou dost net sow, thou shalt net reap," and thus ended primitive Communism by separating the drones from the bees. One who studies this subject will soon be brought face to face with the conclusion that upon the sacredness of property civilization itself depends—the right of the laborer to his hundred dollars in the savings bank, and equally the legal right of the millionaire to his millions. To these who propose to substitute Communism for this intense Individualism the answer, therefore, is: The race has tried that. All progress from that barbarous day to the present time has resulted from its displacement. Not evil, but good, has come to the race from the accumulation of wealth by those who have the ability and energy that produce it. But even if we admit for a moment that it might be better for the race to discard its present foundation, Individualism—that it is a nobler ideal that man should labor, not for himself alone, but in and for a brotherhood of his fellows, and share with them all in common, realizing Swedenborg's idea of Heaven, where, as he says, the angels derive their happiness, not from laboring for self, but for each other—even admit all this, and a sufficient answer is, This is not evolution, but revolution. It necessitates the changing of human nature itself a work of eons, even if it were good to change it, which we cannot know. It is not practicable in our day or in our age. Even if desirable theoretically, it belongs to another and long-succeeding sociological stratum. Our duty is with what is practicable now; with the next step possible in our day and generation. It is criminal to waste our energies in endeavoring to uproot, when all we can profitably or possibly accomplish is to bend the universal tree of humanity a little in the direction most favorable to the production of good fruit under existing circumstances. We might as well urge the destruction of the highest existing type of man because he failed to reach our ideal as favor the destruction of Individualism, Private Property, the Law of Accumulation of Wealth, and the Law of Competition; for these are the highest results of human experience, the soil in which society so far has produced the best fruit. Unequally or unjustly, perhaps, as these laws sometimes operate, and imperfect as they appear to the Idealist, they are, nevertheless, like the highest type of man, the best and most valuable of all that humanity has yet accomplished.

We start, then, with a condition of affairs under which the best interests of the race are promoted, but which inevitably gives wealth to the few. Thus far, accepting conditions as they exist, the situation can be surveyed and pronounced good. The question then arises—and, if the foregoing be correct, it is the only question with which we have to deal—What is the proper mode of administering wealth after the laws upon which civilization is founded have thrown it into the hands of the few? And it is of this great question that I believe I offer the true solution. It will be understood that *fortunes* are here spoken of, not moderate sums saved by many years of effort, the returns on which are required for the comfortable maintenance and education of families. This is not *wealth*, but only *competence* which it should be the aim of all to acquire.

There are but three modes in which surplus wealth can be disposed of. It call be left to the families of the descendants; or it can be bequeathed for public purposes; or, finally, it can be administered during their lives by its possessors. Under the first and second modes most of the wealth of the world that has reached the few has hitherto been applied. Let us in turn consider each of these modes. The first is the most injudicious. In monarchical countries, the estates and the greatest portion of the wealth are left to the first son, that the vanity of the parent may be gratified by the thought that his name and title are to descend to succeeding generations unimpaired. The condition of this class in Europe to-day

teaches the futility of such hopes or ambitions. The successors have become impoverished through their follies or from the fall in the value of land. Even in Great Britain the strict law of entail has been found inadequate to maintain the status of an hereditary class. Its soil is rapidly passing into the hands of the stranger. Under republican institutions the division of property among the children is much fairer, but the question which forces itself upon thoughtful men in all lands is: Why should men leave great fortunes to their children? If this is done from affection, is it not misguided affection? Observation teaches that, generally speaking, it is not well for the children that they should be so burdened. Neither is it well for the state. Beyond providing for the wife and daughters moderate sources of income, and very moderate allowances indeed, if any, for the sons, men may well hesitate, for it is no longer questionable that great suns bequeathed oftener work more for the injury than for the good of the recipients. Wise men will soon conclude that, for the best interests of the members of their families and of the state, such bequests are an improper use of their means.

Poor and restricted are our opportunities in this life; narrow our horizon; our best work most imperfect; but rich men should be thankful for one inestimable boon. They have it in their power during their lives to busy themselves in organizing benefactions from which the masses of their fellows will derive lasting advantage, and thus dignify their own lives. The highest life is probably to be reached, not by such imitation of the life of Christ as Count Tolstoi gives us, but, while animated by Christ's spirit, by recognizing the changed conditions of this age, and adopting modes of expressing this spirit suitable to the changed conditions under which we live; still laboring for the good of our fellows, which was the essence of his life and teaching, but laboring in a different manner.

This, then, is held to be the duty of the man of Wealth: First, to set an example of modest, unostentatious living, shunning display or extravagance; to provide moderately for the legitimate wants of those dependent upon him; and after doing so to consider all surplus revenues which come to him simply as trust funds, which he is called upon to administer, and strictly bound as a matter of duty to administer in the manner which, in his judgment, is best calculated to produce the most beneficial results for the community—the man of wealth thus becoming the mere agent and trustee for his poorer brethren, bringing to their service his superior wisdom, experience and ability to administer, doing for them better than they would or could do for themselves.

We are met here with the difficulty of determining what are moderate sums to leave to members of the family; what is modest, unostentatious living; what is the test of extravagance. There must be different standards for different conditions. The answer is that it is as impossible to name exact amounts or actions as it is to define good manners, good taste, or the rules of propriety; but, nevertheless, these are verities, well known although indefinable. Public sentiment is quick to know and to feel what offends these. So in the case of wealth. The rule in regard to good taste in the dress of men or women applies here. Whatever makes one conspicuous offends the canon. If any family be chiefly known for display, for extravagance in home, table, equipage, for enormous sums ostentatiously spent in any form upon itself, if these be its chief distinctions, we have no difficulty in estimating its nature or culture. So likewise in regard to the use or abuse of its surplus wealth, or to generous, freehanded cooperation in good public uses, or to unabated efforts to accumulate and hoard to the last, whether they administer or bequeath. The verdict rests with the best and most enlightened public sentiment. The community will surely judge and its judgments will not often be wrong.

The best uses to which surplus wealth can be put have already been indicated. These who, would administer wisely must, indeed, be wise, for one of the serious obstacles to the improvement of our race is indiscriminate charity. It were better for mankind that the millions of the rich were thrown in to the sea than so spent as to encourage the slothful, the drunken, the unworthy. Of every thousand dollars spent in so called charity to-day, it is probable that $950 is unwisely spent; so spent, indeed as to produce the very evils which it proposes to mitigate or cure. A well-known writer of philosophic books admitted the other day that he had given a quarter of a dollar to a man who approached him as he was coming to visit the house of his friend. He knew nothing of the habits of this beggar; knew not the use that would be made of this money, although he had every reason to suspect that it would be spent improperly. This man professed to be a disciple of Herbert Spencer; yet the quarter-dollar given that night will probably work more injury than all the money which its thoughtless donor will ever be able to give in true charity will do good. He only gratified his own feelings, saved himself from annoyance—and this was probably one of the most selfish and very worst actions of his life, for in all respects he is most worthy.

In bestowing charity, the main consideration should be to help those who will help themselves; to provide part of the means by which those who desire to improve may do so; to give those who desire to use the aids by which they may rise; to assist, but rarely or never to do all. Neither the individual nor the race is improved by alms-giving. Those worthy of assistance, except in rare cases, seldom require assistance. The really valuable men of the race never do, except in cases of accident or sudden change. Every one has, of course, cases of individuals brought to his own knowledge where temporary assistance can do genuine good, and these he will not overlook. But the amount which can be wisely given by the individual for individuals is necessarily limited by his lack of knowledge of the circumstances connected with each. He is the only true reformer who is as careful and as anxious not to aid the unworthy as he is to aid the worthy, and, perhaps, even more so, for in alms-giving more injury is probably done by rewarding vice than by relieving virtue.

The rich man is thus almost restricted to following the examples of Peter Cooper, Enoch Pratt of Baltimore, Mr. Pratt of Brooklyn, Senator Stanford, and others, who know that the best means of benefiting the community is to place within its reach the ladders upon which the aspiring can rise—parks, and means of recreation, by which men are helped in body and mind; works of art, certain to give pleasure and improve the public taste, and public institutions of various kinds, which will improve the general condition of the people;—in this manner returning their surplus wealth to the mass of their fellows in the forms best calculated to do them lasting good.

Thus is the problem of Rich and Poor to be solved. The laws of accumulation will be left free; the laws of distribution free. Individualism will continue, but the millionaire will be but a trustee for the poor; entrusted for a season with a great part of the increased wealth of the community, but administering it for the community far better than it could or would have done for itself. The best minds will thus have reached a stage in the development of the race in which it is clearly seen that there is no mode of disposing of surplus wealth creditable to thoughtful and earnest men into whose hands it flows save by using it year by year for the general good. This day already dawns. But a little while, and although, without incurring the pity of their fellows, men may die sharers in great business enterprises from which their capital cannot be or has not been withdrawn, and is left chiefly at death for public uses, yet the man who dies leaving behind many millions of available wealth, which was his to administer during life, will pass away "unwept, unhonored, and unsung," no matter to what uses he leaves the dross which he cannot take with him. Of such as these the public verdict will then be: "The man who dies thus rich dies disgraced."

Such, in my opinion, is the true Gospel concerning Wealth, obedience to which is destined some day to solve the problem of the Rich and the Poor, and to bring "Peace on earth, among men Good-Will."

GLOSSARY

Maecenas: Gaius Maecenas, the first Emperor of Rome (as Caesar Augustus)

Herbert Spencer: (1820–1903): British philosopher and sociologist who was a proponent of Social Darwinism (survival of the fittest)

Swedenborg: Emanuel Swedenborg (1688–1772), Swedish philosopher, theologian, and mystic

Document Analysis

When Andrew Carnegie wrote "The Gospel of Wealth" in 1889, he transferred the notion of *noblesse oblige* (the social responsibility of the European nobility) to the context of industrialized America. He believed that the business leaders of the time had a responsibility to use their wealth not just for self-aggrandizement but also for the common good of humanity. The idea of the common good was shaped by one of the most popular ideologies among the wealthy of the time, Social Darwinism.

It is ironic that a man who would become the wealthiest man in the world would state, "the man who dies thus rich dies disgraced," but the saying, which Carnegie often repeated, encapsulated his viewpoint. Carnegie also believed that an increased gap between the wealthy and the poor defined civilization in a positive way. Earlier, less "civilized" societies, Carnegie argues, had equality, but only an equality of poverty, meaning civilization could not progress because there were no wealthy individuals to fund it.

Following the ideas of Herbert Spencer, who coined the term "survival of the fittest" as it relates to societal organization, Carnegie believes that individualism and the drive to become wealthy were "the soil in which society so far has produced the best fruit." He states that collectivism and forced equality were to be abhorred, and the wealthy were obligated by their position in society to lead and to provide opportunities for others who had the ability to achieve more, thus uplifting civilization as a whole. Charity, as it was commonly practiced—giving money or other necessities to the poor—is an unwise use of money according to Carnegie because it only serves to perpetuate the social ills they were trying to cure.

Though a product of the ideas of his time, Carnegie's application of those ideas was far ahead of his contemporaries. He criticizes those who bequeathed their wealth to their children as both depriving society and doing a disservice to their children by not forcing them to earn their success. Instead, the wealthy are obligated by their position to use their wealth "in the manner which, in his judgment, is best calculated to produce the most beneficial results for the community." The wealthy are trustees for the poor, "doing for them better than they would or could do for themselves."

Essential Themes

Carnegie proposed a new and different solution to the crisis of poverty in the United States in his "Gospel of

Wealth" essay. Indeed, the fact that he was so willing to tell his fellow millionaires what to do with their money was controversial, as were his ideas about Social Darwinism and the futility of the most common type of charity. Regardless of the debate his ideas generated, he would not back down and continued to write on the topic of philanthropy. He devoted his life and fortune to realizing his vision after he sold Carnegie Steel. At the time of his death in 1919, he had given away more than ninety-five percent of his personal fortune.

Though very few of the wealthy have followed Carnegie's advice to the extent that he did, many have followed the Carnegie pattern of donating and dispersing their money. Today, the Carnegie Corporation, the Carnegie Foundation for the Advancement of Teaching, and the Carnegie Endowment for the Humanities still carry on the philanthropic work started by Carnegie's fortune.

Even if the terminology has changed, the Social Darwinistic bent of Carnegie's philanthropy has lived far beyond his years. Many among the wealthy see themselves as possessing a unique responsibility to society. Additionally, some political philosophies common to the wealthy hold to this view of the proper use of wealth: not giving direct charity to the poor, but instead enabling them to rise out of poverty if they possess the drive to do so.

—Steven L. Danver, PhD

Bibliography and Additional Reading

Burgoyne, Arthur G. *The Homestead Strike of 1892.* Pittsburgh: U of Pittsburgh P, 1979. Print.

Josephson, Matthew. *The Robber Barons: The Great American Capitalists, 1861–1901.* New Brunswick: Transaction, 2011. Print.

Kahan, Paul. *The Homestead Strike: Labor, Violence, and American Industry.* New York: Routledge, 2014. Print.

Lagemann, Ellen Condliff. *The Politics of Knowledge: The Carnegie Corporation, Philanthropy, and Public Policy.* Chicago: U of Chicago P, 1989. Print.

Nasaw, David. *Andrew Carnegie.* New York: Penguin, 2007. Print.

CONFLICTS FARTHER AFIELD

The year 1898 is known, of course, as the year in which the Spanish-American War unfolded. In this conflict, spurred largely by American territorial interests in the Caribbean and the Pacific, naval and land battles were fought briefly and successfully in Cuba, resulting in that island (together with Puerto Rico) becoming a U.S. possession. In the following year, a more drawn out yet equally one-sided combat situation took root in the Philippines, as U.S. occupiers sought to quell a Filipino insurgency there.

In this section we review a number of documents associated with that war. We read a report on the Battle of Santiago de Cuba, recounting U.S. naval actions. We examine a detailed summary of events in the Philippines, written by a critic of U.S. actions. And we hear the voices of two dissenting parties: the American Anti-Imperialist League, which denounced the war effort as improper and immoral; and Mark Twain, who, in response to the war, penned an imaginative piece of prose that publishers refused to print.

We begin and end the section, however, with docu-ments from conflicts that arose before and after the Spanish-American War. The first is a diplomatic cry for help from Queen Liliuokalani of Hawaii, addressing, in 1893, U.S. president Benjamin Harrison. In her plea Liliuokalani laments the fact that U.S. armed forces, in collaboration with business interests, have taken over her island and dispatched with her and her rule. The American move was the first step toward eventual annexation of Hawaii.

The last conflict reviewed here leaps ahead in time to 1916 but returns us geographically to the North American continent. In a set of three documents we find descriptions of U.S. forces under General John Pershing entering Mexico in pursuit of the famed Pancho Villa. Villa had himself crossed the border into the United States earlier, in a raid for supplies to support his anti-government forces in northern Mexico. Coming before the United States' entry into World War I, the skirmish tested the readiness of the American military and had implications for the larger war to come.

■ Queen Liliuokalani to President Benjamin Harrison

Date: January 18, 1893
Author: Queen Liliuokalani
Genre: letter; petition

Summary Overview

When white American businessmen, assisted by US diplomat John L. Stevens and US Marines, took over the islands of Hawaii in 1893, the overthrown Queen Liliuokalani requested help from American president Benjamin Harrison. Unfortunately for her, no help came. By the 1890s, Hawaii had become important to US officials both as a territory and as a stepping-stone to the vast trade potential of China and other parts of East Asia. Though the United States did not annex Hawaii officially until 1898, white Americans effectively ruled the islands after 1893, culminating a long period of growing Caucasian interest and involvement in the kingdom. In addition to being a plea for help, Queen Liliuokalani's letter sheds light on broader historical questions, including, on one hand, whether or not the United States intended to be a Pacific power and, on the other, whether or not American expansion after victory in the 1898 Spanish-American War was a break with previous policy.

Defining Moment

Queen Liliuokalani's letter marked the most important shift in the relationship between Hawaii and the United States. By the 1820s, American Protestant missionaries were active on the islands, and the United States had signed its first trade deals with the kingdom. From the 1840s to the 1860s, American leaders included Hawaii in their visions of expanding American power and influence in the Pacific. For instance, in the 1842 Tyler Doctrine, President John Tyler declared Hawaii to be an object of US national interest and warned against European encroachments on the islands. In 1851, Secretary of State Daniel Webster declared that the United States would defend Hawaii's independence with force. Many American leaders and businessmen saw Hawaii as important both as a potential source of trade in itself and as a stop on the way to the rumored vast China market, which opened to Western trade after British victory in the First Opium War in the early 1840s and the Taiping Rebellion in the 1850s.

The American Civil War (1861–65) began to change power relations in Hawaii. Because the source of Southern sugar was cut off, sugar production grew rapidly on the islands, leading to the increasing influence of white American planters. These men even helped the Hawaiian king negotiate a treaty with the United States in 1873 that allowed the tariff-free importation of Hawaiian sugar into the United States in exchange for Hawaii's refusal to sign any significant economic or military treaties with European nations. Throughout the 1870s and 1880s, therefore, Hawaii came under American influence even more. In early 1893, Queen Liliuokalani decided to reassert the authority of native Hawaiians by changing the constitution to reconcentrate control in the hands of the monarch—therefore reclaiming control from the white American ministers, who, by then, occupied many important positions in the Hawaiian government—and by extending the vote to indigenous Hawaiians. The American plantation owners had already begun planning to overthrow Queen Liliuokalani because of their opposition to her views, and the new constitution set their plans in motion. With the help of Marines from the USS Boston, sent ashore "to preserve order" by Stevens (who was in league with the plotters), the planters overthrew Queen Liliuokalani and rushed an annexation agreement to the United States.

The American businessmen expected, and initially received, a warm welcome in Washington, DC, from President Harrison, a pro-expansionist; but before the Senate could approve Hawaiian annexation, Grover

Cleveland was elected to his second (nonconsecutive) term as president. As an anti-expansionist, Cleveland put a temporary end to the attempt to annex Hawaii. However, even though Cleveland's investigation into the events of the coup determined that indigenous Hawaiians did not want American rule, he did nothing to reverse what had already happened. Eventually, the United States officially recognized the new, American-dominated Hawaiian government, and in 1898, the United States formally annexed the islands, ending the dispute over their status and making them a US territory.

Author Biography

Queen Liliuokalani was born in 1838 and became well acquainted with American norms as a result of her interaction with influential New England missionaries in Hawaii. She also traveled widely, and was, therefore, familiar with both white worldviews and the power of white nations; thus, she knew she could not combat the United States with force. However, she was willing to do everything else in her power to keep Hawaii independent. As early as 1881, when her brother (who was the king at the time) was abroad, she closed the kingdom's ports to stop the spread of smallpox brought in by some Chinese who came to work on the plantations, and then she stood firm despite the anger of white American businessmen. When she became queen in 1891 upon her brother's death, the white growers knew that she might challenge their growing power. Her new 1893 constitution confirmed their fears. After failing to receive the support of the US government, however, she exited public life. She died in Honolulu in 1917.

HISTORICAL DOCUMENT

His Excellency BENJAMIN HARRISON,
President of the United States:

MY GREAT AND GOOD FRIEND: It is with deep regret that I address you on this occasion. Some of my subjects, aided by aliens, have renounced their loyalty and revolted against the constitutional government of my Kingdom. They have attempted to depose me and to establish a provisional government, in direct conflict with the organic law of this Kingdom. Upon receiving incontestable proof that his excellency the minister plenipotentiary of the United States, aided and abetted their unlawful movements and caused United States troops to be landed for that purpose, I submitted to force, believing that he would not have acted in that manner unless by the authority of the Government which he represents.

This action on my part was prompted by three reasons: The futility of a conflict with the United States; the desire to avoid violence, bloodshed, and the destruction of life and property, and the certainty which I feel that you and your Government will right whatever wrongs may have been inflicted upon us in the premises. In due time a statement of the true facts relating this matter will be laid before you, and I live in the hope that you will judge uprightly and justly between myself and my enemies.

This appeal is not made for myself personally, but for my people who have hitherto always enjoyed the friendship and protection of the United States. My opponents have taken the only vessel which could be obtained here for the purpose, and hearing of their intention to send a delegation of their number to present their side of this conflict before you, I requested the favor of sending by the same vessel an envoy to you, to lay before you my statement, as the facts appear to myself and my loyal subjects. This request has been refused and I now ask you that in justice to myself and to my people that no steps be taken by the Government of the United States until my cause can be heard by you.

I shall be able to dispatch an envoy about the 2nd day of February as that will be the first available opportunity hence, and he will reach you with every possible haste that there may be no delay in the settlement of this matter.

I pray you, therefore, my good friend, that you will not allow any conclusions to be reached by you until my envoy arrives. I beg to assure you of the continuance of my highest consideration.

LILIUOKALANI, R.

HONOLULU, January 18,1893.

GLOSSARY

alien: a nonresident; an outsider

plenipotentiary: a diplomatic agent authorized to fully represent a government

Document Analysis

While the letter is relatively short, many sections reference the events of the coup. The first paragraph announces the overthrow and also demonstrates Queen Liliuokalani's calculated response. It was apparent that the US minister to Hawaii had been directly involved. The queen relates that, because of his involvement, she believes the American government supported the coup: "I submitted to force, believing that he would not have acted in that manner unless by the authority of the Government which he represents," she states. Because of her shrewd understanding of international politics, she may have actually believed that President Harrison and Secretary of State James G. Blaine wanted Hawaii to be part of the United States. Indeed, historians have discovered that these two did support the coup and even gave tacit approval to its planning several months before it occurred. Furthermore, Harrison's rapid approval of an annexation treaty seemed to illustrate his support for the overthrow.

Even if the queen does not believe the US government supported the coup, she realizes that fighting the American Marines and planters would be futile and would likely have repercussions. Indeed, her first reason for not fighting back is her recognition of "the futility of a conflict with the United States." With European colonization rapidly occurring around the world at the end of the nineteenth century, partly because of the superior weaponry and military organization of Western nations, Queen Liliuokalani correctly recognizes that her chances of military success were slim.

However, she reminds the president of Hawaii's long-standing friendship with the United States, which stretched back seven decades, to the 1820s. Previous Hawaiian monarchs had utilized the growing power and influence of the United States to remain independent during European imperialist expansion throughout the Pacific, and many American missionaries and businessmen had strong ties to the islands by the 1890s. Queen Liliuokalani is not only invoking this friendship to remind the United States that Hawaii had long been a willing partner, but she is also trying to strike a middle ground between completely shedding US influence (and therefore opening up Hawaii to predation by European nations) and submitting to complete US control. As many non-Western leaders did during the late nineteenth century, the queen faced a hard choice between attempting to keep Hawaii independent, transitioning to semi-independence, or becoming a territory or colony of a Western power.

Essential Themes

The American takeover and annexation of Hawaii was part of the larger process of the growth of US power in the Pacific in the latter half of the nineteenth century. By 1898, the path to becoming a power whose influence spanned two oceans was set when the United States finally annexed Hawaii (and also took Guam and the Philippines from Spain). Historians debate, however, the extent to which the United States intentionally expanded its imperial influence. Did US leaders simply seize on opportune moments to expand US holdings, or did more extensive planning inform US geopolitical maneuvering in the Pacific during the 1800s? This issue relates to the question of whether the 1898 victory over Spain should be seen as the dividing line between anti-expansionist sentiment and the acceptance of expansion by virtually every US leader of the twentieth century.

During the nineteenth century, most US leaders did

not actively seek to expand the country's power in the Pacific, but the few who did set the course for the United States' eventual global influence. Late eighteenth-century issues—a lack of public enthusiasm for overseas expansion, a lack of experience or resources for US diplomats, and domestic issues such as the Civil War, transcontinental expansion, and the Plains Indian Wars—hampered the ambitions of those US leaders who did lobby for expansion in the Pacific. Nonetheless, President Tyler in the 1840s, Secretary of State Webster in the 1850s, Secretary of State William H. Seward in the 1860s, and Secretary of State Blaine in the 1880s and early 1890s all laid out visions for American power in the Pacific. These plans variously included American influence in Alaska (a territory that Seward successfully purchased from Russia in 1867), Hawaii, the Philippines, and China. Therefore, the takeover of Hawaii by white Americans (and Queen Liliuokalani's response to the coup), was part of the larger story of the growth of American power in the Pacific.

—*Kevin E. Grimm, PhD*

Bibliography and Additional Reading

Herring, George C. *From Colony to Superpower: U.S. Foreign Relations since 1776.* New York: Oxford UP, 2008. Print.

Merry, Sally Engle. *Colonizing Hawaii: The Cultural Power of Law.* Princeton: Princeton UP, 2000. Print.

"Hawaii's Last Queen: The Program." *American Experience.* PBS Online, n.d. Web. 28 Apr. 2014.

"Hawaii's Last Queen: Timeline." *American Experience.* PBS Online, n.d. Web. 28 Apr. 2014.

■ Report on the Battle of Santiago

Date: July 6, 1898
Author: Winfield Scott Schley
Genre: report; letter

Summary Overview

The Battle of Santiago de Cuba represents a pivotal point in US history, as the newly modernized US Navy engaged Spain, one of the world's preeminent naval powers, off the coast of Cuba. The battle itself was relatively one-sided, as American warships quickly captured or destroyed the ships of the Spanish naval squadron as they attempted to escape from Santiago Bay. The commanding officer at the battle, Commodore Winfield Scott Schley, issued a report to his superior officer, Rear Admiral William T. Sampson, summarizing the day's events.

Defining Moment

In the years prior to the outbreak of the Spanish-American War, the American public was strongly in support of the Cuban independence movement, and many Americans called for war against Spain, although President William McKinley repeatedly sought a diplomatic solution to the tensions. After riots broke out in Havana in January 1898, the US government sent an American warship, the USS *Maine*, to Havana Harbor to protect US citizens in Cuba. On February 15, 1898, the *Maine* exploded in Havana Harbor, setting off a chain of events that led to an American declaration of war against Spain in April. The Spanish Navy sent a flotilla of ships, led by Admiral Pascual Cervera y Topete, to Cuba to defend its interests in the Caribbean.

Rear Admiral William T. Sampson was the commander of the US Navy's North Atlantic Squadron and took orders to intercept Cervera's fleet. The Flying Squadron, led by Commodore Winfield Scott Schley, joined the North Atlantic Squadron in the search for Cervera's fleet. Although Schley had been slightly senior in rank before the conflict, he was placed under Sampson's command, leading to some friction between the two officers. After Cervera's fleet was spotted in Santiago Harbor in late May, Schley initially delayed following Sampson's orders to join the blockade at the harbor's entrance, which lasted more than a month. Cervera's fleet was well protected within the harbor, and he hoped to wait out the US Navy; however, American ground forces were approaching Santiago de Cuba on land, prompting Cervera to attempt an escape from the harbor.

On the morning of July 3, Sampson was called away to the mainland for a conference with Major General William Shafter of the US Army. Shortly after Sampson's flagship, the *New York*, left its position in the blockade with the USS *Ericsson*, Cervera's ships made their move to escape the harbor. At the sound of gunfire, Sampson turned his ship around to rejoin his fleet, but he did not return until after the end of the battle. As the Spanish ships emerged from the harbor, Schley quickly maneuvered to catch up with them, nearly causing a collision between his flagship, the *Brooklyn*, and the USS *Texas*. Poor-quality coal slowed the Spanish ships, and the Americans destroyed or ran aground five of Cervera's six ships, effectively destroying the Spanish Navy's Caribbean squadron. Cervera surrendered and the battle came to an end after a few hours.

Within the story of the battle is the rivalry between Schley and Sampson. The public and the press largely credited Schley with the victory, although Schley had issued no special orders during the battle and had followed Sampson's standing orders to run down the Spanish fleet. Following the battle, Schley issued a report to Sampson, offering his perspective on the battle's events, using language that seems intended to remind Sampson of his absence from the battle. Sampson later sent a report to the secretary of the Navy, John D. Long, criticizing Schley's actions. Afterward, Schley was promoted to rear admiral, but Sampson was advanced ahead of Schley on the Navy List (the official list of naval officers), generating a controversy over whether Sampson or Schley deserved credit for the victory at Santiago de Cuba.

Author Biography

Winfield Scott Schley was born on October 9, 1839, near Frederick City, Maryland. He graduated from the US Naval Academy in Annapolis in 1860 and was promoted to the rank of lieutenant just two years later. During the Civil War, Schley fought with the Union against many of his Annapolis classmates who had joined the Confederacy. After the war, he joined the faculty at the US Naval Academy.

Schley continued to gain recognition as a naval officer. In 1888, he was promoted to the rank of captain and placed in command of the cruiser *Baltimore*. In 1898, Schley was promoted to commodore and given command of the Flying Squadron, which was assigned to patrol the Atlantic coast at the outset of the Spanish-American War. Schley retired in 1901 and died on October 2, 1909.

HISTORICAL DOCUMENT

NORTH ATLANTIC FLEET, SECOND SQUADRON
U.S. FLAGSHIP BROOKLYN

Guantanamo Bay, Cuba,
July 6, 1898

SIR: I have the honor to make the following report of that part of the squadron under your command which came under my observation during the engagement with the Spanish fleet on July 3, 1898.

At 9.35 a. m. Admiral Cervera, with the *Infanta Maria Teresa, Viscaya, Oquendo, Cristobal Colon*, and two torpedo boat destroyers, came out of the harbor of Santiago de Cuba in column at distance and attempted to escape to the westward. Signal was made from the *Iowa* that the enemy was coming out, but his movement had been discovered from this ship at the same moment. This vessel was the farthest west, except the *Vixen*, in the blockading line. Signal was made to the western division, as prescribed in your general orders, and there was immediate and rapid movement inward by your squadron and a general engagement at 1,100 yards and varying to 3,000 [yards] until the *Vizcaya* was destroyed, about 10:50 a.m. The concentration of the fire upon the ships coming out was most furious and terrific, and great damage was done them.

About twenty or twenty-five minutes after the engagement began two vessels, thought to be the *Teresa* and *Oquendo*, and since verified as such, took fire from the effective shell fire of the squadron and were forced to run on the beach some 6 or 7 miles west of the harbor entrance, where they burned and blew up later. The torpedo boat destroyers were destroyed early in the action, but the smoke was so dense in the direction that I can not say to which vessel or vessels the credit belongs. This, doubtless, was better seen from your flagship.

The *Vizcaya* and *Colon*, perceiving the disaster to their consorts, continued at full speed to the westward to escape and were followed and engaged in a running fight with the *Brooklyn, Texas, Iowa,* and *Oregon* until 10.50, when the *Vizcaya* took fire from our shells. She put her helm to port and, with a heavy list to port, stood in shore and ran aground at Asseraderos, about 21 miles west of Santiago, on fire fore and aft, and where she blew up during the night. Observing that she had struck her colors, and that several vessels were nearing her to capture and save her crew, signal was made to cease firing. The *Oregon* having proved vastly faster than the other battleships, she and the *Brooklyn*, together with the *Texas* and another vessel which proved to be your flagship, continued westward in pursuit of the *Colon*, which had run close in shore, evidently seeking some good spot to beach if she should fail to elude her pursuers.

This pursuit continued with increasing speed in the *Brooklyn, Oregon,* and other ships, and soon the *Brooklyn* and *Oregon* were within long range of the *Colon,* when the *Oregon* opened fire with her 13-inch guns, landing a shell close to the *Colon*. A moment afterwards the *Brooklyn* opened fire with her 8-inch guns, landing a shell just ahead of her. Several other shells were fired at the *Colon*, now in range of the *Brooklyn's* and *Oregon's* guns. Her commander, seeing all chances of escape cut off, and destruction awaiting his ship, fired a lee gun and struck her flag at 1.15 p. m., and ran ashore at a point some 50 miles west of Santiago Harbor. Your flagship was coming up rapidly at the time, as was also the *Texas* and *Vixen*. A little later, after your arrival, the *Cristobal Colon*, which had struck to the *Brooklyn* and the *Oregon,* was turned over to you as one of the trophies of this great victory of the squadron under your command.

During my official visit, a little later, Commander Eaton, of the *Resolute*, appeared and reported to you the presence of a Spanish battle ship near Altares. Your orders to me were to take the *Oregon* and go eastward to meet her, and this was done by the *Brooklyn*, with the result that the vessel reported as an enemy was discovered to be the Austrian cruiser *Infanta Maria Teresa*, seeking the commander in chief.

I would mention, for your consideration, that the *Brooklyn* occupied the most westward blockading position, with the *Vixen*, and, being more directly in the route taken by the Spanish squadron, was exposed for some minutes, possible ten to the gun fire of three of the Spanish ships and the west battery, as a range of 1,500 yards from the ships and about 3,000 yards from the batteries, but the vessels of the entire squadron, closing in rapidly, soon diverted this fire and did magnificent work at close range. I have never before witnessed such deadly and fatally accurate shooting as was done by the ships of your command as they closed in on the Spanish squadron, and I deem it a high privilege to commend to you, for, such action as you may deem proper, the gallantry and dashing courage, the prompt decision and the skillful handling of their respective vessels of Captain Philip, Captain Evans, Captain Clark, and especially of my chief of staff, Captain Cook, who was directly under my personal observation and whose coolness, promptness, and courage were of the highest order. The dense smoke of the combat shut out from my view the *Indiana* and the *Gloucester*, but, as these vessels were closer to your flagship, no doubt their part in the conflict was under your immediate observation.

Lieutenant Sharp, commanding the *Vixen*, acted with conspicuous courage; although unable to engage the heavier ships of the enemy with his light guns, nevertheless was close in to the battle line under heavy fire, and many of the enemy's shot passed beyond his vessel.

I beg to invite special attention to the conduct of my flag lieutenant James H. Sears, and Ensign Edward McCauley, Jr., aide, who were constantly at my side during the engagement and who exposed themselves fearlessly in discharging their duties; and also to the splendid of my secretary, Lieut. B. W. Wells, Jr., who commanded and directed the fighting of the fourth division with splendid effect.

I would commend the highly meritorious conduct and courage in the engagement of Lieut. Commander N. E. Mason, the executive officer whose presence everywhere over the ship during its continuance did much to secure the good result of this ship's part in the victory.

The navigator, Lieut. A. C. Hodgson, and the division officers, Lieut. T. D. Griffin, Lieut. W. R. Rush, Lieut. Edward Simpson, Lieut. J. G. Doyle, Ensign Charles Webster, and. the junior divisional officers were most steady and conspicuous in every detail of duty contributing to the accurate firing of this ship in her part of the great victory of your forces.

The officers of the Medical, Pay, Engineer, and Marine Corps responded to every demand of the occasion, and were fearless in exposing themselves. The warrant officers, Boatswain William L. Hill, Carpenter G. H. Warford, and Gunner F. T. Applegate, were everywhere exposed, in watching for damage, reports of which were promptly conveyed to me.

I have never in my life served with a braver, better, or worthier crew than that of the *Brooklyn*. During the combat, lasting from 9.35 until 1.15 p. m., much of the time under fire, they never flagged for a moment, and were apparently undisturbed by the storm of projectiles passing ahead, astern, and over the ship.

The result of the engagement was the destruction of the Spanish squadron and the capture of the admiral and some thirteen to fifteen hundred prisoners, with the loss of several hundred killed, estimated by Admiral Cerveraat 600 men.

The casualties on board this ship were: G. H. Ellis,

chief yeoman, killed; J. Burns, fireman, first class, severely wounded. The marks and scars show that the ship was struck about twenty-five times, and she bears in all forty-one scars as the result of her participation in the great victory of your force on July 3, 1898. The speed-cone halyards were shot away, and nearly all the signal halyards. The ensign at the main was so shattered that in hauling it down at the close of the action it fell in pieces.

I congratulate you most sincerely upon this great victory to the squadron under your command, and I am glad that I had an opportunity to contribute in the least to a victory that seems big enough for all of us.

I have the honor to transmit herewith the report of the commanding officer, and a drawing, in profile, of the ship, showing the location of hits and scars, also a memorandum of the ammunition expended and the amount to fill her allowance.

Since reaching this place and holding conversation with several of the captains, viz, Captain Eulate, of the *Vizcaya*, and the second in command of the *Colon*, Commander Contreras, I have learned that the Spanish admirals scheme was to concentrate all fire for awhile on the *Brooklyn* and the *Vizcaya* to ram her, in hopes that if they could destroy her the chance of escape would be increased, as it was supposed she was the swiftest ship of your squadron. This explains the heavy fire mentioned

and the *Vizcaya's* action in the earlier moments of the engagement. The execution of this purpose was promptly defeated, by the fact that all the ships of the squadron advanced into close range and opened an irresistibly furious and terrific fire upon the enemy's squadron as it was coming out of the harbor.

I am glad to say that the injury supposed to be below the waterline was due to a water valve being opened from some unknown cause and flooding the compartment. The injury to the belt is found to be only slight and the leak small.

I beg to inclose a list of the officers and crew who participated in the combat of July 3, 1898.

I cannot close this report without mentioning in high terms of praise the splendid conduct and support of Capt. C. E. Clark, of the *Oregon*. Her speed was wonderful and her accurate fire splendidly destructive.

Very respectfully,

W. S. SCHLEY,
Commodore, United States Navy,
Commanding Second Squadron, North Atlantic Fleet.
THE COMMANDER IN CHIEF U.S. NAVAL FORCE
North Atlantic Station.

Document Analysis

The Battle of Santiago de Cuba was the largest naval engagement in the Spanish-American War. When Rear Admiral Sampson, the commander of the American blockade, was called back to the mainland, no particular officer was named to take his place. Commodore Schley, however, was the ranking officer in Sampson's absence and was responsible for directing the actions of two of the key ships involved in the battle, the *Texas* and the *Brooklyn*. After the engagement, Schley issued his report in the form of a letter to Sampson.

Sampson's absence is a recurring theme in Schley's report. For example, Schley begins his letter by writing, "I have the honor to make the following report of that part of the squadron under your command which came under my observation during the engagement with the Spanish fleet on July 3, 1898." Schley recounts the action of the battle, describing how Sampson's ships

fired upon the two Spanish torpedo boat destroyers, destroying both. Schley admits that he has been unable to determine which vessel deserves credit for disabling the destroyers due to thick smoke of the battle, adding, "This, doubtless, was better seen from your flagship."

Following his comments on the battle, Schley next turns his attention to the valor of the ships' crews. Sampson, who was the commander-in-chief of all ships involved (including Schley's), normally would have been the officer to hand out such accolades on sight. With Sampson absent from the battle itself, Schley took it upon himself to commend the noteworthy performances of the American forces (including those aboard Sampson's individual fleet).

Finally, while turning to damage reports and information gleaned from captured Spanish officers, Schley again highlights his role in the victory, writing, "I congratulate you most sincerely upon this great victory to the squadron under your command, and I am glad that I had an opportunity to contribute in the least to a victory that seems big enough for all of us." He comments on the Spanish plan to shower the *Brooklyn* with fire and then to ram it with the *Vizcaya*. This claim seems to validate Schley's assertion that he made the unusual move of turning away when the other US ships were turning toward the fleeing Spanish fleet; a few days earlier, Schley had told his commanding officer that he disobeyed orders to turn with the other US ships because he believed the *Brooklyn* was being directly targeted for ramming by *Vizcaya*. At the time, naval commanders often made adjustments on the open sea if conditions suddenly arose that required defying orders; however, by disobeying Sampson's general orders, Schley had seemingly endangered another US ship. In his report, Schley suggests that his on-site decision was warranted and ultimately correct.

Essential Themes

The controversy over whether Schley or Sampson deserved credit for the victory at Santiago de Cuba continued for many years, prompting the secretary of the Navy to issue an order forbidding all naval officers on active duty from discussing the controversy in 1899 and leading to a court of inquiry into Schley's actions before and during the battle in 1901. According to accounts, Schley took umbrage that Sampson was his superior officer at the Battle of Santiago de Cuba, despite his absence from the battle and his slightly junior rank.

Prior to the battle, Schley and Sampson had already had some friction, as Schley insisted upon looking for Admiral Cereva in Cienfuego, staying there even after he was ordered by Sampson to come to Santiago. Although Schley's report on the subsequent Battle of Santiago de Cuba credits Sampson with the victory, it nevertheless reflects Schley's apparent disapproval of being commanded by Sampson by repeatedly under-scoring Sampson's absence during the battle itself. In 1901, a court of inquiry mildly censored Schley for failing to follow Sampson's orders to proceed to Santiago with due dispatch and for nearly causing a collision between his flagship and the *Texas*; however, Admiral George Dewey, the president of the court, issued a dissenting opinion commending Schley's actions during the battle and crediting him with the victory.

Schley's report provides a detailed eyewitness account of the Battle of Santiago de Cuba, which was critical in bringing an end to the Spanish Navy's dominance of the Caribbean, and offers insight into the ongoing rivalry between Schley and Sampson. The Sampson-Schley controversy created a minor schism within the US Navy, as officers sided with either man, and it damaged the reputations of both men, as well as of the Navy itself.

—*Michael P. Auerbach, MA*

Bibliography and Additional Reading

Ashbury, John W. *Frederick County Characters: Innovators, Pioneers and Patriots of Western Maryland.* Gloucestershire: History, 2013. Print.

Graham, George Edward. *Schley and Santiago.* Ann Arbor: U of Michigan, 1902. Print.

Halstead, Murat. *The Story of the Philippines and Our New Possessions: Including the Ladrones, Hawaii, Cuba and Porto Rico the Eldorado of the Orient.* 1898. Alexandria: Library of Alexandria, 2006. Print.

Hendrickson, Kenneth E. *The Spanish-American War.* Westport: Greenwood, 2003. Print.

Howarth, Stephen. *To Shining Sea: A History of the United States Navy, 1775–1998.* Norman: U of Oklahoma P, 1999. Print.

Parker, James. *Rear-Admirals Schley, Sampson and Cervera: A Review of the Naval Campaign of 1898.* New York: Neale, 1910. Print.

■ Platform of the American Anti-Imperialist League

Date: 1899
Author: American Anti-Imperialist League
Genre: charter; political tract

Summary Overview

In 1899, after the United States gained possession of Cuba during the Spanish-American War and moved toward occupation of the Philippines, the American Anti-Imperialist League took shape at a conference in Boston. In its charter, the group called the occupations counter to the American notions of liberty. The party argued that the American government, supposedly born of democratic ideals, was subjugating the peoples of these two nations. The document further encouraged the American people not to blindly support their government in this campaign and instead work to defeat any political candidate or party that advocated for what the league called "forcible subjugation" of other nations and peoples.

Defining Moment

Through the sixteenth and seventeenth centuries, Spain possessed one of the world's largest empires. The reach of the Spanish crown extended as far east as the Philippines and as far west as the Pacific coast of North America and South America. However, by the late nineteenth century, Spain's empire had diminished significantly. Most of the Latin American colonies, for example, had freed themselves from Spanish rule. The once-vaunted Spanish Navy simply could not maintain control over nations that lay across the vast Atlantic Ocean.

Such was the case with Cuba, where a violent uprising, beginning in 1895, threatened not only the Spanish occupying forces but also US interests. Many American citizens lived and many American businesses operated in Cuba by the late 1890s, and the Spanish colony's instability placed them at risk. On February 15, 1898, the US battleship *Maine* steamed into Havana Harbor both as a friendly visit to the Spanish government and to evacuate Americans from the city if the conflict escalated. That evening, the *Maine* exploded, killing 260 of the ship's 374 officers and crew and sending the battleship to the floor of the harbor.

For nearly two decades, Americans had sympathized with the Cuban people in their struggle for independence from what many considered an authoritarian Spanish regime. After years of calls for intervention on behalf of the Cubans, the American government had an excuse to take action against Spain. As calls of "Remember the *Maine*!" inspired the country, the increasingly powerful American military went to war in Cuba. The Spanish-American War was brief, lasting less than a year. The first battle between the two foes occurred in Manila Bay in the Philippines, with the US Navy emerging victorious. A month later, American naval ships earned a lopsided victory at the Battle of Santiago, essentially breaking the back of the Spanish Navy in Cuba.

With Spain defeated in Cuba, attention turned to the Philippines, one of Spain's other major holdings. After the American victory over the Spanish, Filipinos were free from Spain, but the United States then occupied their country, which was claimed as a US territory. Filipino revolutionaries clashed with American forces in an effort to establish the Philippines as an independent nation. Unlike the Cuba campaign, this conflict was brutal at times—some viewed the American occupation as more heavy-handed and bloody than Spanish rule.

As the Philippine-American War (1899–1902) continued, Americans remained largely supportive of their government's efforts. However, in 1898, a group of prominent Americans convened in Boston to express their concerns over perceived American imperialism in a Pacific nation, particularly as the violence and bloodshed in the Philippines continued. In 1899, the group known as the American Anti-Imperialist League—which included former US president Grover Cleveland, author Mark Twain, and steel magnate Andrew Carnegie—officially formed as a political party and interest group. The league drafted its platform, seeking to halt the annexation of the Philippines to the United States.

HISTORICAL DOCUMENT

We hold that the policy known as imperialism is hostile to liberty and tends toward militarism, an evil from which it has been our glory to be free. We regret that it has become necessary in the land of Washington and Lincoln to reaffirm that all men, of whatever race or color, are entitled to life, liberty and the pursuit of happiness. We maintain that governments derive their just powers from the consent of the governed. We insist that the subjugation of any people is "criminal aggression" and open disloyalty to the distinctive principles of our Government.

We earnestly condemn the policy of the present National Administration in the Philippines. It seeks to extinguish the spirit of 1776 in those islands. We deplore the sacrifice of our soldiers and sailors, whose bravery deserves admiration even in an unjust war. We denounce the slaughter of the Filipinos as a needless horror. We protest against the extension of American sovereignty by Spanish methods.

We demand the immediate cessation of the war against liberty, begun by Spain and continued by us. We urge that Congress be promptly convened to announce to the Filipinos our purpose to concede to them the independence for which they have so long fought and which of right is theirs.

The United States have always protested against the doctrine of international law which permits the subjugation of the weak by the strong. A self-governing state cannot accept sovereignty over an unwilling people. The United States cannot act upon the ancient heresy that might makes right.

Imperialists assume that with the destruction of self-government in the Philippines by American hands, all opposition here will cease. This is a grievous error. Much as we abhor the war of "criminal aggression" in the Philippines, greatly as we regret that the blood of the Filipinos is on American hands, we more deeply resent the betrayal of American institutions at home. The real firing line is not in the suburbs of Manila. The foe is of our own household. The attempt of 1861 was to divide the country. That of 1899 is to destroy its fundamental principles and noblest ideals.

Whether the ruthless slaughter of the Filipinos shall end next month or next year is but an incident in a contest that must go on until the Declaration of Independence and the Constitution of the United States are rescued from the hands of their betrayers. Those who dispute about standards of value while the foundation of the Republic is undermined will be listened to as little as those who would wrangle about the small economies of the household while the house is on fire. The training of a great people for a century, the aspiration for liberty of a vast immigration are forces that will hurl aside those who in the delirium of conquest seek to destroy the character of our institutions.

We deny that the obligation of all citizens to support their Government in times of grave National peril applies to the present situation. If an Administration may with impunity ignore the issues upon which it was chosen, deliberately create a condition of war anywhere on the face of the globe, debauch the civil service for spoils to promote the adventure, organize a truth-¬suppressing censorship and demand of all citizens a suspension of judgment and their unanimous support while it chooses to continue the fighting, representative government itself is imperiled.

We propose to contribute to the defeat of any person or party that stands for the forcible subjugation of any people. We shall oppose for reelection all who in the White House or in Congress betray American liberty in pursuit of un-American ends. We still hope that both of our great political parties will support and defend the Declaration of Independence in the closing campaign of the century.

We hold, with Abraham Lincoln, that "no man is good enough to govern another man without that other's consent. When the white man governs himself, that is self-government, but when he governs himself and also governs another man, that is more than self-govern-ment—that is despotism." "Our reliance is in the love of liberty which God has planted in us. Our defense is in the spirit which prizes liberty as the heritage of all men in all lands. Those who deny freedom to others deserve it not for themselves, and under a just God cannot long retain it."

We cordially invite the cooperation of all men and women who remain loyal to the Declaration of Independence and the Constitution of the United States.

Document Analysis

In this political tract, the American Anti-Imperialist League reminds readers that the United States was founded on anti-imperialist ideals. The authors state that the US government was operating in direct contradiction to those ideals by engaging in the "subjugation" of the people of the Philippines. Therefore, the league condemns the actions of the United States and calls upon the American people to join it in defeating any political candidate who endorses the US effort in the Philippines.

The league argues that the founders of the United States abhorred despotism and imperialism. Expressing "regret" that it had to remind the public of this point, the league invokes such figures as George Washington and Abraham Lincoln. The latter in particular, the league states, spoke out against forcing governance upon peoples that do not consent to that governance. Lincoln had argued that those who denied freedom and liberty to others did not deserve it themselves. If the United States succeeded in its efforts to defeat the insurrection and the developing self-government in the Philippines, the league argues, the American government would be guilty of betraying its own formative principles, outlined in the Declaration of Independence and the Constitution.

Therefore, the league condemns the actions of the US government in the Philippines and calls for an immediate cessation of the violence in that nation. The authors recognize that such a condemnation will be seen by some as a refusal to show support for the government during time of "grave National peril," but the league emphasizes that citizens must not give carte blanche support to the government to manage wartime activities. In reality, it says, the government should not be allowed to create a war and intimidate, censor, or suppress the people to ensure unanimous support for war.

According to the document, the US military partici-pated in "ruthless slaughter" in the Philippines. In defining its anti-imperialist platform, the American Anti-Imperialist League strongly emphasizes this issue as it seeks support of its ideals and membership in its ranks. Because the violence in the Philippines resulted directly from American military occupation, the Philippines-American War was as destructive to the American way of life as the Civil War. The league notes that conflict threatened to tear apart the country; this war, if left unchecked, would destroy the country's fundamental principles and ideals.

Because of the undemocratic and unjust nature of the war, the league argues, it was not necessary for Americans to rally around a government that had strayed from its founding principles. In fact, the document calls upon Americans to vote against political candidates who vote or act in support of not only the ongoing campaign in the Philippines, but also any effort to satisfy "un-American ends."

Essential Themes

The party platform of the American Anti-Imperialist League served three essential purposes. First, it directly condemned the war in the Philippines, citing its brutality and antidemocratic goals. Second, it challenged Americans to rethink blind support of the government's efforts, especially when those efforts ran counter to the nation's fundamental principles. Third, the league wanted to use this document to gain supporters and even recruit members from the other two major parties.

The document argues that the government was not being completely honest about the Philippine-American War. Americans had heard of the violence, but had been told that it was the insurrectionists who had caused the brutality. The league openly disagreed with this position, claiming that the occupying American military had engaged in despotic behavior with regard to the Filipinos. Americans at home were also to blame for allowing themselves to believe that, with the Spanish removed from the Philippines, the US had a moral obligation to annex and colonize that nation.

Thus, the American Anti-Imperialist League challenged Americans not to blindly accept the government's word on the Philippines war and to defy nondemocratic and imperialistic behavior. Through its platform, therefore, the group sought to gain more supporters, using the war as a rallying cry to generate the public to speak out against any situation in which the US government denied a population liberty and self-governance. The group represented an important, although ultimately minority voice, in American politics around the turn of the century, eventually fading into obscurity before disbanding in 1920.

—*Michael P. Auerbach, MA*

Bibliography and Additional Reading

Churchill, Bernardita Reyes. "The Philippine-American War (1899–1902)." *NCCA*. Philippines National Commission for Culture and the Arts, 2011. Web. 18 Apr. 2014.

Dolan, Edward F. *The Spanish-American War*. Minneapolis: Twenty-First Century, 2001. Print.

Hernandez, Roger E. *The Spanish-American War*. New York: Marshall Cavendish, 2009. Print.

Ignacio, Abe, et al. *The Forbidden Book: The Philippine-American War in Cartoons*. San Francisco: T'Boli, 2004. Print.

Seymour, Richard. *American Insurgents: A Brief History of American Anti-Imperialism*. Chicago: Haymarket, 2012. Print.

■ "Subjugation of the Philippines Iniquitous"

Date: May 1902
Author: George Frisbie Hoar
Genre: speech

Summary Overview

In the aftermath of the Spanish-American War, the United States acquired control over the former Spanish colony of the Philippine Islands. Massachusetts Senator George Frisbie Hoar's speech in the Senate is an attack on the United States' policy of annexing the Philippines rather than granting the country independence, like it did another former Spanish colony, Cuba. Making the Philippines an American colony had led to a war with Philippine nationalists, which Hoar denounces as cruel and inconsistent with both previous American policy and American ideals dating back to the American Revolution. He contrasts the unsuccessful Philippine policy with the successful policy of recognizing Cuba's independence. The reasons he gives for his position are both ideological and practical, pointing out the enormous cost in lives and money of trying to take over the Philippines and the uncharacteristic role of the United States, champion of liberty, waging war to subdue a people fighting for independence.

Defining Moment

The American victory over Spain in the Spanish-American War of 1898 had left the United States in control of several former Spanish colonies. Cuba, Spain's cruel treatment of which was the alleged cause of the war, was allowed its independence, although, in practice, the United States continued to dominate it in many ways until Fidel Castro's Cuban Revolution of the 1950s. Puerto Rico and the Philippines, however, became American territories. The Filipinos resisted under the leadership of Emilio Aguinaldo, a former leader of the Philippine resistance to the Spanish. The United States fought a short, but bloody and controversial, war to put down Filipino resistance. The Philippine-American War of 1899 to 1902 was brutal, and American soldiers committed atrocities. The war was longer and much more costly than the preceding Spanish-American War.

The late nineteenth century was the age of high imperialism, when much of the globe, including nearly the entire continent of Africa, was divided between European powers, with America and Japan joining in by the end of the century. Colonization of the Philippines was extremely controversial in the United States. Many viewed imperialism as a betrayal of American values, although others argued that America's destiny, like that of the major European powers, was as an imperial power. (The United States had already been established as an imperial power in the Pacific with the controversial annexation of the Hawaiian Islands in 1898, shortly before the outbreak of the Spanish-American War.) If the Philippines were not annexed, supporters contended, they might fall into the hands of a European power or even Japan. Many leaders of the Republican Party, including younger politicians such as Vice President Theodore Roosevelt and Indiana Senator Albert Beveridge, supported annexation of the islands. Some imperialists argued that the Filipinos, like other peoples of color, were incapable of self-government, and their best hope was benevolent American rule. This position was most memorably summed up in "The White Man's Burden," a poem by English imperialist Rudyard Kipling first published in 1899. In it, he seeks to persuade white Americans to take up rule over the Philippines by appealing to the idea that civilizing "sullen peoples, half-devil and half-child" was an American responsibility.

Anti-imperialism brought together a broad coalition of Americans, including Republicans, like Hoar; conservative Democrats, like former president Grover Cleveland; and Progressive Democrats, like William Jennings Bryan; along with African American leaders, like W. E. B. Du Bois; and America's leading writer, Mark Twain. Anti-imperialists like Hoar wanted to differentiate the United States from the greedy imperial powers of Europe. South Africa's contemporaneous Boer War, in which Dutch-descended Afrikaner farmers, or Boers, fought the forces of Great Britain, met with considerable popular sympathy for the Afrikaners in the United States.

Author Biography
George Frisbie Hoar (1826–1904) was a descendant of Roger Sherman, a signer of the Declaration of Independence, and a member of New England's social and political elite. He entered politics as an antislavery Republican and was elected to the House of Representa-

tives from Massachusetts in 1868. Integrity in government was one of his principal concerns, and although he believed the Republicans to be the party of honesty in government, as opposed to the corrupt Democrats, he distanced himself from the scandals of the administration of Republican president Ulysses S. Grant. He was elected a senator from Massachusetts in 1877. As a senator, Hoar supported much of the Progressive agenda, including women's suffrage and civil service and antitrust reform, but opposed the popular election of US senators, which he believed would lead to corruption. Hoar took a leading role in opposing the American annexation of Puerto Rico and the Philippines following the Spanish-American War.

HISTORICAL DOCUMENT

We have to deal with a territory ten thousand miles away, twelve hundred miles in extent, containing ten million people. A majority of the Senate think that people are under the American flag and lawfully subject to our authority. We are not at war with them or with anybody. The country is in a condition of profound peace as well as of unexampled prosperity. The world is in a profound peace, except in one quarter, in South Africa, where a handful of republicans are fighting for their independence, and have been doing better fighting than has been done on the face of the earth since Thermopylæ, or certainly since Bannockburn.

You are fighting for sovereignty. You are fighting for the principle of eternal dominion over that people, and that is the only question in issue in the conflict. We said in the case of Cuba that she had a right to be free and independent. We affirmed in the Teller resolution, I think without a negative voice, that we would not invade that right and would not meddle with her territory or anything that belonged to her. That declaration was a declaration of peace as well as of righteousness; and we made the treaty, so far as concerned Cuba, and conducted the war and have conducted ourselves ever since on that theory—that we had no right to interfere with her independence; that we had no right to her territory or to anything that was Cuba's. So we only demanded in the treaty that Spain should hereafter let her alone.

If you had done to Cuba as you have done to the Philippine Islands, who had exactly the same right, you would be at this moment, in Cuba, just where Spain was when she excited the indignation of the civilized world and we compelled her to let go. And if you had done in the Philippines as you did in Cuba, you would be to-day or would soon be in those islands as you are in Cuba.

But you made a totally different declaration about the Philippine Islands. You undertook in the treaty to acquire sovereignty over her for yourself, which that people denied. You declared not only in the treaty, but in many public utterances in this Chamber and elsewhere, that you had a right to buy sovereignty with money, or to treat it as the spoils of war or the booty of battle. The moment you made that declaration the Filipino people gave you notice that they treated it as a declaration of war. So your generals reported, and so Aguinaldo expressly declared. In stating this account of profit and loss I hardly know which to take up first, principles and honor, or material interests—I should have known very well which to have taken up first down to three years ago—what you call the sentimental, the ideal, the historical on the right side of the column; the cost or the profit in honor or shame and in character and in principle and moral influence, in true national glory; or the practical side, the cost in money and gain, in life and health, in wasted labor, in diminished national strength, or in prospects of trade and money getting.

What has been the practical statesmanship which comes from your ideals and your sentimentalities. You have wasted nearly six hundred millions of treasure. You have sacrificed nearly ten thousand American lives—the flower of our youth. You have devastated provinces. You have slain uncounted thousands of the people you desire to benefit. You have established reconcentration camps. Your generals are coming home from their harvest bringing sheaves with them, in the shape of other thousands of sick and wounded and insane to drag out miserable lives, wrecked in body and mind. You make the American flag in the eyes of a numerous people the emblem of sacrilege in Christian churches, and of the burning of human dwellings, and of the horror of the water torture. Your practical statesmanship which disdains to take George Washington and Abraham Lincoln or the soldiers of the Revolution or of the Civil War as models, has looked in some cases to Spain for your example. I believe—nay, I know—that in general our officers and soldiers are humane. But in some cases they have carried on your warfare with a mixture of American ingenuity and Castilian cruelty.

Your practical statesmanship has succeeded in converting a people who three years ago were ready to kiss the hem of the garment of the American and to welcome him as a liberator, who thronged after your men when they landed on those islands with benediction and gratitude, into sullen and irreconcilable enemies, possessed of a hatred which centuries can not eradicate.

The practical statesmanship of the Declaration of Independence and the Golden Rule would have cost nothing but a few kind words. They would have bought for you the great title of liberator and benefactor, which your fathers won for your country in the South American Republics and in Japan, and which you have won in Cuba. They would have bought for you undying gratitude of a great and free people and the undying glory which belongs to the name of liberator. That people would have felt for you as Japan felt for you when she declared last summer that she owed everything to the United States of America.

What have your ideals cost you, and what have they bought for you?

1. For the Philippine Islands you have had to repeal the Declaration of Independence.

For Cuba you had to reaffirm it and give it new luster.

2. For the Philippine Islands you have had to convert the Monroe Doctrine into a doctrine of mere selfishness.

For Cuba you have acted on it and vindicated it.

3. In Cuba you have got the eternal gratitude of a free people.

In the Philippine Islands you have got the hatred and sullen submission of a subjugated people.

4. From Cuba you have brought home nothing but glor.

From the Philippines you have brought home nothing of glory.

5. In Cuba no man thinks of counting the cost. The few soldiers who came home from Cuba wounded or sick carry about their wounds and their pale faces as if they were medals of honor. What soldier glories in a wound or an empty sleeve which he got in the Philippines?

6. The conflict in the Philippines has cost you six hundred million dollars, thousands of American soldiers—the flower of your youth—the health and sanity of thousands more, and hundreds of thousands of Filipinos slain.

Another price we have paid as the result of your practical statesmanship. We have sold out the right, the old American right, to speak out the sympathy which is in our hearts for people who are desolate and oppressed everywhere on the face of the earth.

This war, if you call it war, has gone on for three years. It will go on in some form for three hundred years, unless this policy be abandoned. You will undoubtedly have times of peace and quiet, or pretended submission. You will buy men with titles, or office, or salaries. You will intimidate cowards. You will get pretended and fawning submission. The land will smile and seem at peace. But the volcano will be there. The lava will break out again. You can never settle this thing until you settle it right.

Gentlemen tell us that the Filipinos are savages, that they have inflicted torture, that they have dishonored our dead and outraged the living. That very likely may be true. Spain said the same thing of the Cubans. We have made the same charges against our own countrymen in the disturbed days after the war. The reports of committees and the evidence in the documents in our library are full of them. But who ever heard before of an American gentleman, or an American, who took as a rule for his own conduct the conduct of his antagonist, or who claimed that the Republic should act as savages because she had savages to deal with? I had supposed, Mr. President, that the question, whether a gentleman shall lie or murder or torture, depended on his sense of his own character, and not on his opinion of his victim. Of all the miserable sophistical shifts which have attended this wretched business from the beginning, there is none more miserable than this.

Mr. President, this is the eternal law of human nature. You may struggle against it, you may try to escape it, you may persuade yourself that your intentions are benevolent, that your yoke will be easy and your burden will be light, but it will assert itself again. Government without the consent of the government—an authority which heaven never gave—can only be supported by means which heaven never can sanction.

The American people have got this one question to answer. They may answer it now; they can take ten years, or twenty years, or a generation, or a century to think of it. But it will not down. They must answer it in the end: Can you lawfully buy with money, or get by brute force of arms, the right to hold in subjugation an unwilling people, and to impose on them such constitution as you, and not they, think best for them.

We have answered this question a good many times in the past. The fathers answered it in 1776, and founded the Republic upon their answer, which has been the corner-stone. John Quincy Adams and James Monroe answered it again in the Monroe doctrine, which John Quincy Adams declared was only the doctrine of the consent of the governed. The Republican party answered it when it took possession of the force of government at the beginning of the most brilliant period in all legislative history. Abraham Lincoln answered it when, on that fatal journey to Washington in 1861, he announced that the doctrine of his political creed, and declared, with prophetic vision, that he was ready to be assassinated for it if need be. You answered it again yourselves when you said that Cuba, who had no more title than the people of the Philippine Islands had to their independence, of right ought to be free and independent.

The question will be answered again hereafter. It will be answered soberly and deliberately and quietly as the American people are wont to answer great questions of duty. It will be answered, not in any turbulent assembly, amid shouting and clapping of hands and stamping of feet, where men do their thinking with their heels and not with their brains. It will be answered in the churches and in the schools and in the colleges; and it will be answered in fifteen million American homes; and it will be answered as it has always been answered. It will be answered right.

Document Analysis

"The Subjugation of the Philippines Iniquitous" is a sweeping denunciation of the American war against the Philippine insurgents, attacking both its purposes and conduct. Hoar also discusses the expense of the war both in money and in the lives of American soldiers. He mistrusts the imperialist ideology that supported making the islands an American colony. Hoar's general opposition to European imperialism can be seen in his opening praise of the South Africans fighting the British, although the fighters themselves were members of the white minority in the region rather than the black majority.

Hoar describes the annexation of the Philippines as an exception in an American history he portrays in glowing terms. The tradition of the American Revolution, the Monroe Doctrine, the Civil War (at least the Union side), the American role in the opening of Japan, and the Spanish-American War itself as it pertained to Cuba, was one of nurturing and protecting liberty. Hoar draws parallels between the behavior of the United States in the Philippines and that of Spain in colonial Cuba, arguing that the United States was descending to the level of Spain, a common theme among American anti-imperialists. ("Reconcentration camps," later to be known as "concentration camps," were particularly associated with the Spanish fight against the Cuban independence movement.) He discusses, in general terms, the atrocities committed by the American forces in the Philippines, including the infamous "water torture." This was a particularly powerful argument, given the wide publicity the American press had given to Spanish atrocities against the Cuban people in the period preceding the Spanish-American War. Hoar has a difficult needle to thread here, attacking the atrocities committed by Americans while portraying himself as on the side of the American troops in the Philippines. Although he generally sympathizes with the Filipinos as a people fighting for their freedom, he does not minimize the atrocities with which they were charged, only denying that these provide any justification for reciprocal atrocities committed by Americans.

Hoar contrasts the success of the United States' post–Spanish-American War policy in Cuba, which allowed the island independence, with its failure in the Philippines. The Cuban policy had not involved the United States in a protracted war, and as a war of liberation, it was something that all Americans, particularly veterans of the conflict, could be proud of. The war against the Philippine rebels, by contrast, brought only shame.

Essential Themes

Hoar's call for an independent Philippines was in vain. The rebellion was to be crushed militarily. The official end of the war in July 1902 occurred shortly after Hoar's speech, although scattered Filipino groups continued fighting. The last holdouts, the Muslim Moro people of the southern Philippines, were not defeated until 1913. The islands remained a US colony until July 4, 1946, when the United States relinquished its sovereignty and the modern independent Philippine nation was born. However, Hoar's anti-imperialism and defense of the right of foreign peoples to govern themselves would become a much more common stance in the mid-twentieth century, in the era of decolonization after World War II. Later opponents of other American wars in the postcolonial developing world, such as the Persian Gulf, Iraq, and Afghanistan Wars, have followed Hoar's rhetoric, which attacks the atrocities committed by American troops while avoiding, as much as possible, attack of the troops and their commanders

as individuals; however, these wars, unlike the Philippine-American War, were not fought explicitly to extend American sovereignty over these foreign lands and transform them into colonies.

Hoar's treatment of the Philippine annexation as a sharp break from a generally pro-liberty American history has been questioned, however. Many modern historians, like some contemporaries of Hoar, attack the generally rosy view of American history held by Hoar and others—a viewpoint now frequently identified as American exceptionalism—and regard the conquest of the Philippines as consistent with the nineteenth-century wars against Mexico and the American Indians on the North American continent and with the annexation of Hawaii. Imperialism has also been connected with late-nineteenth-century America's increasingly aggressive stance in Latin America and its mistreatment of African Americans in the Jim Crow era. Much of the American military doctrine and methods applied to the Philippine-American War, in fact, can be traced to the earlier Indian Wars, and much of the racial imagery used to disparage Filipinos had roots in previous caricatures of American Indians, African Americans, and Latin Americans.

—*William E. Burns, PhD*

Bibliography and Additional Readings

Sibley, David J. *A War of Frontier and Empire: The Philippine-American War, 1899–1902.* New York: Hill, 2007. Print.

Welch, Richard E., Jr. *George Frisbie Hoar and the Half-Breed Republicans.* Cambridge: Harvard UP, 1971. Print.

Welch, Richard E., Jr. *Response to Imperialism: The United States and the Philippine-American War, 1899–1902.* Chapel Hill: U of North Carolina P, 1979. Print.

■ The War Prayer

Date: 1904 or 1905
Authors: Mark Twain
Genre: essay

Summary Overview

In 1904 or 1905, famed author and humorist Mark Twain penned a scathing indictment—written as a prose poem—of the Philippine American War (1899–1902). The poem is a reflection of Twain's disdain for American imperialism in the aftermath of the Spanish American War. In his comments, Twain parodies the idea of praying for a victory in battle, as such prayers are exercises in self-indulgence rather than petitions to the God of all people.

Defining Moment

By the 1890s, Samuel Clemens (known by his pen name Mark Twain) was one of America's most celebrated authors. The resident of Hartford, Connecticut, had, by that time, published *The Adventures of Tom Sawyer* (1876), *The Adventures of Huckleberry Finn* (1885), and *A Connecticut Yankee in King Arthur's Court* (1889). In 1891, Twain closed his Hartford residence and moved his family to Europe, from which he began a global tour.

In addition to being a humorist, Twain was also developing into a staunch anti-imperialist in the late 1880s. During the 1870s, he spoke out against the proposed annexation of Hawaii (it would become a US territory in 1898). Twain's views became more pronounced during his travels in Europe and elsewhere abroad. In 1891, Twain cofounded the *American Friends of Russian Freedom*, a Boston-based organization designed to generate support for the opposition movement that would culminate in the Revolution of 1905 in Russia. During the mid-1890s, he traveled to India, South Africa, Australia, and Sri Lanka, all regions of interest to the European colonial powers. In 1895, Twain—by then a resident of Great Britain—even found himself in the middle of a threatened war between the United States and Britain regarding the two countries' dispute over the Monroe Doctrine and the United States's claim to a sphere of influence over Latin America.

In 1898, war broke out between the United States and Spain. Twain was initially under the impression that the United States was attempting liberate Cuba from the oppression of Spanish imperialists and, therefore, supported the war. However, when the Spanish-American War came to a close later that year, the United States was (under the articles of the Treaty of Paris) handed control over Cuba, Puerto Rico, Guam, and the Philippines. According to his writings at the time, Twain was appalled at the transfer of power. He spoke vehemently against America's presence in the Philippines, particularly US forces' brutal efforts to "civilize" and "Christianize" the Muslim population there, as well as efforts to suppress opposition to US occupation from the Christian Filipino population. He returned to the United States in 1900, declaring himself to be an anti-imperialist. Twain later became the vice president of the Anti-Imperialist League of New York and is credited with being a major force behind that group's revitalization. The focus of Twain's anti-imperialist attention was on US occupation in the Philippines. Although the Philippine-American War ended in 1902, conflicts between US forces and the Muslim Moro people, as well as between US forces and the Pulahanes people, lasted until these groups conceded defeat in 1913.

Between 1904 and 1905, Twain penned "The War Prayer," satirizing American military efforts in the Philippines. However, the strong tone of this parody made his family discourage him from trying to publish it, though it was virtually impossible for Twain to find a willing publisher anyway. Even those companies with whom he shared a long-standing relationship, such as *Harper's Bazaar*, refused to publish it. Twain, therefore, shelved the essay, famously uttering, "None but the dead are permitted to tell the truth." He left the essay among a set of documents that were, in fact, to be published after his death.

Author Biography

Samuel Langhorne Clemens was born on November 30, 1835, in Florida, Missouri. In 1839, the Clemens family moved to Hannibal, Missouri, along the Mississippi River. While attending school, Clemens took a number of posts in journalism and typesetting. After traveling throughout the country, including time spent as a riverboat apprentice and pilot on the Mississippi River in the 1850s, Clemens settled in Virginia City, Nevada, in 1861. There, he adopted the pseudonym "Mark Twain," a riverboat term meaning "two fathoms deep." He moved to San Francisco in 1864 and continued his travels, including a trip to Europe and the Middle East in 1867.

In 1865, Twain's short story "Jim Smiley and His Jumping Frog" brought him national acclaim. After a nationwide and European tour, Twain wrote his first best-selling book, *The Innocents Abroad* (1869). In 1870, he married Olivia Langdon and settled in Hartford, Connecticut, where he wrote *The Adventures of Tom Sawyer* and *The Adventures of Huckleberry Finn*. In 1891, he and his family moved to Europe, where he continued writing and guest lecturing, before moving back to the United States in 1900. He died on April 21, 1910, at his home in Redding, Connecticut.

HISTORICAL DOCUMENT

It was a time of great and exalting excitement. The country was up in arms, the war was on, in every breast burned the holy fire of patriotism; the drums were beating, the bands playing, the toy pistols popping, the bunched firecrackers hissing and spluttering; on every hand and far down the receding and fading spread of roofs and balconies a fluttering wilderness of flags flashed in the sun; daily the young volunteers marched down the wide avenue gay and fine in their new uniforms, the proud fathers and mothers and sisters and sweethearts cheering them with voices choked with happy emotion as they swung by; nightly the packed mass meetings listened, panting, to patriot oratory which stirred the deepest deeps of their hearts, and which they interrupted at briefest intervals with cyclones of applause, the tears running down their cheeks the while; in the churches the pastors preached devotion to flag and country, and invoked the God of Battles beseeching His aid in our good cause in outpourings of fervid eloquence which moved every listener. It was indeed a glad and gracious time, and the half dozen rash spirits that ventured to disapprove of the war and cast a doubt upon its righteousness straightway got such a stern and angry warning that for their personal safety's sake they quickly shrank out of sight and offended no more in that way.

Sunday morning came—next day the battalions would leave for the front; the church was filled; the volunteers were there, their young faces alight with martial dreams—visions of the stern advance, the gathering momentum, the rushing charge, the flashing sabers, the flight of the foe, the tumult, the enveloping smoke, the fierce pursuit, the surrender! Then home from the war, bronzed heroes, welcomed, adored, submerged in golden seas of glory! With the volunteers sat their dear ones, proud, happy, and envied by the neighbors and friends who had no sons and brothers to send forth to the field of honor, there to win for the flag, or, failing, die the noblest of noble deaths. The service proceeded; a war chapter from the Old Testament was read; the first prayer was said; it was followed by an organ burst that shook the building, and with one impulse the house rose, with glowing eyes and beating hearts, and poured out that tremendous invocation

God the all-terrible! Thou who ordainest!
Thunder thy clarion and lightning thy sword!

Then came the "long" prayer. None could remember the like of it for passionate pleading and moving and beautiful language. The burden of its supplication was, that an ever-merciful and benignant Father of us all would watch over our noble young soldiers, and aid, comfort, and encourage them in their patriotic work; bless them, shield them in the day of battle and the hour of peril, bear them in His mighty hand, make them strong and confident, invincible in the bloody onset; help them to crush the foe, grant to them and to their flag and country imperishable honor and glory—

An aged stranger entered and moved with slow and noiseless step up the main aisle, his eyes fixed upon the minister, his long body clothed in a robe that reached to his feet, his head bare, his white hair descending in a frothy cataract to his shoulders, his seamy face unnaturally pale, pale even to ghastliness. With all eyes following him and wondering, he made his silent way; without pausing, he ascended to the preacher's side and stood there waiting. With shut lids the preacher, unconscious of his presence, continued with his moving prayer, and at last finished it with the words, uttered in fervent appeal, "Bless our arms, grant us the victory, O Lord our God, Father and Protector of our land and flag!"

The stranger touched his arm, motioned him to step aside—which the startled minister did—and took his place. During some moments he surveyed the spellbound audience with solemn eyes, in which burned an uncanny light; then in a deep voice he said:

"I come from the Throne—bearing a message from Almighty God!" The words smote the house with a shock; if the stranger perceived it he gave no attention. "He has heard the prayer of His servant your shepherd, and will grant it if such shall be your desire after I, His messenger, shall have explained to you its import—that is to say, its full import. For it is like unto many of the prayers of men, in that it asks for more than he who utters it is aware of—except he pause and think.

"God's servant and yours has prayed his prayer. Has he paused and taken thought? Is it one prayer? No, it is two—one uttered, the other not. Both have reached the ear of Him Who heareth all supplications, the spoken and the unspoken. Ponder this—keep it in mind. If you would beseech a blessing upon yourself, beware! lest without intent you invoke a curse upon a neighbor at the same time. If you pray for the blessing of rain upon your crop which needs it, by that act you are possibly praying for a curse upon some neighbor's crop which may not need rain and can be injured by it.

"You have heard your servant's prayer—the uttered part of it. I am commissioned of God to put into words the other part of it—that part which the pastor—and also you in your hearts—fervently prayed silently. And ignorantly and unthinkingly? God grant that it was so! You heard these words: 'Grant us the victory, O Lord our God!' That is sufficient. The *whole* of the uttered prayer is compact into those pregnant words. Elaborations were not necessary. When you have prayed for victory you have prayed for many unmentioned results which follow victory—*must* follow it, cannot help but follow it. Upon the listening spirit of God fell also the unspoken part of the prayer. He commandeth me to put it into words. Listen!

"O Lord our Father, our young patriots, idols of our hearts, go forth to battle—be Thou near them! With them—in spirit—we also go forth from the sweet peace of our beloved firesides to smite the foe. O Lord our God, help us to tear their soldiers to bloody shreds with our shells; help us to cover their smiling fields with the pale forms of their patriot dead; help us to drown the thunder of the guns with the shrieks of their wounded, writhing in pain; help us to lay waste their humble homes with a hurricane of fire; help us to wring the hearts of their unoffending widows with unavailing grief; help us to turn them out roofless with little children to wander unfriended the wastes of their desolated land in rags and hunger and thirst, sports of the sun flames of summer and the icy winds of winter, broken in spirit, worn with travail, imploring Thee for the refuge of the grave and denied it—for our sakes who adore Thee, Lord, blast their hopes, blight their lives, protract their bitter pilgrimage, make heavy their steps, water their way with their tears, stain the white snow with the blood of their wounded feet! We ask it, in the spirit of love, of Him Who is the Source of Love, and Who is the ever-faithful refuge and friend of all that are sore beset and seek His aid with humble and contrite hearts. Amen.

(*After a pause.*) "Ye have prayed it; if ye still desire it, speak! The messenger of the Most High waits!"

It was believed afterward that the man was a lunatic, because there was no sense in what he said.

GLOSSARY

benignant: benign; kind and gracious

cataract: a high waterfall

smite (smote): strike (struck), hit

Document Analysis

Mark Twain's "The War Prayer" is a harsh parody of a common occurrence. Twain's piece has two main elements: a criticism of the Philippine-American War and what he perceives as that war's imperialist underpinnings, and a commentary on the idea of praying for God's blessing in battle. Mark Twain's beliefs on this particular war were well known by the time "The War Prayer" was written. Still, the dark humor prevalent in the piece is a major reason why a work by one of America's most prominent authors could not find a publisher until well after his death.

The piece describes a time in which patriotism is running high, with every man, woman, and child celebrating their national pride as they cheer on their soldiers, who are off to war. There is among the throng a small group of opponents to the war; this party is quickly shouted down by the majority and forced to leave. The next day, the war-inspired crowd goes to church, where they intend to pray for their soldiers' success when they depart for the battlefield. When they return, the soldiers will again be celebrated as heroes.

The minister steps to the pulpit and, aided by thunderous bursts from the organ, delivers a fiery prayer to God, asking Him to bless and keep the soldiers as they enter battle. Furthermore, the minister prays that God will "grant us the victory." As he is calling out for God's help, a strange man enters the church, walks down the aisle, and approaches the pulpit. This "unnaturally pale" and cloaked man ushers aside the minister and stands before the congregation.

The man identifies himself as a messenger from God and states that God will grant the minister's prayer, as long as the congregation understands and approves its full meaning—which he suggests they do not grasp. The man then proceeds to reword the nationalistic prayer, asking God—"Who is the Source of Love"—to help tear the enemy soldiers "to bloody shreds with our shells," filling the air with "shrieks of their wounded, writhing in pain," leaving their wives and children to "wander unfriended in the wastes of their desolated land in rags and hunger and thirst." If the congregation wishes for God to hear this revised prayer, the man says, they should say so. The congregation instead dismisses the man as "a lunatic, because there was no sense in what he said."

This story underscores what Twain saw as the blindness-inducing effects of wartime patriotism. God, the universe's ultimate source of love and peace, is called upon to help one side in a war. However, wishing victory for one side is wishing catastrophe for the other, and when the realities of war—the carnage and destruction that occur during such conflicts—are described, the so-called patriots disregard them. Imperialism and war, Twain is arguing, are the stuff of humanity and not of Heaven.

Essential Themes

Mark Twain initially embraced the US effort against the Spanish in the conflict leading up to the Philippine-American War. He later regretted his outspoken patriotism when the Philippines became a bargaining chip rather than an independent nation. "The War Prayer" encapsulates Twain's reversal of opinion, suggesting that he and others were deceived when imperialism was confused with freedom fighting.

At the time Twain wrote "The War Prayer," America had already won the Spanish-American War and was reaping the fruits of that victory in the Philippines. Nationalism was high, with Americans overwhelmingly in support of the American effort in its newly acquired Pacific territory. The raucous crowd in this piece represents that fervor, impassioned by the idea that an American victory—liberating the Filipino people from their backward social and religious ways—was a cause in line with the precepts of Christianity.

Twain's essay also satirizes the notion of praying to God for success in war. The minister in this story echoes the crowd's sentiments—calling upon God to bless the country's soldiers when they engage the enemy. Those who oppose the war are presented here as a small minority whose voices are quickly silenced by the roar of the patriotic crowd. The crowd, representing the America that Twain saw in the opening years of the twentieth century, views the occupation of the Philippines as unquestionably just.

However, the prayer to God is clarified by the stranger who enters the church. He warns the congregation that it is critical to understand the nature of their prayer. War, he explains, involves death and devastation, a scene few non-soldiers would understand or appreciate. In response, the crowd dismisses God's messenger as a lunatic and his revised prayer as nothing but nonsense.

As was the case with Twain and his fellow anti-imperialists, the crowd is blinded by the idea of a just war and dismisses the voice of dissent. In his pursuit of a publisher for "The War Prayer," along with other anti-imperialist essays he penned during American occupation of the Philippines, Twain himself was silenced by the majority while America engaged in what he saw as a brutal war not for independence but for conquest.

—*Michael P. Auerbach, MA*

Bibliography and Additional Reading

Fishkin, Shelly Fisher. *A Historical Guide to Mark Twain*. New York: Oxford UP, 2002. Print.

Phipps, William E. *Mark Twain's Religion*. Macon: Mercer UP, 2003. Print.

Twain, Mark. *Following the Equator and Anti-Imperialist Essays*. Ed. Shelley Fisher Fishkin. Vol. 20. New York: Oxford UP, 1996. Print.

Twain, Mark. *Mark Twain's Weapons of Satire: Anti-Imperialist Writings on the Philippine-American War*. Ed. Jim Zwick. Syracuse: Syracuse UP, 1992. Print.

Zehr, Martin. "The Psychologies of Mark Twain." *Monitor on Psychology* 41.4 (2010): 28. Print.

■ US–Mexico Tensions

Date: March 30, 1916 through June 18, 1916
Authors: General John J. Pershing; Venustiano Carranza, President of Mexico; Secretary of War
   Newton Baker
Genre: report; letter; petition

Summary Overview

These three documents illustrate the closest the United States and Mexico came to a formal state of war in the twentieth century. Written by high-ranking government officials of the two countries, these statements record the thoughts and analyses of these individuals. Mexico had been in a state of revolution since 1910. During most of 1914, the United States had occupied Veracruz, on the east coast of Mexico, in response to the arrest of nine American sailors who were in the process of legally getting oil for their ship. In March 1916, Pancho Villa, the leader of antigovernment forces in northern Mexico, raided Columbus, New Mexico, for supplies, killing Americans in the process. This resulted in the invasion of Mexico by Pershing's forces, partially described here and in the other documents written as the incident unfolded. These documents reflect the attitudes of the two countries, the United States' view that military action was the only response, and Mexico's plea for a diplomatic solution.

Defining Moment

These contemporaneous documents are from a time of great turmoil within Mexico and uncertain relations between the United States and Mexico. Pershing's report on the one-sided encounter between American and Villa's forces demonstrated the decline Villa had been facing for months. Mexico's complaint to the United States made it clear that there was really nothing Mexico could do except protest. And Baker's mobilization of the National Guard demonstrated how small and weak the United States Army was in 1916. Although these three documents do not fully explain why war did not break out between the United States and Mexico, they do give some strong indications.

Pershing, as commander of the American forces in Mexico, gave a very optimistic account regarding his success, with the implication that it would not take long to bring the whole situation to the desired conclusion. This would be the capture, or death, of Pancho Villa. The initial encounter not only resulted in a relatively high casualty rate for Villa's forces, but it caused them to lose much of what they had gained from their New Mexican raid. With United States' forces on the north, and Carranza's allied forces on the south, the future was bleak for Villa and his small army. However, the fact that it took two weeks for the Army to catch up to this section of Villa's forces indicated the major difficulties the United States would have if it expanded its goals.

In response to the movement of 5,000 to 10,000 American soldiers into Mexico, President Carranza could only respond with a plea for cooperation between the two nations. The last time Mexico had detained any American military personnel, the United States had seized Veracruz for seven months. Carranza, the recognized president of Mexico, could not control the northern part of the country, or Villa, demonstrating that he was even more helpless against the United States. Everyone knew this, so Carranza could only appeal to President Wilson's idealism and hope that perhaps other nations would put pressure on the United States for a withdrawal.

The final section of the document illustrated why the United States could not afford a war with Mexico. The small size of the Army did not even allow General Funston, commander of the US forces on the Mexican border, enough troops to protect the United States from possible additional incursions by armed Mexican forces. National Guard forces had to be mobilized to secure the border. As will be discussed below, the need to take this action played a role in the entry of the United States into World War I.

Author Biography

John J. Pershing (1860–1948), best known as the leader of American forces in World War I, was a graduate of the United States Military Academy. He had served as an officer in the cavalry during the last engagements against Native Americans, the Spanish-American War, and the Philippine-American conflict. He was promoted to general by executive order of President Theodore Roosevelt. He led the troops sent to Mexico in 1916.

Jose Venustiano Carranza Garza (1859–1920) was a Mexican leader of the revolution from 1910, became president in 1915, and then was officially elected president in 1917. The constitution he helped create in 1917, although since amended, is the same constitution used today in Mexico. Although a reformer who helped overthrow his dictatorial predecessor, Porfirio Diaz, Carranza gained the presidency by being the least threatening of the revolutionary leaders, although not all were willing to accept him in that role.

Newton D. Baker, Jr. (1871–1937) was a lawyer and Democratic politician. An eloquent speaker, he had no military experience when he became Secretary of War. He selected Pershing as the leader of the American forces and together, during the war, they increased the Army to about eighty times its pre-war size.

HISTORICAL DOCUMENT

Official Report of the Dispersal of Villa's Forces
by General John Pershing
San Geronimo Ranch,
March 30, 1916

Dodd struck Villa's command, consisting of 500, 6 o'clock, March 29th, at Guerrero.

Villa, who is suffering from a broken leg and lame hip, was not present. Number Villa's dead known to be thirty, probably others carried away dead. Dodd captured two machine guns, large number horses, saddles, and arms. Our casualties, four enlisted men wounded, none seriously.

Attack was surprise, the Villa troops being driven in a ten-mile running fight and retreated to mountains northeast of railroad, where they separated into small bands.

Large number Carranzista prisoners, who were being held for execution, were liberated during the fight.

In order to reach Guerrero, Dodd marched fifty-five miles in seventeen hours and carried on fight for five hours.

Eliseo Hernandez, who commanded Villa's troops, was killed in fight. With Villa permanently disabled, Lopez wounded, and Hernandez dead, the blow administered is a serious one to Villa's band.

* * *

Official Letter of Complaint to the U.S. Government
President Carranza
Mexico, D.F.,
May 22, 1916

1. The Mexican Government has ... been informed that a group of American troops, crossing the international boundary, has entered Mexican territory and is at the present time near a place called El Pino, located about sixty miles south of the line.

The crossing of these troops effected again without the consent of the Mexican Government gravely endangers the harmony and good relations which should exist between the Governments of the United States and Mexico.

This Government must consider the above action as a violation of the sovereignty of Mexico, and therefore it requests in a most urgent manner that the Washington Government should consider the case carefully in order to definitely outline the policy it should follow with regard to the Mexican Nation.

In order to afford a clear understanding of the basis of the request involved in this note, it becomes necessary to carefully review the incidents which have occurred up to the present time.

2. On account of the incursion at Columbus, N. M., by a band led by Francisco Villa on the morning of March 9, 1916, the Mexican Government, sincerely deploring the occurrence, and for the purpose of affording efficacious protection to the frontier, advanced its desire that the Governments of the United States and Mexico should enter into an agreement for the pursuit of bandits.

The above proposal was made by the Government of Mexico guided by the precedent established under similar conditions obtaining in the years 1880 to 1884, and requested, in concrete, a permission for Mexican forces to cross into American territory in pursuit of bandits, under a condition of reciprocity which would permit American forces to cross into Mexican territory, if the Columbus incident should be repeated in any other point of the frontier line.

As a consequence of this proposal made in the Mexican note of March 10th the Government of the United States, through error or haste, considered that the good disposition shown by the Mexican Government was sufficient to authorize the crossing of the boundary, and to that effect, without awaiting the conclusion of a formal agreement on the matter, ordered that a column of American forces should cross into Mexican territory in pursuit of Villa and his band....

The Mexican Government firmly desires to preserve peace with the American Government, but to that effect it is indispensable that the American Government should frankly explain its true purposes toward Mexico.

The Mexican Government, therefore, formally invites the Government of the United States to cause the situation of uncertainty between the two countries to cease and to support its declarations and protests of amity with real and affective action which will convince the Mexican people of the sincerity of its purposes.

This action, in the present situation, cannot be other than the immediate withdrawal of the American troops which are now in Mexican territory.

* * *

Proclamation of June 18th, the Calling of the National Guard
Newton Baker

In view of the disturbed conditions on the Mexican border, and in order to assure complete protection for all Americans, the President has called out substantially all the State militia, and will send them to the border wherever and as fully as General Funston determines them to be needed for the purpose stated.

If all are not needed an effort will be made to relieve those on duty there from time to time so as to distribute the duty.

This call for militia is wholly unrelated to General Pershing's expedition, and contemplates no additional entry into Mexico, except as may be necessary to pursue bandits who attempt outrages on American soil.

The militia are being called out so as to leave some troops in the several States. They will be mobilized at their home stations, where necessary recruiting can be done.

GLOSSARY

Carranzista: a supporter of Venustiano Carranza in the Mexican Revolution.

Lopez: Martin "Pablo" Lopez Aguirre, one of Pancho Villa's military leaders killed by Carranza's forces.

Villa: Jose Doroteo Arango Arambula, widely known as Pancho Villa

Document Analysis

General Pershing's report on the first major encounter with Villa's forces was positive regarding the results of the battle, but did indicate the limitations for America's offensive operation. There were only two battles of this scale against Villa's forces, the second occurring just over a month later. Villa's army had consistently lost major battles against the forces of the interim Mexican president, Carranza, and Villa fared no better against Pershing. The much greater losses for his troops in this March engagement and his loss of forty-one men to none for the United States on May 5, 1916, indicated that these types of battles were hopeless for Villa. The result was that Villa's forces hid in the mountains and waited out the Americans, as they did at the conclusion of this battle. Pershing had spotter airplanes and automobiles to assist his forces. However, once the limitations of these in mountainous terrain were known by Villa, there were no encounters with Villa's forces. In the ten-month campaign, it was estimated that about 160 of Villa's men were killed by the American forces.

President Carranza's letter seeking an end to the American invasion follows the form of a plea or statement by country which has no other realistic option. In addition, although Carranza and Villa had worked together earlier in the revolution, they split when Carranza claimed the presidency, even though Villa did not want the position. Thus Carranza wanted American help against Villa, but help on his terms, not American terms. Relations between the two countries had been relatively good during the last half of the nineteenth century. During revolution, the United States basically accepted whoever was president as representing the nation. Thus, it had worked with Carranza on previous issues and, as a result, cut the aid the United States had previously given to Villa. In his objection to the United States, Carranza was very polite and noted that previously an offer had been made allowing either country's forces the right to make pursuits across the border. (The United States had not accepted this, as its leaders believed this should be allowed only in one direction, the US to Mexico.) The United States did not immediately respond to the overture, and just five weeks later American forces attacked a detachment of the Mexican Army, with high losses on each side and the Americans being repelled. Ultimately, there were negotiations and the United States withdrew its forces from Mexico in January 1917.

The short proclamation by Newton Baker, calling up the National Guard, was an indication of how small the United States Army was. With only about 27,000 soldiers in the regular Army, it was stretched thin with the deployment of several thousand men in Mexico. Baker made it clear that none of the National Guard would be sent to Mexico, and that they would be rotated on a regular basis. This was to keep up morale in the Guard units, as well as an indication of the lack of coordination between the Guard and the standing Army. He did not quite tell the truth when he stated that the "call for militia is wholly unrelated to General Pershing's expedition" because if it were not for the expedition, there would have been enough regular troops on the border to respond to any incidents.

Essential Themes

The major point of the three documents is that the United States was going to dictate the terms in its relationship with Mexico. Obviously, this created a great amount of uncertainty and tension between the two countries. The American military leadership was certain it could handle the situation, even though, as it played out, they did not achieve the goal of capturing Pancho Villa. Mexico's president, unable to control his badly divided nation, did not have any way of altering the situation forced on him by the Americans. Finally, even though the United States could exert great pressure, this step mandated the mobilization of people and resources well beyond what was normal at that time. The documents demonstrate that neither side was adequately prepared for this conflict, which many see as one reason there ultimately was a diplomatic, rather than a military solution, to the crisis.

However, the incidents discussed in these documents had a much greater effect than might, at first, seem to be the case. The First World War was raging in Europe and leaders on both sides were analyzing events in North America. The two documents from American sources (Pershing and Baker) indicated something that was a factor in the minds of German leaders. When faced with problems with Mexico, the United States did not declare war because of the known weakness of the American Army. American leaders were uncertain what might be needed militarily if America were dragged into the war in Europe. Thus, when the German leaders were discussing whether to expand their submarine warfare in early 1917, they calculated that the general weakness of the American Army, as demonstrated in Mexico, would keep it from being a factor in Europe for more than a year, if the United States did enter the war in Europe. In early 1917, the Germans decided to attack all supply ships going to Great Britain, including American vessels, believing Germany could defeat a weakened Britain before the United States could expand and strengthen its Army and get it into position to play a major part in World War I. Ultimately, then, the incursion into Mexico was a factor in America entering World War I.

—*Donald A. Watt, PhD*

Bibliography and Additional Reading

Benjamin, Thomas. *La Revolucion: Mexico's Great Revolution as Memory, Myth & History*. Austin: University of Texas Press, 2000.

Blackburn, Marc "Pancho Villa, General Pershing and the U.S. Army Truck." *The Ultimate History Project*. 2014. Web. 22 May 2014.

Eisenhower, John S.D. *Intervention: the United States and the Mexican Revolution, 1913–1917*. New York: W.W. Norton, 1993.

Hurst, James W. *Pancho Villa and Black Jack Pershing: the Punitive Expedition in Mexico*. Westport CT: Praeger, 2008.

U.S. Department of State. "Punitive Expedition in Mexico, 1916–1917." U.S. Department of State Archive. 2001–2009. Web. 22 May 2014.

MINORITIES AND MISTREATMENTS

As noted elsewhere in this volume, little of the wealth in circulation at the commanding heights of the Gilded Age trickled down to the lower echelons of society—unless one counts the fact that employment was plentiful and eagerly taken up by the masses. Labor was exploited, but businesses continued to grow, and the economy, overall, continued to surge. The picture was different, however, for marginalized groups in society. American Indians, Chinese immigrants, African Americans, and Mexican immigrants all faced additional sets of challenges beyond the purely economic.

In this section we explore some of those challenges. For American Indians, for example, the days of open warfare against whites on the frontier had started to draw to a close around the time of the Great Sioux War in the 1870s. By the 1890s Native American tribal lands were being broken up under the Dawes Act and officials were requiring Indian children to attend English-language schools—and to abandon their native tongue. We look here, then, at a document concerning Indian reform and education.

Also on the sidelines of the economic boom were the Chinese immigrants who helped to build the west-ern railroad lines and to support, in the western cities, white middle-class citizens with their services. Yet, as early as 1882, disgruntled white residents and self-serving legislative leaders rallied to enact a ban on further immigration from China. The resulting Chinese Exclusion Act, included here, remained in place for many decades and caused severe hardships among Chinese American families.

Some sought a similar ban, or at least a far more restrictive policy, with respect to Mexican immigrants, who were seen by critics as damaging white workers' prospects by accepting work at cheap rates. We include here a document reflecting such views.

Equally troubling was the treatment accorded to African American citizens. This section includes a statement by a Mississippi governor who opposes black education (and much else). This is countered by three essays by the great African American sociologist and historian W. E. B. Du Bois, laying out how the view looks from the other side, along with a trenchant piece on "What It Means to Be Colored in the Capital" by black activist and journalist Mary Church Terrell.

■ Chinese Exclusion Act

Date: May 6, 1882
Author: Forty-Seventh US Congress
Genre: law

Summary Overview

In the spring of 1882, the Forty-Seventh Congress approved and President Chester A. Arthur signed the Chinese Exclusion Act, which strictly limited the ability of Chinese citizens to immigrate to the United States for a period of ten years. This law represented the first time the United States would restrict a particular ethnic group from immigrating to American shores. It also opened the door to other, similar acts targeting other ethnic groups. The act was seemingly a confluence of two major political forces. On one side were American- and European-born laborers, who lamented the influx of Chinese laborers that began during the California Gold Rush several decades prior. On the other side were leaders who wished to halt what they believed amounted to the importation of slave labor to work in the mines and in the manufacturing sector.

Defining Moment

During the late 1840s, after gold was discovered in the western United States, laborers flocked to the region to work in the mines. Among them were the Chinese, many of whom came overseas to escape the violence, poverty, and instability of the Taiping Rebellion (1850–64). Chinese laborers, however, came in two general groups: individual immigrants and "coolies" (unskilled or semiskilled laborers brought overseas on a contract).

After the Civil War, the United States began its Reconstruction efforts. The Republican-dominated Congress, wary of creating any environment in which slavery could return, pressed for civil rights for all races. In 1870, Senator William Stewart of Nevada, for example, offered legislation that guaranteed legal rights for all immigrants, including Chinese laborers who came to the United States voluntarily. His proposal was tabled at the time, largely because Republicans wavered on whether to regulate both importation and voluntary immigration. Ironically, wartime abolitionists were also divided on this issue, with some active opponents of slavery openly referring to the Chinese as "barbarians." Meanwhile, Chinese immigration and importation continued to increase in the western states. By 1870, even as the Gold Rush came to an end, Chinese workers comprised about a quarter of California's unskilled labor force, engendering animosity among the region's other laborers.

In 1870, the issue of Chinese importation and immigration reached the East Coast, where most of the nation's population (and political power) was based. In North Adams, Massachusetts, seventy-five Chinese laborers were brought in to break a strike at a large factory. The ensuing union protests against Chinese importation, though not immigration, were repeated across several eastern cities. The spotlight cast on the Chinese in the East only helped fan the flames of conflict in the West, where anti-Chinese violence and rhetoric surged as white laborers attacked Chinese workers. One of the chief voices against Chinese workers was labor leader Denis Kearney, himself an Irish immigrant, who raised the cry, "The Chinese must go!"

Kearney's Workingmen's Party of California began the push to ban Chinese labor in 1878, arguing that Chinese labor (which was cheaper than white labor) was forcing down wages in the country. At the same time, the "coolie trade" also remained under scrutiny, after the US consul general to Hong Kong, David Bailey, issued a report that claimed that coolies were frequently tricked or coerced into signing contracts to work in the United States for low wages and in inhumane conditions.

By 1880, anti-Chinese rhetoric had entered the national stage, as aspiring politicians sparred with one another in pursuit of support from the increasingly influential western states. That year, American diplomats successfully renegotiated a long-standing treaty with China regulating Chinese immigration to the United States. The Angell Treaty, as it was known, opened the door for Congress to pass a ten-year moratorium on Chinese laborers. The Chinese Exclusion Act, as the law was known, extended far beyond the decade, remaining in place until 1943.

HISTORICAL DOCUMENT

An Act to execute certain treaty stipulations relating to Chinese.

Whereas in the opinion of the Government of the United States the coming of Chinese laborers to this country endangers the good order of certain localities within the territory thereof: Therefore,

Be it enacted by the Senate and House of Representatives of the United States of America in Congress assembled, That from and after the expiration of ninety days next after the passage of this act, and until the expiration of ten years next after the passage of this act, the coming of Chinese laborers to the United States be, and the same is hereby, suspended; and during such suspension it shall not be lawful for any Chinese laborer to come, or having so come after the expiration of said ninety days to remain within the United States.

SEC. 2. That the master of any vessel who shall knowingly bring within the United States on such vessel, and land or permit to be landed, any Chinese laborer, from any foreign port or place, shall be deemed guilty of a misdemeanor, and on conviction thereof shall be punished by a fine of not more than five hundred dollars for each and every such Chinese laborer so brought, and maybe also imprisoned for a term not exceeding one year.

SEC. 3. That the two foregoing sections shall not apply to Chinese laborers who were in the United States on the seventeenth day of November, eighteen hundred and eighty, or who shall have come into the same before the expiration of ninety days next after the passage of this act, and who shall produce to such master before going on board such vessel, and shall produce to the collector of the port in the United States at which such vessel shall arrive, the evidence hereinafter in this act required of his being one of the laborers in this section mentioned; nor shall the two foregoing sections apply to the case of any master whose vessel, being bound to a port not within the United States, shall come within the jurisdiction of the United States by reason of being in distress or in stress of weather, or touching at any port of the United States on its voyage to any foreign port or place: Provided, That all Chinese laborers brought on such vessel shall depart with the vessel on leaving port.

SEC. 4. That for the purpose of properly identifying Chinese laborers who were in the United States on the seventeenth day of November eighteen hundred and eighty, or who shall have come into the same before the expiration of ninety days next after the passage of this act, and in order to furnish them with the proper evidence of their right to go from and come to the United States of their free will and accord, as provided by the treaty between the United States and China dated November seventeenth, eighteen hundred and eighty, the collector of customs of the district from which any such Chinese laborer shall depart from the United States shall, in person or by deputy, go on board each vessel having on board any such Chinese laborers and cleared or about to sail from his district for a foreign port, and on such vessel make a list of all such Chinese laborers, which shall be entered in registry-books to be kept for that purpose, in which shall be stated the name, age, occupation, last place of residence, physical marks of peculiarities, and all facts necessary for the identification of each of such Chinese laborers, which books shall be safely kept in the custom-house.; and every such Chinese laborer so departing from the United States shall be entitled to, and shall receive, free of any charge or cost upon application therefor, from the collector or his deputy, at the time such list is taken, a certificate, signed by the collector or his deputy and attested by his seal of office, in such form as the Secretary of the Treasury shall prescribe, which certificate shall contain a statement of the name, age, occupation, last place of residence, persona description, and facts of identification of the Chinese laborer to whom the certificate is issued, corresponding with the said list and registry in all particulars. In case any Chinese laborer after having received such certificate shall leave such vessel before her departure he shall deliver his certificate to the master of the vessel, and if such Chinese laborer shall fail to return to such vessel before her departure from port the certificate shall be delivered by the master to the collector of customs for cancellation. The certificate herein provided for shall entitle the Chinese laborer to whom the same is issued to return to and re-enter the United States upon producing and delivering the same to the collector of customs of the district at which such Chinese laborer shall seek to re-enter; and upon delivery of such certificate by such Chinese laborer to the collector of customs at the time of re-entry in the United States said collector shall cause the same to be filed in the custom-house anti duly canceled.

SEC. 5. That any Chinese laborer mentioned in section four of this act being in the United States, and desiring to depart from the United States by land, shall have the right to demand and receive, free of charge or cost, a certificate of identification similar to that provided for in section four of this act to be issued to such Chinese laborers as may desire to leave the United States by water; and it is hereby made the duty of the collector of customs of the district next adjoining the foreign country to which said Chinese laborer desires to go to issue such certificate, free of charge or cost, upon application by such Chinese laborer, and to enter the same upon registry-books to be kept by him for the purpose, as provided for in section four of this act.

SEC. 6. That in order to the faithful execution of articles one and two of the treaty in this act before mentioned, every Chinese person other than a laborer who may be entitled by said treaty and this act to come within the United States, and who shall be about to come to the United States, shall be identified as so entitled by the Chinese Government in each case, such identity to be evidenced by a certificate issued under the authority of said government, which certificate shall be in the English language or (if not in the English language) accompanied by a translation into English, stating such right to come, and which certificate shall state the name, title or official rank, if any, the age, height, and all physical peculiarities, former and present occupation or profession,

and place of residence in China of the person to whom the certificate is issued and that such person is entitled, conformably to the treaty in this act mentioned to come within the United States. Such certificate shall be prima-facie evidence of the fact set forth therein, and shall be produced to the collector of customs, or his deputy, of the port in the district in the United States at which the person named therein shall arrive.

SEC.7. That any person who shall knowingly and falsely alter or substitute any name for the name written in such certificate or forge any such certificate, or knowingly utter any forged or fraudulent certificate, or falsely personate any person named in any such certificate, shall be deemed guilty of a misdemeanor; and upon conviction thereof shall be fined in a sum not exceeding one thousand dollars, and imprisoned in a penitentiary for a term of not more than five years.

SEC.8. That the master of any vessel arriving in the United States from any foreign port or place shall, at the same time he delivers a manifest of the cargo, and if there be no cargo, then at the time of making a report of the entry of the vessel pursuant to law, in addition to the other matter required to be reported, and before landing, or permitting to land, any Chinese passengers, deliver and report to the collector of customs of the district in which such vessels shall have arrived a separate list of all Chinese passengers taken on board his vessel at any foreign port or place, and all such passengers on board the vessel at that time. Such list shall show the names of such passengers (and if accredited officers of the Chinese Government traveling on the business of that government, or their servants, with a note of such facts), and the names and other particulars, as shown by their respective certificates; and such list shall be sworn to by the master in the manner required by law in relation to the manifest of the cargo. Any willful refusal or neglect of any such master to comply with the provisions of this section shall incur the same penalties and forfeiture as are provided for a refusal or neglect to report and deliver a manifest of the cargo.

SEC. 9. That before any Chinese passengers are landed from any such line vessel, the collector, or his deputy, shall proceed to examine such passenger, comparing the certificate with the list and with the passengers; and no passenger shall be allowed to land in the

United States from such vessel in violation of law.

SEC.10. That every vessel whose master shall knowingly violate any of the provisions of this act shall be deemed forfeited to the United States, and shall be liable to seizure and condemnation in any district of the United States into which such vessel may enter or in which she may be found.

SEC. 11. That any person who shall knowingly bring into or cause to be brought into the United States by land, or who shall knowingly aid or abet the same, or aid or abet the landing in the United States from any vessel of any Chinese person not lawfully entitled to enter the United States, shall be deemed guilty of a misdemeanor, and shall, on conviction thereof, be fined in a sum not exceeding one thousand dollars, and imprisoned for a term not exceeding one year.

SEC. 12. That no Chinese person shall be permitted to enter the United States by land without producing to the proper officer of customs the certificate in this act required of Chinese persons seeking to land from a vessel. And any Chinese person found unlawfully within the United States shall be caused to be removed therefrom to the country from whence he came, by direction of the President of the United States, and at the cost of the United States, after being brought before some justice, judge, or commissioner of a court of the United States and found to be one not lawfully entitled to be or remain in the United States.

SEC.13. That this act shall not apply to diplomatic and other officers of the Chinese Government traveling upon the business of that government, whose credentials shall be taken as equivalent to the certificate in this act mentioned, and shall exempt them and their body and house-hold servants from the provisions of this act as to other Chinese persons.

SEC. 14. That hereafter no State court or court of the United States shall admit Chinese to citizenship; and all laws in conflict with this act are hereby repealed.

SEC.15. That the words "Chinese laborers", wherever used in this act shall be construed to mean both skilled and unskilled laborers and Chinese employed in mining.

Approved, May 6, 1882.

GLOSSARY

manifest (of cargo): a list of cargo or passengers

prima facie: (lit. at first view): true and authentic, self-evident

Document Analysis

The Chinese Exclusion Act establishes a broad set of strict regulations on Chinese laborers on two main fronts. First, it places strong restrictions on the Chinese government to prevent Chinese citizens from either immigrating to the United States or accepting contracts from would-be employers. Second, it places strong sanctions on the employers themselves (and/or the ship captains who carry the laborers to the United States), threatening prison and fines for bringing Chinese laborers to the United States. The Act does not clearly define who the laborers are in relation to other workers, however, leaving employers and relevant government officials to make the distinction themselves. The Chinese, the Act alleges, cause discord and disruption in the places in which they work. It is, therefore, deliberately short on such details, expecting workers' employers to take heed of the threat and altogether avoid exploring the use of Chinese workers.

The Act begins with a clear statement that Chinese laborers represent, in the view of the government, a threat to the order of the communities in which they work. The government does not state the basis for this assertion, although the protests (and violence associated with them), such as that which took place in North Adams, could be seen as examples of such disorder. Nevertheless, the Act clearly identifies Chinese laborers as a disruptive presence in the American economy.

In light of this perceived danger to the order of American society, Congress applies a ten-year moratorium on Chinese laborers. In an earlier draft of the bill, the ban actually extended to twenty years, although the president vetoed that version in light of the risks it posed to Sino-American relations. The moratorium would be enforced on two major fronts. The first of these fronts were the merchants who would recruit, contract, carry overseas, and put to work the laborers in question. The "master of any vessel" on which laborers would usually be delivered would receive a fine of up to five hundred dollars per illegal laborer found aboard their ships, for example. The merchants would also need to obtain proper paperwork to present to the customs officials from the ports from which they disembarked and the ports at which they unloaded their cargo. Merchants who brought Chinese laborers across the US border with either Canada or Mexico would receive a similar sanction.

On the second front were the government officials. In the United States, the responsibility of locating and capturing illegal laborers as well as examining the documentation of every merchant vessel would fall to the customs officials. China, too, would bear responsibility for ensuring that laborers would not emigrate or sign a contract that would take them to the United States. US negotiators spent a great deal of time working with Chinese officials on this point. Fourteen years earlier, the United States and China signed the Burlingame-Seward Treaty, which was designed to ease immigration restrictions between the two countries and mitigate perceived American interference in China. The Act references this treaty in section six, taking care to underscore the relationship between the two countries that was improved under that treaty. Additionally, although the Act does not clearly define the term "laborer" (except in section fifteen, where it identifies both "skilled" and "unskilled" laborers and those involved in mining), section thirteen ensures that the term would not apply to any Chinese diplomat or government official.

The Act does not attempt to reconcile the differences between immigration and importation of Chinese laborers. Rather, it strongly regulates both immigrants and workers, threatening illegal Chinese laborers with jail sentences and fines if caught approaching or on American territory. Furthermore, the Act does not attempt to define groups that might be exempted from the law (except the aforementioned diplomats). Instead, the Act requires that any individual who would be exempted from the law be able to produce comprehensive documentation, sanctioned by Chinese authorities, that clearly states in English the lawfulness of his or her presence. Under the Act, any exemption certificate must be approved by both the US and Chinese governments before the Chinese individual in question could enter the United States. Such bureaucracy is deliberate—most potential Chinese immigrants who might be worthy of exemption would undoubtedly be deterred by the certification process.

Terms for Chinese laborers already residing in the United States became harsher as well. Their travel in and out of the country was likewise restricted and monitored with the use of certificates issued by the US government. Under the Act, they were also deemed ineligible for US citizenship.

Essential Themes

The Chinese Exclusion Act of 1882 represents the first government policy designed to prevent certain racial or ethnic groups from entering the United States. Born of pressure from organized labor groups in the western states (where Asian laborers, particularly those of Chinese origin, were rapidly becoming the largest group of minority laborers) and specific incidents of violence, the Act took a bold step that would be repeated with regard to other racial and ethnic groups in the decades leading up to World War II.

The Act, extended repeatedly in the late nineteenth century and repealed in 1943, worked to prevent Chinese laborers from entering the United States, as such laborers allegedly posed a threat to local economies. However, the Act deliberately avoids providing a clear definition of "laborers" and, with the threat of imprisonment and/or fines, provided enough of a deterrent for any possible candidates for exemption to proceed with immigrating to America.

Additionally, the Act does not wade into the immigration-versus-importation issue that vexed previous attempts to curtail the influx of Chinese laborers. Rather, it simply halts both immigration and commercial importation of Chinese nationals, empowering American customs officials and relevant law enforcement entities to investigate and capture Chinese laborers. Those who were found in the United States ninety days or more after the law's implementation would need to produce a certificate, officially issued by the Chinese government and validated by American customs, proving that the holders were exempt from the law. With the amount of bureaucracy involved in obtaining such documents, few Chinese seeking to enter the United States would carry such certificates. Lacking such information, any persons of Asian origin—a race that Reconstruction-era Americans still found alien even in comparison to recently freed blacks—would be considered criminals and subject to prosecution.

—*Michael P. Auerbach, MA*

Bibliography and Additional Reading

Gyory, Andrew. *Closing the Gate: Race, Politics, and the Chinese Exclusion Act*. Chapel Hill: U of North Carolina P, 1998. Print.

Lee, Erika. *At America's Gates: Chinese Immigration During the Exclusion Era, 1882–1943*. Chapel Hill: U of North Carolina P, 2007. Print.

Mills, Charles. *The Chinese Exclusion Act and American Labor*. Alexandria: Apple Cheeks, 2009. Print.

Soennichsen, John. *The Chinese Exclusion Act of 1882*. Westport: Greenwood, 2011. Print.

Tian, Kelly. "The Chinese Exclusion Act of 1882 and Its Impact on North American Society." *Undergraduate Research Journal for the Human Sciences* 9 (2010): n. pag. Web. 16 Jan. 2014.

■ Address of the Lake Mohonk Conference on Indian Affairs

Date: September 1884
Authors: Friends of the Indian members and others
Genre: address

Summary Overview

The Lake Mohonk Conferences of the Friends of the Indian were annual meetings at which government Indian policy was discussed. The meetings were held at the Lake Mohonk resort near New Paltz, New York. Many prominent politicians, government officials, and clergymen interested in Indian affairs attended these meetings. Friends of the Indian was an informal movement rather than an actual organization. Among their goals were education for American Indians, US citizenship for tribal peoples, and the allotment of reservation land in individual homesteads to Indian families. In this report from the 1884 conference, there is strong emphasis on education and the extension of US law over the reservations, including extending citizenship to American Indians. The conference also supported an allotment bill proposed by Senator Richard Coke that was similar to the General Allotment Act eventually passed in 1887.

Defining Moment

In early American history, the general population's attitudes toward the American Indians was often one of fear and distrust, sometimes mingled with a paternalistic view of the Indians as a backward people needing to be "civilized." While this attitude persisted into the late nineteenth century, after the Civil War a more sympathetic view arose—perhaps first manifested in Helen Hunt Jackson's 1881 book, *A Century of Dishonor*, which chronicled the US government's mistreatment of the Indians. This changing sentiment can also be seen in the public backlash against violence toward the Indians involved in the Sand Creek Massacre in Colorado in 1864 and in the Washita Massacre in Indian Territory in 1868. By the 1870s, the Friends of the Indian movement had developed, primarily among

people in the urban areas of the Northeast. The Friends of the Indian was an amorphous movement made up of white reformers, politicians, government bureaucrats, journalists, and clergymen. There was a strong religious sentiment evidenced in the approach of the Friends, and for the most part they were fervent supporters of Christian missionary work among the Indians.

The Lake Mohonk Conferences, which were held annually from 1883 to 1916, were representative of the attitudes and approaches of the broader Friends of the Indian movement. The Lake Mohonk resort was owned by Quaker philanthropist Albert K. Smiley. In 1879, President Rutherford B. Hayes had appointed Smiley to the Board of Indian Commissioners, a group of reformers that advised the government on Indian policy. Smiley began the Lake Mohonk Conferences in part because he believed the brief, infrequent meetings of the Board of Indian Commissioners offered little chance to deeply explore the issues that arose. Virtually everyone who was prominent in the movement for the reform of Indian policy was a regular participant at the Lake Mohonk Conferences. At the 1884 conference, retired general Clinton B. Fisk served as chairman of the meeting. He had been an abolitionist before the Civil War and was involved with the Freedmen's Bureau, working among the freed slaves in the South after the war. The conference's secretary in 1884 was Herbert Welsh, who was one of the founders of the Indian Rights Association.

While these reformers had a genuine interest in the welfare of the Indians, they held an approach to reform that was ethnocentric and dismissive of Indian culture. In the minds of these reformers, education and civilization should aim at "freeing" the Indian from his tribal background. Citizenship and individual land holding were also seen an important steps that would break down the tribal bonds and fit the Indian for assimilation into the general society.

Author Biography

The collective authors of the address are not named in the document, although it was signed by Fisk and Welsh. The address was a general statement of the interests and concerns of those who were a regular part of the Lake Mohonk Conferences. Those who were considered members of the Conference are listed toward the end of the document (not shown here); the list includes most of the men and women in the nation who were prominently involved in Indian policy reform at that time. These people were part of a broader informal movement known as the Friends of the Indian. The Friends of the Indian was not an organization one could join, although it included people who belonged to organizations, such as the Indian Rights Association. Many of the individuals who were part of the Board of Indian Commissioners, an unofficial advisory body formed by President Ulysses S. Grant in 1869, were also part of the Friends of the Indian movement.

HISTORICAL DOCUMENT

...6th. *Resolved*, That from testimony laid before the Conference, our confidence in the good results flowing from the education of Indians has been confirmed, and that we regard with great satisfaction the increasing appropriations made by Congress for Indian schools, for instruction in farming and trades, for supplies of cattle, for irrigation, and for other means to promote self-supporting industries. That our conviction has been strengthened as to the importance of taking Indian youth from the reservations to be trained in industrial schools placed among communities of white citizens, and we favor the use of a larger proportion of the funds appropriated for Indian education for the maintenance of such schools. The placing of the pupils of these schools in the families of farmers or artisans where they may learn the trades and home habits of their employers has proved very useful and should be encouraged by the Government.

Resolved, That from evidence brought before the Conference it is apparent that the plan carried out to a small extent at Hampton and elsewhere, of bringing young men and their wives to industrial schools and there furnishing them with small houses so that they may be instructed in work and a proper home life, has been successful and should be carried out more largely.

Resolved, That while we approve the methods of Indian education pursued at Hampton and Carlisle, we do not fail to recognize that the schools and other methods of instruction, industrial, intellectual, moral, and religious, as carried on within or near the reservations by Christian missionaries for the last fifty years, have lifted up tribe after tribe to civilization and fitted them to take lands in severalty, and the good already achieved should stimulate and encourage Christian people to continued efforts in the same direction.

7th. *Resolved*, That education is essential to civilization. The Indian must have a knowledge of the English language, that he may associate with his white neighbors and transact business as they do. He must have practical industrial training to fit him to compete with others in the struggle for life. He must have a Christian education to enable him to perform duties of the family, the State, and the Church. Such an education can be best acquired apart from his reservation and amid the influences of Christian and civilized society. Such Government industrial training schools as those at Carlisle, Hampton, Forest Grove, Lawrence, Chilocco, and Genoa should be sustained and their number increased. The Government should continue to avail itself of institutions such as the training schools at Albuquerque, New Mexico; Lincoln Institute, Pennsylvania, and others conducted by religious or philanthropic associations, and promote the placing of pupils educated in all these schools in the families of farmers and artisans. But since the great majority of the Indians cannot be educated away from their homes, it is a matter of the highest importance that the Government should provide and liberally sustain good manual labor and day schools on the reservations. These should be established in sufficient number to accommodate all Indian children of school age. The Christian people of the country should exert through the Indian schools a strong moral and religious influence.

This the Government cannot do, but without this the true civilization of the Indian is impossible.

HOW TO SECURE THESE THINGS.

(a)   Public sentiment.
(b)   Legislation.

8th. *Resolved*, That since legislation in Congress and the benevolent work of the Christian people on behalf of the Indian is dependent upon public sentiment, every effort should be made to further the development of such sentiment. To this end we commend to the sympathy and support of the public the Indian Rights Association and the Woman's National Indian Association. We urge the organization of branches of these Societies in the principal cities and towns of the country. We think it extremely desirable that the press be enlisted in bringing the Indian cause to public attention, and we also rejoice in the efforts of the many benevolent societies belonging to the various religious bodies to diffuse information concerning the Indians and to arouse public interest in their behalf....

10th. *Resolved*, That careful observation has conclusively proved that the removal of Indians from reservations which they have long occupied, to other reservations far distant from the former and possessing different soil and climate, is attended by great suffering and loss of life. Such removals destroy the fruits of past industry and discourage the Indians from further effort in the habits of civilized life. These removals are usually made, not for wise reasons, but are instigated by the covetousness of the whites, who desire possession of the Indian lands or wish to rid themselves of the Indians' presence. We, therefore, earnestly protest against such Indian removals in the future, excepting in those cases where they shall be justified by full and sufficient reasons, and shall not be detrimental to the welfare of the Indians. When the removal of an Indian tribe becomes a necessity, individual Indians belonging to the tribe who have formed settled homes should have the privilege of taking homesteads upon the lands they occupy prior to the opening of the reservation and before white men are permitted to make land-entries thereon....

14th. *Resolved*, That immediate efforts should be made to place the Indian in the same position before the law as that held by the rest of the population, but that if it is not advisable, under existing circumstances, to subject the Indian at once to our entire body of law, the friends of the Indian should promptly endeavor: First, to provide for him some method of admission to citizenship so soon as he has prepared himself for its privileges and responsibilities; second, to give him at once the right to sue in our courts; and, third, to provide some system for the administration of certain laws on the reservations. We believe that the laws relating to marriage and inheritance and the criminal law affecting person and property should be extended over the reservations immediately.

As may be seen from the above resolutions, the Conference unites in urging that plain and sensible policy the main points of which have been so long and patiently recommended to Congress by men of practical experience in Indian affairs. As these resolutions show, the Conference recognized that to permanently keep Indians as tribes, under the control of agents on reservations set apart for them, is both impossible and undesirable.

They recognized that the Indian must be forced out into the current of ordinary life; that to make him a citizen is the solution of the Indian problem.

Yet the resolutions express with equal strength the conviction that Indians should not be at once made citizens in a mass. The preparation for citizenship should be general, vigorous, and immediate. The Indian is to be prepared for citizenship by giving him his land in severalty in the manner provided for by the Coke Bill, by larger appropriations for Indian education and the careful use of such appropriations in the establishment and support of schools, industrial and otherwise, and by the education of the race in the broadest and largest sense of the word.

By adequate provision for the administration of law among the Indians, and by giving the Indian the right to sue.

By Christian teaching and the establishing and support of churches.

By the gradual reduction of rations given to Indians, the systematic instruction in farming, and the encouragement in self-support.

By the appointment and support of agents of ability and integrity, uninfluenced by political preference, the only standard being that of individual fitness.

By proper provision for the immediate admission to citizenship of such Indians as are fitted for its duties and responsibilities.

These are substantially the recommendations which the Conference respectfully urges upon Congress and the people of the United States, as the just, obvious, and practical answer to the Indian question.

Signed on behalf of the Conference.

CLINTON B. FISK,
President.

HERBERT WELSH,
Secretary.

GLOSSARY

severalty: divided into separate, individually owned parcels—as opposed to being owned collectively by a tribe

Document Analysis

In these resolutions from the 1884 Lake Mohonk Conference, there is a strong emphasis on education for American Indians. The resolutions especially praise the industrial school model in which students were sent to off-reservation boarding schools where they received a rudimentary academic education and training either in agriculture or in some vocational trade. The Hampton Normal and Agricultural Institute in Hampton, Virginia, is mentioned specifically, as is the United States Indian Training School (also known as the Carlisle Indian Industrial School) at Carlisle, Pennsylvania. The Hampton Institute was originally founded by the American Missionary Association for the education of the freedmen after the Civil War, but beginning in 1878, Indian students were also taught there. The Carlisle School, founded by Captain Richard H. Pratt, was considered the preeminent government Indian school, and Pratt was widely considered the foremost expert on Indian education at that time. Both Pratt and General S. C. Armstrong, the founder of the Hampton Institute, attended the 1884 Lake Mohonk Conference. The address praises the work that had been carried on "within or near the reservations by Christian missionaries for the last fifty years." The reformers tended to see both missionary work and education as necessary for the civilization of American Indians, and both would contribute to breaking down tribal customs and attachments and, ultimately, to assimilation of Indians into the general society.

The tenth resolution of the 1884 conference urges an end to the relocation of Indians from one reserva-

tion to another. As the government confronted the last military resistance by tribes in the American West in the late nineteenth century, these newly pacified tribes were sometimes settled on reservations carved out from existing reservations. Thus, some of the people already living on these reservations would be moved, causing disruption to their attempts to maintain a farm or homestead. In other cases, parts of reservations were being opened to settlement by whites, also disrupting their lives. The resolution notes that such removals were often made "not for wise reasons" and urges ending this practice.

The fourteenth resolution from this conference calls for placing Indians under the jurisdiction of state and territorial laws, and eventually making them US citizens. The reformers recognized that this would be best accomplished gradually, but they do urge that Indians be granted US citizenship as soon as they could be prepared for it. In connection with this, they favorably note a bill recently introduced by Texas senator Coke, which called for giving each Indian individual or family their own homestead, thus breaking up the communal landholding practices of the reservations. This policy became known as allotment in severalty. Coke's bill provided that when an Indian accepted an allotment, the laws of the state or territory in which he or she lived would apply, rather than federal Indian law or tribal law. Coke's bill was never passed, but in 1887, Congress passed the Dawes Act, which began allotment and granted US citizenship to those Indians who accepted an allotment. Over time, the three concepts of education, allotment in severalty, and Indian citizenship became hallmarks of the reforms advocated by the Lake Mohonk Conferences.

Essential Themes

The paternalism and ethnocentrism of the reformers are major themes evident in this address. These reformers were genuinely concerned with the needs of American Indians, but because they were convinced of the superiority of white American culture and American social, religious, and political institutions, they never believed it was necessary to ask what the Indian people themselves might want.

In the late nineteenth century, many Indian parents did want education for their children. However, when they came to realize that government schools were intent on destroying tribal cultures, education became a controversial issue. Eventually, beginning with the Indian New Deal in the 1930s, the government began to move away from a policy that virtually forced assimilation, and eventually many Indian students attended public schools or tribally run schools on reservations.

Initially, many American Indian peoples had little interest in U.S. citizenship. American law had originally considered the Indian tribes as sovereign foreign nations, and many Indian people would have preferred to maintain that standing. But federal legislation and court decisions eroded the concept of tribal sovereignty, and Indian people increasingly lived under the jurisdiction of state and federal law. Citizenship, however, gave American Indian peoples constitutionally protected rights and access to federal courts to see that these rights were respected.

Unlike education and citizenship, however, allotment in severalty was a clear example of good intentions gone awry. Many American Indian tribes and individuals opposed allotment, and it was never carried out on some reservations. But in general, where it was applied, it eventually left a large number of Indian people landless. Some reservations disappeared completely because of allotment, and others were "honeycombed" with non-Indian settlement when Indian landowners sold their lands to white settlers.

In general, while the Friends of the Indian and the members of the Lake Mohonk Conferences had good intentions, their reform agenda exhibited the kinds of problems one might expect from externally derived reform, with little consideration for the self-determination of the people involved.

—*Mark S. Joy, PhD*

Bibliography and Additional Reading

Burgess, Larry E. *The Lake Mohonk Conference of the Friends of the Indian: Guide to the Annual Reports.* New York: Clearwater, 1975. Print.

_____. "'We'll Discuss It at Mohonk.'" *Quaker History* 40 (1971): 14–28. Print.

Prucha, Francis Paul. The Great Father: *The United States Government and the American Indian.* 2 vols. Lincoln: U of Nebraska P, 1984.

■ *Plessy v. Ferguson*

Date: May 18, 1896
Authors: Justice Henry Billings Brown and Justice John Marshall Harlan
Genre: court opinion; law

Summary Overview

In 1890, Louisiana passed a law that required railways to provide separate accommodations for whites and people of color. Attempting to lay the groundwork for a legal challenge to the law, Homer Adolph Plessy (who was one-eighth black) used the white carriage on such a train and was arrested. The case was eventually heard by the US Supreme Court, where Justice Henry Billings Brown, speaking for the other seven justices in the majority, stated that as long as the separate train accommodations were equal in quality, the Fourteenth Amendment to the Constitution was not violated. The lone dissenter, Justice John Marshall Harlan, argued that the law amounted to legalized and institutionalized racism.

Defining Moment

In 1877, Congress withdrew federal troops from the Southern states, effectively bringing to an end the period known as Reconstruction. The era had been a positive one for African Americans; black men were given the power to vote, and African Americans earned the right to attend public schools. Northerners helped redevelop state governments in such a way that equality among blacks and whites could be promoted. However, with the departure of the Reconstruction-era leaders and law enforcement personnel, Southern whites reasserted control and began imposing racial segregation. Leaders imposed poll taxes and other laws and regulations that essentially prevented the poor (meaning most African Americans) from voting. Without the influence of black voters, Southern legislatures were able to pass laws requiring separate facilities for blacks and whites. When such laws were challenged legally, white-dominated courts dismissed the cases.

In 1890, Louisiana passed a law requiring railways to provide separate passenger cars for whites and people of color. These cars would be of equal size and quality. However, people of color were not allowed to use cars designated for white people, and white people were prohibited from traveling on coaches assigned to people of color. Louisiana's new law was not the first of its kind: Florida, Mississippi, Texas, and other states had already passed such measures. Even the US Supreme Court had ruled that segregation laws on common carriers such as trains were legally acceptable. Still, civil rights organizations pursued legal options. Two such groups—Comité des Citoyens (Committee of Citizens) and the activist newspaper *The Crusader*—attempted to challenge Louisiana's law.

Plessy was African American according to the strict definition in use at the time: He was a white-skinned man of Creole descent, with only one-eighth African American blood. In 1892, he boarded a train in New Orleans, bound for Covington, Louisiana. Sitting down in a white car, he refused to move into the "colored only" car. He was arrested for violating the "separate but equal" law. He and his backers filed an appeal with the local circuit court, but Judge John Howard Ferguson denied the appeal. Plessy's team proceeded to bring the case to the Louisiana Supreme Court and, finding no support from that body, later brought the case before the US Supreme Court. On May 18, 1896, the US Supreme Court issued its decision, with eight justices upholding Ferguson's ruling.

Author Biography

Henry Billings Brown was born on March 2, 1836, in South Lee, Massachusetts. In 1856, he graduated from Yale College. A year later, he began practicing law in Connecticut. In 1875, he was appointed to the US District Court for Eastern Michigan. In 1890, President

Benjamin Harrison appointed him to the US Supreme Court. He retired in 1906 and died in 1913.

John Marshall Harlan was born in Boyle County, Kentucky, on June 1, 1833. In 1850, he graduated from Centre College and then studied law at Transylvania University (both in Kentucky). He served as a Union Army officer during the Civil War and ran unsuccessfully for governor of Kentucky in 1875. In 1877, President Rutherford B. Hayes appointed him to the US Supreme Court. He held his seat for thirty-four years before his death on October 14, 1911.

HISTORICAL DOCUMENT

Mr. Justice BROWN delivered the opinion of the court:

This case turns upon the constitutionality of an act of the general assembly of the state of Louisiana, passed in 1890, providing for separate railway carriages for the white and colored races. Acts 1890, No. 111, p. 152.

The first section of the statute enacts "that all railway companies carrying passengers in their coaches in this state, shall provide equal but separate accommodations for the white, and colored races, by providing two or more passenger coaches for each passenger train, or by dividing the passenger coaches by a partition so as to secure separate accommodations: provided, that this section shall not be construed to apply to street railroads. No person or persons shall be permitted to occupy seats in coaches, other than the ones assigned to them, on account of the race they belong to."

By the second section it was enacted "that the officers of such passenger trains shall have power and are hereby required to assign each passenger to the coach or compartment used for the race to which such passenger belongs; any passenger insisting on going into a coach or compartment to which by race he does not belong, shall be liable to a fine of twenty-five dollars, or in lieu thereof to imprisonment for a period of not more than twenty days in the parish prison, and any officer of any railroad insisting on assigning a passenger to a coach or compartment other than the one set aside for the race to which said passenger belongs, shall be liable to a fine of twenty-five dollars, or in lieu thereof to imprisonment for a period of not more than twenty days in the parish prison; and should any passenger refuse to occupy the coach or compartment to which he or she is assigned by the officer of such railway, said officer shall have power to refuse to carry such passenger on his train, and for such refusal neither he nor the railway company which he represents shall be liable for damages in any of the courts of this state."

The third section provides penalties for the refusal or neglect of the officers, directors, conductors, and employees of railway companies to comply with the act, with a proviso that "nothing in this act shall be construed as applying to nurses attending children of the other race." The fourth section is immaterial.

The information filed in the criminal district court charged, in substance, that Plessy, being a passenger between two stations within the state of Louisiana, was assigned by officers of the company to the coach used for the race to which he belonged, but he insisted upon going into a coach used by the race to which he did not belong. Neither in the information nor plea was his particular race or color averred.

The petition for the writ of prohibition averred that petitioner was seven-eighths Caucasian and one-eighth African blood; that the mixture of colored blood was not discernible in him; and that he was entitled to every right, privilege, and immunity secured to citizens of the United States of the white race; and that, upon such theory, he took possession of a vacant seat in a coach where passengers of the white race were accommodated, and was ordered by the conductor to vacate said coach, and take a seat in another, assigned to persons of the colored race, and, having refused to comply with such demand, he was forcibly ejected, with the aid of a police officer, and imprisoned in the parish jail to answer a charge of having violated the above act.

The constitutionality of this act is attacked upon the ground that it conflicts both with the thirteenth amendment of the constitution, abolishing slavery, and the fourteenth amendment, which prohibits certain restrictive legislation on the part of the states....

We consider the underlying fallacy of the plaintiff's

argument to consist in the assumption that the enforced separation of the two races stamps the colored race with a badge of inferiority. If this be so, it is not by reason of anything found in the act, but solely because the colored race chooses to put that construction upon it.... Legislation is powerless to eradicate racial instincts, or to abolish distinctions based upon physical differences, and the attempt to do so can only result in accentuating the difficulties of the present situation. If the civil and political rights of both races be equal, one cannot be inferior to the other civilly [163 U.S. 537, 552] or politically. If one race be inferior to the other socially, the constitution of the United States cannot put them upon the same plane....

Mr. Justice HARLAN dissenting:

By the Louisiana statute the validity of which is here involved, all railway companies (other than street-railroad companies) carry passengers in that state are required to have separate but equal accommodations for white and colored persons, "by providing two or more passenger coaches for each passenger train, or by dividing the passenger coaches by a partition so as to secure separate accommodations." Under this statute, no colored person is permitted to occupy a seat in a coach assigned to white persons; nor any white person to occupy a seat in a coach assigned to colored persons. The managers of the railroad are not allowed to exercise any discretion in the premises, but are required to assign each passenger to some coach or compartment set apart for the exclusive use of is race. If a passenger insists upon going into a coach or compartment not set apart for persons of his race, he is subject to be fined, or to be imprisoned in the parish jail. Penalties are prescribed for the refusal or neglect of the officers, directors, conductors, and employees of railroad companies to comply with the provisions of the act.

Only "nurses attending children of the other race" are excepted from the operation of the statute. No exception is made of colored attendants traveling with adults. A white man is not permitted to have his colored servant with him in the same coach, even if his condition of health requires the constant personal assistance of such servant. If a colored maid insists upon riding in the same coach with a white woman whom she has been employed to serve, and who may need her personal attention while traveling, she is subject to be fined or imprisoned for such an exhibition of zeal in the discharge of duty.

While there may be in Louisiana persons of different races who are not citizens of the United States, the words in the act "white and colored races" necessarily include all citizens of the United States of both races residing in that state. So that we have before us a state enactment that compels, under penalties, the separation of the two races in railroad passenger coaches, and makes it a crime for a citizen of either race to enter a coach that has been assigned to citizens of the other race.

Thus, the state regulates the use of a public highway by citizens of the United States solely upon the basis of race.

However apparent the injustice of such legislation may be, we have only to consider whether it is consistent with the constitution of the United States.

That a railroad is a public highway, and that the corporation which owns or operates it is in the exercise of public functions, is not, at this day, to be disputed. Mr. Justice Nelson, speaking for this court in *New Jersey Steam Nav. Co. v. Merchants' Bank,* 6 How. 344, 382, said that a common carrier was in the exercise "of a sort of public office, and has public duties to perform, from which he should not be permitted to exonerate himself without the assent of the parties concerned." Mr. Justice Strong, delivering the judgment of this court in *Olcott v. Supervisors,* 16 Wall. 678, 694, said: "That railroads, though constructed by private corporations, and owned by them, are public highways, has been the doctrine of nearly all the courts ever since such conveniences for passage and transportation have had any existence. Very early the question arose whether a state's right of eminent domain could be exercised by a private corporation created for the purpose of constructing a railroad. Clearly, it could not, unless taking land for such a purpose by such an agency is taking land for public use. The right of eminent domain nowhere justifies taking property for a private use. Yet it is a doctrine universally accepted that a state legislature may authorize a private corporation to take land for the construction of such a road, making compensation to the owner. What else does this doctrine mean if not that building a railroad, though it be built by a private corporation, is an act done for a public use?"

So, in *Township of Pine Grove v. Talcott*, 19 Wall. 666, 676: "Though the corporation [a railroad company] was private, its work was public, as much so as if it were to be constructed by the state." So, in Inhabitants of *Worcester v. Western R. Corp.*, 4 Metc. (Mass.) 564: "The establishment of that great thoroughfare is regarded as a public work, established by public authority, intended for the public use and benefit, the use of which is secured to the whole community, and constitutes, therefore, like a canal, turnpike, or highway, a public easement." "It is true that the real and personal property, necessary to the establishment and management of the railroad, is vested in the corporation; but it is in trust for the public."

In respect of civil rights, common to all citizens, the constitution of the United States does not, I think, permit any public authority to know the race of those entitled to be protected in the enjoyment of such rights. Every true man has pride of race, and under appropriate circumstances, when the rights of others, his equals before the law, are not to be affected, it is his privilege to express such pride and to take such action based upon it as to him seems proper. But I deny that any legislative body or judicial tribunal may have regard to the race of citizens when the civil rights of those citizens are involved. Indeed, such legislation as that here in question is inconsistent not only with that equality of rights which pertains to citizenship, national and state, but with the personal liberty enjoyed by every one within the United States.

The thirteenth amendment does not permit the withholding or the deprivation of any right necessarily inhering in freedom. It not only struck down the institution of slavery as previously existing in the United States, but it prevents the imposition of any burdens or disabilities that constitute badges of slavery or servitude. It decreed universal civil freedom in this country. This court has so adjudged. But, that amendment having been found inadequate to the protection of the rights of those who had been in slavery, it was followed by the fourteenth amendment, which added greatly to the dignity and glory of American citizenship, and to the security of personal liberty, by declaring that "all persons born or naturalized in the United States, and subject to the jurisdiction thereof, are citizens of the United States and of the state wherein they reside," and that "no state shall make or enforce any law which shall abridge the privileges or immunities of citizens of the United States; nor shall any state deprive any person of life, liberty or property without due process of law, nor deny to any person within its jurisdiction the equal protection of the laws." These two amendments, if enforced according to their true intent and meaning, will protect all the civil rights that pertain to freedom and citizenship. Finally, and to the end that no citizen should be denied, on account of his race, the privilege of participating in the political control of his country, it was declared by the fifteenth amendment that "the right of citizens of the United States to vote shall not be denied or abridged by the United States or by any state on account of race, color or previous condition of servitude."

These notable additions to the fundamental law were welcomed by the friends of liberty throughout the world. They removed the race line from our governmental systems. They had, as this court has said, a common purpose, namely, to secure "to a race recently emancipated, a race that through many generations have been held in slavery, all the civil rights that the superior race enjoy." They declared, in legal effect, this court has further said, "that the law in the states shall be the same for the black as for the white; that all persons, whether colored or white, shall stand equal before the laws of the states; and in regard to the colored race, for whose protection the amendment was primarily designed, that no discrimination shall be made against them by law because of their color." We also said: "The words of the amendment, it is true, are prohibitory, but they contain a necessary implication of a positive immunity or right, most valuable to the colored race—the right to exemption from unfriendly legislation against them distinctively as colored; exemption from legal discriminations, implying inferiority in civil society, lessening the security of their enjoyment of the rights which others enjoy; and discriminations which are steps towards reducing them to the condition of a subject race." It was, consequently, adjudged that a state law that excluded citizens of the colored race from juries, because of their race, however well qualified in other respects to discharge the duties of jurymen, was repugnant to the fourteenth amendment. *Strauder v. West Virginia*, 100 U.S. 303, 306 , 307 S.; *Virginia v. Rives*, Id. 313; *Ex parte Virginia*, Id. 339; *Neal v. Delaware*, 103 U.S. 370, 386; *Bush v. Com.*, 107 U.S. 110, 116, 1 S.

Sup. Ct. 625. At the present term, referring to the previous adjudications, this court declared that "underlying all of those decisions is the principle that the constitution of the United States, in its present form, forbids, so far as civil and political rights are concerned, discrimination by the general government or the states against any citizen because of his race. All citizens are equal before the law." *Gibson v. State*, 162 U.S. 565, 16 Sup. Ct. 904.

The decisions referred to show the scope of the recent amendments of the constitution. They also show that it is not within the power of a state to prohibit colored citizens, because of their race, from participating as jurors in the administration of justice.

It was said in argument that the statute of Louisiana does not discriminate against either race, but prescribes a rule applicable alike to white and colored citizens. But this argument does not meet the difficulty. Every one knows that the statute in question had its origin in the purpose, not so much to exclude white persons from railroad cars occupied by blacks, as to exclude colored people from coaches occupied by or assigned to white persons. Railroad corporations of Louisiana did not make discrimination among whites in the matter of accommodation for travelers. The thing to accomplish was, under the guise of giving equal accommodation for whites and blacks, to compel the latter to keep to themselves while traveling in railroad passenger coaches. No one would be so wanting in candor as to assert the contrary. The fundamental objection, therefore, to the statute, is that it interferes with the personal freedom of citizens. "Personal liberty," it has been well said, "consists in the power of locomotion, of changing situation, or removing one's person to whatsoever places one's own inclination may direct, without imprisonment or restraint, unless by due course of law." 1 Bl. Comm. 134. If a white man and a black man choose to occupy the same public conveyance on a public highway, it is their right to do so; and no government, proceeding alone on grounds of race, can prevent it without infringing the personal liberty of each.

It is one thing for railroad carriers to furnish, or to be required by law to furnish, equal accommodations for all whom they are under a legal duty to carry. It is quite another thing for government to forbid citizens of the white and black races from traveling in the same public conveyance, and to punish officers of railroad companies for permitting persons of the two races to occupy the same passenger coach. If a state can prescribe, as a rule of civil conduct, that whites and blacks shall not travel as passengers in the same railroad coach, why may it not so regulate the use of the streets of its cities and towns as to compel white citizens to keep on one side of a street, and black citizens to keep on the other? Why may it not, upon like grounds, punish whites and blacks who ride together in street cars or in open vehicles on a public road or street? Why may it not require sheriffs to assign whites to one side of a court room, and blacks to the other? And why may it not also prohibit the commingling of the two races in the galleries of legislative halls or in public assemblages convened for the consideration of the political questions of the day? Further, if this statute of Louisiana is consistent with the personal liberty of citizens, why may not the state require the separation in railroad coaches of native and naturalized citizens of the United States, or of Protestants and Roman Catholics?

The answer given at the argument to these questions was that regulations of the kind they suggest would be unreasonable, and could not, therefore, stand before the law. Is it meant that the determination of questions of legislative power depends upon the inquiry whether the statute whose validity is questioned is, in the judgment of the courts, a reasonable one, taking all the circumstances into consideration? A statute may be unreasonable merely because a sound public policy forbade its enactment. But I do not understand that the courts have anything to do with the policy or expediency of legislation. A statute may be valid, and yet, upon grounds of public policy, may well be characterized as unreasonable. Mr. Sedgwick correctly states the rule when he says that, the legislative intention being clearly ascertained, "the courts have no other duty to perform than to execute the legislative will, without any regard to their views as to the wisdom or justice of the particular enactment." Sedg. St. & Const. Law, 324. There is a dangerous tendency in these latter days to enlarge the functions of the courts, by means of judicial interference with the will of the people as expressed by the legislature. Our institutions have the distinguishing characteristic that the three departments of government are co-ordinate and separate. Each much keep within the limits defined by the constitution. And the courts best discharge their duty by executing the will of the law-making power, constitutionally expressed, leaving the results of legislation to be dealt with by the people through their representatives. Statutes must always have a reasonable construction. Sometimes they are to be construed strictly, sometimes literally, in order to carry out the legislative will. But, however construed, the intent of the legislature is to be respected if the particular statute in question is valid, although the courts, looking at the public interests, may conceive the statute to be both unreasonable and impolitic. If the power exists to enact a statute, that ends the matter so far as the courts are concerned. The adjudged cases in which statutes have been held to be void, because unreasonable, are those in which the means employed by the legislature were not at all germane to the end to which the legislature was competent.

The white race deems itself to be the dominant race in this country. And so it is, in prestige, in achievements, in education, in wealth, and in power. So, I doubt not, it will continue to be for all time, if it remains true to its great heritage, and holds fast to the principles of constitutional liberty. But in view of the constitution, in the eye of the law, there is in this country no superior, dominant, ruling class of citizens. There is no caste here. Our constitution is color-blind, and neither knows nor tolerates classes among citizens. In respect of civil rights, all citizens are equal before the law. The humblest is the peer of the most powerful. The law regards man as man, and takes no account of his surroundings or of his color when his civil rights as guaranteed by the supreme law of the land are involved. It is therefore to be regretted that this high tribunal, the final expositor of the fundamental law of the land, has reached the conclusion that it is competent for a state to regulate the enjoyment by citizens of their civil rights solely upon the basis of race.

In my opinion, the judgment this day rendered will, in time, prove to be quite as pernicious as the decision made by this tribunal in the Dred Scott Case.

It was adjudged in that case that the descendants of Africans who were imported into this country, and sold as slaves, were not included nor intended to be included under the word "citizens" in the constitution, and could not claim any of the rights and privileges which that instrument provided for and secured to citizens of the United States; that, at time of the adoption of the constitution, they were "considered as a subordinate and inferior class of beings, who had been subjugated by the dominant race, and, whether emancipated or not, yet remained subject to their authority, and had no rights or privileges but such as those who held the power and the government might choose to grant them." 17 How. 393, 404. The recent amendments of the constitution, it was supposed, had eradicated these principles from our institutions. But it seems that we have yet, in some of the states, a dominant race—a superior class of citizens—which assumes to regulate the enjoyment of civil rights, common to all citizens, upon the basis of race. The present decision, it may well be apprehended, will not only stimulate aggressions, more or less brutal and irritating, upon the admitted rights of colored citizens, but will encourage the belief that it is possible, by means of state enactments, to defeat the beneficent purposes which the people of the United States had in view when they adopted the recent amendments of the constitution, by one of which the blacks of this country were made citizens of the United States and of the states in which they respectively reside, and whose privileges and immunities, as citizens, the states are forbidden to abridge. Sixty millions of whites are in no danger from the presence here of eight millions of blacks. The destinies of the two races, in this country, are indissolubly linked together, and the interests of both require that the common government of all shall not permit the seeds of race hate to be planted under the sanction of law. What can more certainly arouse race hate, what more certainly create and perpetuate a feeling of distrust between these races, than state enactments which, in fact, proceed on the ground that colored citizens are so inferior and degraded that they cannot be allowed to sit in public coaches occupied by white citizens? That, as all will admit, is the real meaning of such legislation as was enacted in Louisiana.

The sure guaranty of the peace and security of each race is the clear, distinct, unconditional recognition by our governments, national and state, of every right that inheres in civil freedom, and of the equality before the law of all citizens of the United States, without regard to race. State enactments regulating the enjoyment of civil rights upon the basis of race, and cunningly devised to defeat legitimate results of the war, under the pretense of recognizing equality of rights, can have no other result than to render permanent peace impossible, and to keep alive a conflict of races, the continuance of which must do harm to all concerned. This question is not met by the suggestion that social equality cannot exist between the white and black races in this country. That argument, if it can be properly regarded as one, is scarcely worthy of consideration; for social equality no more exists between two races when traveling in a passenger coach or a public highway than when members of the same races sit by each other in a street car or in the jury box, or stand or sit with each other in a political assembly, or when they use in common the streets of a city or town, or when they are in the same room for the purpose of having their names placed on the registry of voters, or when they approach the ballot box in order to exercise the high privilege of voting.

There is a race so different from our own that we do not permit those belonging to it to become citizens of the United States. Persons belonging to it are, with few exceptions, absolutely excluded from our country. I allude to the Chinese race. But, by the statute in question, a Chinaman can ride in the same passenger coach with white citizens of the United States, while citizens of the black race in Louisiana, many of whom, perhaps, risked their lives for the preservation of the Union, who are entitled, by law, to participate in the political control of the state and nation, who are not excluded, by law or by reason of their race, from public stations of any kind, and who have all the legal rights that belong to white citizens, are yet declared to be criminals, liable to imprisonment, if they ride in a public coach occupied by citizens of the white race. It is scarcely just to say that a colored citizen should not object to occupying a public coach assigned to his own race. He does not object, nor, perhaps, would he object to separate coaches for his race if his rights under the law were recognized. But he does object, and he ought never to cease objecting, that citizens of the white and black races can be adjudged criminals because they sit, or claim the right to sit, in the same public coach on a public highway. The arbitrary separation of citizens, on the basis of race, while they are on a public highway, is a badge of servitude wholly inconsistent with the civil freedom and the equality before the law established by the constitution. It cannot be justified upon any legal grounds.

If evils will result from the commingling of the two races upon public highways established for the benefit of all, they will be infinitely less than those that will surely come from state legislation regulating the enjoyment of civil rights upon the basis of race. We boast of the freedom enjoyed by our people above all other peoples. But it is difficult to reconcile that boast with a state of the law which, practically, puts the brand of servitude and degradation upon a large class of our fellow citizens,- our equals before the law. The thin disguise of "equal" accommodations for passengers in railroad coaches will not mislead any one, nor atone for the wrong this day done.

The result of the whole matter is that while this court has frequently adjudged, and at the present term has recognized the doctrine, that a state cannot, consistently with the constitution of the United States, prevent white and black citizens, having the required qualifications for jury service, from sitting in the same jury box, it is now solemnly held that a state may prohibit white and black citizens from sitting in the same passenger coach on a public highway, or may require that they be separated by a "partition" when in the same passenger coach. May it not now be reasonably expected that astute men of the dominant race, who affect to be disturbed at the possibility that the integrity of the white race may be corrupted, or that its supremacy will be imperiled, by contact on public highways with black people, will endeavor to procure statutes requiring white and black jurors to be separated in the jury box by a "partition," and that, upon retiring from the court room to consult as to their verdict, such partition, if it be a movable one, shall be taken to their consultation room, and set up in such way as to prevent black jurors from coming too close to their brother jurors of the white race. If the "partition" used in the court room happens to be stationary, provision could be made for screens with openings through which jurors of the two races could confer as to their verdict without coming into personal contact with each other. I cannot see but that, according to the principles this day announced, such state legislation, although conceived in hostility to, and enacted for the purpose of humiliating, citizens of the United States of a particular race, would be held to be consistent with the constitution.

I do not deem it necessary to review the decisions of

state courts to which reference was made in argument. Some, and the most important, of them, are wholly inapplicable, because rendered prior to the adoption of the last amendments of the constitution, when colored people had very few rights which the dominant race felt obliged to respect. Others were made at a time when public opinion, in many localities, was dominated by the institution of slavery; when it would not have been safe to do justice to the black man; and when, so far as the rights of blacks were concerned, race prejudice was, practically, the supreme law of the land. Those decisions cannot be guides in the era introduced by the recent amendments of the supreme law, which established universal civil freedom, gave citizenship to all born or naturalized in the United States, and residing ere, obliterated the race line from our systems of governments, national and state, and placed our free institutions upon the broad and sure foundation of the equality of all men before the law.

I am of opinion that the state of Louisiana is inconsistent with the personal liberty of citizens, white and black, in that state, and hostile to both the spirit and letter of the constitution of the United States. If laws of like character should be enacted in the several states of the Union, the effect would be in the highest degree mischievous. Slavery, as an institution tolerated by law, would, it is true, have disappeared from our country; but there would remain a power in the states, by sinister legislation, to interfere with the full enjoyment of the blessings of freedom, to regulate civil rights, common to all citizens, upon the basis of race, and to place in a condition of legal inferiority a large body of American citizens, now constituting a part of the political community, called the "People of the United States," for whom, and by whom through representatives, our government is administered. Such a system is inconsistent with the guaranty given by the constitution to each state of a republican form of government, and may be stricken down by congressional action, or by the courts in the discharge of their solemn duty to maintain the supreme law of the land, anything in the constitution or laws of any state to the contrary notwithstanding.

For the reason stated, I am constrained to withhold my assent from the opinion and judgment of the majority.

GLOSSARY

argument ("in argument"): the period in a case brought before a court in which litigants present and defend their positions

eminent domain: the right of a state to claim private land for public use

Document Analysis

The Supreme Court decision known as *Plessy v. Ferguson* is broken into two segments. The first is the majority decision, penned by Justice Brown on behalf of seven other justices. The second is the dissent, written by Justice Harlan. Plessy and his supporters argued that the Louisiana law segregating the rails violated citizens' rights under the Thirteenth and Fourteenth Amendments.

Brown's comments focus primarily on the merits of the law and the majority's belief that such a law did not violate either amendment. The law, he says, was passed appropriately by the Louisiana legislature and was presented to that state's citizenry with clarity. All public railways, the law stated, should provide separate but equal accommodations for people of white and "colored" racial groups, and the agents of the railroad companies were responsible for enforcing these laws. Even the exemptions—an African American nurse tending to white children, for example—were detailed in the law, Brown states, and Plessy knowingly and purposefully defied that law.

The question, Brown continues, is whether the law itself is unconstitutional. He takes great care to state that the Thirteenth and Fourteenth Amendments are vital in the post-Reconstruction era. Such amendments promote the equality of all races in the United States. However, continues Brown, the Louisiana law does not place one racial group ahead of another. Rather, he says, it simply separates the two groups. Absent any sort of language that places whites ahead of nonwhites (or vice versa), Brown says, the law is constitutional.

Harlan's dissent speaks not to the facts but to the clear intent of the law in question. The law is designed to impose "badges of slavery or servitude" upon non-whites by requiring people of color to identify themselves as separate from whites. The Thirteenth and Fourteenth Amendments, he says, were designed to prevent such differentiations and instead foster "universal civil freedom."

Furthermore, Harlan dismisses the argument that the Louisiana legislature made a law that simply separates the races but still provides both sides with equal protection. "Every one knows," he argues forcefully, that the law was not designed to prohibit white people from riding on trains with black passengers. Instead, he says, the Louisiana government passed a law that prohibits blacks from traveling on public transportation with whites, a policy that runs counter to the color-blind nature of the Constitution. Harlan acknowledges that the court made the error of supporting racist laws in the past, citing the *Dred Scott v. Sandford* case of 1857, which denied citizenship to imported slaves, and he warns that government should not continue to foster racial divides. Harlan concludes that the Louisiana law is inconsistent with the ideals of personal liberty for all races and is therefore in contradiction to the principles of the Constitution.

Essential Themes

Plessy v. Ferguson was one of the first examples of the federal government's endorsement of the "separate but equal" concept. From this point through the middle of the twentieth century, segregation was a legally acceptable practice. At the heart of the issue was the question of whether segregation amounted to state-sponsored racism. The Supreme Court decision in Plessy's case impacted the American social order for decades to come.

Justice Brown, writing on behalf of the majority of his Supreme Court peers, argued that separating the races on public transportation would not necessarily establish the superiority of one race over another. The majority acknowledged that opponents to segregation laws would argue to the contrary. However, Brown and his peers asserted, such a position was grounded in perception and not in matters of fact or constitutionality.

Justice Harlan, the lone dissenter, argued that the Constitution was based on the notion that all Americans were equal in standing. Legal segregation, he stated, amounted to defiance of that principle and the reinstatement of black servitude. Furthermore, he argued, the separation of blacks from whites aboard public transportation perpetuated a feeling of distrust between the two racial groups and fostered interracial hate.

Despite Harlan's dissent, the Supreme Court upheld Louisiana's law and similar statutes. Not until 1954, when the court issued a landmark decision in favor of desegregation in *Brown v. Topeka Board of Education*, did Harlan's counterargument find support in the US Supreme Court.

—*Michael P. Auerbach, MA*

Bibliography and Additional Reading

Hoffer, William James Hull. Plessy v. Ferguson: *Race and Inequality in Jim Crow America*. Lawrence: UP of Kansas, 2012. Print.

Kelly, Blair L. M. R*ight to Ride: Streetcar Boycotts and African American Citizenship in the Era of Plessy v. Ferguson*. Chapel Hill: U of North Carolina P, 2010. Print.

Medley, Keith. *We as Freemen:* Plessy v. Ferguson. Gretna: Pelican, 2012. Print.

Thomas, Brook, and Waldo E. Martin. *Brown v. Board and Plessy v. Ferguson: A Brief History with Documents*. New York: Bedford, 1999. Print.

■ W.E.B. Du Bois: "Strivings of the Negro People"

Date: August 1, 1897
Author: W.E.B. Du Bois
Genre: essay

Summary Overview

Published in 1897, W.E.B. Du Bois's essay "Strivings of the Negro People" reflects on the unique challenges facing the African American population at a time of dismal race relations and legally sanctioned racism. In explaining his own struggle to develop a unified identity as both a black man who experiences discrimination and an educated man who seeks and deserves equal opportunity in the world, Du Bois presented the idea of the "double consciousness" that characterized the African American experience. Du Bois also argued that African Americans should be proud of their race and culture despite the negative perception of their community by the white majority. To best fulfill that potential—and in opposition to the dominant, accepted thinking on the position of African Americans supported by Booker T. Washington—Du Bois suggested that African Americans must actively seek the liberties denied them under the contemporary social system, including educational, economic, and political opportunity.

Defining Moment

Historians generally consider the late 1800s to be the nadir, or absolute low point, in US race relations. African Americans had first reached the Americas centuries before as part of the trans-Atlantic slave trade. The colonies became the agricultural heart of the southern United States and developed a significant enslaved African population. The question of slavery became one of the dominant problems of the early US republic; the framers of the Constitution made several compromises over the institution in order to garner cross-regional support, including a ban of the mere discussion of the slave trade in the US Congress for two decades. During the early 1800s, another series of compromises allowed the nation to maintain a fragile peace between pro-slavery Southern interests and increasingly pro-emancipation Northern interests. Contention over slavery greatly contributed to the outbreak of the Civil War. A Union victory allowed for the passage of constitutional amendments ending slavery and ensuring freedmen citizenship rights supported by additional federal legislation.

These legislative changes made little difference in the social view of African Americans, however. A Southern society that viewed African Americans as intellectually, spiritually, and morally inferior as a race before the Civil War maintained those views after slaves' civil status changed. The Ku Klux Klan arose to terrorize African Americans and their white supporters. State legislatures worked to limit African American rights, with increasing success after direct federal involvement in the South ended in the late 1870s. Even in the North, prejudice and discrimination were a social norm. The situation only worsened through the 1880s and 1890s. Violence against African Americans, often in the form of murderous lynchings, increased, but the federal government remained reluctant to intervene. Southern states passed laws that essentially disenfranchised African American voters, barred interracial marriages, and legally required the segregation of the races in public places and on mass transportation. African Americans had limited educational or work opportunities.

Some African Americans, such as Du Bois, nevertheless managed to make great personal achievements. A Northerner, Du Bois received a prestigious education both in the United States and Europe and found work as a university professor after completing his studies. At a time when Booker T. Washington, the leading African American spokesperson of the 1890s, was arguing that African Americans should accept racial discrimination and put aside the immediate quest for legal equality, Du Bois was becoming frustrated by the treatment of

African Americans. He experienced discrimination firsthand while teaching in Atlanta and saw the negative social and economic effects of discrimination while completing an in-depth study of the African American community of Philadelphia.

Author Biography

Born in 1868 in Massachusetts, sociologist, professor, and civil rights activist W.E.B. Du Bois emerged as a powerful voice against the policies of accommodation and gradualism supported by the most important African American spokesperson of the late 1800s, Washington. In the course of his sociological research, Du

Bois came to believe that acceptance of racial discrimination was a threat to the social, political, and economic well-being of the African American community. His speeches and writings in favor of the immediate expansion of civil rights and racial equality made him a prominent Washington dissenter, and his views led him to help found the Niagara Movement and, later, the National Association for the Advancement of Colored People (NAACP). In his role as editor of the NAACP's publication *The Crisis*, Du Bois helped set the agenda for African American protest action for more than two decades. He eventually parted ways with the organization. He died in Ghana in 1963.

HISTORICAL DOCUMENT

Between me and the other world there is ever an unasked question: unasked by some through feelings of delicacy; by others through the difficulty of rightly framing it. All, nevertheless, flutter round it. They approach me in a half-hesitant sort of way, eye me curiously or compassionately, and then, instead of saying directly, How does it feel to be a problem? they say, I know an excellent colored man in my town; or I fought at Mechanicsville; or, Do not these Southern outrages make your blood boil? At these I smile, or am interested, or reduce the boiling to a simmer, as the occasion may require. To the real question, How does it feel to be a problem? I answer seldom a word.

And yet, being a problem is a strange experience,—peculiar even for one who has never been anything else, save perhaps in babyhood and in Europe. It is in the early days of rollicking boyhood that the revelation first burst upon one, all in a day, as it were. I remember well when the shadow swept across me. I was a little thing, away up in the hills of New England, where the dark Housatonic winds between Hoosac and Taghanic to the sea. In a wee wooden schoolhouse, something put it into the boys' and girls' heads to buy gorgeous visiting-cards—ten cents a package—and exchange. The exchange was merry, till one girl, a tall newcomer, refused my card,—refused it peremptorily, with a glance. Then it dawned upon me with a certain suddenness that I was different from the others; or like, mayhap, in heart and life and longing, but shut out from their world by a vast veil. I had thereafter

no desire to tear down that veil, to creep through; I held all beyond it in common contempt, and lived above it in a region of blue sky and great wandering shadows. That sky was bluest when I could beat my mates at examination-time, or beat them at a foot-race, or even beat their stringy heads. Alas, with the years all this fine contempt began to fade; for the world I longed for, and all its dazzling opportunities, were theirs, not mine. But they should not keep these prizes, I said; some, all, I would wrest from them. Just how I would do it I could never decide: by reading law, by healing the sick, by telling the wonderful tales that swam in my head,—some way. With other black boys the strife was not so fiercely sunny: their youth shrunk into tasteless sycophancy, or into silent hatred of the pale world about them and mocking distrust of everything white; or wasted itself in a bitter cry, Why did God make me an outcast and a stranger in mine own house? The "shades of the prison-house" closed round about us all: walls strait and stubborn to the whitest, but relentlessly narrow, tall, and unscalable to sons of night who must plod darkly against the stone, or steadily, half hopelessly watch the streak of blue above.

After the Egyptian and Indian, the Greek and Roman, the Teuton and Mongolian, the Negro is a sort of seventh son, born with a veil, and gifted with second-sight in this American world,—a world which yields him no self-consciousness, but only lets him see himself through the revelation of the other world. It is a peculiar sensation, this double-consciousness, this sense of always looking at one's self through the eyes of others, of measuring one's soul by the tape of a world that looks on in amused contempt and pity. One feels his two-ness,—an American, a Negro; two souls, two thoughts, two unreconciled strivings; two warring ideals in one dark body, whose dogged strength alone keeps it from being torn asunder. The history of the American Negro is the history of this strife,—this longing to attain self-conscious manhood, to merge his double self into a better and truer self. In this merging he wishes neither of the older selves to be lost. He does not wish to Africanize America, for America has too much to teach the world and Africa; he does not with to bleach his Negro blood in a flood of white Americanism, for he believes—foolishly, perhaps, but fervently—that Negro blood has yet a message for the world. He simply wishes to make it possible for a man to be both a Negro and an American without being cursed and spit upon by his fellows, without losing the opportunity of self-development.

This is the end of his striving: to be a co-worker in the kingdom of culture, to escape both death and isolation, and to husband and use his best powers. These powers, of body and of mind, have in the past been so wasted and dispersed as to lose all effectiveness, and to seem like absence of all power, like weakness. The double-aimed struggle of the black artisan, on the one hand to escape white contempt for a nation of mere hewers of wood and drawers of water, and on the other hand to plough and nail and dig for a poverty-stricken horde, could only result in making him a poor craftsman, for he had but half a heart in either cause. By the poverty and ignorance of his people the Negro lawyer or doctor was pushed toward quackery and demagogism, and by the criticism of the other world toward an elaborate preparation that overfitted him for his lowly tasks. The would-be black-savant was confronted by the paradox that the knowledge his people needed was a twice-told tale to his white neighbors, while the knowledge which would teach the white world was Greek to his own flesh and blood. The innate love of harmony and beauty that set the ruder souls of his people a-dancing, a-singing, and a-laughing raised but confusion and doubt in the soul of the black artist; for the beauty revealed to him was the soul-beauty of a race which his larger audience despised, and he could not articulate the message of another people.

This waste of double aims, this seeking to satisfy two unreconciled ideals, has wrought sad havoc with the courage and faith and deeds of eight thousand people, has sent them often wooing false gods and invoking false means of salvation, and has even at times seemed destined to make them ashamed of themselves. In the days of bondage they thought to see in one divine event the end of all doubt and disappointment; eighteenth-century Rousseauism never worshiped freedom with half the unquestioning faith that the American Negro did for two centuries. To him slavery was, indeed, the sum of all villainies, the cause of all sorrow, the root of all prejudice; emancipation was the key to a promised land of sweeter beauty than ever stretched before the eyes of wearied Israelites. In his songs and exhortations swelled one refrain, liberty; in his tears and curses the god he implored had freedom in his right hand. At last it came,—suddenly, fearfully, like a dream. With one wild carnival of blood and passion came the message in his own plaintive cadences: —

> Shout, O children!
> Shout, you're free!
> The Lord has bought your liberty!

Years have passed away, ten, twenty, thirty. Thirty years of national life, thirty years of renewal and development, and yet the swarthy ghost of Banquo sits in its old place at the national feast. In vain does the nation cry to its vastest problem, —

> Take any shape but that, and my firm nerves
> Shall never tremble!

The freedman has not yet found in freedom his promised land. Whatever of lesser good may have come in these years of change, the shadow of a deep disappointment rests upon the Negro people,—a disappointment all the more bitter because the unattained ideal was unbounded save by the simple ignorance of a lowly folk.

The first decade was merely a prolongation of the vain search for freedom, the boon that seemed ever barely to elude their grasp,—like a tantalizing will-o'-the wisp, maddening and misleading the headless host. The holocaust of war, the terrors of the Kuklux Klan, the lies of carpet-baggers, the disorganization of industry, and the contradictory advice of friends and foes left the bewildered serf with no new watchword beyond the old cry for freedom. As the decade closed, however, he began to grasp a new idea. The ideal of liberty demanded for its attainment powerful means, and these the Fifteenth Amendment gave him. The ballot, which before he had looked upon as a visible sign of freedom, he now regarded as the chief means of gaining and perfecting the liberty with which war had partially endowed him. And why not? Had not votes made war and emancipated millions? Had not votes enfranchised the freedmen? Was anything impossible to a power that had done all this? A million black men started with renewed zeal to vote themselves into the kingdom. The decade fled away,—a decade containing, to the freedman's mind, nothing but suppressed votes, stuffed ballot-boxes, and election outrages that nullified his vaunted right of suffrage. And yet that decade from 1875 to 1885 held another powerful movement, the rise of another ideal to guide the unguided, another pillar of fire by night after a clouded day. It was the ideal of "book-learning;" the curiosity, born of compulsory ignorance, to know and test the power of the cabalistic letters of the white man, the longing to know. Mission and night schools began in the smoke of battle, ran the gauntlet of reconstruction and at last developed into permanent foundations. Here at last seemed to have been discovered the mountain path to Canaan; longer than the highway of emancipation and law, steep and rugged, but straight, leading to heights high enough to overlook life.

Up the new path the advance guard toiled, slowly, heavily, doggedly; only those who have watched and guided the faltering feet, the misty minds, the dull understandings, of the dark pupils of these schools know how faithfully, how piteously, this people strove to learn. It was weary work. The cold statistician wrote down the inches of progress here and there, noted also where here and there a foot had slipped or some one had fallen. To the tired climbers, the horizon was ever dark, the mists were often cold, the Canaan was always dim and far away. If, however, the vistas disclosed as yet no goal, no resting-place, little but flattery and criticism, the journey at least gave leisure for reflection and self-examination; it changed the child of emancipation to the youth with dawning self-consciousness, self-realization, self-respect. In those sombre forests of his striving his own soul rose before him, and he saw himself,—darkly as through a veil; and yet he saw in himself some faint revelation of his power, of his mission. He began to have a dim feeling that, to attain his place in the world, he must be himself, and not another. For the first time he sought to analyze the burden he bore upon his back, that dead-weight of social degradation partially masked behind a half-named Negro problem. He felt his poverty; without a cent, without a home, without land, tools, or savings, he had entered into competition with rich landed, skilled neighbors. To be a poor man is hard, but to be a poor race in a land of dollars is the very bottom of hardships. He felt the weight of his ignorance,—not simply of letters, but of life, of business, of the humanities; the accumulated sloth and shirking and awkwardness of decades and centuries shackled his hands and feet. Nor was his burden all poverty and ignorance. The red stain of bastardy, which two centuries of systematic legal defilement of Negro women had stamped upon his race, meant not only the loss of ancient African chastity, but also the hereditary weight of a mass of filth from white whoremongers and adulterers, threatening almost the obliteration of the Negro home.

A people thus handicapped ought not to be asked to race with the world, but rather allowed to give all its time and thought to its own social problems. But alas! while sociologists gleefully count his bastards and his prostitutes, the very soul of the toiling, sweating black man is darkened by the shadow of a vast despair. Men call the shadow prejudice, and learnedly explain it as the natural defense of culture against barbarism, learning against ignorance, purity against crime, the "higher" against the "lower" races. To which the Negro cries Amen! and swears that to so much this strange prejudice as is founded on just homage to civilization, culture, righteousness, and progress he humbly bows and meekly does obeisance. But before that nameless prejudice that leaps beyond all this he stands helpless, dismayed, and well-nigh speechless; before that personal disrespect and mockery, the ridicule and systematic humiliation, the distortion of fact and wanton license of fancy, the cynical ignoring of the better and boisterous welcoming of the worse, the all-pervading desire to inculcated disdain for everything black, from Toussaint to the devil,—before this there rises a sickening despair that would disarm and discourage any nation save that black host to whom "discouragement" is an unwritten word.

They still press on, they still nurse the dogged hope,—not a hope of nauseating patronage, not a hope of reception into charmed social circles of stock-jobbers, pork-packers, and earl-hunters, but the hope of a higher synthesis of civilization and humanity, a true progress, with which the chorus "Peace, good will to men,"

> May make one music as before,
> But vaster.

Thus the second decade of the American Negro's freedom was a period of conflict, of inspiration and doubt, of faith and vain questionings, of Sturm und Drang. The ideals of physical freedom, of political power, of school training, as separate all-sufficient panaceas for social ills, became in the third decade dim and overcast. They were the vain dreams of credulous race childhood; not wrong, but incomplete and over-simple. The training of the schools we need to-day more than ever,—the training of deft hands, quick eyes and ears, and the broader, deeper, higher culture of gifted minds. The power of the ballot we need in sheer self-defense, and as a guarantee of good faith. We may misuse it, but we can scarce do worse in this respect than our whilom masters. Freedom, too, the long-sought, we still seek,—the freedom of life and limb, the freedom to work and think. Work, culture, and liberty—all these we need, not singly, but together; for to-day these ideals among the Negro people are gradually coalescing, and finding a higher meaning in the unifying ideal of race,—the ideal of fostering the traits and talents of the Negro, not in opposition to, but in conformity with, the greater ideals of the American republic, in order that some day, on American soil, two world races may give each to each those characteristics which both so sadly lack. Already we come not altogether empty-handed: there is to-day no true American music but the sweet wild melodies of the Negro slave; the American fairy tales are Indian and African; we are the sole oasis of simple faith and reverence in a dusty desert of dollars and smartness. Will America be poorer if she replace her brutal, dyspeptic blundering with the light-hearted but determined Negro humility; or her coarse, cruel wit with loving, jovial good humor; or her Annie Rooney with *Steal Away*?

Merely a stern concrete test of the underlying principles of the great republic is the Negro problem, and the spiritual striving of the freedmen's sons is the travail of souls whose burden is almost beyond the measure of their strength, but who bear it in the name of an historic race, in the name of this the land of their fathers' fathers, and in the name of human opportunity.

GLOSSARY

Annie Rooney: a cartoon character—an orphan—similar to Little Orphan Annie

Banquo: a ghost in Shakespeare's *Macbeth*

demagogism: demagoguery; the practice of gaining power and popularity by arousing the prejudices and emotions in others

Housatonic: the Housatonic River, in western Massachusetts, where Du Bois grew up

mayhap: perhaps, perchance

Rousseauism: a reference to the Swiss philosopher Jean Jacques Rousseau (1712–1778)

Steal Away: a Negro spiritual song

Sturm und Drang: (literally, storm and stress): turmoil, upheaval

sycophancy: servile flattery, fawning behavior

visiting-card: a small card identifying the holder and dropped into a box upon visiting someone

Document Analysis

Du Bois opens his essay with the question, "How does it feel to be a problem?" This language harks back to what commentators on the African American experience at the time commonly referred to as "the Negro problem." By stating the "real question" bluntly, Du Bois opens a discussion about what it means to characterize a group of individuals not as people but as a concept.

Much of the rest of the essay addressed itself to the response. Du Bois presents anecdotal evidence of his own experience, using stories to which his presumably educated readers would connect in order to humanize his experience as a "problem." In describing his time as a student, he focuses on successes shared by all who have pursued an education—attending a pleasant school, achieving a top score on an examination, deciding on an advanced field of study. Yet his triumphs were weakened, he notes, by the knowledge that he was unwelcome in the very society that he sought to join. This knowledge, he explains, is not a direct knowledge of oneself, but rather a knowledge of oneself "through the revelation of the other world," or what Du Bois calls a "double consciousness."

This knowledge, Du Bois suggests, is the answer to his guiding question. He briefly traces the history of African Americans through the era of slavery into the complicated years following emancipation, focusing on the promise of true freedom and the failure of that promise. The writer emphasizes the immense challenge facing African Americans: "war, the terrors of the Kuklux Klan, the lies of carpet-baggers, the disorganization of industry, and the contradictory advice of friends and foes." He contrasts the poverty and political repression of African Americans with the wealth and opportunity afforded their "rich landed, skilled neighbors." The greatness of these struggles meant that African Americans deserved the right to solve their problems rather than accept an inferior status.

Du Bois concludes by returning the themes of Americanism and freedom introduced earlier in the essay, offering another definition in answer to his opening question—that to be a "problem" is to provide a litmus test for the ideals of liberty and justice on which the United States was founded.

Essential Themes

In this essay, Du Bois explores the concept of what he termed the African American "double consciousness," or the experience of being simultaneously a person and, specifically, a black person, subject to the expectations of and restrictions imposed by white-dominated US society. The effects of this dichotomy on the African American psyche and experience became one of Du Bois's key points of exploration in his later works; "Strivings of the Negro People" was incorporated with only minor changes into Du Bois's seminal 1903 work *The Souls of Black Folk.*

Du Bois's propositions of African American pride foreshadow the later black nationalist movement. Under the influence of Jamaican immigrant Marcus Garvey, this movement encouraged African Americans to be proud of their race, support black economic opportunity, and to create their own independent nation through emigration to Africa. Black nationalism inspired African American leaders of later decades, perhaps most notably Malcolm X.

The concept of racial separation remains a discussion in modern US society. At the time when Du Bois wrote the "Strivings of the Negro People," segregation and racial discrimination were written into state laws in parts of the United States; although those laws no longer remain, de facto segregation continues to occur across the nation. African Americans of all socioeconomic groups tend to reside in largely black neighborhoods, and these neighborhoods tend to suffer higher rates of crime and poverty along with lower access to public services. Equally, some US educators encourage African American youth to learn to "code switch," or change their word choice and manner of speaking depending on whether they are interacting with other young African Americans or with outsiders. This type of lingual switch reflects the idea of a modern double consciousness. Thus, Du Bois's explanation of the double consciousness remains relevant, albeit in a different political, social, and economic landscape.

—*Vanessa E. Vaughn, MA*

Bibliography and Additional Reading

Jones, Gavin. "'Whose Line Is It Anyway?' W. E. B. Du Bois and the Language of the Color-Line." *Race Consciousness: African-American Studies for the New Century.* Eds. Judith Jackson Fossett and Jeffrey A. Tucker. New York: NYUP, 1997. 19–34. Print.

Lewis, David Levering. *W. E. B. Du Bois, 1868–1919: Biography of a Race.* New York: Holt, 1993. Print.

Zamir, Shamoon. Dark Voices: *W. E. B. Du Bois and American Thought, 1888–1903.* Chicago: U of Chicago P, 1995. Print.

■ W.E.B. Du Bois: "The Study of the Negro Problems"

Date: January 1898
Author: W. E. B. Du Bois
Genre: essay

Summary Overview

Written at a time of great national debate over the role of African Americans in society, W. E. B. Du Bois's "The Study of the Negro Problems" applied a systematic sociological lens to the discussion. Arguing that African Americans were excluded from full participation in the nation's economic, social, and political life, Du Bois postulated that the ability of African Americans to overcome these circumstances was hampered by a history of oppression and discrimination. Discrimination and segregation, he argued, meant African Americans started life with an automatic disadvantage. Du Bois's claims set the stage for the activist stance toward civil rights and African American social integration that characterized African American issues during the early twentieth century.

Defining Moment

Although African Americans had been among the earliest, albeit forced, immigrants to North America and even, at times, formed a majority population in certain Southern regions, their position in late nineteenth-century US society was tenuous at best. The Civil War, the Emancipation Proclamation, and the Thirteenth Amendment had combined to end the institution of slavery nationwide. But integrating freed African Americans and their descendants into a reluctant and often hostile society proved difficult, especially after the end of Reconstruction in 1877.

Without active federal enforcement of civil rights measures, many states passed Jim Crow laws requiring racial segregation and hampering black political involvement. The 1896 US Supreme Court decision in *Plessy v. Ferguson* supported the constitutionality of legal segregation, and a series of state-level laws adopted across the South used literacy tests and poll taxes to essentially disenfranchise African American voters. At the same time, violence against African Americans increased, with hundreds of individuals lynched during the 1880s and 1890s.

African Americans struggled to chart a course amid these turbulent waters. During the 1880s, a former slave named Booker T. Washington had become a leading voice of the African American community. A teacher, he believed that education and vocational training were the foundations for black economic advancement. At the Cotton States and International Exposition in Atlanta in 1895, Washington gave a famous speech in favor of a policy of gradualism, encouraging African Americans to accept racial discrimination for the time being. Hard work, patience, and personal discipline, he argued, would allow for the eventual development of equal political and social rights. In the meantime, accommodation would allow African Americans to receive access to at least a minimal education and perhaps protection under the law from a separate and superior white society. White Americans and some black activists supported Washington's positions, believing them to be true solutions to problems faced by African Americans.

Others did not support his position, however. During the mid-1890s, Du Bois served as a professor at Wilberforce College in Ohio and then at Atlanta University. At the same time, he undertook a detailed sociological study of the African American community in the city of Philadelphia. His experiences living in the South combined with the conclusions he drew from the Philadelphia study caused him to arrive at a different conclusion than that promoted by Washington. Du Bois presented his thoughts on the subject of the "negro problem" in a paper at a Philadelphia social sciences conference in late 1897, and a few months later, he published the paper as "The Study of the Negro Problems" in the organization's journal.

Author Biography

Born in 1868, sociologist W. E. B. Du Bois was among the leading African American reformers and civil rights activists of his time. By the time he produced "The Study of the Negro Problems" in 1898, he had already completed a doctorate in history at Harvard University and become interested in the study of race in society. During the late 1890s, he undertook the first case study of an African American community in Philadel-phia. Work of this type provided the basis for a new understanding of the African American experience, a field that had been overwhelmingly neglected in both popular and academic studies to that time.

Du Bois's application of sociology to the African American condition convinced him that widespread racism was a significant barrier to black advancement. Beginning in the early 1900s, he sought to combat this problem through active resistance. He later established the National Association for the Advancement of Colored People. He died in 1963.

HISTORICAL DOCUMENT

Such are some of the changes of condition and social movement which have, since 1619, altered and broadened the social problems grouped about the American Negro. In this development of successive questions about one centre, there is nothing peculiar to American history. Given any fixed condition or fact—a river Nile, a range of Alps, an alien race, or a national idea—and problems of society will at every stage of advance group themselves about it. All social growth means a succession of social problems—they constitute growth, they denote that laborious and often baffling adjustment of action and condition which is the essence of progress, and while a particular fact or circumstance may serve in one country as a rallying point of many intricate questions of adjustment, the absence of that particular fact would not mean the absence of all social problems. Questions of labor, caste, ignorance and race were bound to arise in America; they were simply complicated here and intensified there by the presence of the Negro.

Turning now from this brief summary of the varied phases of these questions, let us inquire somewhat more carefully into the form under which the Negro problems present themselves to-day after 275 years of evolution. Their existence is plainly manifested by the fact that a definitely segregated mass of eight millions of Americans do not wholly share the national life of the people; are not an integral part of the social body. The points at which they fail to be incorporated into this group life constitute the particular Negro problems, which can be divided into two distinct but correlated parts, depending on two facts:

First—Negroes do not share the full national life because as a mass they have not reached a sufficiently high grade of culture.

Secondly—They do not share the full national life because there has always existed in America a conviction—varying in intensity, but always widespread—that people of Negro blood should not be admitted into the group life of the nation no matter what their condition might be.

Considering the problems arising from the backward development of Negroes, we may say that the mass of this race does not reach the social standards of the nation with respect to

(a) Economic condition.

(b) Mental training.

(c) Social efficiency.

Even if special legislation and organized relief intervene, freedmen always start life under an economic disadvantage which generations, perhaps centuries, cannot overcome. Again, of all the important constituent parts of our nation, the Negro is by far the most ignorant; nearly half of the race are absolutely illiterate, only a minority of the other half have thorough common school training, and but a remnant are liberally educated. The great deficiency of the Negro, however, is his small knowledge of the art of organized social life—that last expression of human culture. His development in group life was abruptly broken off by the slave ship, directed into abnormal channels and dwarfed by the Black Codes, and suddenly wrenched anew by the Emancipation Proclamation. He finds himself, therefore, peculiarly weak in that nice adaptation of individual life to the life of the group which is the essence of civilization. This is shown in the grosser forms of sexual immorality, disease and crime, and also in the difficulty of race organization for common ends in economic or in intellectual lines.

For these reasons the Negro would fall behind any average modern nation, and he is unusually handicapped in the midst of a nation which excels in its extraordinary economic development, its average of popular intelligence and in the boldness of its experiments in organized social life.

These problems of poverty, ignorance and social degradation differ from similar problems the world over in one important particular, and that is the fact that they are complicated by a peculiar environment. This constitutes the second class of Negro problems, and they rest, as has been said, on the widespread conviction among Americans that no persons of Negro descent should become constituent members of the social body. This feeling gives rise to economic problems, to educational problems, and nice questions of social morality; it makes it more difficult for black men to earn a living or spend their earnings as they will; it gives them poorer school facilities and restricted contact with cultured classes; and it becomes, throughout the land, a cause and excuse for discontent, lawlessness, laziness and injustice.

GLOSSARY

Black Codes: harsh "Jim Crow"-like laws passed in many Southern states after the Civil War to restrict the rights of African Americans

Document Analysis

In his "The Study of the Negro Problems," Du Bois identifies and outlines the challenges of fully integrating African Americans into US society. Du Bois begins with a discussion of the historical origins of these challenges by fully documenting the contentious "Negro problems" of his day. His sociological bent is evident throughout his identification of these problems; he points to the existence of a "definitely segregated mass . . . [who] do not wholly share the national life of the people" nor participate in society as clear proof of the severity of the issue. This life, he suggests, includes economic, social, and political components sorely lacking in African American society.

Throughout the piece, Du Bois returns to the complicated factor of racial discrimination. Exclusion from mainstream US society, he argues, has left African Americans in an especially difficult quandary. Discrimination has made earning either an education or a living harder for African Americans than for whites; these challenges could not be readily overcome through good intentions or legislation. Therefore, Du Bois argues, discrimination becomes both "a cause and excuse for discontent, lawlessness, laziness and injustice." At the same time, he posits that exclusion from human society has left African Americans poorly adapted to participation in mainstream American society. Du Bois argues that because African Americans have been assigned to artificial groups because of slavery and the laws enforcing it, they have been unable to develop a proper social order; furthermore, emancipation has not been able to unloose the societal structures developed under the slave system.

Although Du Bois does not suggest that an oppressed status is the sole cause of the problems facing African Americans, he asserts that discrimination puts African Americans at a strong disadvantage, hampering their ability to take the necessary steps, particularly educational, to better their position. Thus, he rejects the arguments postulated by Washington that mainstream white society would eventually accept and integrate black Americans if only they proved themselves through self-betterment and hard work, stating that "freedmen always start life under an economic disadvantage which generations, perhaps centuries, cannot overcome."

Essential Themes

Key themes that characterized Du Bois's writings and ideas during the pivotal early 1900s are present in his "The Study of the Negro Problems." As Du Bois's ideas developed, he became increasing convinced that active racism and discrimination severely impeded the abilities of African Americans to progress in US society. In this essay, Du Bois pointed to discrimination as an inherent setback for African Americans, whom he argued did not enjoy a level playing field in US social, economic, or political life. Later, Du Bois would argue that one solution to the problems of discrimination was active political agitation to bring about the passage of federal antilynching laws and civil rights protections.

These positions set him in opposition to the ideas of Washington, who had seen the natural role of African Americans to be one step behind their white counterparts. Because Washington was the leading African American thinker of the late 1800s and enjoyed an unusual degree of respect from white leaders, Du Bois's positions established him as one of Washington's greatest critics. Du Bois's activism helped pave the way for the sweeping social changes of the 1950s and 1960s.

Also apparent in Du Bois's outline of the "negro problems" was his support for the transformative power of education¬—an opinion shared by Washington. Du Bois suggested that preventing African Americans from earning proper educations was the primary negative effect of discrimination; such prevention limited economic opportunity. Not long after the publication of this essay, Du Bois began to argue for the role of a "Talented Tenth" of highly educated, elite African Americans who would serve as role models for contemporary black society. Because Du Bois believed that a college education was vital to the intellectual development of the Talented Tenth, he naturally saw illiteracy and a lack of formal education as among the most crucial of the problems facing African Americans.

—*Vanessa E. Vaughn, MA*

Bibliography and Additional Reading

Green, Dan S., and Edwin D. Driver, eds. *W. E. B. Du Bois on Sociology and the Black Community*. Chicago: U of Chicago P, 1978. Print.

Lewis, David Levering. *W. E. B. Du Bois, 1868–1919: Biography of a Race*. New York: Holt, 1993. Print.

Outlaw, Lucius T. "W. E. B. Du Bois on the Study of Social Problems." *Annals of the American Academy of Political and Social Science* 568.1 (2000): 281–97. Print.

■ A Mississippi Governor Opposes Black Education

Date: February 4, 1904
Author: James K. Vardaman
Genre: editorial; article

Summary Overview

By the end of the nineteenth century, an issue had developed in the post-Reconstruction South over the rights of black Americans to receive a quality public school education. Governor James K. Vardaman of Mississippi, in office from 1904 to 1908, argued vehemently against such a policy, expressing his unapologetic belief that blacks were morally and socially inferior to whites. He also opposed African Americans voting, running for public office, and exercising other rights legally afforded to them after the Civil War, on the basis of what he believed to be their propensity for criminal and otherwise corrupt behavior.

Defining Moment

By the latter nineteenth century, the Southern states—whose rabid defense of slavery helped fuel the Civil War—saw black political empowerment thrust upon them by the federally imposed Reconstruction program. The Fourteenth and Fifteenth Amendments, for example, granted citizenship to former slaves and gave them the right to vote and hold elected office. However, the Reconstruction era had come to a formal close in 1877, with the withdrawal of the last federal troops from the South, and despite the nominal political equality given to black Americans, Southern white racists quickly returned to political power and began systematically undermining the rights of black Southerners.

During the post-Reconstruction era, a number of fronts opened in the struggle for black equality in these states. One area was the aforementioned power to vote. To be sure, the restored power of white leaders (particularly Democrats) could not force the repeal of the Fourteenth and Fifteenth Amendments, but the imposition of poll taxes and other obstructions kept black Southerners away from the polls. Jim Crow laws im-

posed legal segregation, and in 1896, the US Supreme Court ruled in *Plessy v. Ferguson* that "separate but equal" facilities in public transportation were constitutional.

In the public education arena, a similar struggle was taking place. White leaders actively opposed the idea of providing a public education—one that was comparable to that offered to white children—to black children. Even some of the South's most progressive education leaders called for the creation of a special curriculum that addressed the particular needs of a race perceived by many as fit for little more than manual labor. Prevailing attitudes in the United States (in the North as well as in the South) held that blacks were socially and morally inferior to whites. Statistics unfortunately supported this sentiment in the minds of many—crime rates among African Americans were significantly higher than those among whites, particularly in the South. Even activists, such as W. E. B. Du Bois, whose lifelong pursuit of black equality included the establishment of the National Association for the Advancement of Colored People (NAACP), were troubled by the growing issues of black illiteracy and crime. White Southern leaders, using these statistics and with popular support, were able to continue the fight against black public education.

In Mississippi, the state's first primary election in 1904 sent Vardaman into the governor's office. Vardaman, a Democrat, was well known as a progressive, advocating for increased government regulation of large corporations and pursuing laws prohibiting child labor. However, he was also an unabashed and outspoken racist, particularly with regard to African Americans. Complaining that education was "ruining our Negroes," he closed black public schools in Mississippi one month after his election. He also took out an editorial in *Les-*

lie's Weekly expressing his views on black public education.

Author Biography

James Kimble Vardaman was born on July 26, 1861, in Jackson County, Texas, where his family had moved from Mississippi in the 1850s. In 1868, he and his family moved back to Mississippi, and he was raised in Yalobusha County, where he received his public school education. He studied law while living with an uncle in Carrollton and gained admittance to the Mississippi bar in 1882. Thereafter, he practiced law in Winona while also editing a number of newspapers. Vardaman served in the Mississippi House of Representatives from 1890 to 1896 and later served as an officer in the Spanish-American War. He served one four-year term as governor from 1904 to 1908 (during which he was dubbed the "White Chief"), and was then elected to the US Senate, serving from 1913 to 1919; he actively opposed US involvement in World War I, and thus lost his reelection bid. He retired to Alabama and died on June 25, 1935.

HISTORICAL DOCUMENT

The race question is one of the most serious problems which confront the civilization of the present century. The entire republic is interested in it; but the South, where the nigger lives in such large numbers, is of course more widely affected and therefore more materially and vitally interested. The election in Maryland, and the interest manifested by the people of the whole republic, bids me hope that a way may be discovered whereby destructive attrition will be avoided—for many years at least. The first thing to be done to bring about the beginning of the process which works matters to a satisfactory issue is to bring our statesmen, philanthropists, sociologists, conservative business men, and misinformed preachers to a sane consideration of the real, inbred, God-planted, and time fixed moral and mental qualities of the nigger.

In the solution of this problem we must recognize in the very outset what Thomas Jefferson recognized a hundred years ago and what Abraham Lincoln indorsed fifty years later, that the nigger cannot live in the same country with the white man on terms of social or political equality. It is one of the impossible things. One of the other of the races will rule. They will not mix. Another thing must be done—the truth must be told about these matters and the nigger given to understand just what is expected of him and what will be done for him. I am very much in favor of protecting the nigger in the pursuit of happiness and the full enjoyment of the products of his labor. I believe in being honest in all business dealing with him as I believe in being candid in the discussion of his political and civil rights.

I am opposed to the nigger's voting, it matters not what his advertised moral and mental qualifications may be. I am just as much opposed to Booker Washington as I am to voting by the cocoanut-headed, chocolate colored typical little coon, Andy Dotson, who blacks my shoes every morning. Neither one is fit to perform the supreme functions of citizenship. Some people may say that that is prejudice. It may be. But it is a wise prejudice founded upon the experience of all the ages. Did you ever think what we are indebted to this prejudice for? It is to this prejudice we are indebted for the purity of the Anglo-Saxon race—the master race of the world. We are indebted to it for the literature of the English-speaking people, for all the great discoveries in science, for the incomparable original plan of the government under which we live—in a word, all the glories which crown and glorify the civilization of the twentieth century. But it matters little what I may think or others may say, that prejudice will live as long as the Anglo-Saxon race retains its virility, its genius for government, and its unconquerable will to rule. When it shall cease to exist, then, indeed, will the scepter of world-rulership pass to other hands, and the glorious achievements of the "heir of all the ages" shall crumble and fall, and over it all will drift the Sahara sands of oblivion. The absolute domination by the white race means race purity. It means order, good government, progress, and general prosperity both for the nigger and white man. But when the nigger is taken into partnership in the government of the country, demoralization, retrogression, and decay ensue—just as surely as the night follows the day

I want to do what is best for both races. I am the nigger's best friend. But I am friendly to him as a nigger whom I expect to live, act, and die as a nigger. A great deal of money, more than $250,000,000, has been spent since the years 1861–65 by the white people of the North and the South in a foolish endeavor to make more of the nigger than God Almighty every intended. How well these efforts have succeeded, this extract from an address by a Northern man attests. I want to call attention to the fact that these statistics are entirely free from the suspicion of "race prejudice," for they were collected by Professor Wilcox, of Cornell University, a native of Massachusetts, and Dr. Winston, president of the North Carolina Agricultural College. These are the conclusions.

1. The negro element is the most criminal in our population.

2. The negro is much more criminal as a free man than he was as a slave.

3. The negro is increasing in criminality with fearful rapidity being one-third more criminal in 1890 than 1880.

4. The negroes who can read and write are more criminal than the illiterate, which is true of no other element of our population.

5. The negro is nearly three times as criminal in the Northeast, where he has not been a slave for a hundred years, and three and a half times as criminal in the Northwest, where he has never been a slave, as in the South, where he was a slave until 1865.

6. The negro is three times as criminal as a native white, and once and a half as criminal as the foreign white, consisting in many cases of the scum of Europe.

7. More than seven-tenths of the negro criminals are under thirty years of age.

But Dr. Wilcox is not the only man who has demonstrated the fallacy of the contention of the superficial student who sees in the school-house and booklearning the panacea for the ills which render the nigger unfit to perform any other function in the economy of the world than that of a servant or menial. Read this clipping from the New Orleans *Times-Democrat*:

These conclusions are sustained by an article by Professor J. R. Stratton printed in the *North American Review* for June 1900. Professor Stratton points out that, according to the census of 1890, the minimum illiteracy of the negro is found in New England, where it is 21.7 per cent.; and the maximum illiteracy of the negro is to be found in the so-called 'black belt' of South Carolina, Mississippi, and Alabama, where it is 65.7 per cent. And yet the negro is four and a half times more criminal in New England, hundred for hundred of the population, than he is in the 'black belt.' You cannot deny or question the correctness of the conclusions reached by these gentlemen. They are irrefragable and stand a Gibraltar against the waves of ignorance, fanaticism, sectional hatred, and Rooseveltian stupidity. We squander money on their education and make criminals of what should be efficient laborers.

It is a grave question and should be handled with consummate skill. The services of the wise, fearless, and patriotic statesman are demanded. We must be just to the nigger, and we must at the same time be true to the white man and true to the civilization of the age. A long way toward the solution of this question would be effected by repealing the amendments to the Federal Constitution which gave the nigger the right to pollute politics. Congress should submit that question to the people, or rather to the States. A mistake was made and it should be corrected. It is urged by some men that it is "too early to discuss that matter." I do not think it is ever too early to tell the truth, correct a mistake, or explode a lie. The people of some of the Southern States have already in effect repealed those amendments. They have eliminated the nigger from politics, and I think and hope they will be able to keep him eliminated; but I prefer doing it in a different way. It would be infinitely better botch for the nigger and the white man if it could be done.

I do not know what will be done along the line we have been discussing by the Legislature of Mississippi. I should like to see Section 206 of the State constitution so amended as to put the public schools entirely in the hands of the Legislature. I am exceedingly desirous of improving the educational facilities of our rural white population. I want the white country boys and girls who are to rule Mississippi in the future equipped, in so far as the school can equip them, for the services, serious duties, and responsibilities which must soon devolve upon them. The hope of the republic, the Ark of the Cov-enant of American ideals, is in the keeping of the great common people, more especially those who live in the rural districts. In these days of sordid materialism and greed for gain, when the dollar has almost become the god, it is pleasant to contemplate the superb qualities of

"The old-fashioned people—
The hale, hard-working people
The kindly country people,
'At uncle used to know."

GLOSSARY

"The old-fashioned people…": from a poem, "The Good, Old-Fashioned People," by James Whitcomb Riley (1849–1916)

Document Analysis

Vardaman's comments stem from his perception that the "race question" was slowly being answered in a way that validated the notion of white superiority over black Americans. Vardaman expresses "hope" that, in spite of the largely ineffectual policies of the Reconstruction era, the United States was starting to embrace the truth: that black Americans simply could not exist on equal social or political footing with white Americans. More than a century earlier, he says, Thomas Jefferson made such a point, and Abraham Lincoln made a similar argument half a century later. Now, he says, state governments (such as Maryland, which was in the process of sending a black disenfranchisement referendum to the voters) were starting to follow suit by recognizing the "truth" about the mental and moral limitations of blacks.

Vardaman speaks in scathing, unapologetically racist terms: he says that blacks—whether educated, like prominent activist Booker T. Washington, or illiterate, like the young man who shines Vardaman's shoes every day—are all equally unworthy of the great social responsibility of voting, for example. Some may call his comments prejudiced, he admits, but he states that history is on his side: the Anglo-Saxon (white) race, he says, is responsible for every major advance in literature, technology, and government in history. If blacks were to replace the "order, good government, progress, and general prosperity" associated with white rule, Vardaman states, the country would fall into a state of demoralization and decay.

Vardaman cites as his evidence crime statistics reported by two university professors. These statistics, he says, show that black men are more likely to be involved in criminal activity as free men than they were as slaves. He even states that educated black men are more "criminal" than illiterate black men. He further cites a study from the journal North American Review, which reports that African Americans in New England, about three-quarters of whom are literate, are four times as likely to commit crime as blacks in the South, where only about one-third are literate.

Having wasted millions of dollars on the Reconstruction effort to educate and empower blacks, government should change course, Vardaman argues. He says it is time to repeal the Fourteenth and Fifteenth Amendments, which made the "mistake" of giving African Americans "the right to pollute politics." After all, Southern states had, by this time, largely done away with the substance of these amendments, barring blacks from the political process, and it was now time to allow the popular vote to remove these amendments from the Constitution. At the same time, blacks should be stripped of the right to receive an equitable public education and take part in government, Vardaman concludes, and the state of Mississippi should invest its money in improving rural white schools so the future white leaders of the state would have the best education possible.

Essential Themes

Although Governor Vardaman states that he thinks black citizens should have the right to the pursuit of happiness and to enjoy the fruits of their labor, he is also clear that black Americans should understand their status as "unfit to perform any other function in the economy of the world than that of a servant or menial." Vardaman is unrepentant in his belief that blacks are the inferior race in comparison to whites, and that they should be encouraged to remain in positions of virtual servitude.

He criticizes the efforts of civil rights activists and others to educate black children and give black Americans the right to vote. Vardaman believes that the inferior status of black people was given to them by God and has been validated throughout human history. Thus, he says, the mistakes of the Reconstruction era—particularly black citizenship and suffrage—were overdue for correction.

Vardaman cites the success of discriminatory policies (such as disenfranchisement) throughout the South as proof that more Americans are embracing the "truth" about what he dubbed the "race question." Still, there remained a push for equality, especially through the public school system. Vardaman dismisses activists who continued the call for racial equality, returning to what he saw as the fundamental truth about blacks: that they should be socially subordinate to whites.

—*Michael P. Auerbach, MA*

Bibliography and Additional Reading

Dean, Edward Ayers, and Hugh P. Kelley. *The Promise of the New South: Life after Reconstruction*. Oxford: Oxford UP, 2007. Print.

Holland, Antonio Frederick. Nathan B. *Young and the Struggle over Black Higher Education*. Columbia: U of Missouri P, 2006. Print.

Lambert, Frank. *The Battle of Ole Miss: Civil Rights v. States Rights*. Oxford: Oxford UP, 2009. Print.

Muhammad, Khalil Gibran. *The Condemnation of Blackness: Race, Crime, and the Making of Modern Urban America*. Cambridge: Harvard UP, 2010. Print.

Sansing, David. "James Kimble Vardaman: Thirty-Sixth Governor of Mississippi: 1904–1908." *Mississippi History Now*. Mississippi Historical Society, Jan. 2004. Web. 16 Apr. 2014.

■ "What It Means to Be Colored in the Capital of the U.S.A."

Date: October 10, 1906
Author: Mary Church Terrell
Genre: speech

Summary Overview

One of the first African American women to earn a college degree, Mary Church Terrell was a prominent public figure in Washington, DC, when she delivered a speech to the United Women's Club on October 10, 1906. The nation's capital had been officially segregated since the late nineteenth century, and Terrell pointed out the injustice of a system that denied citizens all manner of services and opportunities based solely on their race. By the year of her speech, Terrell had earned a master's degree from Oberlin College (a level of education typically reserved for white men), served as the first president of the newly formed National Association of Colored Women, and been appointed to the District of Columbia Board of Education. She was an accomplished public speaker and used her position to argue against the racism and prejudice she encountered. In her speech, Terrell argues that far from being a place of opportunity for African Americans, Washington, DC, was a city where prejudice and segregation made their lives "almost impossible."

Defining Moment

Before the Civil War, Washington, DC, had a significant free black population. Slavery was legal in the city as well, and slaves were transported to Washington for sale until 1850. Slavery was abolished in the capital on April 16, 1862, when President Abraham Lincoln signed the District of Columbia Compensated Emancipation Act. The Act, delivered nearly nine months before Lincoln issued the Emancipation Proclamation, paid slave owners to free their slaves and provided financial incentives for freed slaves to leave the United States. Despite those incentives, a large, active African American community, including a significant educated elite, developed in the city, establishing thriving businesses, supporting the arts, and founding schools and colleges.

The period after the Civil War was one of significant growth for the city's African American citizens. The Fourteenth Amendment (1868) extended citizenship and equal protection under the law to African Americans, and the Fifteenth Amendment (1870) outlawed racial discrimination in voting. Black Washingtonians successfully fought discriminatory practices in public transportation and in schools and the workplace. Efforts were bolstered by the Civil Rights Act of 1875, which attempted to prohibit racial discrimination in public accommodations. In 1883, the Supreme Court of the United States declared the statute unconstitutional. The judges' decision that private companies and facilities, such as theaters and trains, could not be regulated by federal statute marked the beginning of increasingly repressive Jim Crow segregation laws. This, along with a white Southern backlash against the integrated Reconstruction governments in the South, meant that rights for black Southerners, including residents of Washington, DC, quickly eroded. In *Plessy v. Ferguson* (1896), the United States Supreme Court essentially legalized segregation, stating in the majority decision that the establishment of separate but equal facilities for African Americans was not unconstitutional.

In 1872, Lewis Douglass, son of influential abolitionist and statesman Fredrick Douglass, had successfully introduced a bill banning segregation in public places in Washington. Though this law was not officially repealed, segregation laws were later passed that governed public schools and facilities. When not enforced through laws, segregation was maintained through custom and intimidation. In her 1906 speech, Terrell outlined many of the ways that segregation, even when not enforced by law, hampered freedom of movement and restricted employment opportunities for African Americans in Washington, DC. The city's African American residents were not able to rent a hotel room, sit at a lunch counter, or expect service in a department store. They were restricted to but a few trades, and preference was nearly always given to white applicants for employment. In Terrell's view, African Americans were "sacrificed on the altar of prejudice in the Capital of the United States."

Author Biography

Mary Church Terrell was born in Memphis, Tennessee, on September 23, 1863. Her parents were former slaves, and her father, Robert Church, became quite wealthy as a real estate investor. Terrell attended Ober-

lin College, one of the first colleges in the United States to admit both white and black students. She earned a bachelor's degree from Oberlin in 1884 and a master's degree in 1888. After college, Terrell taught school in Washington, DC, and studied in Europe. In 1891, she married Robert Heberton Terrell, Washington's first black municipal court judge. Terrell was appointed to the District of Columbia Board of Education in 1895, becoming the first African American woman to hold the post. Terrell was a well-respected journalist and public speaker who argued against segregation and in favor of women's suffrage. In 1909, she played a key role in the founding of the National Association for the Advancement of Colored People (NAACP). Terrell continued to fight for civil rights and desegregation until her death in 1954.

HISTORICAL DOCUMENT

Thank you very much.

Washington, D.C., has been called "The Colored Man's Paradise." Whether this sobriquet was given to the national capital in bitter irony by a member of the handicapped race, as he reviewed some of his own persecutions and rebuffs, or whether it was given immediately after the war by an ex-slaveholder who for the first time in his life saw colored people walking about like free men, minus the overseer and his whip, history saith not. It is certain that it would be difficult to find a worse misnomer for Washington than "The Colored Man's Paradise" if so prosaic a consideration as veracity is to determine the appropriateness of a name.

For fifteen years I have resided in Washington, and while it was far from being a paradise for colored people when I first touched these shores it has been doing its level best ever since to make conditions for us intolerable. As a colored woman I might enter Washington any night, a stranger in a strange land, and walk miles without finding a place to lay my head. Unless I happened to know colored people who live here or ran across a chance acquaintance who could recommend a colored boarding-house to me, I should be obliged to spend the entire night wandering about. Indians, Chinamen, Filipinos, Japanese and representatives of any other dark race

can find hotel accommodations, if they can pay for them. The colored man alone is thrust out of the hotels of the national capital like a leper.

As a colored woman I may walk from the Capitol to the White House, ravenously hungry and abundantly supplied with money with which to purchase a meal, without finding a single restaurant in which I would be permitted to take a morsel of food, if it was patronized by white people, unless I were willing to sit behind a screen. As a colored woman I cannot visit the tomb of the Father of this country, which owes its very existence to the love of freedom in the human heart and which stands for equal opportunity to all, without being forced to sit in the Jim Crow section of an electric car which starts form the very heart of the city—midway between the Capital and the White House. If I refuse thus to be humiliated, I am cast into jail and forced to pay a fine for violating the Virginia laws....

As a colored woman I may enter more than one white church in Washington without receiving that welcome which as a human being I have the right to expect in the sanctuary of God....

Unless I am willing to engage in a few menial occupations, in which the pay for my services would be very poor, there is no way for me to earn an honest living, if

I am not a trained nurse or a dressmaker or can secure a position as teacher in the public schools, which is exceedingly difficult to do. It matters not what my intellectual attainments may be or how great is the need of the services of a competent person, if I try to enter many of the numerous vocations in which my white sisters are allowed to engage, the door is shut in my face.

From one Washington theater I am excluded altogether. In the remainder certain seats are set aside for colored people, and it is almost impossible to secure others....

With the exception of the Catholic University, there is not a single white college in the national capitol to which colored people are admitted.... A few years ago the Columbian Law School admitted colored students, but in deference to the Southern white students the authorities have decided to exclude them altogether.

Some time ago a young woman who had already attracted some attention in the literary world by her volume of short stories answered an advertisement which appeared in a Washington newspaper, which called for the services of a skilled stenographer and expert typewriter.... The applicants were requested to send specimens of their work and answer certain questions concerning their experience and their speed before they called in person. In reply to her application the young colored woman...received a letter from the firm stating that her references and experience were the most satisfactory that had been sent and requesting her to call. When she presented herself there was some doubt in the mind of the man to whom she was directed concerning her racial pedigree, so he asked her point-blank whether she was colored or white. When she confessed the truth the merchant expressed...deep regret that he could not avail himself of the services of so competent a person, but frankly admitted that employing a colored woman in his establishment in any except a menial position was simply out of the question....

Not only can colored women secure no employment in the Washington stores, department and otherwise, except as menials, and such positions, of course, are few, but even as customers they are not infrequently treated with discourtesy both by the clerks and the proprietor himself....

Although white and colored teachers are under the same Board of Education and the system for the children of both races is said to be uniform, prejudice against the colored teachers in the public schools is manifested in a variety of ways. From 1870 to 1900 there was a colored superintendent at the head of the colored schools. During all that time the directors of the cooking, sewing, physical culture, manual training, music and art departments were colored people. Six years ago a change was inaugurated. The colored superintendent was legislated out of office and the directorships, without a single exception, were taken from colored teachers and given to the whites....

Now, no matter how competent or superior the colored teachers in our public schools may be, they know that they can never rise to the height of a directorship, can never hope to be more than an assistant and receive the meager salary therefore, unless the present regime is radically changed....

Strenuous efforts are being made to run Jim Crow cars in the national capital....

Representative Heflin, of Alabama, who introduced a bill providing for Jim Crow street cars in the District of Columbia last winter, has just received a letter from the president of the East Brookland Citizens' Association "indorsing the movement for separate street cars and sincerely hoping that you will be successful in getting this enacted into a law as soon as possible." Brookland is a suburb of Washington.

The colored laborer's path to a decent livelihood is by no means smooth. Into some of the trades unions here he is admitted, while from others he is excluded altogether. By the union men this is denied, although I am personally acquainted with skilled workmen who tell me they are not admitted into the unions because they are colored. But even when they are allowed to join the unions they frequently derive little benefit, owing to certain tricks of the trade. When the word passes round that help is needed and colored laborers apply, they are often told by the union officials that they have secured all the men they needed, because the places are reserved for white men, until they have been provided with jobs, and colored men must remain idle, unless the supply of white men is too small....

And so I might go on citing instance after instance to show the variety of ways in which our people are sacrificed on the altar of prejudice in the Capital of the United States and how almost insurmountable are the obstacles which block his path to success....

It is impossible for any white person in the United States, no matter how sympathetic and broad, to realize what life would mean to him if his incentive to effort were suddenly snatched away. To the lack of incentive to effort, which is the awful shadow under which we live, may be traced the wreck and ruin of score of col-

ored youth. And surely nowhere in the world do oppression and persecution based solely on the color of the skin appear more hateful and hideous than in the capital of the United States, because the chasm between the principles upon which this Government was founded, in which it still professes to believe, and those which are daily practiced under the protection of the flag, yawn so wide and deep.

Document Analysis

On October 10, 1906, Terrell delivered her speech to the United Women's Club of Washington, DC, an overwhelmingly white audience. Terrell's speech begins with a denunciation of the reputation that Washington, DC, had as "the Colored Man's Paradise." The city could only be thought of as paradise to one accustomed to slavery, she argues. Terrell goes on to give examples of sweeping segregation and widespread discrimination, describing "the variety of ways in which our people are sacrificed on the altar of prejudice in the Capital of the United States and how almost insurmountable are the obstacles which block his path to success."

Washington presented a host of difficulties to African American travelers and residents alike. Terrell begins with the problem of room and board. Any other race of people, she argues, would have a place to sleep and food to eat so long as they could pay their bill. Not so with African Americans. "Unless I happened to know colored people who live here or ran across a chance acquaintance who could recommend a colored boarding-house to me, I should be obliged to spend the entire night wandering about," she explains. Terrell also lays out the difficulties inherent in finding a place to eat, using public transportation, finding a seat in a theater, or visiting a department store.

Perhaps most egregious to Terrell was the lack of employment opportunities available to African American men and women. A single drop of African blood was enough to cost someone a job or prevent him or her from being hired in the first place, regardless of skills or qualifications. She explains, "It matters not what my intellectual attainments may be or how great is the need of the services of a competent person, if I try to enter many of the numerous vocations in which my

white sisters are allowed to engage, the door is shut in my face." Terrell provides examples of discrimination in various professions, noting that African American teachers had lost jobs as department heads, even in segregated schools, and so incoming teachers had no way to move up within the system. Terrell argues that even when African American men joined unions that had a nondiscriminatory policy, the system was often rigged so black men were the last to be given work and were not promoted.

Terrell closes her speech with her conclusion that segregation and discrimination render African Americans helpless and hopeless. Even sympathetic white men and women could not fully "realize what life would mean to [them if their] incentive to effort were suddenly snatched away." Terrell's catalogue of prejudice and injustice was made more poignant by its place in the capital of the United States, which should have protected and defended the rights of its citizens. Despite the nation's lofty ideals, Terrell concludes, "the chasm between the principles upon which this Government was founded, in which it still professes to believe, and those which are daily practiced under the protection of the flag, yawn[s] so wide and deep."

Essential Themes

The primary theme of this speech is the grave injustice suffered by African Americans in the very home of American government, which should have been devoted to the protection of its citizens. Terrell outlines the ways that segregation made even routine travel difficult, prevented gainful employment, and robbed African Americans of the ability to better themselves. Her speech is made the more poignant by her location. She notes that if she attempted to visit George Washington's grave to pay tribute to the man who founded a country that "stands for equal opportunity to all," she would be forced to sit in the back of a streetcar, and she would likewise find it difficult to get a meal while on her way to the White House. Even in Washington, DC, whose government was meant to protect all of its citizens, segregation had made life for African Americans "intolerable."

—*Bethany Groff, MA*

Bibliography and Additional Reading

Fradin, Dennis Brindell, and Judith Bloom Fradin. *Fight On! Mary Church Terrell's Battle for Integration*. New York: Clarion, 2005. Print.

Holland, Jesse J. *Black Men Built the Capitol: Discovering African-American History in and around Washington*. Guilford: Globe Pequot, 2007. Print.

Lightman, David. "Racial Barriers Fell Slowly in Capital." *Journal Sentinel* [Milwaukee]. Journal Sentinel, 16 Jan. 2009. Web. 28 Apr. 2014.

A Skeptical View of Mexican Immigrants in the United States

Date: September 1912
Author: Samuel Bryan
Genre: editorial; article

Summary Overview

During the early twentieth century, the increasing number of Mexican immigrants entering the United States became a major political issue. In this editorial, economist Samuel Bryan wrote that increased Mexican immigration was to be expected, since the country's growing railway industry was enabling Mexicans to easily cross the border into and out of the United States. Bryan also suggested that Mexicans were, as a race, illiterate and predisposed to living in poverty. Such qualities, said Bryan, made Mexican immigrants undesirable and likely to engage in criminal activity that would undermine American society.

Defining Moment

Starting in the early nineteenth century, waves of immigrants came from all over the world to be a part of the new and independent United States. Europeans of all classes came across the Atlantic, while East Asians (most of whom were Chinese and Japanese) came across the Pacific. The discovery of gold in California in the middle of the nineteenth century hastened arrivals from the latter regions, however, as Chinese laborers were brought to the American West to support gold excavation operations. Anglo-American (white) prejudices, however, resulted in the passage of the Chinese Exclusion Act in 1882, effectively putting an end to Chinese immigration to the United States for decades.

Meanwhile, however, another major group was continuing to pour into the United States. By the late nineteenth century, large waves of Mexican immigrants were leaving their homes and crossing the border into the United States in search of jobs. However, unlike Chinese laborers (the largest concentration of whom were found in California and other western regions), by the end of the nineteenth century, Mexican immigrants were found in Chicago and Wyoming, as well as other areas of the country far from the Mexican border, working in a wide range of industries, including mining, farming, and ranching.

One such industry was the same sector that helped these immigrants move about the country rapidly. In the early twentieth century, the US transportation infrastructure continued to expand. As railways spread to virtually every corner of the nation, Mexican laborers played a major role in their construction. The US-Mexican border was largely unprotected—people could cross with relative ease. Therefore, American employers saw in Mexico an opportunity to aggressively recruit laborers and, using the rails, transport these workers across the border.

American attitudes about Mexican immigrants were relatively neutral (at least when compared to sentiments about Chinese immigrants). To be sure, white Americans largely saw Mexicans as an "inferior" race. However, they also valued the presence of Mexican immigrants in the country's agricultural, mining, and transportation sectors. As a result, there was not as much of a backlash against Mexican workers as there was with other immigrant groups.

Still, there was a noticeable growth in the number of Mexican immigrants throughout the country. They were working and living as far north as Chicago in addition to the American Southwest. According to Bryan, wherever these immigrants settled, they did so in closely knit communities that were, in the eyes of other Americans, segregated from the rest of the community. Because of the unique and widespread presence of

Mexicans, conversations arose during the early twentieth century about the influences and impacts of Mexican immigrants on American society. In September 1912, Bryan penned this article, which was published in the progressive periodical *The Survey*. In the article, Bryan offered his opinions of Mexican immigrants, how they compared to other immigrants, and how their lifestyle impacted American society at large.

HISTORICAL DOCUMENT

Previous to 1900 the influx of Mexicans was comparatively unimportant. It was confined almost exclusively to those portions of Texas, New Mexico, Arizona and California which are near the boundary line between Mexico and the United States. Since these states were formerly Mexican territory and have always possessed a considerable Mexican population, a limited migration back and forth across the border was a perfectly natural result of the existing blood relationship. During the period from 1880 to 1900 the Mexican-born population of these border states increased from 66,312 to 99,969—a gain of 33,657 in twenty years. This increase was not sufficient to keep pace with the growth of the total population of the states. Since 1900, however, there has been a rapid increase in the volume of Mexican immigration, and also some change in its geographical distribution....

In 1908, it was estimated that from 60,000 to 100,000 Mexicans entered the United States each year. This estimate, however, should be modified by the well-known fact that each year a considerable number of Mexicans return to Mexico. Approximately 50 percent of those Mexicans who find employment as section hands upon the railroads claim the free transportation back to El Paso which is furnished by the railroad companies to those who have been in their employ six months or a year. Making allowance for this fact, it would be conservative to place the yearly accretion of population by Mexican immigration at from 35,000 to 70,000. It is probable, therefore, that the Mexican-born population of the United States has trebled since the census of 1900 was taken.

This rapid increase within the last decade has resulted from the expansion of industry both in Mexico and in the United States. In this country the industrial development of the Southwest has opened up wider fields of employment for unskilled laborers in transportation, agriculture, mining, and smelting. A similar expansion in northern Mexico has drawn many Mexican laborers from the farms of other sections of the country farther removed from the border, and it is an easy matter to go from the mines and section gangs of northern Mexico to the more remunerative employment to be had in similar industries of the southwestern United States. Thus the movement from the more remote districts of Mexico to the newly developed industries of the North has become largely a stage in a more general movement to the United States. Entrance into this country is not difficult, for employment agencies in normal times have stood ready to advance board, lodging, and transportation to a place where work was to be had, and the immigration officials have usually deemed no Mexican likely to become a public charge so long as this was the case. This was especially true before 1908....

Most of the Mexican immigrants have at one time been employed as railroad laborers. At present they are used chiefly as section hands and as members of construction gangs, but a number are also to be found working as common laborers about the shops and powerhouses. Although a considerable number are employed as helpers. Few have risen above unskilled labor in any branch of the railroad service. As section hands on the two more important systems they were paid a uniform wage of $1.00 per day from their first employment in 1902 until 1909, except for a period of about one year previous to the financial stringency of 1907, when they were paid $1.25 per day. In 1909 the wages of all Mexican section hands employed upon the Santa Fe lines were again raised to $1.25 per day. The significant feature is, however, that as a general rule they have earned less than the members of any other race similarly employed. For example, of the 2,455 Mexican section hands from whom data were secured by the Immigration Commission in 1908 and 1909, 2,111 or 85.9 percent, were earning less than $1.25 per day, while the majority of the

Greeks, Italians, and Japanese earned more than $1.25 and a considerable number more than $1.50 per day.

In the arid regions of the border states where they have always been employed and where the majority of them still live, the Mexicans come into little direct competition with other races, and no problems of importance result from their presence. But within the last decade their area of employment has expanded greatly. They are now used as section hands as far east as Chicago and as far north as Wyoming. Moreover, they are now employed to a considerable extent in the coal mines of Colorado and New Mexico, in the ore mines of Colorado and Arizona, in the smelters of Arizona, in the cement factories of Colorado and California, in the beet sugar industry of the last mentioned states, and in fruit growing and canning in California. In these localities they have at many points come into direct competition with other races, and their low standards have acted as a check upon the progress of the more assertive of these.

Where they are employed in other industries, the same wage discrimination against them as was noted in the case of railroad employees is generally apparent where the work is done on an hour basis, but no discrimination exists in the matter of rates for piecework. As pieceworkers in the fruit canneries and in the sugar beet industry the proverbial sluggishness of the Mexicans prevents them from earning as much as the members of other races. In the citrus fruit industry their treatment varies with the locality. In some instances they are paid the same as the "whites," in others the same as the Japanese, according to the class with which they share the field of employment. The data gathered by the Immigration Commission show that although the earnings of Mexicans employed in the other industries are somewhat higher than those of the Mexican section hands, they are with few exceptions noticeably lower than the earnings of Japanese, Italians, and members of the various Slavic races who are similarly employed. This is true in the case of smelting, ore mining, coal mining, and sugar refining. Specific instances of the use of Mexicans to curb the demands of other races are found in the sugar beet industry of central California, where they were introduced for the purpose of showing the Japanese laborers that they were not indispensable, and in the same industry in Colorado, where they were used in a similar

way against the German-Russians. Moreover, Mexicans have been employed as strikebreakers in the coal mines of Colorado and New Mexico, and in one instance in the shops of one important railroad system.

Socially and politically the presence of large numbers of Mexicans in this country gives rise to serious problems. The reports of the Immigration Commissions show that they lack ambition, are to a very large extent illiterate in their native language, are slow to learn English, and most cases show no political interest. In some instances, however, they have been organized to serve the purposes of political bosses, as for example in Phoenix, Arizona. Although more of them are married and have their families with them than is the case among the south European immigrants, they are unsettled as a class, move readily from place to place, and do not acquire or lease land to any extent. But their most unfavorable characteristic is their inclination to form colonies and live in a clannish manner. Wherever a considerable group of Mexicans are employed, they live together, if possible, and associate very little with members of other races. In the mining towns and other small industrial communities they live ordinarily in rude adobe huts outside of the town limits. As section hands they of course live as the members of the other races have done, in freight cars fitted with windows and bunks, or in rough shacks along the line of the railroad. In the cities their colonization has become a menace.

In Los Angeles the housing problem centers largely in the cleaning up or demolition of the Mexican "house courts," which have become the breeding ground of disease and crime, and which have now attracted a considerable population of immigrants of other races. It is estimated that approximately 2,000 Mexicans are living in these "house courts." Some 15,000 persons of this race are residents of Los Angeles and vicinity. Conditions of life among the immigrants of the city, which are molded to a certain extent by Mexican standards, have been materially improved by the work of the Los Angeles Housing Commission.... However, the Mexican quarter continues to offer a serious social problem to the community....

In conclusion it should be recognized that although the Mexicans have proved to be efficient laborers in certain industries, and have afforded a cheap and elastic labor supply for the southwestern United States, the evils to the community at large which their presence in large numbers almost invariably brings may more than overbalance their desirable qualities. Their low standards of living and of morals, their illiteracy, their utter lack of proper political interest, the retarding effect of their employment upon the wage scale of the more progressive races, and finally their tendency to colonize in urban centers, with evil results, combine to stamp them as a rather undesirable class of residents.

GLOSSARY

house court: a collection of temporary dwellings; a shantytown

piecework: work for which one is paid by the number of pieces completed

section hand: one who works as part of a crew on a section of railroad track

Document Analysis

In his article, Bryan attempts to present to the readers an educated perspective on the growing issue of Mexican immigration to the United States in the early 1900s. Bryan argues that the rate of Mexican immigrants entering and dispersing throughout the United States increased markedly in the late 1800s and early 1900s, an upward trend that could be easily explained. He attributes the increase to the railway industry, which either gave employment to these immigrants or transported them to work opportunities in other industries. Finally, Bryan, reflecting the everyday racism of the time, states that the social characteristics of Mexicans limits these workers to unskilled labor and fosters their willingness to live in makeshift "colonies" that breed disease and crime.

Bryan begins his commentary by stating that Mexican immigration in the United States—which, prior to the 1900s, grew at a sustainable rate and was limited to Texas, California, and the southwestern states—was increasing considerably both in terms of numbers and prevalence. In 1908, for example, Bryan says that as many as one hundred thousand Mexicans entered the country. In fact, he says, since the first census was taken in 1900, the Mexican population in the US appears to have tripled (though, he notes, this might not be entirely accurate, because it does not account for Mexicans returning to Mexico after finishing stints of employment). Furthermore, immigrants were appearing in not only the usual states but also in states far to the North and East.

Bryan attributes this growth and spread to the growing American rail industry. Mexicans were used in a wide range of capacities, including in construction gangs and as powerhouse workers and section hands. The railroads commonly paid for these immigrants' transportation to and from Mexico, a practice that facilitated an increase in cross-border traffic. While the railroad industry was one of the main foci of Mexican workers, Bryan says, it was not the only one: by 1912, Mexicans were working in mines, on farms and ranches, and in smelting facilities. These immigrants were willing to work for even less than other immigrant workers, such as Europeans and East Asians, Bryan argues. The pay imbalance had a "retarding effect" on the wage scale for all racial and ethnic labor groups.

Although Mexican workers presented a viable and less expensive labor pool that benefited the US economy, Bryan's article claims a sociopolitical downside. He says that, in areas close to the US–Mexican border, Mexicans had little competition from other racial and ethnic groups, creating few disruptions to the area. However, in more populated and diverse areas, Mexicans' preference for living together in "colonies" was creating an issue. In Los Angeles, for example, Mexican immigrants were forming "house courts," which were essentially Mexican communes. Crime was a major issue in these courts, as was the spread of disease. Furthermore, the combination of Mexican illiteracy and lack of "political interest" made these immigrants a major target for recruitment by local party bosses and other corrupt officials. For example, Mexicans had been used to break strikes in Colorado and New Mexico mines, Bryan states.

In his conclusion, Bryan weighs the positives and negatives of increased Mexican immigration. He argues that Mexicans present an inexpensive and reliable labor pool to a number of key industries. On the other hand, Mexicans' low standard of living, illiteracy, supposed lack of morals and political interest, and their insistence on living outside American society made this group an "undesirable class," Bryan states.

Essential Themes

Bryan's article on Mexican immigration in the early twentieth-century United States demonstrates two major characteristics of this period in modern American history. First, the increasing volume of immigrants entering the United States reflected the tremendous development the nation was undergoing. Second, despite the value placed on immigrant laborers in some of the nation's most expansive industries, prejudice among Anglo-Americans against immigrant (particularly nonwhite) laborers contributed to a lack of economic success among these ethnic groups.

Bryan begins by acknowledging that Mexican immigration was increasing significantly. This growth was attributable to the wide range of unskilled and/or manual job opportunities available in the United States. The railroad industry was largely responsible for this growth, as the industry was one of the country's leading employers of Mexican immigrants. This industry even made it possible for Mexicans to cross the US border without issue. The rise in Mexican populations in areas far from the border was also attributable to the rails. By the beginning of the twentieth century, Mexicans had access to myriad opportunities: if they were not transported via train to a job within the railroad industry, Bryan writes, Mexicans could easily travel to mines, smelting facilities, and farms throughout the United States.

Mexicans, however, were different from other immigrant groups, Bryan argues. They were apparently willing to accept lower wages than other laborers, for example. This characteristic made Mexicans an attractive pool from which to recruit laborers, Bryan says. However, he adds that Mexicans seemingly lacked certain motivations (including political interest) and were more interested in living a nomadic, communal lifestyle that fostered crime and racial segregation in the areas where they worked. Mexicans, he concluded, presented the US economy with opportunities for inexpensive labor. However, he stated, they offered American society little else of value.

—*Michael P. Auerbach, MA*

Bibliography and Additional Reading

Garcia, Mario T. *Desert Immigrants: The Mexicans of El Paso, 1880–1920.* New Haven: Yale UP, 1981. Print.

Link, William A., and Susannah J. Link. *The Gilded Age and Progressive Era: A Documentary Reader.* Malden: Wiley, 2012. Print.

Lorey, David E. *The U.S.–Mexican Border in the Twentieth Century: A History of Economic and Social Transformation.* Lanham: Rowman, 1999. Print.

Mintz, Steven, ed. *Mexican American Voices: A Documentary Reader.* Malden: Wiley, 2009. Print.

Weber, David J., ed. *Foreigners in Their Native Land: Historical Roots of the Mexican Americans.* Albuquerque: U of New Mexico P, 2003. Print.

Zolberg, Aristide R. *A Nation by Design: Immigration Policy in the Fashioning of America.* Cambridge: Harvard UP, 2009. Print.

■ W.E.B. Du Bois: "Socialism and the Negro Problem"

Date: February 1, 1913
Author: W. E. B. Du Bois
Genre: editorial; article; essay

Summary Overview

Nearly fifty years after the conclusion of the American Civil War and the abolition of slavery, most African Americans were still living in oppression and poverty, and many black leaders were looking for answers. Racial segregation mandated by Jim Crow laws, sharecropping arrangements, and violence on the part of white supremacist organizations such as the Ku Klux Klan combined to keep many black Americans economically and socially repressed. One suggested panacea for the problems facing African Americans was socialism, an ideology and economic model that places a high value on equality for the working class. One of the most prominent early advocates of African American equality was W. E. B. Du Bois, a cofounder of the National Association for the Advancement of Colored People (NAACP). In his essay "Socialism and the Negro Problem," Du Bois addresses socialism as an ideology that had considerable support in the United States at the time and outlines how it cannot be truly successful in achieving its goals unless American socialists are willing to confront the unique challenges facing African Americans, which largely stemmed from racial discrimination.

Defining Moment

The decades following the American Civil War were extremely difficult for most African Americans, especially in the South. Beginning with the Emancipation Proclamation in 1863 and extending through the passage of the Civil Rights Act of 1866 and the three Reconstruction Amendments (the Thirteenth, Fourteenth, and Fifteenth Amendments), many African Americans had high hopes of a more just society coming out of the social and political tumult that followed the abolition of slavery. However, for the vast majority, life did not change as they had hoped. Even before the Reconstruction era came to an official end in 1877 with the withdrawal of the last federal troops from the South, white Southerners had reasserted their political, economic, and social dominance over black Americans, rolling back many of the economic, educational, and political advancements achieved by black Americans in the wake of the Civil War. Further, many white Southerners joined organizations such as the Ku Klux Klan to enforce a hierarchical, white supremacist social order. Black Southerners, working under sharecrop agreements that kept them indebted to white landowners, had very few alternatives but to continue to farm cotton, just as their enslaved forebears had.

Radicalism in the United States has a long history, but possibly at no other point in time were working-class Americans more willing to experiment with new ideologies than during the late nineteenth and early twentieth century, largely due to the monumental economic changes brought on by the Industrial Revolution. However, the majority of prominent socialist thinkers considered the plight of white working-class individuals to be separate from the problems facing African Americans. For one thing, most of the industrial unrest and socialist political organization was taking place in the Northern states, while most of the African American oppression was happening in the South, making it easier for white socialists to ignore the problems facing African Americans. Furthermore, many working-class whites in the North were reluctant to advocate for racial equality due to decades of rhetoric, which told them that if African Americans were to achieve equality, they would only be competition for the factory jobs on which white workers depended. Worse yet, African Americans could be (and often were) brought in by factory owners as scab labor in the event of a strike, further undermining the incentive for white and black workers to ally with one another in the fight for the socialist ideal of economic equality.

In the thirteen years prior to the publication of Du Bois's essay, three large race riots had rocked the nation: in New Orleans in 1900, Atlanta in 1906, and even one in the Northern city of Springfield, Illinois, in 1908. During the Atlanta riot, the threat that African Americans posed as economic competition to white workers—in a city where one of the first nascent black middle classes had taken shape—drove many white Atlantans to violent retaliation. At about the same time, the Socialist Party of America, formed in 1901, became a significant force in US politics. By 1912, the Socialist Party boasted nearly 120,000 members and the party's presidential candidate, Eugene V. Debs, received about 6 percent of the vote in the presidential election of 1912. It was at the nexus of these two historical arcs— between the movements for economic equality and racial equality—that Du Bois wrote "Socialism and the Negro Problem."

Author Biography

Born on February 23, 1868 in Great Barrington, Massachusetts, W. E. B. Du Bois grew up to be a scholar and a civil rights leader. In 1895, Du Bois became the first African American to receive a PhD from Harvard University. He published numerous books, including *Black Reconstruction in America* (1935), which is still in print and widely studied. In 1905, Du Bois was among the founders of the Niagara Movement, a civil rights group made up of scholars dedicated to ensuring equality between the races in the United States. Four years later, Du Bois helped to found the NAACP and served as the editor of the group's monthly periodical, *The Crisis*. He was a member of the Socialist Party from 1910 until 1912, and although he harshly criticized the racism of many prominent socialist thinkers of the time, his belief in socialism's model for a just society never wavered. Late in his life, in 1961, he joined the Communist Party and left the United States for Ghana, where he passed away two years later, on August 27, 1963.

HISTORICAL DOCUMENT

One might divide those interested in Socialism into two distinct camps: On the one hand, those farsighted thinkers who are seeking to determine from the facts of modern industrial organization just what the outcome is going to be; on the other hand, those who suffer from the present industrial situation and who are anxious that, whatever the broad outcome may be, at any rate the present suffering which they know so well shall be stopped.

It is this second class of social thinkers who are interested particularly in the Negro problem. They are saying that the plight of 10,000,000 human beings in the United States, predominantly of the working class, is so evil that it calls for much attention in any program of future social reform. This paper, however, is addressed not to this class, but rather to the class of theoretical Socialists; and its thesis is: In the Negro problem, as it presents itself in the United States, theoretical Socialism of the twentieth century meets a critical dilemma.

There is no doubt as to the alternative presented. On the one hand, here are 90,000,000 white people who, in their extraordinary development, present a peculiar field for the application of Socialistic principles; but on the whole, these people are demanding to-day that just as under capitalistic organization the Negro has been the excluded (i.e., exploited) class, so, too, any Socialistic program shall also exclude the 10,000,000. Many Socialists have acquiesced in this program. No recent convention of Socialists has dared to face fairly the Negro problem and make a straightforward declaration that they regard Negroes as men in the same sense that other persons are. The utmost that the party has been able to do is not to rescind the declaration of an earlier convention. The general attitude of thinking members of the party has been this: We must not turn aside from the great objects of Socialism to take up this issue of the American Negro; let the question wait; when the objects of Socialism are achieved, this problem will be settled along with other problems.

That there is a logical flaw here, no one can deny. Can the problem of any group of 10,000,000 be properly considered as "aside" from any program of Socialism? Can the objects of Socialism be achieved so long as the Negro is neglected? Can any great human problem "wait"? If Socialism is going to settle the American problem of race prejudice without direct attack along these lines by Socialists, why is it necessary for Socialists to fight along other lines? Indeed, there is a kind of fatalistic attitude on the part of certain transcendental Socialists, which often assumes that the whole battle of Socialism is coming by a kind of evolution in which active individual effort on their part is hardly necessary.

As a matter of fact, the Socialists face in the problem of the American Negro this question: Can a minority of any group or country be left out of the Socialistic problem? It is, of course, agreed that a majority could not be left out. Socialists usually put great stress on the fact that the laboring class form a majority of all nations and, nevertheless, are unjustly treated in the distribution of wealth. Suppose, however, that this unjust distribution affected only a minority, and that only a tenth of the American nation were working under unjust economic conditions: Could a Socialistic program be carried out which acquiesced in this condition? Many American Socialists seem silently to assume that this would be possible. To put it concretely, they are going to carry on industry so far as this mass is concerned; they are going to get rid of the private control of capital and they are going to divide up the social income among these 90,000,000 in accordance with some rule of reason, rather than in the present haphazard way. But at the same time, they are going to permit the continued exploitation of these 10,000,000 workers. So far as these 10,000,000 workers are concerned, there is to be no active effort to secure for them a voice in the Social Democracy, or an adequate share in the social income. The idea is that ultimately when the 90,000,000 come to their own, they will voluntarily share with the 10,000,000 serfs. Does the history of the world justify us in expecting any such outcome? Frankly, I do not believe it does. The program is that of industrial aristocracy which the world has always tried; the only difference being that such Socialists are trying to include in the inner circle a much larger number than have ever been included before. Socialistic as this program may be called, it is not real Social Democracy. The essence of Social Democracy is that there shall be no excluded or exploited classes in the Socialistic state; that there shall be no man or woman so poor, ignorant or black as not to count one. Is this simply a far-off ideal, or is it a possible program? I have come to believe that the

test of any great movement toward social reform is the Excluded Class. Who is it that Reform does not propose to benefit? If you are saving dying babies, whose babies are you going to let die? If you are feeding the hungry, what folk are you (regretfully, perhaps, but nonetheless truly) going to let starve? If you are making a juster division of wealth, what people are you going to permit at present to remain in poverty? If you are giving all men votes (not only in the "political" but also in the economic world), what class of people are you going to allow to remain disfranchised?

More than that, assuming that if you did exclude Negroes temporarily from the growing Socialistic state, the ensuing uplift of humanity would in the end repair the temporary damage, the present question is, can you exclude the Negro and push Socialism forward? Every tenth man in the United States is of acknowledged Negro descent; if you take those in gainful occupations, one out of every seven Americans is colored; and if you take laborers and workingmen in the ordinary acceptation of the term, one out of every five is colored. The problem is then to lift four-fifths of a group on the backs of the other fifth. Even if the submerged fifth were "dull driven cattle," this program of Socialistic opportunism would not be easy. But when the program is proposed in the face of a group growing in intelligence and social power and a group made suspicious and bitter by analogous action on the part of trade unionists, what is anti-Negro Socialism doing but handing to its enemies the powerful weapon of 4,500,000 men, who will find it not simply to their interest, but a sacred duty, to underbid the labor market, vote against labor legislation, and fight to keep their fellow laborers down? Is it not significant that Negro soldiers in the army are healthier and desert less than whites? Nor is this all: What becomes of Socialism when it engages in such a fight for human downfall? Whither are gone its lofty aspiration and high resolve—its songs and comradeship?

The Negro Problem, then, is the great test of the American Socialist. Shall American Socialism strive to train for its Socialistic state 10,000,000 serfs, who will serve or be exploited by that state, or shall it strive to incorporate them immediately into that body politic? Theoretically, of course, all Socialists, with few exceptions, would wish the latter program. But it happens that in the United States there is a strong local opinion in the South which violently opposes any program of any kind of reform that recognizes the Negro as a man. So strong is this body of opinion that you have in the South a most extraordinary development. The whole radical movement there represented by men like Blease and Vardaman and Tillman and Jefferson Davis, and attracting such demagogues as Hoke Smith, includes in its program of radical reform a most bitter and reactionary hatred of the Negro. The average modern Socialist can scarcely grasp the extent of this hatred; even murder and torture of human beings holds a prominent place in its philosophy; the defilement of colored women is its joke, and justice toward colored men will not be listened to.

The only basis on which one can even approach these people with a plea for the barest tolerance of colored folk, is that the murder and mistreatment of colored men may possibly hurt white men. Consequently, the Socialist Party finds itself in this predicament: If it acquiesces in race hatred, it has a chance to turn the tremendous power of Southern white radicalism toward its own party; if it does not do this, it becomes a "party of the Negro," with its growth South and North decidedly checked. There are signs that the Socialist leaders are going to accept the chance of getting hold of the radical South, whatever its cost. This paper is written to ask such leaders: After you have gotten the radical South and paid the price which they demand, will the result be Socialism?

GLOSSARY

Blease … Smith: persons expressing strongly racist views: Coleman Blease (1868–1942), James K. Vardaman (1861–1930), Benjamin Tillman (1842–1918), and M. Hoke Smith (1855–1931)

Document Analysis

In this essay, aimed squarely at American socialists, W. E. B. Du Bois bluntly points out the utter hypocrisy inherent in a movement that, although based on the ideal of economic equality for all, had done, up to that point, almost nothing to address or even acknowledge the inherent inequality under which African Americans lived. Written at a point when the Socialist Party's influence in American society had never been greater, Du Bois points out that the main tenet of socialism "is that there shall be no excluded or exploited classes in the Socialistic state; that there shall be no man or woman so poor, ignorant or black as not to count one." He paints the choice facing socialists in stark terms: to live up to their rhetoric and a fight for the economic equality of all Americans, including African Americans, or to seek greater acceptance among white voters and betray their ideals.

In his argument, Du Bois contrasts what he characterizes as the ninety million white Americans, for whom the socialists had shown great concern, with the ten million African Americans, who were mostly members of the working class, yet whom American socialists had largely ignored. Du Bois accuses socialists of having shown no concern for these ten million workers, going so far as to accuse white, working-class socialists of working for improved economic opportunities for themselves while ignoring the plight of the black minority. He lampoons their justification that once equality is gained for the white majority, white Americans would then voluntarily share society's abundance with the black minority. Du Bois responds to this by contending that this is not the way that social movements have operated in the history of the world and that the truest test of a social reform movement is how it treats those who have been historically excluded from society's bounty. He criticizes the "fatalistic attitude" held by many white socialists that "assumes the whole battle of Socialism is coming by a kind of evolution in which active individual effort on their part is hardly necessary."

Finally, Du Bois asserts that, in the long run, socialists are undermining their goal of achieving economic equality by excluding African Americans from their efforts. The ongoing tension between the intertwined issues of race and class left socialists in the American South in a peculiar quandary. They could choose the more expedient path of achieving economic equality for white workers by appealing to Southern whites and excluding African Americans from their political and social agenda, or they could choose the more difficult strategy but the one more likely to succeed: addressing African Americans as equals from the start.

Essential Themes

The challenge that Du Bois posed to American socialists presented them with a difficult choice; but in the short term, it ended up being a choice they did not have to make. The year 1912 proved to be the high point for the American socialist movement, with Debs's presidential run. When the United States entered World War I in 1917, the Socialist Party split over whether to support US involvement in the war. The patriotic fervor generated by the war effort led to an increase in nationalism among white and black Americans that made radical ideologies less appealing. Following the violent Bolshevik Revolution in Russia in 1917, American socialists were seen as a significant threat to national security and became targets of the First Red Scare of 1919 and 1920. Labor unions, where socialism once appeared earlier as a plausible means of attaining economic justice for workers, were singled out by both government officials and factory owners for scrutiny and harassment. Because of this and the generally booming economy of the 1920s, socialism and many other radical ideologies lost a large portion of their supporters and ultimately faded into the background of American politics.

Despite the declining influence of the Socialist Party of America in the years immediately following the publication of "Socialism and the Negro Problem," Du Bois's essay touches on a larger theme of the tension between race and class that continues to be explored by modern scholars. Later socialist thinkers, including the civil rights leader Malcolm X, have argued that there is in inextricable link between capitalism and racism, in which racism is used to divide and control the working class. This line of thought posits that racism prevents workers of various races from recognizing their commonality of interest and joining together in the fight for improved economic opportunities for the poor and the working class, thereby benefiting the interests of the ruling class.

—Steven L. Danver, PhD

Bibliography and Additional Reading
Bell, Daniel. *Marxian Socialism in the United States.* Rev. ed. Ithaca: Cornell UP, 1995. Print.
Hays, Samuel P. *The Response to Industrialism: 1885–1914.* 2nd ed. Chicago: U of Chicago P, 1995. Print.
McPherson, James M. *The Abolitionist Legacy: From Reconstruction to the NAACP.* Princeton: Princeton UP, 1975. Print.
Synnestvedt, Sig. *The White Response to Black Emancipation.* New York: Macmillan, 1972. Print.
Woodward, C. Vann. *The Strange Career of Jim Crow.* New York: Oxford UP, 1955. Print.

WOMEN, SUFFRAGE, AND SOCIETY

Women's push for a voice in politics through the vote, or suffrage, surged ahead during the period covered in this volume, although it was not until passage of the Nineteenth Amendment in 1920 that women finally achieved their goal. In this section we include a number of documents related to women's suffrage. One is an early (1874) petition to Congress by Susan B. Anthony, in the wake of her having been arrested for attempting to vote. Another document, from 1915, presents a well-considered argument by Anna H. Shaw on the democratic necessity of allowing women to vote. A third one (1891), by the Christian temperance activist Frances Willard, speaks more broadly about the role of women in society and the injustice of treating them as second-class citizens. We hear, too, from a group of anti-suffrage women activists at the dawn of World War I about the need to cease discussing the vote altogether in order, they say, to focus society's attention on the war.

Filling out this section are two additional documents of interest: 1) a statement by Theodore Roosevelt on the value of motherhood in society, and the need to keep matters between men and women on an equitable basis; and 2) an excerpt from a book of etiquette for young people, wherein correct behavior and proper relations between men and women in high society are described.

■ Petition to US Congress for Women's Suffrage

Date: January 12, 1874
Author: Susan B. Anthony
Genre: petition; political tract

Summary Overview

One of the most prominent women's rights campaigners of her time, Susan B. Anthony was particularly interested in winning the right to vote (suffrage) for women and spent the better part of her life advocating for such. On November 5, 1872, she and fourteen other women in the first district of Rochester, New York's Eighth Ward tested the American electoral system by attempting to register and vote in the national election. She and the other women were arrested two weeks after the election and charged with voting illegally, but only Anthony's case was pursued; she was tried in federal court in June 1873. In *United States v. Susan B. Anthony* the court eventually decided against Anthony and fined her $100, along with court costs. At this point, Anthony petitioned the US Congress to revoke the fine, which she never paid and which the government never compelled her to pay. In this way, these women were the first to actually vote in a US election, which did not become a legal right for women nationwide until the Nineteenth Amendment came into force in 1920.

Defining Moment

Although the women's rights movement had been active before the Civil War, the movement was mainly put on hold as the nation decided its stance on slavery. The 1848 Seneca Falls Convention in New York and the 1850 National Women's Rights Convention in Worcester, Massachusetts, were evidence that the antebellum women's rights movement was gaining momentum. Many women's rights activists had been deeply involved in the abolition movement as well, which gave them invaluable experience in how to organize and communicate their reform platforms. After the Civil War concluded, many women returned their attention to women's rights and, in particular, to women's suffrage. This was a time in American history when many other social reforms and civil rights were emerging. Many fought for more than women's rights to vote, pushing for equal pay and equal access to higher education for women. Others took up the cause of temperance (the abolition of the sale of alcohol and certain drugs), as they were seen as detrimental to stable family life, an issue in which women had a vested interest.

As for suffrage, Anthony, along with other activists, saw the newly enacted Fourteenth Amendment as an opportunity to test the system. This amendment to the Constitution, ratified in 1868, was part of the Reconstruction efforts after the Civil War, and was designed to grant former slaves US citizenship, with due process and equal protection under the law. It was the citizenship clause of the amendment on which Anthony focused, reasoning that because women were US citizens, they too had the right to vote. The Fifteenth Amendment (1870), which gave the federal government oversight of elections, was also seen to be in their favor, as it too had a clause stipulating that citizen's right to vote "shall not be denied or abridged by the United States or by any state on account of race, color, or previous condition of servitude." Anthony and the National Woman Suffrage Association decided to challenge the new laws through the courts to see if women's suffrage could be gained by such means. As such, in 1872, a group of women including Anthony tried to register to vote in Rochester, New York. As they were successful in this, many returned to actually vote in the election, and they were allowed to do so by the federal election inspectors. Anthony used this challenge as a key theme of one of her speaking tours, which she undertook before her trial in June 1873. At the trial, the judge gave a directed guilty verdict to the jury. Anthony was ordered to pay a fine, but instead, she petitioned

Congress to overturn the fine.

Author Biography

Susan Brownell Anthony, born on February 15, 1820, in Adams, Massachusetts, was one of the most prominent civil rights activists in the nineteenth century. She was a particular proponent of women's right to vote (or suffrage) and to higher education and equal pay for equal work, although she was also active in the abolitionist and temperance movements. She had a working partnership for most of her life with Elizabeth Cady Stanton. While Stanton wrote copiously, Anthony traveled and lectured tirelessly, sharing their ideas for reform far and wide, which included petitioning state and federal legislatures. A leader in the suffrage movement, Anthony organized the National Woman Suffrage Association with Stanton, which eventually merged with the American Woman Suffrage Association to form the National American Woman Suffrage Association. With her suffrage colleagues, Anthony ensured the history of the early movement was documented and disseminated to school and university libraries. She died on March 13, 1906.

HISTORICAL DOCUMENT

To the Congress of the United States.

The petition of Susan B. Anthony, of the city of Rochester in the county of Monroe and state of New York, respectfully represents:

That prior to the late Presidential election your petitioner applied to the board of registry in the Eighth ward of the city of Rochester, in which city she had resided for more than 25 years, to have her name placed upon the register of voters, and the board of registry, after consideration of the subject, decided that your petitioner was entitled to have her name placed upon the register, and placed it there accordingly.

On the day of the election, your petitioner, in common with hundreds of other American citizens, her neighbors, whose names had also been registered as voters, offered to the inspectors of election, her ballots for electors of President and Vice President, and for members of Congress, which were received and deposited in the ballot box by the inspectors.

For this act of your petitioner, an indictment was found against her by the grand jury, at the sitting of the District Court of the United States for the Northern District of New York at Albany, charging your petitioner, under the nineteenth section of the Act of Congress of May 31, 1870, entitled, "An act to enforce the rights of citizens of the United States to vote in the several states of this union, and for other purposes," with having "*knowingly* voted without having a lawful right to vote."

To that indictment your petitioner pleaded not guilty,

and the trial of the issue thus joined took place at the Circuit Court in Canandaigua, in the county of Ontario, before the Honorable Ward Hunt, one of the Justices of the Supreme Court of the United States, on the eighteenth day of June last.

Upon that trial, the facts of voting by your petitioner, and that she was a woman, were not denied—nor was it claimed on the part of the government, that your petitioner lacked any of the qualifications of a voter, unless disqualified by reason of her sex.

It was shown on behalf of your petitioner on the trial, that before voting she called upon a respectable lawyer and asked his opinion whether she had a right to vote, and he advised her that she had such right; and the lawyer was examined as a witness in her behalf, and testified that he gave her such advice, and that he gave it in good faith, believing that she had such right.

It also appeared that when she offered to vote, the question, whether, as a woman she had a right to vote, was raised by the inspectors, and considered by them in her presence, and they decided that she had a right to vote, and received her vote accordingly.

It was shown on the part of the government, that on the examination of your petitioner before the commissioner on whose warrant she was arrested, your petitioner stated that she should have voted if allowed to vote, without reference to the advice of the attorney whose opinion she had asked; that she was not induced to vote by that opinion; that she had before determined to offer her vote, and had no doubt about her right to vote.

At the close of the testimony, your petitioner's counsel proceeded to address the jury and stated that he desired to present for consideration three propositions, two of law and one of fact:

First—That your petitioner had a lawful right to vote.

Second—That whether she had a right to vote or not, if she honestly believed that she had that right, and voted in good faith in that belief, she was guilty of no crime.

Third—That when your petitioner gave her vote she gave it in good faith, believing that it was her right to do so.

That the two first propositions presented questions for the Court to decide, and the last a question for the jury.

When your petitioner's counsel had proceeded thus far, the Judge suggested that the counsel had better discuss in the first place the questions of law; which the counsel proceeded to do, and having discussed the two legal questions at length, asked leave then to say a few words to the jury on the question of fact. The Judge then said to the counsel that he thought that had better be left until the views of the court upon the legal questions should be made known.

The district attorney thereupon addressed the court at length upon the legal questions, and at the close of his argument the Judge delivered an opinion adverse to the positions of your petitioner's counsel upon both of the legal questions presented, holding, that your petitioner was not entitled to vote; and that if she voted in good faith in the belief in fact that she had a right to vote, it would constitute no defense—the ground of the decision on the last point being that your petitioner was bound to know that by law she was not a legal voter, and that even if she voted in good faith in the contrary belief, it constituted no defence to the crime with which she was charged.

The decision of the Judge upon those questions was read from a written document, and at the close of the reading the Judge said, that the decision of those questions disposed of the case, and left no question of fact for the jury, and that he should therefore direct the jury to find a verdict of guilty. The judge then said to the jury that the decision of the Court had disposed of all there was in the case, and that he directed them to find a verdict of guilty; and he instructed the clerk to enter such a verdict.

At this time, before any entry had been made by the clerk, your petitioner's counsel asked the Judge to submit the case to the jury, and to give to the jury the following several instructions:

First—That if the defendant at the time of voting, believed that she had a right to vote, and voted in good faith in that belief, she was not guilty of the offence charged.

Second—That in determining the question whether she did or did not believe that she had a right to vote, the jury might take into consideration as bearing upon that question, the advice which she received from the counsel to whom she applied.

Third—That they might also take into consideration as bearing upon the same question, the fact that the inspectors considered the question, and came to the conclusion that she had a right to vote.

Fourth—That the jury had a right to find a general verdict of guilty or not guilty, as they should believe that she had or had not been guilty of the offense described in the statute.

The Judge declined to submit the case to the jury upon any question whatever, and directed them to render a verdict of guilty against your petitioner.

Your petitioner's counsel excepted to the decision of the Judge upon the legal questions, and to his direction to the jury to find a verdict of guilty; insisting that it was a direction which no court had a right to give in any criminal case.

The Judge then instructed the clerk to take the verdict, and the clerk said, "Gentlemen of the jury, hearken to your verdict as the court hath recorded it. You say you find the defendant guilty of the offence charged. So say you all."

No response whatever was made by the jury either by word or sign. They had not consulted together in their seats or otherwise. Neither of them had spoken a word, nor had they been asked whether they had or had not agreed upon a verdict.

Your petitioner's counsel then asked that the clerk be requested to poll the jury. The Judge said, "that cannot be allowed, gentlemen of the jury you are discharged," and the jurors left the box. No juror spoke a word during the trial, from the time when they were empannelled to the time of their discharge.

After denying a motion for a new trial, the Judge proceeded upon the conviction thus obtained to pass sentence upon your petitioner, imposing upon her, a fine of one hundred dollars, and the costs of the prosecution.

Your petitioner respectfully submits, that in these proceedings she has been denied the rights guarantied by the constitution to all persons accused of crime, the right of trial by jury, and the right to have the assistance of counsel for their defence. It is a mockery to call her trial a trial by jury; and unless the assistance of counsel may be limited to the argument of legal questions, without the privilege of saying a word to the jury upon the question of the guilt or innocence in fact of the party charged, or the privilege of ascertaining from the jury whether they do or do not agree to the verdict pronounced by the court in their name, she has been denied the assistance of counsel for her defence.

Your petitioner, also, respectfully insists, that the decision of the Judge, that good faith on the part of your petitioner in offering her vote did not constitute a defence, was not only a violation of the deepest and most sacred principle of the criminal law, that no one can be guilty of crime unless a criminal intent exists; but was also, a palpable violation of the statute under which the conviction was had; not on the ground that good faith could, in this, or in any case justify a criminal act, but on the ground that *bad faith* in voting was an indispensable ingredient in the offence with which your petitioner was charged. Any other interpretation strikes the word

"knowingly," out of the statute, the word which alone describes the essence of the offence.

The statute means, as your petitioner is advised, and humbly submits, a *knowledge in fact*, not a knowledge falsely imputed by law to a party not possessing it in fact, as the Judge in this case has held. Crimes cannot either in law, or in morals, be established by judicial falsehood. If there be any crime in the case, your petitioner humbly insists, it is to be found in such an adjudication.

To the decision of the Judge upon the question of the right of your petitioner to vote she makes no complaint. It was a question properly belonging to the court to decide, was fully and fairly submitted to the Judge, and of his decision, whether right or wrong, your petitioner is well aware she cannot here complain.

But in regard to her conviction of crime, which she insists, for the reasons above given, was in violation of the principles of the common law, of common morality, of the statute under which she was charged, and of the Constitution; a crime of which she was as innocent as the Judge by whom, she was convicted, she respectfully asks, inasmuch as the law has provided no means of reviewing the decisions of the Judge, or of correcting his errors, that the fine imposed upon your petitioner be remitted, as an expression of the sense of this high tribunal that her conviction was unjust.

Dated January 12, 1874.
Susan B. Anthony.

GLOSSARY

empanel: (or impanel): to situate on a panel or jury; to establish as a jury

except to: take exception to, disagree with

hearken: listen to, hear

Document Analysis

By the time Anthony sent her petition to Congress in 1874, she had already been found guilty of voting illegally. She felt she had done nothing wrong and did not agree to pay the fine. In this document, Anthony appeals her conviction to Congress and asks for her fine to be overturned. In her appeal, Anthony relies upon legal arguments involving the Fourteenth and Fifteenth Amendments, as well as prior legal arguments made by her lawyer designed to appeal her conviction.

Throughout the document, Anthony addresses members of Congress in language they would easily understand. As they are in charge of making the laws, she speaks to them in legal terms. She quotes verbatim from her lawyer, Henry Selden, at times, knowing that the words of a man, and a lawyer, may well hold more weight with them than the words of a woman found guilty of a crime. Anthony presents the facts of her case, and the history of how her case came before the courts, in a concise, dispassionate, and logical manner, which is in direct opposition to the more passionate tones of her public speeches on suffrage. She makes the point that before attempting to vote, she asked the opinion of a respected (male) lawyer, and that he "advised her that she had such right" (he repeated this when called as a witness at her trial). She also makes the point that the election inspectors also "decided that she had a right to vote, and received her vote accordingly."

Anthony also insists that because of this, she truly believes she has the right to vote and, therefore, voted in good faith. She is also concerned that her verdict and sentence were directed to the jury by the judge in the case and that, therefore, she was denied her constitutional right to a trial by jury. She feels that because of these irregularities, her conviction is unjust. Further, she states that because the court system gives her no access to appeal or "no means of reviewing the decisions of the Judge, or of correcting his errors," she should not have to pay the fine and, therefore, asks Congress to overturn her sentence by remitting the fine.

Essential Themes

As a woman, Anthony could not legally vote in elections in 1872, and yet she dared to do so. Change was in the air, and progressive women and men began advocating for a woman's right to vote. As amendments had been introduced to ensure that some black men were able to vote after the Civil War, many women saw this as an opportunity for them to gain the same right.

Anthony's legal and constitutional challenge for the right of women to vote set the stage for the growth of the suffrage movement over the following several de-

cades. These events also provided her with an opportunity to embark on a speaking tour about suffrage and to sway many other women, and especially men, to her cause. Anthony actually wanted to be arrested, for the sake of publicity, and published three thousand copies of her lawyer's argument in 1873 as pamphlets, mailing them to key newspapers. In 1874, she also published an account of her trial.

After losing her case, Anthony was portrayed as either a martyr for the suffrage cause or as a common criminal. However, Anthony is remembered as a feminist icon and a champion of women's rights. Americans did not forget this trailblazing woman, and she was the first woman to appear on a US dollar coin. Although Anthony died more than a decade before American women finally won the right to vote in 1920, her life's work set the stage for change.

—*Lee Tunstall, PhD*

Bibliography and Additional Reading

Barry, Kathleen. *Susan B. Anthony: A Biography of a Singular Feminist*. New York: NYUP, 1988. Print.

Gordon, Ann D., ed. *The Selected Papers of Elizabeth Cady Stanton and Susan B. Anthony*. 6 Vols. New Brunswick: Rutgers UP, 1997–2013. Print.

_____. *The Trial of Susan B. Anthony*. Washington, DC: Federal Judicial Center, 2005. Digital file.

Hull, N. E. H. *The Woman Who Dared to Vote*. Lawrence: U of Kansas P, 2012. Digital file.

Sherr, Lynn. *Failure Is Impossible: Susan B. Anthony in Her Own Words*. New York: Times Books, 1995. Print.

Stanton, Elizabeth Cady, and Susan Brownell Anthony. *The Elizabeth Cady Stanton–Susan B. Anthony Reader: Correspondence, Writings, Speeches*. Ed. Ellen Carol DuBois. Boston: Northeastern UP, 1992. Print.

Frances Willard: Address to the National Council of Women

Date: February 22–25, 1891
Authors: Frances E. Willard
Genre: speech

Summary Overview

In February of 1891, social reformer and feminist Frances Willard, president of the National Council of Women of the United States, spoke at that organization's first triennial meeting in Washington, DC. During her address to the group, she commented on the long-standing inferior position of women in American society, particularly in the realms of labor and politics. Citing the examples of international female leaders as well as the observations of prominent American thinkers, she expressed hope that women would one day be considered equal members of American society.

Defining Moment

The temperance movement, an effort to halt alcohol consumption in the United States, began during the years before the Civil War. The war drew attention away from the movement, but many religious groups and reformers nevertheless sought to address the issue. During the late nineteenth century, the cause of temperance was taken up by women's groups, who argued that alcohol posed a danger to American women and families.

In 1879, one such group, the Woman's Christian Temperance Union (WCTU), chose as its newest president Frances E. Willard, who had been involved in the temperance movement for much of her life. The WCTU had grown rapidly since its official formation in 1873, and by the time Willard assumed her position of leadership, the group had evolved into one of the United States' leading temperance organizations.

Although the WCTU continued to focus primarily on temperance during her tenure as president, Willard saw an opportunity to build and expand the organization beyond the prohibition arena. She inspired the group's members to develop an interest in a wide range of issues, including women's suffrage. Willard also introduced a new phrase, *home protection*, as a driving force in encouraging women to take an interest in issues outside of the home as well as within it. Under the auspices of home protection, the WCTU began speaking out against such issues as prostitution and the spread of venereal disease. Willard was also interested in forming alliances with like-minded international reformers. The WCTU encouraged world leaders to fight alcoholism as well as consumption of addictive drugs such as opiates, and chapters of the WCTU came into being in countries around the world.

Back in the United States, Willard continued to gain supporters. She offered a different approach to achieving women's suffrage than other activists: rather than calling for a constitutional amendment, which would require the support of the all-male Congress, Willard encouraged women to work at the local level to bolster support for suffrage. Willard also drew the public's attention to a variety of labor and education issues.

In 1888, the National Council of Women (NCW) formed under the leadership of Willard and Susan B. Anthony, among other noted suffragists. Willard was named president of the organization that year. In February of 1891, the organization held its first meeting in Washington, DC.

Author Biography

Frances Elizabeth Caroline Willard was born on September 28, 1839, in Churchville, New York. She and her parents moved to Oberlin, Ohio, when she was two years old, and later to Wisconsin. She attended Milwaukee Female College and North Western Female College. Willard began her career in education, but after traveling abroad for a time, she returned to become president of Evanston College for Ladies. In the early

1870s, she joined the WCTU's Illinois chapter. Soon after, she became secretary of the national organization. Over time, she became the WCTU's global leader as well as a prominent writer and public speaker. In 1888 she was named president of the NCW, a position she held for several years. She continued to lead the WCTU until February 18, 1898, when she died of influenza.

HISTORICAL DOCUMENT

In the epoch on which we have entered labor will doubtless come to be the only potentate, and, "for value received," will have the skilled toil of the human species as its sole basis of any "specie payment"; "a note of hand" having no offset save the human hand at work. For man added to nature, is all the capital there is on earth; and "the best that any mortal hath is that which every mortal shares." But nature belongs equally to all men; hence the only genuine capital and changeless medium of exchange, always up to par value is labor itself, and there will eventually be no more antagonism between capital and labor than between the right hand and the left. Labor is the intelligent and beneficent reaction of man upon nature. This reaction sets force enough in motion to float him in all waters and carry him across all continents. His daily labor, then, is the natural equivalent he furnishes for food and clothing, fuel and shelter, and it is the supreme interest of the State of prepare the individual in head, hand, and heart to put forth his highest power. Carried to its legitimate conclusion, this is the socialism of Christ; the Golden Rule in action; the basis of that golden age which shall succeed this age of gold. There is no devil's delusion so complete as that "blue blood" is best. That it is really the cheapest and thinnest blood of all is proved by the fact that the blue veins, from which we get the phrase, are but the symptoms of poor health, and he who has poor health is poor indeed. That a white hand is to be desired is another first-class delusion, and in time to come the white hand will be a badge of inferiority and progressive paralysis, while the brown hand of self-help will be the hand of holiness. Women are beginning to study the labor question, that whale to which politicians are now throwing tubs, and which spouts so foamily in the deep sea of living issues. Women, as a class, have been the world chief toilers; it is a world-old proverb that "their work is never done." But the value put upon that work is pointedly illustrated in the reply recently given by an ancient Seminole to one of our white ribboners who visited the reservation of that tribe in Florida, where she saw oxen grazing and a horse roaming the pasture, while two women were grinding at the mill, pushing its wheels laboriously by hand. Turning to the old Indian chief who sat by, the temperance woman said, with pent-up indignation:

"Why don't you yoke the oxen or harness the horses and let them the turn the mill?" The "calm view" set forth in his answer contains a whole body of evidence touching the woman question. Hear him:

"Horse cost money; ox cost money; squaw cost nothing."

After all, there were tons of philosophy in the phrase; for, by the laws of mind, each person in a community is estimated according to his relation to the chief popular standard of value. To-day, in this commercial civilization of ours, money is that standard. Hence the emancipation of women must come, first of all, along industrial lines. She must, in her skilled head and hands, represent financial values. To-day the standard is gold; to-morrow it will be gifts; the next day character. But, in the slow, systematic process of evolution it is only through financial freedom, that she will rise to that truer freedom which is the measure of all her faculties in trained, harmonious, and helpful exercise. ...

Just thirty years ago, in 1861, General Spinner, of grateful memory, proposed the admission of women to employment in the United States Treasury. As Salmon P. Chase was Secretary of that Department, his permission was sought and freely obtained, but so much difficulty was made by men who wanted the work that Attorney-General Edward Bates had to render an opinion favorable to the women, and we may well believe that Abraham Lincoln, always our friend, was in sympathy with the movement. Not a little annoyance was endured by the three officers who publicly took up the women's cause. A variegated and complete assortment of nightcaps, labeled with the word "Grandmother," and other epithets intended to be equally opprobrious, was sent them through the post-office, also letters containing vituperative threats that failed of their intention.

It is not too much to claim that a new era dawned for woman, industrially and officially, when the imperial people's Government thus for the first time recognized her right to a share in the good things it has to give.

For my part, I would have woman everywhere treated as an individual and not as belonging to a tribe. I would have her portion under the sun assigned to her in severalty, and would teach her as rapidly as possible to become a citizen of the world on equal terms with every other citizen.

No words more cogent have been spoken on the industrial disenthrallment of women than by Edward Bellamy, who told me once that when he felt the touch of his little girl's hand upon his cheek the exclamation of Luther, "This is a hard world for girls," came to his lips, and he set about advocating social conditions that should make it less difficult and dangerous.

The February issue of that breezy magazine, *The Ladies Home Journal*, is of especial interest. Compare it with a twenty-year-old *Godey*, and, in spite of its puny-waisted fashion-plates, see how much more roomy now is woman's world. And its most significant article this month is Edward Bellamy's "Woman in the Year 2000." Here he shows the supreme importance to society of industrial independence among women. He claims that within two or three generations there will be but one great business corporation—the state—in which all men and women shall have an equal share—say one, three, or five thousand a year, which, as matters now stand, is certainly most generous of him, especially as it is to come through no masculine intermediary, but straight into our own, in that day, ample and numerous pockets. For woman is to "share and share alike" in this national income with the noblest Roman of them all, and, being thus rendered perfectly "secure and comfortable" for life, she will not marry except for love; and, if she does not marry at all, will be under no pecuniary or social disadvantage. He says:

Would you gain a realization of the position of the old maid in the year 2000. If so, look at the lordly bachelor of today, the hero of romance, the cynosure of the drawing-room and of the promenade. Even as that bright being,

like him self-poised, serenely insouciant, free as air will the old maid of the year 2000 be. It is altogether probable, by the way, that the term old maid will by that time have fallen into disuse. But while the unmarried woman of the year 2000, whether young or old, will enjoy the dignity and independence of the bachelor of to-day, the insolent prosperity at present enjoyed by the latter will have passed into salutary, if sad, eclipse. No longer profiting by the effect of the pressure of economic necessity upon woman, to make him indispensable, but dependent exclusively upon his intrinsic attractions, instead of being able to assume the fastidious airs of a sultan surrounded by languishing beauties, he will be fortunate if he can secure by his merits the smiles of one… In the year 2000 no man, whether lover or husband, may hope to win the favor of maid or wife save by desert.

Surely desert is a vast improvement upon desertion as the divorce courts illustrate the latter in these unpoetic days!

The *Boston Globe*, analyzing the recent statistics of the Massachusetts Labor Bureau, says:

> The figures simply show that in the employments in which the very lowest wages are paid, women constitute over 70 per cent of the workers, while in the employments where as high as $20 a week are paid they constitute hardly over 3 per cent. In addition to all this is the humiliating fact that in the same occupations, standing side by side with men, the females are paid less wages for the same work; or, what amounts to the same thing, a woman of twenty years or upwards is made to work side by side with a boy of ten at the same wages. Women are compelled, then, to fill most of the cheap places, and paid less wages for the same work at that. We have no hesitation in saying that this is an indefensible injustice, and one so gross as to shame civilization. Why do legislators sit passively under such discriminations of sex in the matter of work and wages: Simply because they know that the women carry no votes, and that mere sentiment, however just, can

neither seat nor unseat a politician. But it will not always be thus.

Now there can be no more constant source of moral deterioration among women than these figures furnish ....

Jacob Riis, in his new book, entitled "How the Other Half Lives," portrays the life of "the submerged tenth" in New York city after a fashion that makes us wonder if our Siberian exile petitions ought not to be duplicated to the governor of the proud Empire State of our own land. Now, in face of all this abomination of desolation, I believe that when, for every child born into the world, the problems of food and clothing, fuel and shelter are already and forevermore settled questions (the great, kind foresighted human family as a corporate firm of We, Us & Company, having arranged all that as an offset to the labor of that child when old enough to work), then will have come the very first fair chance ever yet given for the survival of the fittest in true character and the highest conquest.

The whole rationale of women's place in finance and politics is set forth in the remark of a Knight of Labor, who, referring to an undesirable locality, said, "It's not a fit place for a woman," and the quick reply of a comrade, "Then it's time for women to go down there and make it fit." ...

A philosopher has said (he was the father of Louisa M. Alcott) that individualism grows behind the ears, personality over the eyes. To me the distinction seems a good one and I could wish that in all our woman's work we might insist on the motherly, the social, the unifying power of personality with its gracious instinct of motherhood rather than on individualism with selfhood as its everlasting and colossal shadow.

The man-sided woman question has invaded all realms, even to those where crowns are worn. Never before in history were so many of the word's chief rulers women. Victoria of England has been for fifty-three years queen of the greatest nation on earth except our own. Spain has its queen regent; Holland its queen regent and princess royal; Hawaii a queen; Madagascar another queen, and it seems but yesterday since the Republic of Brazil was ruled by the princess regent, who abolished slavery.

In all the line of English history only two epochs have received a gracious name, and they are the two when great queens reigned—the "Elizabethan" and the "Victorian" ages. Besides them, we have affectionate mention of "the good Queen Anne, whom God defended." So far as I have learned, there is nothing analogous to this in the reign of any English king. Surely these facts have high significance in helping to work out a solution of the mightiest problem of our time: woman in government.

GLOSSARY

disenthrallment: release from bondage; emancipation

fashion-plate: an illustration (of clothing or accessories) appearing in a book or magazine

opprobrious: scornful or abusive

potentate: a ruler with great power

severalty: individually, as opposed to collectively

vituperative: harshly critical; mean

Document Analysis

Willard's address to the NCW centers on the theme that women, long considered inferior in a male-dominated society, were starting to take an interest in being more influential in many key areas. The first of these areas was labor, which she underscores as an arena of high value to all members of modern society. The second area was politics, as issues such as hunger, child welfare, and housing were, in her estimation, being given attention thanks to the advocacy of women. Women, she explains, were increasingly playing a role in the leadership of other nations, and in the United States, they were starting to rise as well.

Willard begins this portion of her speech by highlighting the significance of labor to modern society. Labor, she says, is the "intelligent and beneficent reaction" of humanity to nature. In other words, when people went to work, they did so to ensure that they had food, shelter, and other critical amenities. There was a misperception, she explains, that only certain people were qualified to perform the most important duties in society; she characterizes this belief, that rich white men were the only people whose contributions to society were vital, as a "devil's delusion." In reality, poor, nonwhite, and female Americans also had an important stake in the success of society.

Women in particular, Willard notes, were, in the late nineteenth century, positioning themselves to be valuable members of the American labor force. However, women continued to receive far less pay for their work, and despite the support of some progressive men, this inequality remained in place. Willard supports her comments with statistics and the words of a number of key figures, including socialist and utopian Edward Bellamy, whom she quotes as having said, "This is a hard world for girls." Bellamy predicted that by the year 2000, the notion that women were inferior to men in the workplace would be history, as women would be far more independent and dignified.

Willard also commented on woman's increasing relevance in government and politics. To be sure, she notes, some of the most pressing issues facing the United States during its ongoing industrialization—the need for food, housing, and fuel, for example—were issues brought to light by women. However, women should not be treated in a political sense as a single interest group or "tribe," as she puts it. Rather, American women were starting to show individual leadership on those and other issues. Although the United States lagged far behind other nations with women in leadership positions, such as England, Spain, and Holland, Willard argues that the tide in the United States was slowly starting to turn toward female political leadership.

Essential Themes

Although Willard was particularly concerned with the effects of alcohol on American society, she was also interested in a wide range of other issues, including women's suffrage and labor equality. Her address delivered at the NCW's first major conference illustrated her thoughts on these issues.

With regard to labor, Willard acknowledged two important facts: first, that labor was an absolutely essential component of modern society, and second, that labor should be considered as a broad spectrum. The work of wealthy white men, she argued, should be considered as but a part of this spectrum, and the labor performed by women, minorities, and the poor should be valued equally. Women were woefully underpaid and relegated to more menial jobs than men, but although this trend had long held true throughout American history, Willard expressed optimism at the fact that a growing group of progressive-minded leaders and thinkers advocated for a change in course.

Connected to what Willard saw as a rise of women's influence in labor was the fact that women were increasingly positioning themselves as influential in American politics, even though suffrage was not yet a reality. Women, Willard noted, had become the chief advocates for a wide range of key issues facing the nineteenth-century American economy. Children's welfare, housing, food, and energy, all major matters facing both state and federal governments, were issues of great familiarity to women, whose long-standing position as homemakers made them direct witnesses to these political matters. Willard believed that women's expertise would be of great benefit in addressing those domestic issues.

To be sure, Willard argued, American women had a long way to go. While contemporary queens, princesses, and other female leaders held considerable authority and influence in their respective nations, American women remained at a political and economic disadvantage in comparison to men. Nevertheless, she said, the presence of those female leaders, as well as the slow changes in the status of women in the United States, provided a great deal of encouragement where there had previously been little.

—*Michael P. Auerbach, MA*

Bibliography and Additional Reading

Fletcher, Holly Berkley. *Gender and the American Temperance Movement of the Nineteenth Century.* London: Routledge, 2008. Print.

"Frances Elizabeth Caroline Willard (1839–1898)." *National Women's History Museum.* National Women's History Museum, n.d. Web. 25 Feb. 2014.

Gusfield, Joseph R. *Symbolic Crusade: Status Politics and the American Temperance Movement.* Champaign: U of Illinois P, 1986. Print.

Satter, Beryl. *Each Mind a Kingdom: American Women, Sexual Purity, and the New Thought Movement, 1875–1920.* Berkeley: U of California P, 2001. Print.

Willard, Frances E. *Let Something Good Be Said: Speeches and Writings of Frances E. Willard.* Champaign: U of Illinois P, 2007. Print.

From *Youth's Educator for Home and Society*

Date: 1896
Author: Anna R. White
Genre: essay

Summary Overview

Published during the late Victorian era, *Youth's Educator for Home and Society* was written for American middle-class youth and provided a guide to socially accepted behaviors. The work, which explains the common practices regarded as correct etiquette, includes specific direction for interactions between men and women in public and private life. Appropriate behavior for day-to-day activities, such as making conversation, dressing appropriately, and dining politely, is also covered. Although imperfect as a full snapshot of the social and economic diversity of US life during the time period, the excerpts reprinted here reflect not only the everyday lives of the American middle classes but their vision of themselves and the accepted ideals of this group. The excerpts also serve to help illustrate a culture, in which self-discipline, modesty, and adherence to common social rules and accepted roles serve as the backbone of what the author would term "good society."

Defining Moment

Throughout its history, US society has been divided into several social classes, each with its own distinctive social practices. During the nineteenth century, the American middle class expanded greatly in size and influence as the nation's changing economy allowed for the accumulation of at least modest wealth by an expanding number of people. The United States prior to the Civil War had been a largely agricultural nation with wealth concentrated in the hands of large landowners and a few commercial scions. But in the post-Reconstruction era, the rapid industrialization of much of the Northeast and Midwest, along with the growth of major urban centers, changed that pattern. Urban factories, rather than rural farms, employed an increasing share of working-class laborers, and a new division of labor meant that business professionals, shop owners, and others with jobs not tied to control of property could join the ranks of the middle class.

By the mid-to-late nineteenth century, a separate middle-class society had emerged. These households had wealth sufficient to own their own homes, educate their children, and engage in leisure activities. Middle-class women frequently shifted the brunt of housework to one or more working-class servants, leaving their own time more open to engage in the betterment of themselves or their communities through volunteer work or involvement in the rising women's club movement. Society considered these women to be moral guardians of the family, and a separate "women's sphere" emerged. Middle-class children did not have to work in order to help support their families and may have fallen under the care of a nanny or tutor for the development of socially and economically desirable skills. Rising household wealth also meant that middle-class families no longer lived in tight quarters and instead had separate rooms in their homes in order to entertain guests, cook, dine, sleep, and so on. This increased privacy meant that individual behavior was not under continuous observation by others but instead, in the eyes of society, required a certain amount of self-discipline.

At the same time, new social mobility meant that those who were currently members of the middle classes had not necessarily been born to that station. Families of what may have been considered the American aristocracy had enjoyed wealth and privilege for generations with the accompanying education in social graces and deportment. But the children of working-class immigrants, who managed to attain a higher economic status, lacked the same background and exposure. Learning to follow social rules, therefore, showed that an individual more truly belonged to the middle class in a way more significant than one's net worth. Reference guides outlined correct behavior, and mass media publications assisted in building a national consumer culture with shared tastes in entertainment, fashion, and other lifestyle choices. Individuals could then rely on this stable basis of agreed-upon ways of life in order to demonstrate their middle-class status.

Author Biography

Little verifiable information about the life and work of Anna R. White exists today. Along with her authorship of the *Youth's Educator for Home and Society*, she wrote and edited other publications for young people. These included the *Young Folks' Monthly* and the *Western Rural*, both published in the Chicago area during the late 1800s; she may also have edited *Youth's Instructor*, a religious publication for young people published during the same time period.

Women made up a relatively small but vital portion of the mass media during this time period. Rising literacy and improved technology allowed for the growth of newspapers and magazines as popular entertainment, and many middle-class American women pursued socially accepted intellectual endeavors, such as writing, club work, or volunteering. Because women's roles were largely confined to the domestic sphere, women who published articles or books were, therefore, likely to focus on matters seen as relevant to the family or household.

HISTORICAL DOCUMENT

For YOUNG WOMEN

Women do not know how great are their privileges. Abroad a lady would not find it safe or proper to walk out alone. Here [in America] two or three ladies may, if they so desire, attend places of amusement, ride in the cars, or promenade unaccompanied by a gentleman...

It is understood, however, that very young girls are never seen anywhere without some older person as an escort...

A true lady always dresses simply and quietly when in street costume. She does not adopt gay and showy colors and load herself down with jewelry, which is entirely out of place, and conveys a very great anxiety to "show off"...

Quiet, subdued shades give an air of refinement, and never subject their wearer to unfavorable criticisms...

A lady should always walk in an easy, unassuming manner, neither looking to the right or to the left...

A lady who desires a reputation for elegant manners does not giggle or whisper in a meaning way on the cars or in theaters or lecture rooms. ...Neither do ladies commence to laugh as soon as the door has closed upon a retiring guest. They may be laughing about something entirely foreign to the present, but it is not in human nature to help imagining the laugh is aimed at the one who has just left the circle, and they will feel uncomfortable in consequence. ...

No lady ever flirts on the street, or allows a stranger to make her acquaintance...

She should never permit one of the opposite sex to address her in a slangy fashion, touch her on the shoulder, call her by her first name before strangers. All such little familiarities ... will give others the impression that she is not held in the highest esteem...

A lady may accept the assistance of a strange gentleman in getting on or off a car, or in crossing a muddy or crowded street. Such attentions should be accepted in the spirit in which they are offered, and acknowledged with thanks...

For YOUNG MEN

A gentleman never swaggers along the street, shouting and laughing with his companions, his hat on one side, a cigar between his fingers, or switching a cane to the danger or discomfort of passers-by...

If attending a lady in the evening, it is customary to offer her the arm. If he has the care of two ladies, he should give his arm to but one, and they should both walk on the same side of him...

A gentleman removes his hat when entering a room where there are ladies. When he meets a lady friend, he should raise his hat gracefully, and if she is with another lady, he should include her in the salutation even though he is unacquainted with her...

In passing through a door, the gentleman holds it open for the lady, even though he never saw her before. He also precedes the lady in ascending stairs, and allows her to precede him in descending...

In assisting a lady to alight from a carriage, he should step out first, and then turn and offer her both hands, particularly if the vehicle be some distance from the ground...

Lord Chesterfield, the most elegant gentleman in all Europe, is quoted as saying "Civility is particularly due to all women; and remember that no provocation whatever can justify any man in not being civil to every woman; and the greatest man would justly be reckoned a brute if he were not civil to the meanest woman... It is due to their sex, and is the only protection they have against the superior strength of ours."

For BOTH

SWEET BREATHS. Both ladies and gentlemen will be very careful to keep their breaths sweet and pure. We wish there were some law to prevent people from polluting their breaths with onions and tobacco when they are going into a mixed company. No one has a right to make himself in any manner offensive to others. All the laws of good breeding forbid it...

TRAVELING MANNERS. ...A lady who acts with propriety, can journey from one end of our country to the other with safety. Women are held in high esteem, and are certain of protection when they require it. It is always more desirable to have an escort when traveling, for there are many little anxieties which he can assume, thus making a lady's journey more enjoyable...

The first office of such escort is to:

1. ... meet her there in ample time to obtain her tickets, check her baggage, and procure a good seat in the car for her.

2. ...looks after her hand baggage, assists her in and out of the car, makes all inquiries about the route,

3. ...brings her a glass of water when she wishes it, and performs many acts of politeness

4. ....pointing out the objects of interest from the car window; or if she is disinclined for further conversation, he lets her relapse into thought, or else provides her with reading matter. ...

5... the journey he sees to obtaining a carriage for her, and looks after her baggage.

6... He may accompany her to the home of her friends, or to the hotel which she is to stop at.

7...The next day he calls on her to inquire how she bore the fatigue of her journey. ...

A lady should not concern herself with any of the details of her trip, when she has an escort. It is presumed that he knows more about traveling than she does...

Ladies should not have a myriad of packages for an escort to guard...

TABLE MANNERS. NO surer gauge of the native refinement of any person can be found than the manners which they show at the table. It is incumbent upon parents to train their children in those niceties of etiquette which will grow with their growth, and make their progress through life far easier...

POLITENESS TO ALL. The enjoyment of the family meal is greatly enhanced when each member is polite and attentive to the others; when parents and children alike are cheerful, agreeable and look after each other's comfort....

TALKING AT TABLE. The children in a household should be encouraged to talk, but not permitted to show off, and say smart things... Require them in asking for an article out of their reach to preface the request with, "Please pass me the salt," and also to call the one whom they address by his name, as "Mr. Willis, will you please pass the salt?"...

When they are invited to have more of an article, which they do not desire, they should answer politely, "I do not wish any more, thank you."

LOUD TALKING PROHIBITED. Loud talking on their part should be prohibited, as also interrupting conversation. They should not whisper, however, or glance around the table and giggle.

WHEN CHILDREN LEAVE THE TABLE. If children are compelled to leave the table before the rest of the family, so as to reach school, they should rise quietly, ask to be excused and leave the apartment so as not to disturb anyone.

DO NOT LET THEM EAT GREEDILY. They should not eat greedily, cramming their mouths full, nor smack their lips, tilt their chairs back, or drop their knives carelessly on the table-cloth. The knife and fork should be laid across the plate, with the handles to the right, when the meal is finished...

GROWN PEOPLE AT FAULT. While children's manners are thus alluded to, we regret to say that they are not the sole violators of good breeding. To any one who observes much, it is astonishing that so many well-dressed people, who seem to know so much, are so shockingly rude at the table...

REFUSING AN ARTICLE OF FOOD. If a guest does not care for a certain article on the table, or for some reason does not wish to partake of it, he should not refuse it by stating that "Cheese don't agree with me," or "I can't endure tomatoes," but simply say "I do not care for any, thank you." We well remember the horror and disgust with which an apparently well-bred lady filled her listeners at the table by declining a certain dish with the assertion that "It took too long to digest, and her doctor had forbidden it"...

RUDENESS AT TABLE. There are many little rudenesses which can be avoided at the table, and which a little thought would instinctively pronounce offensive. Among these are coughing or breathing into your neighbor's face...

Fidgeting in your seat, or moving about restlessly; drumming upon the table with your fingers; whispering confidentially with your neighbor; emphasizing your remarks by flourishing your fork, to the risk of your neighbor's eyes; leaning the elbows upon the table; standing up and reaching across the table in place of requesting that what you want be passed you. All these acts of ill-breeding or thoughtlessness we have seen perpetrated by those who should know better...

MANNERS AT TABLE. Sit upright at the table without bending over or lowering your head to partake of your food. Do not sit either too far away or too near the table. Keep your mouth closed as much as possible while you are masticating your food...

THINGS TO AVOID. Do not talk loudly or boisterously, but be cheerful and companionable, not monopolizing the conversation, but joining in it. Bones and fragments should be deposited on the edge of your plate, so as not to soil the table-cloth...

It is very rude to pick your teeth at the table after a meal is completed. Napkins are to wipe the mouth with, not to mop the forehead or nose. Never put your own knife, fork or spoon into a dish from which others are to be helped...

DRESS FOR THE OCCASION. The table being a meeting place where everything should be nice and conducive to good manners, a gentleman will never appear at it in his shirt sleeves. If it is excessively warm weather, and he wishes to enjoy the freedom of his own home table, he can don a light coat of seersucker, farmer's satin, or similar material; but in public he will always retain the coat which he wears through the day, save of course, on dress occasions, of which we have spoken elsewhere. A lady should observe the same care in her dress. Untidy hair and dirty nails are especially repellant...

CHOOSING COMPANIONS....The friends young people should select, should have moral worth, rather than position in society. Their courteous conduct toward others is of the greatest consequence...

Document Analysis

In *Youth's Educator for Home and Society*, the author outlines a series of personal behaviors quite unlike those of the generally casual modern world. At the basis of these social rules is a sense of formality and self-possession that infused correct behavior and discouraged unwanted attention toward the self. The proper, moral world is shown to be one in which each individual adheres to the mandates of society by following its etiquette.

One key to the practice of good manners in everyday life was the observance of established gender roles through all interactions. Doing so, the author suggests, provides what Victorians would have considered the weaker sex with a measure of personal and social security: "Women do not know how great are their privileges" in being able to take part in everyday activities in the company of other women rather than under the watchful eye of a husband, brother, or father. To protect these privileges, however, both women and men were bound by social rules that ensured their behavior could not be called into question or mistaken for immoral. Women must dress conservatively and behave demurely rather than act childishly or with too much familiarity. Men, in turn, must show respect for women and take care of practical or commercial matters that women could not be expected to attend to. Adhering to these rules assured women a limited level of independence while keeping them under the watchful eye of men.

The practice of etiquette was on clear display at the dining table, a focal point of Victorian society. Appropriate dress showed respect for one's companions, and talking politely gave the affair an air of civility. Table manners also shielded others from unpleasant sights or smells, and in adhering to proper manners, adults set an example for any young people in attendance.

Indeed, learning to participate in society was one of children's most important tasks and equally, one of their parents' "incumbent" jobs. A foundation in the "niceties of etiquette" was one that the author argues would serve young people throughout their lives. The author suggests that mastering these arts was a true gauge of a person's character, with polite interaction with others being "of the greatest consequence" and a better guide to the selection of friends than money or position. Following the rules laid out in the manual, therefore, assured the reader of a happy and fulfilling life, free from worries over the judgment of others and replete with the company of other respectable members of the community.

Essential Themes

Perhaps the guiding theme of White's etiquette manual is its emphasis on adherence to the prescribed roles assigned to each type of individual in American middle-class society. In order to win acknowledgement as a "lady" or a "gentleman," an individual needed more than money and must demonstrate a set pattern of good breeding. Doing so with ease showed that an individual was capable of exhibiting the modesty and self-discipline valued by Victorian mores. It also announced that one was a member of a cultured class, capable of spending time on personal improvement and application to moral matters rather than laboring. The working classes had no need for guidelines explaining how one was to behave at a dinner party or while traveling because members of this class had little to no opportunity to apply these practices.

Holding to these roles also reinforced the existing social order. Men and women resided in largely separate spheres of activity, and their interactions across those spheres were tightly regulated. An emphasis on a retiring modesty subtly deterred women from pressing against the male-dominated worlds of politics and commerce. In a time before the development of a separate youth culture, etiquette helped indoctrinate children in the ways of adult life.

The rules governing correct behavior changed greatly during the twentieth century, especially as middle-class women rejected social strictures confining them to the domestic sphere—inspired in part by women like White, who established the ability of women to succeed in educated, professional roles. Yet some of the key ideals displayed in the *Youth's Educator* endured. Society continues to expect parents to actively participate in the social education of their children by establishing guidelines for respectful behavior in public and at home. Those guidelines also continue to form through consensus; equally, they continue to find published form in newspaper articles, magazine advice columns, and hefty manuals derived from works such as White's and Emily Post's seminal *Etiquette*. As White herself noted in her manual's preface, the exact form that manners take over time varies, but the underlying themes of discipline and courteous respect remain.

—*Vanessa E. Vaughn, MA*

Bibliography and Additional Reading

Calvert, Karin. "Children in the House: 1890 to 1930." *American Home Life, 1880–1930: A Social History of Spaces and Services.* Ed. Jessica H. Foy and Thomas J. Schlereth. Knoxville: U of Tennessee P, 1997. 75–93. Print.

Grier, Katherine C. *Culture and Comfort: Parlor Making and Middle-Class Identity, 1850–1930.* Washington: Smithsonian Inst. P, 1997. Print.

Okker, Patricia. *Our Sister Editors: Sarah J. Hale and the Tradition of Nineteenth-Century American Women Editors.* Athens: U of Georgia P, 1995. Print.

Schlereth, Thomas J. *Victorian America: Transformation in Everyday Life, 1876–1915.* New York: Harper, 1991. Print.

Smith-Rosenberg, Carroll. *Disorderly Conduct: Visions of Gender in Victorian America.* New York: Knopf, 1985. Print.

White, Anna R. *Youth's Educator for Home and Society.* Chicago: Monarch, 1896. Print.

■ On American Motherhood

Date: March 13, 1905
Authors: Theodore Roosevelt
Genre: speech

Summary Overview

President Theodore Roosevelt, speaking before the National Congress of Mothers, offered his thoughts on the need for greater equality between men and women. There are many different occupations that are critical to the development of modern America, he said, but none more so than serving one's own family. He argued that mothers have one of the most difficult jobs—protecting their children and ensuring that their family is cohesive and nurturing. Men and women, he said, both equally share a responsibility for ensuring that children have every resource necessary to develop strong character and a healthy mind.

Defining Moment

Theodore Roosevelt is considered by many to be one of the nation's first "modern" presidents. He took full advantage of the fact that, in the post–Civil War era, Congress had been ceding greater responsibility to the executive branch. He used this increased power to protect the country's natural resources as well as to develop a modern foreign policy that launched the United States into the international arena. Although he demonstrated many of the biases and prejudices of other white Americans who were born in the late nineteenth century (he considered the black race on the whole to be subordinate to whites, for example), he still showed an appreciation and respect for the many different kinds of Americans, a characteristic that endeared him to the electorate as a populist president.

One issue area, in which this characteristic was evident, was women's rights. As president, Roosevelt did not advocate for women's suffrage, which was not included on the Republican Party platform during the 1904 election, and consistently showed a belief that, at the time, changing the law to allow for women's suffrage was unnecessary. However, he did take a pro-suffrage position when he unsuccessfully ran for president as the Progressive Party's candidate in 1912. He also spoke a great deal about equality and respect for women throughout his career: he wrote his college thesis on women's rights; authored legislation authorizing corporal punishment for domestic abusers in New York; and even elevated women to senior-level positions during his tenure as commissioner of the New York Police Department.

Roosevelt frequently invoked his experiences on the American frontier when addressing issues during his presidency (a characteristic historians have dubbed "the frontier myth"). The frontier myth provided the backdrop for his attitudes toward women. In the undeveloped wilds of the western United States, even if women's roles were different from those of men, they showed the same ruggedness, strength, and intelligence that men did. In Roosevelt's presidential rhetoric, he, therefore, characterized women as the moral equals of men, even if he did not see the two genders as political equals.

Although Roosevelt only embraced the equality of the sexes within the context of the frontier, there were issue areas in which the women's rights movement and Roosevelt found commonality. For example, Roosevelt was a strong advocate for moral reform, particularly within the home. He even called for some forms of censorship in order to protect American culture and enhance the moral strength of children. Several organizations, such as the National Congress of Mothers and the Women's Christian Temperance Union, shared such ideals, calling for the suppression of certain forms of entertainment that they deemed impure and, therefore, detrimental to families. This shared opinion on the need for moral reform at home became the basis of

Roosevelt's speech to the National Congress of Mothers in Washington, DC, in March of 1905.

Author Biography

Theodore Roosevelt was born on October 27, 1858, in New York City. On February 14, 1884, his first wife and his mother both died; Roosevelt spent about two years thereafter in the Badlands of Dakota Territory, hunting and recovering from his grief. As a lieutenant colonel in the Spanish-American War, he famously led a charge up San Juan Hill and earned distinction as a war hero. Shortly thereafter, he was elected governor of New York and later, at the age of forty-two, became the nation's youngest president. After choosing William Howard Taft as his successor in 1908, Roosevelt left office (although he ran for president again unsuccessfully in 1912) and went on a safari. He later returned to his home in Oyster Bay, New York. He died on January 6, 1919.

HISTORICAL DOCUMENT

In our modern industrial civilization there are many and grave dangers to counterbalance the splendors and the triumphs. It is not a good thing to see cities grow at disproportionate speed relatively to the country; for the small land owners, the men who own their little homes, and therefore to a very large extent the men who till farms, the men of the soil, have hitherto made the foundation of lasting national life in every State; and, if the foundation becomes either too weak or too narrow, the superstructure, no matter how attractive, is in imminent danger of falling.

But far more important than the question of the occupation of our citizens is the question of how their family life is conducted. No matter what that occupation may be, as long as there is a real home and as long as those who make up that home do their duty to one another, to their neighbors and to the State, it is of minor consequence whether the man's trade is plied in the country or in the city, whether it calls for the work of the hands or for the work of the head.

No piled-up wealth, no splendor of material growth, no brilliance of artistic development, will permanently avail any people unless its home life is healthy, unless the average man possesses honesty, courage, common sense, and decency, unless he works hard and is willing at need to fight hard; and unless the average woman is a good wife, a good mother, able and willing to perform the first and greatest duty of womanhood, able and willing to bear, and to bring up as they should be brought up, healthy children, sound in body, mind, and character, and numerous enough so that the race shall increase and not decrease.

There are certain old truths which will be true as long as this world endures, and which no amount of progress can alter. One of these is the truth that the primary duty of the husband is to be the home-maker, the breadwinner for his wife and children, and that the primary duty of the woman is to be the helpmate, the housewife, and mother. The woman should have ample educational advantages; but save in exceptional cases the man must be, and she need not be, and generally ought not to be, trained for a lifelong career as the family breadwinner; and, therefore, after a certain point, the training of the two must normally be different because the duties of the two are normally different. This does not mean inequality of function, but it does mean that normally there must be dissimilarity of function. On the whole, I think the duty of the woman the more important, the more difficult, and the more honorable of the two; on the whole I respect the woman who does her duty even more than I respect the man who does his.

No ordinary work done by a man is either as hard or as responsible as the work of a woman who is bringing up a family of small children; for upon her time and strength demands are made not only every hour of the day but often every hour of the night. She may have to get up night after night to take care of a sick child, and yet must by day continue to do all her household duties as well; and if the family means are scant she must usually enjoy even her rare holidays taking her whole brood of children with her. The birth pangs make all men the debtors of all women. Above all our sympathy and regard are due to the struggling wives among those whom Abraham Lincoln called the plain people, and whom he so loved and trusted; for the lives of these women are often led on the lonely heights of quiet, self-sacrificing heroism.

Just as the happiest and most honorable and most useful task that can be set any man is to earn enough for the support of his wife and family, for the bringing up and starting in life of his children, so the most important, the most honorable and desirable task which can be set any woman is to be a good and wise mother in a home marked by self-respect and mutual forbearance, by willingness to perform duty, and by refusal to sink into self-indulgence or avoid that which entails effort and self-sacrifice. Of course there are exceptional men and exceptional women who can do and ought to do much more than this, who can lead and ought to lead great careers of outside usefulness in addition to—not as substitutes for—their home work; but I am not speaking of exceptions; I am speaking of the primary duties, I am speaking of the average citizens, the average men and women who make up the nation.

Inasmuch as I am speaking to an assemblage of mothers, I shall have nothing whatever to say in praise of an easy life. Yours is the work which is never ended. No mother has an easy time, the most mothers have very hard times; and yet what true mother would barter her experience of joy and sorrow in exchange for a life of cold selfishness, which insists upon perpetual amusement and the avoidance of care, and which often finds its fit dwelling place in some flat designed to furnish with the least possible expenditure of effort the maximum of comfort and of luxury, but in which there is literally no place for children?

The woman who is a good wife, a good mother, is entitled to our respect as is no one else; but he is entitled to it only because, and so long as, she is worthy of it. Effort and self-sacrifice are the law of worthy life for the man as for the woman; tho neither the effort nor the self-sacrifice may be the same for the one as for the other. I do not in the least believe in the patient Griselda type of woman, in the woman who submits to gross and long continued ill treatment, any more than I believe in a man who tamely submits to wrongful aggression. No wrong-doing is so abhorrent as wrong-doing by a man toward the wife and the children who should arouse every tender feeling in his nature. Selfishness toward them, lack of tenderness toward them, lack of consideration for them, above all, brutality in any form toward them, should arouse the heartiest scorn and indignation in every upright soul.

I believe in the woman keeping her self-respect just as I believe in the man doing so. I believe in her rights just as much as I believe in the man's, and indeed a little more; and I regard marriage as a partnership, in which each partner is in honor bound to think of the rights of the other as well as of his or her own. But I think that the duties are even more important than the rights; and in the long run I think that the reward is ampler and greater for duty well done, than for the insistence upon individual rights, necessary tho this, too, must often be. Your duty is hard, your responsibility great; but greatest of all is your reward. I do not pity you in the least. On the contrary, I feel respect and admiration for you.

Into the woman's keeping is committed the destiny of the generations to come after us. In bringing up your children you mothers must remember that while it is essential to be loving and tender it is no less essential to be wise and firm. Foolishness and affection must not be treated as interchangeable terms; and besides training your sons and daughters in the softer and milder virtues, you must seek to give them those stern and hardy qualities which in after life they will surely need. Some children will go wrong in spite of the best training; and some will go right even when their surroundings are most unfortunate; nevertheless an immense amount depends upon the family training. If you mothers through weakness bring up your sons to be selfish and to think only of themselves, you will be responsible for much sadness among the women who are to be their wives in the future. If you let your daughters grow up idle, perhaps under the mistaken impression that as you yourselves have had to work hard they shall know only enjoyment, you are preparing them to be useless to others and burdens to themselves. Teach boys and girls alike that they are not to look forward to live spent in avoiding difficulties, but to lives spent in overcoming difficulties. Teach them that work, for themselves and also for others, is not a curse but a blessing; seek to make them happy, to make them enjoy life, but seek also to make them face life with the steadfast resolution to wrest success from labor and adversity, and to do their whole duty before God and to man. Surely she who can thus train her sons and her daughters is thrice fortunate among women.

There are many good people who are denied the supreme blessing of children, and for these we have the respect and sympathy always due to those who, from no fault of their own, are denied any of the other great blessings of life. But the man or woman who deliberately forego these blessings, whether from viciousness, coldness, shallow-heartedness, self-indulgence, or mere failure to appreciate aright the difference between the all-important and the unimportant—why, such a creature merits contempt as hearty as any visited upon the soldier who runs away in battle, or upon the man who refuses to work for the support of those dependent upon him, and who tho able-bodied is yet content to eat in idleness the bread which others provide.

The existence of women of this type forms one of the most unpleasant and unwholesome features of modern life. If any one is so dim of vision as to fail to see what a thoroughly unlovely creature such a woman is I wish they would read Judge Robert Grant's novel "Unleavened Bread," ponder seriously the character of Selma, and think of the fate that would surely overcome any nation which developed its average and typical woman along such lines. Unfortunately it would be untrue to say that this type exists only in American novels. That it also exists in American life is made unpleasantly evident by the statistics as to the dwindling families in some localities. It is made evident in equally sinister fashion by the census statistics as to divorce, which are fairly appalling; for easy divorce is now as it ever has been, a bane to any nation, a curse to society, a menace to the home, an incitement to married unhappiness and to immorality, an evil thing for men and a still more hideous evil for women. These unpleasant tendencies in our American life are made evident by articles such as those which I actually read not long ago in a certain paper, where a clergyman was quoted, seemingly with approval, as expressing the general American attitude when he said that the ambition of any save a very rich man should be to rear two children only, so as to give his children an opportunity "to taste a few of the good things of life."

This man, whose profession and calling should have made him a moral teacher, actually set before others the ideal, not of training children to do their duty, not of sending them forth with stout hearts and ready minds to win triumphs for themselves and their country, not of allowing them the opportunity, and giving them the privilege of making their own place in the world, but, forsooth, of keeping the number of children so limited that they might "taste a few good things!" The way to give a child a fair chance in life is not to bring it up in luxury, but to see that it has the kind of training that will give it strength of character. Even apart from the vital question of national life, and regarding only the individual interest of the children themselves, happiness in the true sense is a hundredfold more apt to come to any given member of a healthy family of healthy-minded children, well brought up, well educated, but taught that they must shift up, well educated, but taught that they must shift for themselves, must win their own way, and by their own exertions make their own positions of usefulness, than it is apt to come to those whose parents themselves have acted on and have trained their children to act on, the selfish and sordid theory that the whole end of life is to "taste a few good things."

The intelligence of the remark is on a par with its morality; for the most rudimentary mental process would have shown the speaker that if the average family in which there are children contained but two children the nation as a whole would decrease in population so rapidly that in two or three generations it would very deservedly be on the point of extinction, so that the people who had acted on this base and selfish doctrine would be giving place to others with braver and more robust ideals. Nor would such a result be in any way regrettable; for a race that practised such doctrine—that is, a race that practised race suicide—would thereby conclusively show that it was unfit to exist, and that it had better give place to people who had not forgotten the primary laws of their being.

To sum up, then, the whole matter is simple enough. If either a race or an individual prefers the pleasure of more effortless ease, of self-indulgence, to the infinitely deeper, the infinitely higher pleasures that come to those who know the toil and the weariness, but also the joy, of hard duty well done, why, that race or that individual must inevitably in the end pay the penalty of leading a life both vapid and ignoble. No man and no woman really worthy of the name can care for the life spent solely or chiefly in the avoidance of risk and trouble and labor. Save in exceptional cases the prizes worth having in life must be paid for, and the life worth living must be a life of work for a worthy end, and ordinarily of work more for others than for one's self.

The woman's task is not easy—no task worth doing is easy—but in doing it, and when she has done it, there shall come to her the highest and holiest joy known to mankind; and having done it, she shall have the reward prophesied in Scripture; for her husband and her children, yes, and all people who realize that her work lies at the foundation of all national happiness and greatness, shall rise up and call her blessed.

Document Analysis

Theodore Roosevelt uses the pulpit provided to him by the National Congress of Mothers to share his view that there is no more pressing issue facing America than creating a strong home environment. Indeed, there are many different issues that require a national response, he says, but none are more important than ensuring that American families are strong and healthy. He extols the central role women have played in this issue and implores them to continue their efforts to bring moral strength to American households.

Roosevelt begins his speech by commenting on the many dangers facing the still-developing United States. The nation, he says, was at risk of growing at a rate that its foundations could not sustain. However, the most pressing issue facing the country is not its infrastructure but the American home. Regardless of the level of wealth or talent in a household, he says, the most important characteristics homes should possess are intangible: courage, honesty, decency, and an ethic of hard work are among these characteristics. There are those individuals whose job responsibilities outside of the home are indubitably important, he says, but there is no greater responsibility than that of a parent.

Roosevelt invokes his frontier views of women to extol their roles as mothers and wives. While a man was traditionally supposed to be the breadwinner and a woman was expected to be the "helpmate, the housewife, and mother," the latter's role is, in Roosevelt's view, more crucial and more difficult. Women's jobs at the home lasted twenty-four hours a day and involved the stress of child care and the pain of childbirth (which Roosevelt says makes men "the debtors of all women"). Women, Roosevelt says, deserve respect for their hard work and dedication in the home. Referring to the growing women's rights movement, Roosevelt says that women's duties are far more important (and, therefore, more rewarding) than their rights in compari-

son to men's.

Roosevelt next focuses on the roles of women as mothers. He encourages mothers to continue to teach their children to be morally upright and, in a general sense, upstanding members of society through parental affection, attention, and education. Parents, who are blessed enough to have children, he says, should therefore take seriously their responsibilities as mothers and fathers. That there are women who do not wish to be parents is, in Roosevelt's opinion, an "unpleasant and unwholesome" fact that needs correction.

Men, Roosevelt says, also have a responsibility regarding the moral education of their children but instead defer to women to play this role. Mothers, thus, have the obligation to train their children in this area. If women fail to procreate and foster healthy and happy home environments, Roosevelt concludes, the vacuum that will be left in their place will result in what he terms "race suicide."

Essential Themes

Theodore Roosevelt was, perhaps paradoxically, both a social conservative and a progressive. On the social front, he believed in a morally upright society. At the same time, he advocated for a wide range of social and political changes. While these two concepts might appear divergent, they appeared to converge somewhat with regard to women and family. In his speech to the National Congress of Mothers, he attempts to demonstrate the connective role mothers played (and for which they should be revered) in both of these arenas.

Roosevelt mentions that, although there are a great many important issues and dangers facing the twentieth-century United States, none is more important than the strength of the American home. Tradition and society continued to assign the greatest degree of responsibility on this issue to women and, in particular, to mothers. Mothers, he says, should be held in the highest regard, as their responsibilities as parents were the most valuable and difficult to perform. Mothers, Roosevelt argues, were the keys to ensuring that children were raised in healthy, strong, and morally upright homes.

To be sure, he adds, there were many households from which American society was receiving negative influences. Children were being raised in unloving and non-nurturing environments, a fact that Roosevelt deplores as the biggest danger to society. All parents had a role to play in correcting this issue, but he says that mothers should take particular heed of such problems and foster positivity in their own homes.

In his speech, Roosevelt expresses great concern that the crime and moral issues evident in modern America suggested that American society was—like the country's rapid economic and infrastructural development—in danger of collapsing inward upon itself, particularly because some women were choosing not to have children, a situation he describes as "race suicide." It should be noted that the phrase "race suicide" was often used at the time by white supremacists, who felt that ethnic and racial minorities were a threat to white dominance. In the face of increasing immigration in the late nineteenth and early twentieth century, the perceived threat to native-born Anglo-Americans seemed to be growing. This factor, coupled with women's increasing use of birth control, is what drove Roosevelt to implore the women in his audience to fulfill their duties and become good mothers. Although he ultimately championed women's political rights, Roosevelt was clearly a social conservative on such issues as race and procreation.

—Michael P. Auerbach, MA

Bibliography and Additional Reading

"American President: Theodore Roosevelt (1858–1919)." *Miller Center*. U of Virginia, 2013. Web. 8 Apr. 2014.

Dalton, Kathleen. *Theodore Roosevelt: A Strenuous Life*. New York: Random, 2007. Print.

Dorsey, Leroy G. "Managing Women's Equality: Theodore Roosevelt, the Frontier Myth, and the Modern Woman." *Rhetoric and Public Affairs* 16.3 (2013): 423–56. Print.

Freeman, Jo. *A Room at a Time: How Women Entered Party Politics*. Lanham: Rowman, 2002. Print.

Gable, John. Interview. *PBS.org*. WGBH Educational Foundation, 2013. Web. 8 Apr. 2014.

Morris, Edmund. *Theodore Rex*. New York: Random, 2001. Print.

Ricard, Serge. *A Companion to Theodore Roosevelt*. Hoboken: Wiley, 2011. Print.

■ "Women's Suffrage in a Democratic Republic"

Date: June 21, 1915
Author: Anna Howard Shaw
Genre: speech

Summary Overview

In June 1915, suffragist and social reformer Anna Howard Shaw delivered one of many similarly themed speeches she gave across New York State. Speaking in Ogdensburg, in the far north of the state, Shaw argued that the United States could not be considered a true democratic republic when not all of its citizens could participate in the democratic process. With World War I raging in Europe, Shaw proposed that women's suffrage could help foster future peace.

Defining Moment

The women's movement in the United States, which began in earnest in the mid-nineteenth century and continued through the twentieth century, coincided with (and in many cases was overshadowed by) some of the key events of this pivotal period. Early in its life, the movement linked women's empowerment with social issues, such as temperance and family matters. Prior to the Civil War, however, two key figures in the movement—Susan B. Anthony and Elizabeth Cady Stanton—met to launch a formal, national campaign for women's rights. The two led an unsuccessful push to include women in the Fourteenth and Fifteenth Amendments, which were already controversial by granting citizenship and suffrage to freed slaves.

During the post–Civil War era, the movement found new life, but it was marred by a disagreement over how to achieve suffrage. Anthony, Stanton, and Anna Howard Shaw believed that change should occur at the federal level, while activists like Lucy Stone pushed for a state-level approach. Neither approach gained much traction, despite garnering some sympathy from leaders in Congress and some state legislatures. This trend changed during the last decade of the nineteenth century. Anthony, Stanton, and Shaw's National American

Women's Suffrage Association (NAWSA)—created in 1889 by the merger of the Anthony and Stanton's National Women's Suffrage Association with the American Woman Suffrage Association with which Shaw had been affiliated—returned to the movement's roots, recruiting new supporters by focusing on social issues that were in the eye of the general public, such as labor, child protection, and temperance.

Stanton died in 1902 and Anthony in 1906. Leadership of NAWSA fell to Shaw in 1904, whose exceptional oratory skills had been well known since the late nineteenth century. Shaw was able to attract more than 150,000 new suffrage activists to NAWSA during her tenure and tripled the number of states in which NAWSA sought legislative changes. During this period of growth, however, war broke out in Europe. Americans' attention was diverted from domestic issues to foreign matters—specifically, whether the United States should enter the war.

US neutrality was called into question in 1915, when German U-boats sank the British ocean liner *Lusitania* on May 7, 1915, shortly after it departed New York for Liverpool, England, with a large number of American passengers aboard—128 of them were among the nearly 1,200 people killed in the tragedy. Shaw was delivering presentations across New York State at the time. With Americans focused on the Great War, Shaw modified her speeches to suggest that a truly unified United States—with men, women, and people of all races sharing equal power in the spirit of democracy—would see the greatest success in the war and in the future establishment of world peace. Her speech—dubbed "The Fundamental Principle of a Republic"—was never written down verbatim. However, she echoed its verbiage throughout the state, including on June 21, 1915, when she delivered it in Ogdensburg as part of the New York state equal suffrage campaign.

Author Biography

Anna Howard Shaw was born in Newcastle-on-Tyne, England, on February 14, 1847. She and her parents immigrated to Massachusetts in 1851 and, in 1859, moved to the wilderness in Michigan. Shaw began her career as a teacher at the age of fifteen. She paid her way through Albion College in Michigan until 1875 and then attended the Theological School at Boston University, graduating in 1878. She was a pastor in East Dennis, Massachusetts, and sought ordination in the Methodist Episcopal Church before being ordained as a Methodist Protestant elder in 1880. She also went on to earn her medical degree in 1886 and worked as a paramedic for the poor in South Boston. During the late 1880s, she became involved in the suffrage and temperance movements, joining the Massachusetts Women's Suffrage Association and the Women's Christian Temperance Union. In 1900, when Anthony resigned as president of NAWSA, Carrie B. Chapman became NAWSA's president and Shaw was named vice president at large. Shaw later became the association's president, serving from 1904 to 1915. During World War I, she was an outspoken advocate for the American effort, receiving numerous honors for her leadership. She died from pneumonia on July 2, 1919, in Moylan, Pennsylvania.

HISTORICAL DOCUMENT

When I came into your hall tonight, I thought of the last time I was in your city. Twenty-one years ago I came here with Susan B. Anthony, and we came for exactly the same purpose as that for which we are here tonight. Boys have been born since that time and have become voters, and the women are still trying to persuade American men to believe in the fundamental principles of democracy, and I never quite feel as if it was a fair field to argue this question with men, because in doing it you have to assume that a man who professes to believe in a Republican form of government does not believe in a Republican form of government, for the only thing that woman's enfranchisement means at all is that a government which claims to be a Republic should be a Republic, and not an aristocracy. The difficulty with discussing this question with those who oppose us is that they make any number of arguments but none of them have anything to do with Woman's Suffrage; they always have something to do with something else, therefore the arguments which we have to make rarely ever have anything to do with the subject, because we have to answer our opponents who always escape the subject as far as possible in order to have any sort of reason in connection with what they say.

Now one of two things is true: either a Republic is a desirable form of government, or else it is not. If it is, then we should have it, if it is not then we ought not to pretend that we have it. We ought at least to be true to our ideals, and the men of New York have, for the first time in their lives, the rare opportunity, on the second day of next November, of making the state truly a part of a Republic. It is the greatest opportunity which has ever come to the men of the state. If Woman's Suffrage is wrong, it is a great wrong; if it is right, it is a profound and fundamental principle, and we all know, if we know what a Republic is, that it is the fundamental principle upon which a Republic must rise. Let us see where we are as a people; how we act here and what we think we are. The difficulty with the men of this country is that they are so consistent in their inconsistency that they are not aware of having been inconsistent; because their consistency has been so continuous and their inconsistency so consecutive that it has never been broken, from the beginning of our Nation's life to the present time. If we trace our history back we will find that from the very dawn of our existence as a people, men have been imbued with a spirit and a vision more lofty than they have been able to live; they have been led by visions of the sublimest truth, both in regard to religion and in regard to government that ever inspired the souls of men from the time the Puritans left the old world to come to this country, led by the Divine ideal which is the sublimest and supremest ideal in religious freedom which men have ever known, the theory that a man has a right to worship God according to the dictates of his own conscience, without the intervention of any other man or any other group of men. And it was this theory, this vision of the right of the human soul which led men first to the shores of this country.

Now, nobody can deny that they are sincere, honest and earnest men. No one can deny that the Puritans were men of profound conviction, and yet these men who gave up everything in behalf of an ideal, hardly established their communities in this new country before they began to practice exactly the same sort of persecutions on other men which had been practiced upon them. They settled in their communities on the New England shores and when they formed their compacts by which they governed their local societies, they permitted no man to have a voice in the affairs unless he was a member of the church, and not a member of any church, but a member of the particular church which dominated the particular community in which he happened to be. In Massachusetts they drove the Baptists down to Rhode Island; in Connecticut they drove the Presbyterians over to New Jersey; they burned the Quakers in Massachusetts and ducked the witches, and no colony, either Catholic or Protestant allowed a Jew to have a voice. And so a man must worship God according to the conscience of the particular community in which he was located, and yet they called that religious freedom, they were not able to live the ideal of religious liberty, and from that time to this the men of this government have been following along the same line of inconsistency, while they too have been following a vision of equal grandeur and power.

And God said in the beginning, "It is not good for man to stand alone." That is why we are here tonight, and that is all that woman's suffrage means; just to repeat again and again that first declaration of the Divine, "It is not good for man to stand alone," and so the women of this state are asking that the word "male" shall be stricken out of the constitution altogether and that the constitution stand as it ought to have stood in the beginning and as it must before this state is any part of a Republic. Every citizen possessing the necessary qualifications shall be entitled to cast one vote at every election, and have that vote counted. We are not asking, as our Anti-Suffrage friends think we are, for any of the awful things that we hear will happen if we are allowed to vote: we are simply asking that that government which professes to be a Republic shall be a Republic and not pretend to be what it is not.

Now what is a Republic? Take your dictionary, encyclopedia, lexicon or anything else you like and look up the definition and you will find that a Republic is a form of government in which the laws are enacted by representatives elected by the people. Now when did the people of New York ever elect their representatives? Never in the world. The men of New York have, and I grant you that men are people, admirable people, as far as they go, but they only go half way. There is still another half of the people who have not elected representatives, and you never read a definition of a Republic in which half of the people elect representatives to govern the whole of the people. That is an aristocracy and that is just what we are. We have been many kinds of aristocracies. We have been a hierarchy of church members, [then] an oligarchy of sex.

There are two old theories which are dying today. Dying hard but dying. One of them is dying on the plains of Flanders and the Mountains of Galicia and Austria, and that is the theory of the divine right of kings. The other is dying here in the state of New York and Massachusetts and New Jersey and Pennsylvania and that is the divine right of sex. Neither of them had a foundation in reason, or justice or common sense.

Now I want to make this proposition, and I believe every man will accept it. Of course he will if he is intelligent. Whenever a Republic prescribes the qualifications as applying equally to all the citizens of the Republic, when the Republic says in order to vote, a citizen must be twenty-one years of age, it applies to all alike, there is no discrimination against any race or sex. When the government says that a citizen must be a native born citizen or a naturalized citizen, that applies to all; we are either born or naturalized, somehow or other we are here. Whenever the government says that a citizen, in order to vote, must be a resident of a community a certain length of time, and of the state a certain length of time and of the nation a certain length of time, that applies to all equally. There is no discrimination. We might go further and we might say that in order to vote the citizen must be able to read his ballot. We have not gone that far yet. We have been very careful of male ignorance in these United States. I was much interested, as perhaps many of you, in reading the Congressional Record this last winter over the debate over the immigration bill, and when that illiteracy clause was introduced into the immigration bill, what fear there was in the souls of men for fear we would do injustice to some of the people who might want to come to our shores, and I was much interested in the language in which the President vetoed the bill, when he declared that by inserting the clause we would keep out of our shores a large body of very excellent people. I could not help wondering then how it happens that male ignorance is so much less ignorant than female ignorance. When I hear people say that if women were permitted to vote a large body of ignorant people would vote, and therefore because an ignorant woman would vote, no intelligent women should be allowed to vote. I wonder why we have made it so easy for male ignorance and so hard for female ignorance.

Where is the difficulty? Just in one thing and one thing only, that men are so sentimental. We used to believe that women were the sentimental sex, but they cannot hold a tallow candle compared with the arc light of the men. Men are so sentimental in their attitude about women that they cannot reason about them. Now men are usually very fair to each other. I think the average man recognizes that he has no more right to anything at the hands of the government than has every other man. He has no right at all to anything to which every other man has not an equal right with himself. He says why have I a right to certain things in the government; why have I a right to life and liberty; why have I a right to this or this? Does he say because I am a man? Not at all, because I am human, and being human I have a right to everything which belongs to humanity, and every right which any other human being has, I have. And then he says of his neighbor, and my neighbor he also is human, therefore every right which belongs to me as a human being, belongs to him as a human being, and I have no right to anything under the government to which he is not equally entitled. And then up comes a woman, and then they say now she's a woman; she is not quite human, but she is my wife, or my sister, or my daughter or an aunt, or my cousin. She is not quite human, she is only related to a human, and being related to a human a human will take care of her. So we have had that care taking human being to look after us and they have not recognized that women too are equally human with men. Now if men could forget for a minute—I believe the anti-suffragists say that we want men to forget that we are related to them, they don't know me—if for a minute they could forget our relationship and remember that we are equally human with themselves, then they would say—yes, and this human being, not because she is a woman, but because she is human is entitled to every privilege and every right under the government which I, as a human being am entitled to. The only reason men do not see as fairly in regard to women as they do in regard to each other is because they have looked upon us from an altogether different plane than what they have looked at men; that is because women have been the homemakers while men have been the so-called protectors, in the period of the world's civilization when people needed to be protected. I know that they say that men protect us now and when we ask them what they are protecting us from the only answer they can give is from themselves. I do not think that men need any very great credit for protecting us from themselves. They are not protecting us from any special thing from which we could not protect ourselves except themselves. Now this old time idea of protection was all right when the world needed this protection, but today the protection in civilization comes from within and not from without. . .

When suffragettes are feminists, and when I ask what that is no one is able to tell me. I would give anything to know what a feminist is. They say, would you like to be a feminist? If I could find out I would, you either have to be masculine or feminine and I prefer feminine. Then they cry that we are socialists, and anarchists. Just how a human can be both at the same time, I really do not know. If I know what socialism means it means absolute government and anarchism means no government at all. So we are feminists, socialists, anarchists and mormons or spinsters. Now that is about the list. I have not heard the last speech. Now as a matter of fact, as a unit we are nothing, as individuals we are like all other individuals.

We have our theories, our beliefs, but as suffragettes we have but one belief, but one principle, but one theory and this is the right of a human being to have a voice in the government under which he or she lives, on that we agree, if on nothing else. Whether we agree or not on religion or politics we are not concerned. . . .

Now what does it matter whether the women will vote as their husbands do or will not vote; whether they have time or have not; or whether they will vote for prohibition or not. What has that to do with the fundamental question of democracy, no one has yet discovered. But they cannot argue on that; they cannot argue on the fundamental basis of our existence so that they have to get off on all these side tricks to get anything approaching an argument. So they tell you that democracy is a form of government. It is not. It was before governments were; it will prevail when governments cease to be; it is more than a form of government; it is a great spiritual force emanating from the heart of the Infinite, transforming human character until some day, some day in the distant future, man by the power of the spirit of democracy, will be able to look back into the face of the Infinite and answer, as man cannot answer today, "One is our Father, even God, and all we people are the children of one family." And when democracy has taken possession of human lives no man will ask for him to grant to his neighbor, whether that neighbor be a man or a woman; no man will then be willing to allow another man to rise to power on his shoulders, nor will he be willing to rise to power on the shoulders of another prostrate human being. But that has not yet taken possession of us, but some day we will be free, and we are getting nearer and nearer to it all the time; and never in the history of our country had the men and women of this nation a better right to approach it than they have today; never in the history of the nation did it stand out so splendidly as it stands today, and never ought we men and women to be more grateful for anything than that there presides in the White House today a man of peace.

The other resolution was on peace. We believed then and many of us believe today, notwithstanding all the discussion that is going on, we believe and we will continue to believe that preparedness for war is an incentive to war, and the only hope of permanent peace is the systematic and scientific disarmament of all the nations of the world, and we passed a resolution and passed it unanimously to that effect. A few days afterward I attended a large reception given by the American Ambassador and there was an Italian diplomat there and he spoke rather superciliously and said, "You women think you have been having a very remarkable convention, and I understand that a resolution on peace was offered by the Germans, the French women seconded it, and the British presiding officer presented it and it was carried unanimously." We none of us dreamed what was taking place at that time, but he knew and we learned it before we arrived home, that awful, awful thing that was about to sweep over the nations of the world. The American ambassador replied to the Italian diplomat and said, "Yes Prince, it was a remarkable convention, and it is a remarkable thing that the only people who can get together internationally and discuss their various problems without acrimony and without a sword at their side are the women of the world, but we men, even when we go to The Hague to discuss peace, we go with a sword dangling at our side." It is remarkable that even at this age men cannot discuss international problems and discuss them in peace.

No we women do not want the ballot in order that we may fight, but we do want the ballot in order that we may help men to keep from fighting, whether it is in the home or in the state, just as the home is not without the man, so the state is not without the woman, and you can no more build up homes without men than you can build up the state without women. We are needed everywhere where human life is. We are needed everywhere where human problems are to be solved. Men and women must go through this world together from the cradle to the grave, it is God's way and it is the fundamental principle of a Republican form of government.

Document Analysis

Speaking before her New York state audience, Anna Howard Shaw linked the women's rights movement—which she said had taken place over decades of her own life—to the idea of a true democratic republic. She argued that the nation was founded and developed by men, who were initially well-meaning and earnest but who eventually succumbed to the same sorts of prejudices that had driven them from Europe. Through universal suffrage, she said, the country would be stronger and free from discrimination. It was time, therefore, for men to share governance of the country with the rest of its citizens. Women in particular, she said, could help promote peace and stability in the postwar era.

In her speech, Shaw reminds the audience of how long it has been since the women's suffrage movement began (she and Anthony stood on that very stage twenty-one years earlier, she said, addressing this very issue) and how much had changed during that period. Men, who centuries earlier had established the colonies and then founded the nation, continued to entrench themselves in positions of leadership, promoting the idea of the nation as a democratic republic. However, she said, men had given in to many of the same prejudices that they escaped while under British rule—male religious leaders had driven out different-minded people from New England during the colonial era, and had excluded other religious and social groups from power throughout history.

The central issue, Shaw said, was whether the nation wished to be a democratic republic. Such a political structure, she argued, was designed to be all-inclusive, fed by the votes and participation of every citizen. The present form of government, Shaw said, strayed considerably from this ideal and more resembled an "aristocracy"—the male-dominated political machines, for example, limited open political participation. The notions that fueled this approach to male-dominated government—the divine right of kings and the divine right of sex—were slowly "dying," she said. Leadership was starting to take note of the need to embrace a more literal idea of a republic.

Standing in the way of this progress, however, were "sentimental" men who were unwilling to change the country's ways. Men clung to the notions of women as homemakers and wives and not as citizens, she said (adding that some men even saw women as lesser humans). Suffragists, women's rights activists, and feminists, she said, were seen by men as threats. Thus, the men confronted with such groups would label them "socialists" and "anarchists" and seek to keep them out of mainstream politics.

An acceptance of women's suffrage, Shaw said, posed little risk. Women would not necessarily vote in a way that would disrupt the government. However, she said, their vote on any number of topics would represent a greater sample of Americans' preferences. Still, the issues of interest to women would be brought to light and addressed, she said. One such issue was world peace; she suggested that the intransigence of men had created the ongoing war, while the initiative of multinational women's groups resulted in peaceful resolutions (which had not been adopted by the warring nations'

governments, however). Women were created to provide a balance for men. In this case, she said, the balance created by acceptance of women's suffrage could keep men from fighting and instead foster international peace.

Essential Themes

Anna Howard Shaw recognized the fact that the women's rights movement—specifically in the area of suffrage—had been developing slowly since the mid-1800s and yet had produced few tangible results. Men, as they had throughout American history, continued to dominate the US political system. In the shadow of World War I, Shaw spoke to the ideals of the democratic republic to which Americans were endeared, and said that if these ideals were indeed invaluable to Americans, women should be allowed to vote and participate in government.

Shaw was one of the last living icons of the women's suffrage movement when she delivered this address (with Stanton and Anthony dying during the previous decade). Shaw said that the reason why women had not yet accomplished suffrage (and why the movement itself was consistently met with resistance) was simple: men would not relinquish power. Men had long been America's primary leaders, she said, while women and people of color were relegated to subordinate positions. Men continued to hold all seats in Congress and in other legislative bodies. When faced with the increased influence of suffragists, she added, these men would resist. In fact, in a desperate attempt to defend a male-dominated United States system, Shaw said, men would inevitably dub these activists anarchists or socialists as the rising voice of women captured the nation's attention.

Because men held fast to their positions, Shaw said, the nation was not a true democratic republic, instead resembling an aristocracy. Still, Shaw said, the "divine right" of kings and gender that men presumed to enjoy in the past was slowly dying as women and minority groups sought the opportunity to participate. Ironically, Americans were considering entering a war in an effort to defeat the ideals of discrimination and royalty while America itself was clinging to some of these virtues in its own political system. If given a chance to vote, she added, women would play a role in finally defeating these principles and promoting the peaceful democratic ideals Americans professed to embrace.

—*Michael P. Auerbach, MA*

Bibliography and Additional Reading

Bausum, Ann. *With Courage and Cloth: Winning the Fight for a Woman's Right to Vote*. Washington, DC: Natl. Geographic, 2004. Print.

Crawford, Elizabeth. *The Women's Suffrage Movement: A Reference Guide, 1866–1928*. London: Routledge, 2001. Print.

Franzen, Trisha. Anna Howard Shaw: *The Work of Woman Suffrage*. Champaign: U of Illinois P, 2014. Print.

Frost-Knappman, Elizabeth, and Kathryn Cullen-DuPont. *Women's Suffrage in America: An Eyewitness History*. New York: Facts on File, 1992. Print.

Shaw, Anna Howard. *The Story of a Pioneer*. Teddington: Echo Lib., 2006. Print.

■ Petition from the Women Voters Anti-Suffrage Party

Date: 1917
Authors: Women Voters Anti-Suffrage Party of New York
Genre: petition

Summary Overview

The Women Voters Anti-Suffrage Party of New York drafted and gathered more than three dozen signatures for a petition to the US Senate. The petition mentioned the fact that the country was, at the time, mired in the tremendous crisis that was World War I. For the Senate to turn its attention away from this conflict and address ratification of a constitutional amendment on suffrage, the petition reads, would amount to an unnecessary distraction for the country's men. The signatories urged the Senate not to take up debate on a constitutional amendment, particularly when so many men were unable to join the debate because they were fighting overseas.

Defining Moment

The push for women's equality and, in particular, for women's suffrage, was born in the early to mid-nineteenth century as part of the temperance movement. Prior to the Civil War, suffrage icons including Susan B. Anthony and Elizabeth Cady Stanton began organizing a national campaign for women's rights, including an unsuccessful push for women to be included in the Fourteenth and Fifteenth Amendments, the latter of which was already controversial for granting suffrage to freed slaves. After the Civil War, the women's suffrage movement again gathered momentum, but it fractured into two groups: those who pushed for a constitutional amendment and those—like Lucy Stone—who advocated for a state-level approach to the issue. Anthony and Stanton both died early in the twentieth century, but one of the most enduring products of their work—the National American Woman Suffrage Associa-

tion—gained traction with bolstered membership and a renewed push for federal legislative changes and an amendment to the US Constitution.

The suffragists were not alone, however. Acting as a counterbalance was a growing women's anti-suffrage movement. Organizations such as the Women's Anti-Suffrage Party of New York—one of the first states to adopt suffrage, doing so in 1917—launched propaganda campaigns that argued most women were not concerned with suffrage, preferring to live in harmony and balance with men rather than "in competition" with them. One of the main elements separating the anti-suffragists from the suffragists was the fact that the former considered themselves women first, with a great many responsibilities. Anti-suffragists argued that to assume the additional responsibilities of participating in the political realm—which many believed to be a motivating factor for suffragists—only stifled women's role in society. There is no method by which a "mud-stained reputation" may be cleaned, read one anti-suffrage pamphlet.

During this period of activism, war broke out in Europe. The collective American attention was diverted from domestic issues to foreign matters—specifically, whether the United States should enter the war. With New York and other states adopting suffrage during wartime, the suffrage movement turned its attention to Congress. The Women's Anti-Suffrage Party of New York, in an effort to halt this push, drafted a petition to the US Senate, where such an amendment would originate, asking the members to forgo any debate on suffrage at least until the war came to an end.

HISTORICAL DOCUMENT

Whereas, This country is now engaged in the greatest war in history, and

Whereas, The advocates of the Federal Amendment, though urging it as a war measure, announce, through their president, Mrs. Catt, that its passage "means a simultaneous campaign in 48 States. It demands organization in every precinct; activity, agitation, education in every corner. Nothing less than this nation-wide, vigilant, unceasing campaign will win the ratification," therefore be it

Resolved, That our country in this hour of peril should be spared the harassing of its public men and the distracting of its people from work for the war, and further

Resolved, That the United States Senate be respectfully urged to pass no measure involving such a radical change in our government while the attention of the patriotic portion of the American people is concentrated on the all-important task of winning the war, and during the absence of over a million men abroad.

Document Analysis

The petition introduced by the Women's Anti-Suffrage Party echoes themes that the anti-suffrage movement had invoked long before the start of World War I. The petition's authors took issue with the fact that suffrage activists looked to advance the cause to the national stage during a time of conflict. Doing so, the petition reads, would require a response from every voter in every voting precinct in the United States—a campaign that would distract the nation from issues of higher priority. Furthermore, any suffrage campaign would undermine the focus of the millions of Americans overseas by changing the country's political structure without their input, the petition argues.

The petition criticizes the suffrage movement's timing. The fact that activists, like National American Woman Suffrage Association president Carrie Chapman Catt wished to make suffrage an issue worthy of debate during wartime was particularly unconscionable to the petition's signatories. After all, they wrote, it was not simply a campaign that would require debate in the Senate—every state in the nation would need to take up ratification if Congress approved the proposed amendment. This issue would require full examination by a wide range of interested parties, education for the uninformed voters, protests, and events as part of a comprehensive campaign in virtually every voting district in the country.

In reality, the petition states, the country is in a precarious position that demands the attention and focus of both the government and the people. By commanding the active commentary of the voting electorate and every level of government, the "campaign" for women's suffrage only serves as an unwelcome distraction. After all, what was being proposed—a change to the nation's most important legal document—represented what the petition's authors termed a "radical change in our government."

The American people, according to the petition, should not be forced to redirect their attention and energy at this time of great "peril." In fact, the authors wrote, the mere fact that an enormous percentage of American men were overseas should be enough to table the issue. Meanwhile, the men at home should also be spared from what amounted to "harassment," the petition's authors said.

The position taken by the anti-suffrage activists in this petition demonstrates a philosophy in which women and men retain their traditional roles in society. Despite the fact that this issue would only serve the interests of American women, the anti-suffragists believed that such a change would dramatically change the nation's political landscape, forcing men to take up an analysis and generate an opinion of the proposed amendment. The petition argues that, given the war, it would be ill-advised for the Senate to give the amendment life at this point.

Essential Themes

The petition presented to the US Senate by the Women's Anti-Suffrage Party of New York is representative of some of the foundations of the anti-suffrage philosophy. Women who disagreed with such figures as Anthony, Stanton, and Catt believed that women had their own duties and responsibilities and should not seek to add to them by getting involved in political issues. Furthermore, men—who traditionally handled matters of politics and governance—were justifiably focused on the war—as either observers at home or participants on the battlefields of Europe—and did not need to redirect their attention to such a national campaign, the petition states.

The petition reminds the Senate that a suffrage amendment to the Constitution required a complex, nationwide political endeavor that would take place in not only the US Capitol but also in state capitols, city halls, and in every voting precinct. The petition takes issue with the fact that suffragists pushed this cause to the fore of American public discourse, even connecting it with the war. Rather, anti-suffragists argued, such a campaign would only serve as an unnecessary distraction.

The Senate, according to the petition, stood in the way of allowing this campaign to take shape. The petition's authors reminded senators of the fact that millions of American men were not even in the country, having been sent to the battlefields of Europe. However, the petition does not attempt to convince senators to reject the idea of women's suffrage wholesale. In fact, the petition's authors wrote from one of several states in which suffrage had been passed, an indication that the country was moving toward acceptance of the movement. Rather, it appealed to the Senate to avoid passage of the amendment at that particular time.

—*Michael P. Auerbach, MA*

Bibliography and Additional Reading

Barkhorn, Eleanor. "'Vote No on Women's Suffrage': Bizarre Reasons for Not Letting Women Vote." *Atlantic*. Atlantic Monthly Group, 6 Nov. 2012. Web. 23 Apr. 2014.

Benjamin, Anne M. G. *A History of the Anti-Suffrage Movement in the United States from 1895 to 1920: Women against Equality*. Lewiston: Mellen, 1991. Print.

Cholmeley, Robert Francis. *The Women's Anti-Suffrage Movement*. London: Natl. Union of Women's Suffrage Soc., 1908. Print.

Goodier, Susan. *No Votes for Women: The New York State Anti-Suffrage Movement*. Urbana: U of Illinois P, 2013. Print.

Ruthsdotter, Mary. "Years of Hope, Years of Struggle." *University of Maryland—Maryland Institute for Technology in the Humanities*. Natl. Women's Hist. Project, 2014. Web. 23 Apr. 2014.

REFORMERS AND REMEDIES

In this penultimate section we consider views regarding the matter of social reform and what could be expected of it. Not everyone, of course, believes that social reform is a worthwhile enterprise. On varying grounds, individuals may object to the size, scope, approach, or ultimate value of a reform effort. One of the more prominent perspectives on this topic before the turn of the century was that of Social Darwinism. Social Darwinists argued that society advanced according to set principles of evolution, and human actors were foolish to think that they could somehow alter the trajectory. It was a matter of "survival of the fittest." We hear from one adherent of this philosophy, William Graham Sumner, in this section.

Also included here are statements from 1) temperance leader Frances Willard on the social responsibilities that Christians must bear and bring forward to aid others; 2) social worker Jane Addams on the need to create settlement houses to serve families in need; 3) philosopher John Dewey on the social responsibility that come with the possession of freedom; and 4) Theodore Roosevelt and a conference of state governors on the need to preserve the natural environment for the use and enjoyment of all. We end the section with a document by a temperance advocate arguing for the prohibition of alcohol—or at least its sale. In that effort, however, like the effort to secure the vote for women, supporters would have to wait until after World War I to see their hopes realized.

■ "The Absurd Effort to Make the World Over"

Date: March 1894
Author: William Graham Sumner
Genre: editorial

Summary Overview

Writing in the *Forum*, a leading American general-interest intellectual magazine, Yale sociologist William Graham Sumner published an essay critiquing the push for "social reform" in the late nineteenth century. Sumner attacks Progressive-Era efforts to bring about social and economic reform, claiming that these efforts were both wrong-headed and doomed to failure because of the Progressive inability to come to grips with the intractable nature of social reality. According to Sumner, Progressives are also frequently in error in their assertions about change for the conditions of the working class, which had actually improved since the colonial era despite the Progressive claims that industrialization harmed workers. Sumner sketches a picture of economic progress celebrating the rise of the industrial organization that dominates society and provides a level of prosperity unequaled in history.

Defining Moment

The late nineteenth century in the United States was a time of capitalist economic transformation. The wealth and power of business magnates or "robber barons" was being challenged by Progressive reformers hoping to regulate it and by nascent labor unions organizing workers seeking better working conditions and higher wages. The extremely wealthy, whose wealth was not based as in the colonial era on land but rather on money, were an increasingly prominent presence in American life. Businesses, particularly large businesses, were more frequently organized into corporations. In reaction, socialism, an import from Europe, was also attracting much interest among Americans. The so-called Gilded Age saw a dramatic increase in the influence of business on government.

The growing power of capitalists was connected to an even more fundamental economic transformation: the rise of industry with the growth of the railroad system and the expansion of manufacturing. America, which had since colonial times had been a predominantly agricultural economy, was becoming a more industrialized one. The Northeast, where Sumner spent his life, was a leading region in this transformation. Along with this transformation, the relatively high wages paid by American industry attracted increasing immigration from Europe and elsewhere. By fostering immigration, industrialization made the United States a more diverse and multicultural country, and by concentrating populations in industrial and commercial cities, it made the nation more urbanized. As enterprises grew larger, managers and business owners grew more removed from workers than they had been in small workshop enterprises.

Sumner was also writing at a time when the study of society was becoming professionalized and secularized, as exemplified by his own decision to leave the ministry and enter the world of the university. Influences from Europe were leading to the creation of the discipline of sociology, the study of society, of which Sumner was a leading early practitioner. Along with secularism went a growing tendency toward materialism, analyzing society not in terms of abstract principles but material benefits. Classical economics, with its exaltation of free trade and suspicion of government intervention in the economy, had arrived in the United States from Britain in the mid-nineteenth century, but its influence was continuing to grow in Sumner's time. This was frequently combined with the influence of Darwinian ideas about advances through struggle and the positivist prioritizing of facts over theory. The new ideas were arriving at a time when the academic curriculum was in turmoil, as the old curriculum based on religion and the Greek and Roman classics was increasingly seen as irrelevant to modern life, and academics like Sumner contended over what students should be required and expected to learn.

Author Biography

William Graham Sumner (1840–1910) was born to an English immigrant couple in Paterson, New Jersey. He briefly served as an Episcopal clergyman, but in 1872, he left the ministry to become professor of political economy at Yale University. Although his interests later shifted to the study of society, Sumner remained deeply influenced by the orthodox free-trade economics of the nineteenth century. Like other American economic conservatives, he supported a gold-backed currency, opposing the free silver movement and protectionism. He was also highly suspicious of labor unions, although he believed that they served morale-building and information-disseminating purposes. Later deemed a Social Darwinist (a term not widely used at the time), he became embroiled in a controversy with the Yale administration for employing the English Social Darwinist Herbert Spencer's *The Study of Sociology* (1873) as a textbook. Sumner pioneered the establishment of sociology as an academic discipline in America, teaching the first sociology course at an American university in 1875 and being elected the second president of the American Sociological Society in 1908.

HISTORICAL DOCUMENT

The burden of proof is on those who affirm that our social condition is utterly diseased and in need of radical regeneration! My task at present, therefore, is entirely negative and critical: to examine the allegations of fact and the doctrines which are put forward to prove the correctness of the diagnosis and to warrant the use of the remedies proposed.

The propositions put forward by social reformers nowadays are chiefly of two kinds. There are assertions in historical form, chiefly in regard to the comparison of existing with earlier social states, which are plainly based on defective historical knowledge, or at most on current stock historical dicta which are uncritical and incorrect....

The other class of propositions consists of dogmatic statements which, whether true or not, are unverifiable. This class of propositions is the pest and bane of current economic and social discussion. [Upon a more or less superficial view of some phenomenon a suggestion arises which is embodied in a philosophical proposition and promulgated as a truth. From the form and nature of such propositions they can always be brought under the head of "ethics." This word at least gives them an air of elevated sentiment and purpose, which is the only warrant they possess....

When anyone asserts that the class of skilled and unskilled manual laborers of the United States is worse off now in respect to diet, clothing, lodgings, furniture, fuel, and lights; in respect to the age at which they can marry; the number of children they can provide for; the start in life which they can give to their children, and their chances accumulating capital, than they ever have been at any former time, he makes a reckless assertion for which no facts have been offered in proof. Upon an appeal to facts, the contrary of this assertion would be clearly established. It suffices, therefore, to challenge those who are responsible for the assertion to make it good.

If it is said that the employed class are under much more stringent discipline than they were thirty years ago or earlier, it is true. It is not true that there has been any qualitative change in this respect within thirty years, but it is true that a movement which began at the first settlement of the country has been advancing with constant acceleration and has become a noticeable feature within our time.

This movement is the advance in the industrial organization. The first settlement was made by agriculturists, and for a long time there was scarcely any organization. There were scattered farmers, each working for himself, and some small towns with only rudimentary commerce and handicrafts. As the country has filled up, the arts and professions have been differentiated and the industrial organization has been advancing.

This fact and its significance has hardly been noticed at all; but the stage of the industrial organization existing at any time, and the rate of advance in its development, are the absolutely controlling social facts. Nine-tenths of the socialistic and semi-socialistic, and sentimental or ethical, suggestions by which we are overwhelmed come from failure to understand the phenomena of the industrial organization and its expansion. It controls us all because we are all in it. It creates the conditions of our existence, sets the limits of our social activity, regulates the bonds of our social relations, determines our conceptions of good and evil, suggests our life-philosophy, molds our inherited political institutions, and reforms the oldest and toughest customs, like marriage and property.

I repeat that the turmoil of heterogeneous and antagonistic social whims and speculations in which we live is due to the failure to understand what the industrial organization is and its all-pervading control over human life, while the traditions of our school of philosophy lead us always to approach the industrial organization, not from the side of objective study, but from that of philosophical doctrine. Hence it is that we find that the method of measuring what we see happening by what are called ethical standards, and of proposing to attack the phenomena by methods thence deduced, is so popular.

* * *

All organization implies restriction of liberty. The gain of power is won by narrowing individual range. The methods of business in colonial days were loose and slack to an inconceivable degree. The movement of industry has been all the time toward promptitude, punctuality, and reliability. It has been attended all the way by lamentations about the good old times; about the decline of small industries; about the lost spirit of comradeship between employer and employee; about the narrowing of the interests of the workman; about his conversion into a machine or into a "ware," and about industrial war.

These lamentations have all had reference to unquestionable phenomena attendant on advancing organization. In all occupations the same movement is discernible—in the learned professions, in schools, in trade, commerce, and transportation. It is to go on faster than ever, now that the continent is filled up by the first superficial layer of population over its whole extent and the intensification of industry has begun. The great inven-

tions both make the intention of the organization possible and make it inevitable, with all its consequences, whatever they may be....

Now the intensification of the social organization is what gives us greater social power. It is to it that we owe our increased comfort and abundance. We are none of us ready to sacrifice this. On the contrary, we want more of it. We would not return to the colonial simplicity and the colonial exiguity if we could. If not, then we must pay the price. Our life is bounded on every side by conditions. We can have this if we will agree to submit to that. In the case of industrial power and product the great condition is combination of force under discipline and strict coordination. Hence the wild language about wage-slavery and capitalistic tyranny.

In any state of society no great achievements can be produced without great force. Formerly great force was attainable only by slavery aggregating the power of great numbers of men. Roman civilization was built on this. Ours has been built on steam. It is to be built on electricity. Then we are all forced into an organization around these natural forces and adapted to the methods or their application; and although we indulge in rhetoric about political liberty, nevertheless we find ourselves bound tight in a new set of conditions, which control the modes of our existence and determine the directions in which alone economic and social liberty can go.

If it is said that there are some persons in our time who have become rapidly and in a great degree rich, it is true; it if is said that large aggregations of wealth in the control of individuals is a social danger, it is not true. . . .

If this poor old world is as bad as they say, one more reflection may check the zeal of the headlong reformer. It is at any rate a tough old world. It has taken its trend and curvature and all its twists and tangles from a long course of formation. All its wry and crooked gnarls and knobs are therefore stiff and stubborn. If we puny men by our arts can do anything at all to straighten them, it will only be by modifying the tendencies of some of the forces at work, so that, after a sufficient time, their action may be changed a little and slowly the lines of movement may be modified. This effort, however, can at most be only slight, and it will take a long time. In the meantime spontaneous forces will be at work, compared with which our efforts are like those of a man trying to deflect a river, and these forces will have changed the whole problem before our interferences have time to make themselves felt.

The great stream of time and earthly things will sweep on just the same in spite of us. It bears with it now all the errors and follies of the past, the wreckage of all the philosophies, the fragments of all the civilizations, the wisdom of all the abandoned ethical systems, the debris of all the institutions, and the penalties of all the mistakes. It is only in imagination that we stand by and look at and criticize it and plan to change it. Everyone of us is a child of his age and cannot get out of it. He is in the stream and is swept along with it. All his sciences and philosophy come to him out of it.

Therefore the tide will not be changed by us. It will swallow up both us and our experiments. It will absorb the efforts at change and take them into itself as new

but trivial components, and the great movement of tradition and work will go on unchanged by our fads and schemes. The things which will change it are the great discoveries and inventions, the new reactions inside the social organism, and then changes in the earth itself on account of changes in the cosmic forces.

These causes will make of it just what, in fidelity to them, it ought to be. The men will be carried along with it and be made by it. The utmost they can do by their cleverness will be to note and record their course as they are carried along, which is what we do now, and is that which leads us to the vain fancy that we can make or guide the movement. That is why it is the greatest folly of which a man can be capable, to sit down with a slate and pencil to plan out a new social world.

GLOSSARY

dicta: (pl. of dictum): authoritative pronouncements; maxims

exiguity: meagerness or scantiness

warrant: justification

Document Analysis

Sumner's focus in this essay is less on the ends of progressive reform than on the "absurd" reforming instinct itself, which he finds incompatible with the enormous difficulty of changing social habits and customs. Sumner believes that the reformers are intellectually sloppy, using words without a rigorous understanding of their meaning and making assertions, particularly about past societies, without awareness of their truth or falsity. This leads them to paint contemporary society as declining when it is in many ways improving.

All claims about the deteriorating condition of American workers are, in Sumner's belief, false and based on an inadequate knowledge of the past. Sentimentality and a tendency for making broad, abstract statements without a basis in social reality are also problems for Progressive activists and thinkers. Calling for more rigorous fact-checking of claims about society would also benefit his position as an academic by promoting professionalization of social thought. All social analysis that is not based on rigorous factual analysis Sumner

attacks as "sentimental" or "ethical"; his use of the word "ethical" in a derogatory sense broke with its use in mainstream American culture.

Sumner's picture of history is one where the great forces underlying social and historical change are largely immune to conscious action. (In his emphasis on changes in economic relations driving history, his awareness of the significance of the rise of industry, and his materialism, Sumner resembles his older contemporary, Karl Marx, whose politics he held in low regard.) The great economic change of Sumner's own period as he saw it was the rise of large, disciplined organizations associated with the growth of industry. Sumner does not use the term "Industrial Revolution," generally accepted as having been popularized by the British economic historian Arnold Toynbee (1852–83), but it is clear he sees the rise of industry as connected to major social transformation. These organizations regulate the life of the worker to a degree unprecedented in the less organized enterprises of the colonial and early national periods, giving rise to (in his view) baseless charges of "wage slavery," but they have also, and far more importantly, delivered an unparalleled prosperity. Trying to pass laws to moderate the impact of these changing social forces is a waste of time, in Sumner's view.

Economic prosperity is close to a supreme good for Sumner, although he seems to prefer that all classes benefit. He argues that the material condition of American workers has improved greatly since the colonial era and that the increasing regimentation of work is a small price to pay.

Essential Themes

Sumner became one of America's leading and most respected intellectuals. His brand of laissez-faire conservatism, built on the defense of capitalism and economic inequality, has had a great influence on the politics of American business and has always had its champions among university professors (more economists than practitioners of Sumner's own discipline of sociology) and other scholars. There has also been a revival of interest in Sumner's economic thought among libertarians. However, if he thought his essay would stop the Progressive movement in its tracks, he was destined for disappointment. The anti-trust campaign under the administrations of Republicans Theodore Roosevelt and William Howard Taft attempted to rein in the power of the wealthy with some success, and the New Deal of the 1930s saw the further expansion of the regulatory state as a response to the Great Depression. Labor unions, which attempted to ameliorate the conditions of work and increase wages through collective action, also survived and grew in the subsequent decades. Although Sumner believed that government should interfere with business as little as possible, he also feared the influence of business on government, and there is some evidence that by the early twentieth century, he was more skeptical of the extremely wealthy.

Debates about the effectiveness of social reform and the value of economic controls versus economic freedom have continued to the present day. Although Sumner and his intellectual allies are often referred to as "classical liberals," the skeptical position against reform movements and the belief that large enterprises and wealthy people should be allowed to go their own ways with minimal interference he put forth is now identified with conservative forces in American political and intellectual life. Furthermore, great concentrations of wealth and their effect on American society are now usually discussed under the heading of inequality.

—*William E. Burns, PhD*

Bibliography and Additional Readings

Curtis, Bruce. *William Graham Sumner*. Boston: Twayne, 1981. Print.

Hofstadter, Richard. *Social Darwinism in American Thought*. Boston: Beacon, 1992. Print.

McCloskey, Robert Green. *American Conservatism in the Age of Enterprise 1865–1910: A Study of William Graham Sumner, Stephen J. Field, and Andrew Carnegie*. New York: Harper, 1964. Print.

Sumner, William Graham. *On Liberty, Society and Politics: The Essential Essays of William Graham Sumner*. Ed. Robert C. Bannister. Indianapolis: Liberty Fund, 1992. Print.

Frances Willard on Christian Social Responsibility

Date: November 1890
Author: Frances E. Willard
Genre: speech

Summary Overview

The Woman's Christian Temperance Union (WCTU) and its founder Frances Willard were key participants in the social reform movements that emerged after the Civil War. Although the issue of the abolition of slavery had been decided by the Civil War, there were many other social movements that emerged in the latter part of the nineteenth century. One of the more active and influential was the WCTU, which took on a variety of social causes and whose membership grew to over 100,000 under Willard's leadership. As the name suggests, Christianity was a key tenet of the WCTU, and it was used as a basis to promote a range of social reforms. The WCTU also provided women a place in the public and political sphere, as opposed to being relegated solely to domestic duties. The address Willard made to the membership in 1890 was meant to reinforce the Christian foundation of WCTU's social responsibility and humanitarian reform efforts.

Defining Moment

Frances Willard and the organization she led, the Woman's Christian Temperance Union (WCTU), were in the forefront of the struggle for social reform in the post–Civil War era. Under Willard's leadership, the temperance movement, which initially focused on banning alcohol and some drugs, also broadened its focus to include women's rights, women's suffrage, prison reform, an eight-hour work day, free school lunches, and the abolition of prostitution. Willard was aware of the moral boundaries of her time, and in order to appear nonthreatening, she advocated for change on the basis of a strong Christian message, which then created an appropriate platform for her to speak publicly, something that would otherwise have been viewed as improper during the time period. Women were expected to keep within the separate sphere of domestic issues and focus on the home and on child rearing, while men were granted the freedom move within public and political spheres. However, because alcohol had such destructive effects on the family as a whole, temperance was seen as a suitable issue on which women could speak out. Having secured a platform for this one issue, Willard was able to use her traditional values to bring forward other radical ideas for reform.

She emphasized in many of her speeches the conservative values of Christianity and of women's moral superiority. In this way, the WCTU was not seen as a threat to the status quo of society and especially men's leadership within it. One campaign that worked well for the WCTU was the "Home Protection" campaign, which promoted giving women over the age of twenty-one the vote in order to allow them a voice in prohibiting strong alcohol as a threat to the family unit and domestic life.

As a result of her leadership in the WCTU, Willard was one of the best-known women of her time. She appealed to both women and men by adapting conservative values to promote social reforms. Willard was well respected among such contemporaries as Susan B. Anthony and Elizabeth Cady Stanton. She lost prominence in the eyes of later historians, however, and was virtually ignored by feminist scholars because of those strong conservative and Christian values. Many of her other, more progressive reform attempts were overshadowed by her leadership of a temperance movement. When prohibition ended in 1933, her reputation as a reformer faded along with the movement with which she was so closely associated.

Author Biography

Frances Elizabeth Willard was the leader of the Woman's Christian Temperance Union (WCTU) for almost twenty years, from 1879 until her death in 1898. During her leadership, she transformed the organization from a one-issue focus (the prohibition of alcohol) to a much broader social reform platform. She was born in 1839, and held a variety of teaching positions, eventually being named president of Evanston College for Ladies in 1871. Evanston was later absorbed by Northwestern University, where Willard became the first dean of women in 1873. During her tenure at the WCTU, she expanded its focus to include women's rights and women's right to vote, the moral reform of prostitutes, prison reform, and the kindergarten movement. At the time of her death, she was one of the best-known and most well-respected women of her time, with tens of thousands of mourners paying their respects in both New York and Chicago.

HISTORICAL DOCUMENT

I wish we were all more thorough students of the mighty past, for we should thus be rendered braver prophets of the future, and more cheerful workers in the present. History shows us with what tenacity the human race survives. Earthquake, famine, and pestilence have done their worst, but over them rolls a healing tide of years and they are lost to view; on sweeps the great procession, and hardly shows a scar. Rulers around whom clustered new forms of civilization pass away; but greater men succeed them. Nations are rooted up; great hopes seem blighted; revolutions rise and rivers run with the blood of patriots; the globe itself seems headed toward the abyss; new patriots are born; higher hopes bloom out like stars; humanity emerges from the dark ages vastly ahead of what it was on entering that cave of gloom, and ever the right comes uppermost; and now is Christ's kingdom nearer than when we first believed.

Only those who have not studied history lose heart in great reforms; only those unread in the biography of genius imagine themselves to be original. Except in the realm of material invention, there is nothing new under the sun. There is no reform which some great soul has not dreamed of centuries ago; there is not a doctrine that some father of the Church did not set forth. The Greek philosophers and early Christian Fathers boxed the compass once for all; we may take our choice of what they have left on record. Let us then learn a wise humility, but at the same time a humble wisdom, as we remember that there are but two classes of men—one which

declares that our times are the worst the world has seen, and another which claims our times as best; and he who claims this, all revelation, all science, all history witness, is right, and will be right forevermore.

The most normal and the most perfect human being is the one who most thoroughly addresses himself to the activity of his best powers, gives himself most thoroughly to the world around him, flings himself out into the midst of humanity, and is so preoccupied by his own beneficent reaction on the world that he is practically unconscious of a separate existence. Introspection, and retrospection were good for the cloister; but the uplook, the outlook, and the onlook are alone worthy [of] the modern Christian. To change the figure, a normal Christian stands in the midst of a great, beautiful and varied landscape. It is the landscape of beneficent work. Above him reaches the boundless skies, brilliant with the stars of God and Heaven.

Love and friendship form a beautiful rainbow over his landscape and reach up toward his sky. But the only two great environments of the soul are work for humanity and faith in God. Those wounded in love will find that affection, dear and vital as it is, comes to us not as the whole of life, not as its wide wondrous landscape of the earth, not as its beautiful vision of the sky, but as its beautiful embellishment, its rainbow fair and sweet. But were it gone there would still remain the two greatest and most satisfying pictures on which the soul can gaze—humanity and God.

Document Analysis

Frances Willard gained prominence and a public profile by advocating social responsibility and humanitarianism while retaining a very conservative and Christian position that belied her activism and allowed for support of important social reforms. Views on women's suffrage, women's rights, prohibition, and education reform were thereby kept within a conventional and traditional societal view that was able to attract a wide group of people—both women and men—to her cause.

Her 1890 "Work Done for Humanity" speech to the World's Woman's Christian Temperance Union, an affiliated organization she founded, was designed around strong Christian themes. Notice in particular that, although her audience would have been composed primarily of women, she uses the masculine pronoun "he" throughout the speech to refer to people in general, which, although common usage at the time, also points to her conservative leanings.

Her message in this speech focuses on the concepts of social responsibility and humanitarianism and that people should come to the aid of their neighbors. She uses history to frame her messages and claims that all reform has been thought of by someone else in the past. She notes both "Greek philosophers and early Christian Fathers" in her speech as examples of this. Again, this helps portray her not as a radical, but as a student of history and one who can deliver a message that addresses the current structure of society. Her clever rhetorical strategy points out for the audience that if society only knew its own history, then the reforms to which she refers would not seem as foreign or innovative.

She describes the sense of communion with all humanity that comes from altruistic activity, such that a person who dedicates their life to helping others is "practically unconscious of a separate existence." Willard then expands on this and creates a connection between "beneficent work" (good works) and a closer connection to God. She explains that each person's soul should focus its work on only two things, "work for humanity and faith in God," and by doing the one, the other will naturally be enhanced. She puts service to others as a higher calling than affection or love between people because, as she explains, such affection is not a foundation of one's life, but is rather a "beautiful embellishment" or addition to it. In this way, Willard is attempting to sway her audience to join her in her efforts to make American society a better place for all concerned.

Essential Themes

Frances Willard's view of social reform and communal social responsibility to make American society a better place resonates to modern times, and this period in American history can be seen as the genesis of the modern nonprofit sector. Today, the key tenets of humanitarianism are kept alive by myriad not-for-profit organizations that work to enhance and improve the quality of life around the globe. Many groups are still closely associated with Christian values and operate within church-based organizations. Others are independent of a connection to religion and are therefore free to advocate much more secular social reforms. Ironically, the social reform Willard was best known for—temperance—was ultimately a failed social experiment in the United States: the production and sale of alcohol was banned by constitutional amendment from 1920 to 1933, but the ban was widely flouted and ultimately repealed. As of the early twenty-first century, the WCTU and its global equivalent are still in operation, but they have lost the prominence that they once enjoyed.

Willard's world view was clear: social reforms were necessary, and they needed to be achieved within a society strongly rooted in Christian values. Although Willard believed that women should remain in the traditional role of wife and mother in order for society to operate effectively, she herself never married or had any children. She spoke out on social reforms she felt would make women's lives easier to bear, and she believed that all humanitarian reforms are closely connected to faith in God. By grounding one's life in service to others, one could also find a closer relationship to God. This message is still being used by many Christian leaders in America, as many churches run considerable charitable and humanitarian activities. It is not, however, a message that resonates within a multicultural nation that guarantees freedom of religion to all of its citizens. As such, her message would not have been as universally accepted today as it was during her own time period.

—*Lee Tunstall, PhD*

Bibliography and Additional Reading

Bordin, Ruth. *Frances Willard: A Biography*. Chapel Hill: U of North Carolina P, 1986. Print.

Gifford, Carolyn De Swarte, ed. *Writing Out My Heart: Selections from the Journal of Frances E. Willard, 1855–96*. Urbana: U of Illinois P, 1995. Print.

Gifford, Carolyn De Swarte, and Amy R. Slagell, eds. *Let Something Good Be Said: Speeches and Writings of Frances E. Willard*. Urbana: U of Illinois P, 2007. Print.

Willard Frances E. *How I Learned to Ride the Bicycle: Reflections of an Influential 19th Century Woman*. Sunnyvale: Fair Oaks, 1991. Print.

■ Jane Addams on Settlement Houses

Date: 1892
Authors: Jane Addams
Genre: speech; address

Summary Overview

In the summer of 1892, social activist Jane Addams addressed a conference of settlement house proponents and workers. She shared with the audience what she believed to be the three underlying principles behind social settlements: a desire to interpret democracy in social terms, to share the ways of life of people of different socioeconomic strata, and to remain true to Christian humanitarianism.

Defining Moment

While pursuing her bachelor's degree at Rockford Female Seminary, Addams planned a career in medicine. She entered medical school, but she suffered from poor health associated with a congenital spinal defect and had to halt her training. Surgery corrected her spinal curve, but Addams did not return to medical school. Instead, in 1883, she embarked on a journey across Europe, where she studied and explored her future options. She returned home for two years, then decided to return to Europe in 1887. This time, she was accompanied by a friend, Ellen Starr.

During their travels, Addams and Starr visited Toynbee Hall in London. Toynbee Hall was the first settlement house, an institution that housed, educated, and provided resources for the city's poorest citizens. However, Toynbee Hall was different from other charities: also residing at the settlement house were volunteers from middle- and upper-class backgrounds. The premise behind Toynbee Hall was not only to aid the poor but also to foster better understanding between people from different socioeconomic strata. Founded in 1884 by Church of England curate Samuel Barnett and his wife Henrietta, Toynbee Hall was part of a growing movement in social service and philanthropy that came to be known as the "settlement movement." An important element of

Toynbee's founding spirit was to help foster within England's future leaders an understanding and appreciation of poverty in England, so that the policies they would later introduce would be effective in alleviating it.

Inspired by their experience at Toynbee Hall, Addams and Starr returned to Chicago, an industrialized city with a large population of poor residents. In 1889, they rented a large mansion owned by real estate baron Charles Hull. The building was rooted in a neighborhood that was particularly impacted by poverty. Addams and Starr established a social settlement house similar to Toynbee Hall, recruiting wealthy citizens to live there while providing a wide range of services to the neighborhood's poor. The residents of Hull House were not considered "clients" by the volunteers; they were considered the volunteers' "neighbors," an important distinction, as it fostered equality among the house's diverse resident population. Hull House would quickly grow in popularity: by its second year, it was serving two thousand people every week. Over time, Hull House (which would continue to operate under the leadership of Addams and Starr) expanded to include a wide range of amenities. Among the new wings added were an art school and gallery, full-service kitchen, pool, gymnasium, coffee house, museum, library, and a theater group. Hull House offered educational programs all day and evening, serving students from kindergarten through their adult years.

With Addams serving as the face of the growing social settlement movement in the United States, she was in high demand for presentations and guest speaking engagements. In 1892, three years after Hull House's establishment, she was invited to speak on the topic of social progress and her successes at Hull House at a summer session at the School of Applied Ethics in Plymouth, Massachusetts.

Author Biography

Laura Jane Addams was born on September 6, 1860, in Cedarville, Illinois. Her father, John, was a prominent Illinois state legislator and friend to President Abraham Lincoln. Her mother, Sarah, died in childbirth when Jane was two years old. Addams attended Rockford Female Seminary (later Rockford College for Women), graduating as class valedictorian. Due to health prob- lems, she halted her medical school training and in- stead traveled throughout Europe. After founding Hull House, she became a prominent Chicago city leader and an internationally renowned feminist and activist. She received the Nobel Peace Prize in 1931, but was admitted to a Baltimore hospital with a heart condition on the day she was to receive it. She died on May 21, 1935, from cancer.

HISTORICAL DOCUMENT

Hull House, which was Chicago's first Settlement, was established in September, 1889. It represented no asso- ciation, but was opened by two women, backed by many friends, in the belief that the mere foothold of a house, easily accessible, ample in space, hospitable and toler- ant in spirit, situated in the midst of the large foreign colonies which so easily isolate themselves in American cities, would be in itself a serviceable thing for Chicago. Hull House endeavors to make social intercourse express the growing sense of the economic unity of society. It is an effort to add the social function to democracy. It was opened on the theory that the dependence of classes on each other is reciprocal; and that as "the social relation is essentially a reciprocal relation, it gave a form of expres- sion that has peculiar value.". . .

I have divided the motives which constitute the sub- jective pressure toward Social Settlements into three great lines: the first contains the desire to make the entire social organism democratic, to extend democ- racy beyond its political expression; the second is the impulse to share the race life, and to bring as much as possible of social energy and the accumulation of civili- zation to those portions of the race which have little; the third springs from a certain renaissance of Christianity, a movement toward its early humanitarian aspects.

It is not difficult to see that although America is pledged to the democratic ideal, the view of democracy has been partial, and that its best achievement thus far has been pushed along the line of the franchise. Democ- racy has made little attempt to assert itself in social affairs. We have refused to move beyond the position of its eighteenth-century leaders, who believed that political equality alone would secure all good to all men.

We conscientiously followed the gift of the ballot hard upon the gift of freedom to the negro, but we are quite unmoved by the fact that he lives among us in a practi- cal social ostracism. We hasten to give the franchise to the immigrant from a sense of justice, from a tradition that he ought to have it, while we dub him with epi- thets deriding his past life or present occupation, and feel no duty to invite him to our houses. We forced to acknowledge that it is only in our local and national poli- tics that we try very hard for the ideal so dear to those who were enthusiasts when the century was young. We have almost given it up as our ideal in social intercourse. There are city wards in which many of the votes are sold for drinks and dollars; still there is a remote pretence, at least a fiction current, that a man's vote is his own. The judgment of the voter is consulted and an opportunity for remedy given. There is not even a theory in the social order, not a shadow answering to the polls in politics. The time may come when the politician who sells one by one to the highest bidder all the offices in his grasp, will not be considered more base in his code of morals, more hardened in his practice, than the woman who con- stantly invites to her receptions those alone who bring her an equal social return, who shares her beautiful sur- roundings only with those who minister to a liking she has for successful social events. In doing this is she not just as unmindful of the common weal, as unscrupulous in her use of power, as is any city "boss" who consults only the interests of the "ring"?

In politics "bossism" arouses a scandal. It goes on in society constantly and is only beginning to be challenged. Our consciences are becoming tender in regard to the lack of democracy in social affairs. We are perhaps entering upon the second phase of democracy, as the French philosophers entered upon the first, somewhat bewildered by its logical conclusions. The social organism has broken down through large districts of our great cities. Many of the people living there are very poor, the majority of them without leisure or energy for anything but the gain of subsistence. They move often from one wretched lodging to another. They live for the moment side by side, many of them without knowledge of each other, without fellowship, without local tradition or public spirit, without social organization of any kind. Practically nothing is done to remedy this. The people who might do it, who have the social tact and training, the large houses, and the traditions and custom of hospitality, live in other parts of the city. The clubhouses, libraries, galleries, and semi-public conveniences for social life are also blocks away. We find working-men organized into armies of producers because men of executive ability and business sagacity have found it to their interests thus to organize them. But these workingmen are not organized socially; although living in crowded tenement-houses, they are living without a corresponding social contact. The chaos is as great as it would be were they working in huge factories without foreman or superintendent. Their ideas and resources are cramped. The desire for higher social pleasure is extinct. They have no share in the traditions and social energy which make for progress. Too often their only place of meeting is a saloon, their only host a bartender; a local demagogue forms their public opinion. Men of ability and refinement, of social power and university cultivation, stay away from them. Personally, I believe the men who lose most are those who thus stay away. But the paradox is here: when cultivated people do stay away from a certain portion of the population, when all social advantages are persistently withheld, it may be for years, the result itself is pointed at as a reason, is used as an argument, for the continued withholding.

It is constantly said that because the masses have never had social advantages they do not want them, that they are heavy and dull, and that it will take political or philanthropic machinery to change them. This divides a city into rich and poor; into the favored, who express their sense of the social obligation by gifts of money, and into the unfavored, who express it by clamoring for a "share"—both of them actuated by a vague sense of jus-

tice. This division of the city would be more justifiable, however, if the people who thus isolate themselves on certain streets and use their social ability for each other gained enough thereby and added sufficient to the sum total of social progress to justify the withholding of the pleasures and results of that progress from so many people who ought to have them. But they cannot accomplish this. The social spirit discharges itself in many forms, and no one form is adequate to its total expression. We are all uncomfortable in regard to the sincerity of our best phrases, because we hesitate to translate our philosophy into the deed.

These hopes may be loosely formulated thus: that if in a democratic country nothing can he permanently achieved save through the masses of the people, it will be impossible to establish a higher political life than the people themselves crave; that it is difficult to see how the notion of a higher civic life can be fostered save through common intercourse; that the blessings which we associate with a life of refinement and cultivation can be made universal and must be made universal if they are to be permanent; that the good we secure for ourselves is precarious and uncertain, is floating in mid-air, until it is secured for all of us and incorporated into our common life.

I find it somewhat difficult to formulate the second line of motives which I believe to constitute the trend of the subjective pressure toward the Settlement. There is something primordial about these motives, but I am perhaps over-bold in designating them as a great desire to share the race life. We all bear traces of the starvation struggle which for so long made up the life of the race. Our very organism holds memories and glimpses of that long life of our ancestors which still goes on among so many of our contemporaries. Nothing so deadens the sympathies and shrivels the power of enjoyment as the persistent keeping away from the great opportunities for helpfulness and a continual ignoring of the starvation struggle which makes up the life of at least half the race. To shut one's self away from that half of the race life is to shut one's self away from the most vital part of it; it is to live out but half the humanity which we have been born heir to and to use but half our faculties. We have all had longings for a fuller life which should include the use of these faculties. These longings are the physical complement of the "Intimations of Immortality" on which no ode has yet been written. To portray these would be the work of a poet, and it is hazardous for any but a poet to attempt it.

We have in America a fast-growing number of cultivated young people who have no recognized outlet for their active faculties. They bear constantly of the great social maladjustment, but no way is provided for them to change it, and their uselessness bangs about them heavily. Huxley declares that the sense of uselessness is the severest shock which the human system can sustain, and that, if persistently sustained, it results in atrophy of function. These young people have had advantages of college, of European travel and economic study, but they are sustaining this shock of inaction. They have pet phrases, and they tell you that the things that make us all alike are stronger than the things that make us different. They say that all men are united by needs and sympathies far more permanent and radical than anything that temporarily divides them and sets them in opposition to each other. If they affect art, they say that the decay in artistic expression is due to the decay in ethics, that art when shut away from the human interests and from the great mass of humanity is self-destructive. They tell their elders with all the bitterness of youth that if they expect success from them in business, or politics, or in whatever lines their ambition for them has run, they must let them consult all of humanity; that they must let them find out what the people want and how they want it. It is only the stronger young people, however, who formulate this. Many of them dissipate their energies in so-called enjoyment. Others, not content with that, go on studying and go back to college for their second degrees, not that they are especially fond of study, but because they want something definite to do, and their powers have been trained in the direction of mental accumulation. Many are buried beneath mere mental accumulation with lowered vitality and discontent. Walter Besant says they have had the vision that Peter had when he saw the great sheet let down from heaven, wherein was neither clean nor unclean. He calls it the sense of humanity. It is not philanthropy nor benevolence. It is a thing fuller and wider than either of these. This young life, so sincere in its emotion and good phrases and yet so undirected, seems to me as pitiful as the other great mass of destitute lives.

One is supplementary to the other, and some method of communication can surely be devised. Mr. Barnett, who urged the first Settlement,—Toynbee Hall, in East London,—recognized this need of outlet for the young men of Oxford and Cambridge, and hoped that the Settlement would supply the communication. It is easy to see why the Settlement movement originated in England, where the years of education are more constrained and definite than they are here, where class distinctions are more rigid. The necessity of it was greater there, but we are fast feeling the pressure of the need and meeting the necessity for Settlements in America. Our young people feel nervously the need of putting theory into action, and respond quickly to the Settlement form of activity.

The third division of motives which I believe make toward the Settlement is the result of a certain renaissance going forward in Christianity. The impulse to share the lives of the poor, the desire to make social service, irrespective of propaganda, express the spirit of Christ, is as old as Christianity itself. We have no proof from the records themselves that the early Roman Christians, who strained their simple art to the point of grotesqueness in their eagerness to record a "good news" on the walls of the catacombs, considered this "good news" a religion. Jesus had no set of truths labelled "Religious." On the contrary, his doctrine was that all truth is one, that the appropriation of it is freedom. His teaching had no dogma to mark it off from truth and action in general. He himself called it a revelations life. These early Roman Christians received the Gospel message, a command to love all men, with a certain joyous simplicity. The image of the Good Shepherd is blithe and gay beyond the gentlest shepherd of Greek mythology; the hart no longer pants, but rushes to the water brooks. The Christians looked for the continuous revelation, but believed what Jesus said, that this revelation to be held and made manifest must be put into terms of action; that action is the only medium man has for receiving and appropriating truth. "If any man will do His will, he shall know of the doctrine."

That Christianity has to be revealed and embodied in the line of social progress is a corollary to the simple proposition that man's action is found in his social relationships in the way in which he connects with his fellows, that his motives for action are the zeal and affection with which he regards his fellows. By this simple process was created a deep enthusiasm for humanity, which regarded man as at once the organ and object of revelation; and by this process came about that wonderful fellowship, that true democracy of the early Church, that so captivates the imagination. The early Christians were pre-eminently nonresistant. They believed in love as a cosmic force. There was no iconoclasm during the minor peace of the Church. They did not yet denounce, nor tear down temples, nor preach the end of the world. They grew to a mighty number, but it never occurred to them, either in their weakness or their strength, to regard other men for an instant as their foes or as aliens. The spectacle of the Christians loving all men was the most astounding Rome had ever seen. They were eager to sacrifice themselves for the weak, for children and the aged. They identified themselves with slaves and did not avoid the plague. They longed to share the common lot that they might receive the constant revelation. It was a new treasure which the early Christians added to the sum of all treasures, a joy hitherto unknown in the world, the joy of finding the Christ which lieth in each man, but which no man can unfold save in fellowship. A happiness ranging from the heroic to the pastoral enveloped them. They were to possess a revelation as long as life had new meaning to unfold, new action to propose.

I believe that there is a distinct turning among many young men and women toward this simple acceptance of Christ's message. They resent the assumption that Christianity is a set of ideas which belong to the religious consciousness, whatever that may be, that it is a thing to be proclaimed and instituted apart from the social life of the community. They insist that it shall seek a simple and natural expression in the social organism itself. The Settlement movement is only one manifestation of that wider humanitarian movement which throughout Christendom, but pre-eminently in England, is endeavoring to embody itself, not in a sect, but in society itself. Tolstoi has reminded us all very forcibly of Christ's principle of non resistance. His formulation has been startling and his expression has deviated from the general movement, but there is little doubt that he has many adherents, men and women who are philosophically convinced of the futility of opposition, we believe that evil can be overcome only with good and cannot be opposed. If love is the creative force of the universe, the principle which binds men together, and by their interdependence on each other makes them human, just so surely is anger and the spirit of opposition the destructive principle of the universe, that which tears down, thrusts men apart, and makes them isolated and brutal.

I cannot, of course, speak for other Settlements, but it would, I think, be unfair to Hull House not to emphasize the conviction with which the first residents went there, that it would be a foolish and an unwarrantable expenditure of force to oppose or to antagonize any individual or set of people in the neighborhood; that whatever of good the House had to offer should be put into positive terms; that its residents should live with opposition to no man, with recognition of the good in every man, even the meanest, I believe that this turning, this renaissance of the early Christian humanitarianism, is going on in America, in Chicago, if you please, without leaders who write or philosophize, without much speaking, but with a bent to express in social service, in terms of action, the spirit of Christ. Certain it is that spiritual force is found in the Settlement movement, and it is also true that this force must be evoked and must be called into play before the success of any Settlement is assured. There must be the overmastering belief that all that is noblest in life is common to men as men, in order to accentuate the likenesses and ignore the differences which are found among the people whom the Settlement constantly brings into juxtaposition. It may be true, as Frederic Harrison insists, that the very religious fervor of man can be turned into love for his race and his desire for a future life into content to live in the echo of his deeds. How far the Positivists' formula of the high ardor for humanity can carry the Settlement movement, Mrs. Humphry Ward's house in London may in course of time illustrate. Paul's formula of seeking for the Christ which lieth in each man and founding our likenesses on him seems a simpler formula to many of us.

If you have heard a thousand voices singing in the Hallelujah Chorus in Handel's "Messiah," you have found that the leading voices could still be distinguished, but that the differences of training and cultivation between them and the voices of the chorus were lost in the unity of purpose and the fact that they were all human voices lifted by a high motive. This is a weak illustration of what a Settlement attempts to do. It aims, in a measure, to lead whatever of social life its neighborhood may afford, to focus and give form to that life, to bring to bear upon it the results of cultivation and training; but it receives in exchange for the music of isolated voices the volume and strength of the chorus. It is quite impossible for me to say what proportion or degree the subjective necessity, which led to the opening of Hull House, combined the three trends: first the desire to interpret democracy in social terms; secondly, the impulse beating at the very source of our lives urging us to aid in the race progress;

and, thirdly, the Christian movement toward Humanitarianism. It is difficult to analyze a living thing; the analysis is at best imperfect. Many more motives may blend with the three trends; possibly the desire for a new form of social success due to the nicety of imagination, which refuses worldly pleasures unmixed with the joys of self sacrifice; possibly a love of approbation, so vast that is it not content with the treble clapping of delicate hands, but wishes also to bear the bass notes from toughened palms, may mingle with these.

GLOSSARY

franchise: the vote

Huxley: Thomas Henry Huxley (1825–1895), British biologist and supporter of Charles Darwin

Positivist: one who holds that society operates according to underlying laws or principles, in the same way in which the physical world operates

ring: a syndicate or circle of corrupt individuals

social relation … reciprocal relation: Addams is here quoting herself from a previously published statement

Document Analysis

As cofounder of Hull House, Jane Addams—speaking to a conference of like-minded social settlement activists—comments on the need for such a house in the city of Chicago. The city was divided into many different neighborhoods, each made up of diverse groups of residents who, without a central institution like Hull House, would otherwise "isolate themselves" within this major city, she says. The driving idea behind Hull House, she adds, is to use social intercourse—bringing these diverse groups and individuals together under one roof—to foster a sense of economic unity in American society.

Addams points to three main "motives" behind the social settlement movement. The first of these is to move the idea of democracy—which she says is considered a predominantly political concept—into a social context. In other words, she says that the political application of democracy has given black Americans the power of the vote and justice to immigrants but has done little to halt ongoing prejudices against these so-

cial groups. American political candidates, she argues, frequently buy votes with "drinks and dollars," paying little attention to the different social groups casting their votes. Such attention, she says, only perpetuates social inequality and disadvantage. Only through social intercourse—the mutual acknowledgement and interaction between leaders and diverse populations—can democracy foster social as well as political equality, she suggests.

Her second motive is to "share the race life." This phrase refers, she says, to the idea that interaction with other members of the human race fosters a sense of usefulness and purpose for which each person may spend his or her life searching; art and education are among the areas she cites in which this pursuit of purpose is evident. Young people, she says, are particularly receptive to the notion that, in order to find a sense of purpose, they must interact with different members of the human race. The willingness to help others, she says, is prevalent in young people, as it is not necessarily a matter of philanthropy or benevolence—it is simply part of being human. Therefore, she finds great connectivity with younger people as the driving force behind the social settlement movement.

The third motive she cites is a Christian one. The desire to serve the poor—and indeed to live among and share life with the poor—was a concept as old as Christianity itself, Addams says. Love of one's fellow human beings—"finding the Christ which lieth in each man"—was the core teaching of Christianity, she says, and is not embodied in religious institutions, but in humanitarian social action. Such a principle is pure, she says—there would be no adversarial relationships borne of such attitudes.

Addams states that humanity, particularly young people, were increasingly showing appreciation of this notion as well as the other motivations behind social settlements. She concludes that these motivations were the driving force behind Hull House and a general influence on the social settlement movement.

Essential Themes

Addams was so inspired by the social settlement she encountered at Toynbee Hall that she and her friend, Ellen Starr, decided to create a similar settlement house in Chicago. When she was invited to speak to a group of social settlement proponents, she offered what she saw as the main motivating factors driving the works being performed at Hull House.

The first of these motives was to encourage the expansion of democracy from the political application for which it was best known into a more social setting. Political democracy was limited, she argued, giving nominal legal protections to all economic strata and social groups but not encouraging social equality. By placing people from different sectors of society—the poor and the wealthy, for example—in the same house, Addams believed the social equality anticipated in a democratic nation could actually be achieved.

The second motivation was to make life more fulfilling and to give all members of the human race a sense of purpose. Many young people used art and other diversions to find their meaning and focus in life, but Addams said Hull House and its social settlement approach gave volunteers a connection to their fellow human beings.

The third motivation was the Christian concept of being good to one another. From its earliest roots, Addams said, Christianity encouraged people to share with one another—a principle early Christians embraced, fostering no aversion or antagonism toward any other people. Christianity had been at the heart of the Toynbee Hall model, and Addams said that a similar desire to help and interact with others was a central driving force in the success of Hull House as well.

Addams did not offer these motivations as an exclusive model for other social settlements to follow. Rather, she used this occasion to underscore what she believed to be a major influence on the continued success of her own social settlement house. Similarly, she saw these motivations as generating what she saw as the purely positive characteristics of the social settlement movement.

—*Michael P. Auerbach, MA*

Bibliography and Additional Reading

Addams, Jane. *Twenty Years at Hull House*. London: Penguin, 1910. Print.

Barbuto, Domenica M. *American Settlement Houses and Progressive Social Reform: An Encyclopedia of the American Settlement Movement*. Westport: Greenwood, 1999. Print.

Friedman, Michael, and Brett Friedman. *Settlement Houses: Improving the Social Welfare of America's Immigrants*. London: Rosen, 2006. Print.

"Jane Addams—Biographical." *NobelPrize.org*. Nobel Media, 2014. Web. 28 Feb. 2014.

Joslin, Katherine. *Jane Addams: A Writer's Life*. Champaign: U of Illinois P, 2004. Print.

Linn, James Weber. *Jane Addams: A Biography*. Champaign: U of Illinois P, 1935. Print.

■ John Dewey on Social Organization and the Individual

Date: 1908
Authors: John Dewey and James Tufts
Genre: essay

Summary Overview

In 1908, former University of Chicago colleagues John Dewey and James Tufts published *Ethics*, a seminal textbook for teaching the philosophy of ethics. As part of the Chicago school of pragmatism, they favored the application of ethical theories to current affairs over the study of abstract concepts and emphasized the impact of society on each individual's responsibilities, freedoms, rights, and obligations. They also acknowledged that rapidly changing societies require a more flexible approach to ethics than older philosophical traditions typically followed; thus, they focused on identifying a process for ethical decision-making, rather than establishing concrete principles to apply uniformly in all situations. In this excerpt from *Ethics*, Dewey and Tufts broadly define the concepts of responsibility, freedom, rights, and obligations as they relate to individuals within a broader society.

Defining Moment

Dewey and Tufts's emphasis on the significance of social context to moral theories is clear throughout *Ethics*. For example, the textbook begins by reviewing the moral theories of ancient civilizations and observing their limitations in the context of the societies that created them. The two philosophers strongly believed in studying the application of ethics, particularly in respect to societies as a whole and how they are structured, rather than just in respect to individual behavior—and indeed, their theories suggest that the two cannot truly be separated.

Dewey and Tufts wrote *Ethics* during a time of significant social change within the United States. Slavery had officially been abolished several decades prior, and African American men technically had most of the same rights as white men, but continued discrimina-

tion and fear for personal safety often made it nearly impossible to exercise those rights. Women of all races still fought for the right to vote and faced discrimination in activities necessary to participate fully in society, such as obtaining an education and owning property. As industry prospered, easily exploitable workers, such as children and immigrants, were often placed in dangerous conditions, working long hours for little pay in factories, mills, and mines. Political unrest in Europe seemed to be leading toward war, as well as domestic disagreement about whether and how the United States should become involved.

In the context of these rapidly changing times, Dewey and Tufts posited that the old philosophical approach to ethics and value judgments—namely, identifying specific moral principles to apply uniformly in all situations—was no longer viable. The core of their belief was that responsibility, freedom, rights, and obligations may belong to the individual, but ultimately they stem from society as a whole. As more people with different backgrounds and experiences began actively participating in society, it became nearly impossible to identify static, concrete ethical principles to govern all actions and circumstances. As new situations arose that simply did not exist before—for example, deplorable working conditions in factories—it was necessary to adopt a new approach to ethics. To achieve this, Dewey and Tufts focused on the process of making moral and value judgments, identifying the factors that should be considered when making such judgments rather than naming static, unchanging principles that could not adjust with the changing times.

Author Biography

John Dewey was born in 1859 in Burlington, Vermont. He received his undergraduate degree from the University of Vermont and his PhD in philosophy from Johns Hopkins University in Maryland. He taught at several universities, including the University of Chicago, and served as president of the American Psychological Association and the American Philosophical Association. Over the course of his career, Dewey published hundreds of journal articles and numerous books. Dewey made significant contributions to psychology and philosophy, particularly with regard to the interaction of social environment and the mind and the intersection of education and politics. He died in New York in 1952. James Tufts was born in 1862 in Monson, Massachu-

setts. He attended Amherst College and Yale Divinity School and later spent a year in Germany, obtaining his PhD from Albert-Ludwigs-Universitat. He returned to a faculty position at the newly founded University of Chicago, where he later served as chair of the philosophy department, dean, vice president, and acting president. During his career, Tufts published ten books and more than one hundred articles. His focus on economics and social justice led to political involvement, including chairing the garment industry arbitration board and serving as president of the Illinois Association for Labor Legislation. Tufts died in California in 1942.

HISTORICAL DOCUMENT

RESPONSIBILITY AND FREEDOM

The more comprehensive and diversified the social order, the greater the responsibility and the freedom of the individual. His freedom is the greater, because the more numerous are the effective stimuli to action, and the more varied and the more certain the ways in which he may fulfill his powers. His responsibility is greater because there are more demands for considering the consequences of his acts; and more agencies for bringing home to him the recognition of consequences which affect not merely more persons individually, but which also influence the more remote and hidden social ties.

Liability—Freedom and responsibility have a relatively superficial and negative meaning and a relatively positive central meaning. In its external aspect, responsibility is *liability*. An agent is free to act; yes, but—. He must stand the consequences, the disagreeable as well as the pleasant, the social as well as the physical. He may do a given act, but if so, let him look out. His act is a matter that concerns others as well as himself, and they will prove their concern by calling him to account; and if he cannot give a satisfactory and credible account of his intention, subject him to correction. Each community and organization informs its members what it regards as obnoxious, and serves notice upon them that they have to answer if they

offend. The individual then is (1) likely or liable to have to explain and justify his behavior, and is (2) liable or open to suffering consequent upon inability to make his explanation acceptable.

Positive Responsibility—In this way the individual is made aware of the stake the community has in his behavior; and is afforded an opportunity to take that interest into account in directing his desires and making his plans. If he does so, he is a responsible person. The agent who does not take to heart the concern which others show that they have in his conduct, will note his liability only as an evil to which he is exposed, and will take it into consideration only to see how to escape or evade it. But one whose point of view is sympathetic and reasonable will recognize the justice of the community interest in his performances; and will recognize the value to him of the instruction contained in its assertions of its interest. Such an one responds, answers, to the social demands made; he is not merely called to answer. He holds himself responsible for the consequences of his acts; he does not wait to be held liable by others. When society looks for responsible workmen, teachers, doctors, it does not mean merely those whom it may call to account; it can do that in any case. It wants men and women who habitually form their purpose after consideration of the social consequences of their execution. Dislike of disapprobation, fear of penalty, play a part in generating this responsive habit; but fear, operating directly, occasions only cunning or servility. Fused, through reflection, with other motives which prompt to action, it helps bring about that apprehensiveness, or susceptibility to the rights of others, which is the essence of responsibility, which in turn is the sole *ultimate* guarantee of social order.

The Two Senses of Freedom—In its external aspect, freedom is negative and formal. It signifies freedom *from* subjection to the will and control of others; exemption from bondage; release from servitude; capacity to act without being exposed to direct obstructions or interferences from others. It means a clear road, cleared of impediments, for action. It contrasts with the limitations of prisoner, slave, and serf, who have to carry out the will of others.

Effective Freedom—Exemption from restraint and from interference with overt action is only a condition, though an absolutely indispensable one, of effective freedom. The latter requires (1) positive control of the resources necessary to carry purposes into effect, possession of the means to satisfy desires; and (2) mental equipment with the trained powers of initiative and reflection requisite for free preference and for circumspect and far-seeing desires. The freedom of an agent who is merely released from direct external obstruction is formal and empty. If he is without resources of personal skill, without control of the tools of achievement, he must inevitably lend himself to carrying out the directions and ideas of others. If he has not powers of deliberation and invention, he must pick up his ideas casually and superficially from the suggestions of his environment and appropriate the notions which the interests of some class insinuate into his mind. If he had not powers of intelligent self-control, he will be in bondage to appetite, enslaved to routine, imprisoned within the monotonous round of an imagery flowing from illiberal interests, broken only by wild forays into the illicit.

Legal and Moral—Positive responsibility and freedom may be regarded as moral, while liability and exemption are legal and political. A particular individual at a given time is possessed of certain secured resources in execution and certain formal habits of desire and reflec-

tion. In so far, he is positively free. Legally, his sphere of activity may be very much wider. The laws, the prevailing body of rules which define existing institutions, would protect him in exercising claims and powers far beyond those which he can actually put forth. He is exempt from interference in travel, in reading, in hearing music, in pursuing scientific research. But if he has neither material means nor mental cultivation to enjoy these legal possibilities, mere exemption means little or nothing. It does, however, create a moral demand that the practical limitations which hem him in should be removed; that practical conditions should be afforded which will enable him effectively to take advantage of the opportunities formally open. Similarly, at any given time, the liabilities to which an individual is actually held come far short of the accountability to which the more conscientious members of society hold themselves. The morale of the individual is in advance of the formulated morality, or legality, of the community.

Regulation of Legal to Moral—It is, however, absurd to separate the legal and the ideal aspects of freedom from one another. It is only as men are held liable that they become responsible; even the conscientious man, however much in some respects his demands upon himself exceed those which would be enforced against him by others, still needs in other respects to have his unconscious partiality and presumption steadied by the requirements of others. He needs to have his judgment balanced against crankiness, narrowness, or fanaticism, by reference to the sanity of the common standard of his times. It is only as men are exempt from external obstruction that they become aware of the possibilities, and are awakened to the demand and strive to obtain more positive freedom. Or, again, it is the possession by the more favored individuals in society of an effectual freedom to do and to enjoy things with respect to which the masses have only a formal and legal freedom, that arouses a sense of inequity, and that stirs the social judgment and will to such reforms of law, of administration and economic conditions as will transform the empty freedom of the less favored individuals into constructive realities.

RIGHTS AND OBLIGATIONS

The Individual and Social in Rights and Obligations.— That which, taken at large or in a lump, is called freedom breaks up in detail into a number of specific, concrete abilities to act in particular ways. These are termed *rights*. Any right includes within itself in intimate unity the individual and social aspects of activity upon which we have been insisting. As a capacity for exercise of power, it resides in and proceeds from some special agent, some individual. As exemption from restraint, a secured release from obstruction, it indicates at least the permission and sufferance of society, a tacit social assent and confirmation; while any more positive and energetic effort on the part of the community to guarantee and safeguard it, indicates an active acknowledgment on the part of society that the free exercise by individuals of the power in question is positively on its own interest. Thus a right, individual in residence, is social in origin and intent. The social factor in rights is made explicit in the demand that the power in question be exercised in certain ways. A right is never a claim to a wholesale, indefinite activity, but to a *defined* activity; to one *carried on*, that is, *under certain conditions*. This limitation constitutes the obligatory phases of every right. But he is free to act only according to certain regular and established conditions. That is the obligation imposed upon him. He has a right to use public roads, but he is obliged to turn in a certain way. He has a right to use his property, but he is obliged to pay taxes, to pay debts, not to harm others in its use, and so on.

Correspondence of Rights and Obligations—Rights and obligations are thus strictly correlative. This is true both in their external employment and in their intrinsic natures. Externally the individual is under obligation to use his right in a way which does not interfere with the rights of others. He is free to drive on the public highways, but not to exceed a certain speed, and on condition that he turns to right or left as the public order requires. He is entitled to the land which he has bought, but this possession is subject to the conditions of public registration and taxation. He may use his property, but not so that it menaces others or becomes a nuisance. Absolute rights, if we mean by absolute those not relative to any

social order and hence exempt from any social restriction, there are none. But rights correspond even more intrinsically to obligations. The right is itself a social outcome: it is the individual's only so far as he is himself a social member not merely physically, but in his habits of thought and feeling. He is under obligation to use his rights in social ways. The more we emphasize the free right of an individual to his property, the more we emphasize what society has done for him: the avenues it has opened to him for acquiring; the safeguards it has put about him for keeping; the wealth achieved by others which he may acquire by exchanges themselves socially buttressed. So far as an individual's own merits are concerned these opportunities and protections are "unearned increments," no matter what credit he may deserve for initiative and industry and foresight in using them. The only fundamental anarchy is that which regards rights as private monopolies, ignoring their social origin and intent.

Classes of Rights and Obligations—We may discuss freedom and responsibility with respect to the social organization which secures and enforces them; or from the standpoint of the individual who exercises and acknowledges them. From the latter standpoint, rights are conveniently treated as physical and mental: not that the physical and mental can be separated, but that emphasis may fall primarily on control of the conditions required to execute ideas and intentions, or upon the control of the conditions involved in their personal formation and choice. From the standpoint of the public order, rights and duties are civil and political. We shall consider them in the next chapter in connection with the organization of society in the state. Here we consider rights as inhering in an individual in virtue of his membership in society.

Physical Rights—These are the rights to the free unharmed possession of the body (the rights to life and limb), exemptions from homicidal attack, from assault and battery, and from conditions that threaten health in more obscure ways; and positively, the right to free movement of the body, to use its members for any legitimate purpose, and the right to unhindered locomotion. Without the exemption, there is no security in life, no assurance; only a life of constant fear and uncertainty, of loss of limb, of injury from others, and of death. Without some positive assurance, there is no chance of carrying ideas into effect. Even if sound and healthy and extremely protected, a man lives a slave or prisoner. Right to the control and use of physical conditions of life takes effect then in property rights, command of the natural tools and materials which are requisite to the maintenance of the body in a due state of health and to an effective and competent use of the person's powers. These physical rights to life, limb, and property are so basic to all achievement and capability that they have frequently been termed "natural rights." They are so fundamental to the existence of personality that their insecurity or infringement is a direct menace to the social welfare. The struggle for human liberty and human responsibility has accordingly been more acute at this than at any other point. Roughly speaking, the history of personal liberty is the history of the efforts which have safeguarded the security of life and property and which have emancipated bodily movement from subjection to the will of others.

Unsolved Problems: War and Punishment—While history marks great advance, especially in the last four or five centuries, as to the negative aspect of freedom or release from direct and overt tyranny, much remains undone in the positive side. It is at this point of free physical control that all conflicts of rights concentrate themselves. While the limitation by war of the right to life may be cited as evidence for the face that even this right is not absolute but is socially conditioned, yet that kind of correspondence between individual activity and the social well-being which exacts exposure to destruction as its measure, is too suggestive of the tribal morality in which the savage shows his social nature by participation in a blood feud, to be satisfactory. Social organization is clearly defective when its constituent portions are so set at odds with one another as to demand from individuals their death as their best service to the community. While one may cite capital punishment to enforce, as if in large type, the fact that the individual holds even his right to life subject to the social welfare, the moral works the other way to underline the failure of society to socialize its members, and its tendency to put undesirable results out of sight and mind rather than to face responsibility for causes. The same limitation is seen in methods of imprisonment, which, while supposed to be protective rather than vindictive, recognize only in a few and sporadic cases that the sole sure protection of society is through education and correction of individual character, not by mere physical isolation under harsh conditions.

Security of Life—In civilized countries the blood feud, infanticide, putting to death the economically useless and aged, have been abolished. Legalized slavery, serfdom, the subjection of the rights of wife and child to the will of husband and father, have been done away with. But many modern industries are conducted with more reference to financial gain than to life, and the annual roll of killed, injured, and diseased in factory and railway practically equals the list of dead and wounded in a modern war. Most of these accidents are preventable. The willingness of parents on one side and of employers on the other, conjoined with the indifference of the general public, makes child-labor an effective substitute for exposure of children and other methods of infanticide practiced by savage tribes. Agitation for old-age pensions shows that faithful service to society for a lifetime is still inadequate to secure a prosperous old age.

Document Analysis

Dewey and Tufts begin by discussing the negative and positive aspects of responsibility. In the negative sense of the concept, responsibility is similar to liability, as it requires an individual to accept the consequences of his or her actions. Importantly, people's actions affect not only themselves but also those around them. Each community or organization, therefore, defines the behaviors it finds acceptable and "serves notice" to its members when they do something offensive. In contrast, positive responsibility occurs when an individual voluntarily considers the community's interest, rather than acting as he or she wishes and waiting to be notified that his or her behavior was inappropriate.

Next, Dewey and Tufts distinguish between two senses of freedom. In one sense, freedom "in its external aspect" is freedom from the control of others, while in the other sense, which they refer to as "effective freedom," freedom means having the resources and ability to execute one's own plans. They note that without effective freedom, freedom is "formal and empty." They also observe that positive responsibility and effective freedom are moral in nature, while liability and external freedom are legal and political. Laws can grant individuals more freedom than they are effectively able to exercise—for example, an individual might have the right to travel but not the financial means to do so. While the legal aspects are a necessary element of freedom, they also create a moral demand for society to remove the limitations that prevent individuals from exercising effective freedom. Dewey and Tufts recognize that the legal and moral aspects of freedom cannot be easily separated and that unrest and reform often occur when social injustices prevent specific groups of individuals from exercising their effective freedoms, even if they already possess the requisite external freedoms.

Dewey and Tufts also address the notion of rights and obligations. Rights are "specific, concrete abilities to act in particular ways" but are subject to the conditions imposed by society; for example, one has the right to drive on public roads on the condition that one obeys the speed limit. Individuals must use their rights in ways that do not interfere with the rights of others, and because of this, there cannot be any "absolute" rights. The obligation of individuals to use their rights in socially appropriate ways arises because rights themselves only exist as a result of the individual's membership in the group that provides the rights. Dewey and Tufts note that any opportunities and protections individuals may experience are only theirs by the grace of society and that such rights are "unearned," regardless of how clever individuals may be in using them.

Finally, Dewey and Tufts address physical rights, which include the right to "free unharmed possession of the body," among others. They note that without positive assurance of these physical rights, individuals cannot be free to pursue other ideas; indeed, they are "so basic to all achievement and capability" that they are sometimes called "natural rights." However, Dewey and Tufts point out that many societies, even those that are quite advanced in other ways, condone activities such as war and dangerous working conditions that directly contradict this right.

Essential Themes

As part of the Chicago school of pragmatism, Dewey and Tufts focused on moral theory as it applied to eco-

nomics, society, and social justice. The concepts they express in *Ethics* are particularly notable given their historical context. During the early twentieth century, various groups of people in the United States—including African Americans, women, and immigrants from all over the world—were struggling for equal rights and freedom from discrimination. Dewey and Tufts's description of effective freedom highlights an important practical implication of these struggles: laws that ensure freedoms are meaningless if communities place socially discriminatory boundaries that effectively prevent individuals from exercising those freedoms. For example, although African American men legally had the right to vote in 1908, discriminatory practices such as poll taxes and literacy tests prevented many would-be voters from exercising that right.

This notion is further reflected in Dewey and Tufts's remark that the opportunities and protections of effective freedom are "unearned increments." Individuals possessed effective freedoms because society permitted them to do so and granted them access to the tools necessary to capitalize on their external freedoms. In contrast, society often denied others access to those same tools—by restricting educational opportunities based on race or gender, for example. These kinds of society-imposed barriers to effective freedom raised questions of social justice and equality and often led to unrest and ultimately legal and moral reform.

The concept of physical rights highlighted a contradiction inherent in many societies. The mills, factories, and mines of the United States notoriously employed many people, including children, in dangerous conditions for long hours. Dewey and Tufts observed that in many countries, laws prevented conditions such as outright slavery but nonetheless permitted industries to endanger the lives and limbs of workers and the general public. Additionally, political unrest in Europe pointed to the likelihood of war within the decade. Dewey and Tufts argued that a society is "clearly defective" when it "demand[s] from individuals their death as their best service to the community." Despite recognizing the vital importance of an individual's right to life, health, and physical safety, society nonetheless contained many constructs that routinely violated this right in a socially acceptable way.

—*Tracey M. DiLascio, JD*

Bibliography and Additional Reading

Campbell, James, ed. *Selected Writings of James Hayden Tufts*. Carbondale: Southern Illinois UP, 1992. Print.

Dewey, John, and John J. McDermott. *The Philosophy of John Dewey*. New York: Putnam, 1981. Print.

Feffer, Andrew. *The Chicago Pragmatists and American Progressivism*. Ithaca: Cornell UP, 1993. Print.

Menand, Louis. *Pragmatism: A Reader.* New York: Vintage, 1997. Print.

President Theodore Roosevelt on the Conservation of Natural Resources

Date: December 3, 1907
Author: Theodore Roosevelt
Genre: address; speech; petition

Summary Overview

President Theodore Roosevelt, in his seventh annual message to Congress, puts forward a set of proposals designed to protect the nation's national resources. Americans, he says, take for granted the abundance of natural resources available to them, a perspective he considers foolish. He cites the need for more efficient mining and agricultural practices, updated irrigation projects, and the establishment of protected open spaces. The responsibility for each of these actions, he says, rests with the only entity capable of effectively carrying them out: the federal government.

Defining Moment

Perhaps to a degree unequalled by his predecessors, Theodore Roosevelt was an ardent wildlife enthusiast. Early in his presidency, he occasionally burst into cabinet meetings unexpectedly in order to tell the group of the birds he had just seen outside. Even before becoming president, Roosevelt once wrote to a curator at the American Museum of Natural History in New York, saying that he would like to see all wildlife given every protection possible. To some, Roosevelt's love of nature stemmed from his affinity for hunting. To others, his passion for the natural world went far beyond the animals he and his upper-class friends hunted.

Roosevelt's ascendency to the presidency in 1901 was unexpected: Republican Party officials had thrown him into the vice presidential slot with candidate William McKinley in 1900, but McKinley's assassination a year later brought Roosevelt and his ideals to the executive office. Although he assumed office without a popular mandate, he quickly established himself as a dynamic and popular leader. Meanwhile, the balance of power in government, which had through the Civil War greatly favored Congress over the president, had been slowly shifting toward the executive, a trend Roosevelt used to his advantage.

In addition to his well-known "big stick" approach to foreign policy, Roosevelt saw a need to expand the reach of the federal government in order to protect the America's natural resources. Since the Civil War, the United States had been consuming its timber, mineral, and water resources at a nearly breakneck pace. Entire species of animals—such as the bison—were nearly wiped out by rampant and unregulated hunting. Conservationists such as John Muir, the Scottish-born American founder of the Sierra Club, called for more federal oversight of the country's resources, a push that was well received by the new president. A year after assuming office, Roosevelt introduced plans for more efficient irrigation projects and established federal agencies to gauge and protect the long-term health of the country's natural resources. Following his successful 1904 election campaign, Roosevelt established five national parks and five national natural monuments (including part of the Grand Canyon in 1906). His efforts to protect the nation's natural resources were largely successful—forest reserves alone grew from about 43 million acres to about 194 million acres by the end of Roosevelt's presidency. Meanwhile, the establishment of such nature preserves as the Florida Everglades ensured the protection of a wide range of animal and bird species.

In December 1907, Roosevelt, in one his last addresses to Congress as president, reiterated his belief that the federal government should play a more active role in regulating the country's growth. Part of his address focused on the need for commercial and business regulation. Later in the address, however, he stresses the need for government to play a similar oversight role in ensuring the long-term stability of the country's natural resources.

Author Biography

Theodore Roosevelt was born on October 27, 1858, in New York City. On February 14, 1884, his first wife and his mother both died; Roosevelt spent about two years thereafter in the Badlands of Dakota Territory, hunting and recovering from his grief. As a lieutenant colonel with the US Army in the Spanish-American War, he famously led a charge up San Juan Hill and earned distinction as a war hero. Shortly thereafter, he was elected governor of New York, and later, at the age of forty-two, became the nation's youngest president. After endorsing William Howard Taft as his successor in 1908, Roosevelt left office (although he ran for president again unsuccessfully in 1912) and went on a safari. He later returned to his home in Oyster Bay, New York. He died on January 6, 1919.

HISTORICAL DOCUMENT

To the Senate and House of Representatives:

...The conservation of our natural resources and their proper use constitute the fundamental problem which underlies almost every other problem of our national life.... As a nation we not only enjoy a wonderful measure of present prosperity but if this prosperity is used aright it is an earnest of future success such as no other nation will have. The reward of foresight for this nation is great and easily foretold. But there must be the look ahead, there must be a realization of the fact that to waste, to destroy, our natural resources, to skin and exhaust the land instead of using it so as to increase its usefulness, will result in undermining in the days of our children the very prosperity which we ought by right to hand down to them amplified and developed. For the last few years, through several agencies, the government has been endeavoring to get our people to look ahead and to substitute a planned and orderly development of our resources in place of a haphazard striving for immediate profit. Our great river systems should be developed as national water highways, the Mississippi, with its tributaries, standing first in importance, and the Columbia second, although there are many others of importance on the Pacific, the Atlantic, and the Gulf slopes. The National Government should undertake this work, and I hope a beginning will be made in the present Congress; and the greatest of all our rivers, the Mississippi, should receive special attention. From the Great Lakes to the mouth of the Mississippi there should be a deep waterway, with deep waterways leading from it to the East and the West. Such a waterway would practically mean the extension of our coastline into the very heart of our country. It would be of incalculable benefit to our people. If begun at once it can be carried through in time appreciably to relieve the congestion of our great freight-carrying lines of railroads. The work should be systematically and continuously carried forward in accordance with some well-conceived plan. The main streams should be improved to the highest point of efficiency before the improvement of the branches is attempted; and the work should be kept free from every taint of recklessness or jobbery. The inland waterways which lie just back of the whole Eastern and Southern coasts should likewise be developed. Moreover, the development of our waterways involves many other important water problems, all of which should be considered as part of the same general scheme. The government dams should be used to produce hundreds of thousands of horse-power as an incident to improving navigation; for the annual value of the unused water-powered of the United States perhaps exceeds the annual value of the products of all our mines. As an incident to creating the deep waterways down the Mississippi, the government should build along its whole lower length levees which, taken together with the control of the headwaters, will at once and forever put a complete stop to all threat of floods in the immensely fertile delta region. The territory lying adjacent to the Mississippi along its lower course will thereby become one of the most prosperous and populous, as it already is one of the most fertile, farming regions in all the world. I have appointed an inland waterways commission to study and outline a comprehensive scheme of development along all the lines indicated. Later I shall lay its report before the Congress.

Irrigation should be far more extensively developed than at present, not only in the States of the great plains and the Rocky Mountains, but in many others, as, for instance, in large portions of the South Atlantic and Gulf States, where it should go hand in hand with the reclamation of swampland. The Federal Government should seriously devote itself to this task, realizing that utilization of waterways and water-power, forestry, irrigation, and the reclamation of lands threatened with overflow, are all interdependent parts of the same problem. The work of the Reclamation Service in developing the larger opportunities of the Western half of our country for irrigation is more important than almost any other movement. The constant purpose of the government in connection with the Reclamation Service has been to use the water resources of the public lands for the ultimate greatest good of the greatest number; in other words, to put upon the land permanent home-makers, to use and develop it for themselves and for their children and children's children....

The effort of the government to deal with the public land has been based upon the same principle as that of the Reclamation Service. The land law system which was designed to meet the needs of the fertile and well-watered regions of the Middle West has largely broken down when applied to the drier regions of the Great Plains, the mountains, and much of the Pacific slope, where a farm of 160 acres is inadequate for self-support....Three years ago a public-lands commission was appointed to scrutinize the law, and defects, and recommend a remedy. Their examination specifically showed the existence of great fraud upon the public domain, and their recommendations for changes in the law were made with the design of conserving the natural resources of every part of the public lands by putting it to its best use. Especial attention was called to the prevention of settlement by the passage of great areas of public land into the hands of a few men, and to the enormous waste caused by unrestricted grazing upon the open range. The recommendations of the Public-Lands Commission are sound, for they are especially in the interest of the actual home-maker; and where the small home-maker cannot at present utilize the land they provide that the government shall keep control of it so that it may not be monopolized by a few men. The Congress has not yet acted upon these recommendations, but they are so just and proper, so essential to our national welfare, that I feel confident, if the Congress will take time to consider them, that they will ultimately be adopted.

Some such legislation as that proposed is essential in order to preserve the great stretches of public grazing-land which are unfit for cultivation under present methods and are valuable only for the forage which they supply. These stretches amount in all to some 300,000,000 acres, and are open to the free grazing of cattle, sheep, horses, and goats, without restriction. Such a system, or lack of system, means that the range is not so much used as wasted by abuse. As the West settles, the range becomes more and more overgrazed. Much of it cannot be used to advantage unless it is fenced, for fencing is the only way by which to keep in check the owners of nomad flocks which roam hither and thither, utterly destroying the pastures and leaving a waste behind so that their presence is incompatible with the presence of home-makers. The existing fences are all illegal.... All these fences, those that are hurtful and those that are beneficial, are alike illegal and must come down. But it is an outrage that the law should necessitate such action on the part of the Administration. The unlawful fencing of public lands for private grazing must be stopped, but the necessity which occasioned it must be provided for. The Federal Government should have control of the range, whether by permit or lease, as local necessities may determine. Such control could secure the great benefit of legitimate fencing, while at the same time securing and promoting the settlement of the country.... The government should part with its title only to the actual home-maker, not to the profit-maker who does not care to make a home. Our prime object is to secure the rights and guard the interests of the small ranchman, the man who ploughs and pitches hay for himself. It is this small ranchman, this actual settler and home-maker, who in the long run is most hurt by permitting thefts of the public land in whatever form.

Optimism is a good characteristic, but if carried to an excess it becomes foolishness. We are prone to speak of the resources of this country as inexhaustible; this is not so. The mineral wealth of the country, the coal, iron, oil, gas, and the like, does not reproduce itself, and therefore is certain to be exhausted ultimately; and wastefulness in dealing with it today means that our descendants will feel the exhaustion a generation or two before they otherwise would. But there are certain other forms of waste which could be entirely stopped-the waste of soil by washing, for instance, which is among the most dangerous of all wastes now in progress in the United States, is easily preventable, so that this present enormous loss of fertility is entirely unnecessary. The preservation or replacement of the forests is one of the most important means of preventing this loss. We have made a beginning in forest preservation, but...so rapid has been the rate of exhaustion of timber in the United States in the past, and so rapidly is the remainder being exhausted, that the country is unquestionably on the verge of a timber famine which will be felt in every household in the land.... The present annual consumption of lumber is certainly three times as great as the annual growth; and if the consumption and growth continue unchanged, practically all our lumber will be exhausted in another generation, while long before the limit to complete exhaustion is reached the growing scarcity will make itself felt in many blighting ways upon our national welfare. About twenty per cent of our forested territory is now reserved in national forests, but these do not include the most valuable timberlands, and in any event the proportion is too small to expect that the reserves can accomplish more than a mitigation of the trouble which is ahead for the nation.... We should acquire in the Appalachian and White Mountain regions all the forest-lands that it is possible to acquire for the use of the nation. These lands, because they form a national asset, are as emphatically national as the rivers which they feed, and which flow through so many States before they reach the ocean.

Document Analysis

Roosevelt's address touches on a number of topics, but his theme is consistent: the federal government must play a larger role in regulating the systems and resources that enable the nation to continue to enjoy its prosperity. During the latter part of his speech, he stresses the need for government to help conserve the nation's myriad natural resources.

One of the areas on which this policy would bear was the nation's waterways. The rivers, lakes, and other waterways throughout the United States could become "national water highways," he says, transporting freight not just to the major ports of the East and West Coasts, but to the nation's interior as well. The country's rail system was heavily congested, he states, an issue that would be alleviated by the development of this "highway." In order to make this vision possible, Roosevelt proposes a series of government projects designed to widen and deepen rivers and shores in order to accommodate larger boats. He also proposes the construction of dams and levees to facilitate water-based transportation.

As part of the development of the country's waterways, Roosevelt says, the government should also undertake the development of improved and more efficient irrigation systems. Such projects, coupled with the presence of levees (which would safeguard against the flooding common in the watersheds of the Mississippi and Columbia Rivers as well as the Great Lakes), would aid in the economic development of the Midwest, South, and Northwest by attracting more farmers and commerce.

Additionally, Roosevelt says, it was essential for the government to continue its efforts to reclaim open wetlands in places such as the Gulf states. Roosevelt had already established a special Public Lands Commission designed to analyze existing laws governing the country's fertile farmlands. Here he references this commission's findings and recommendations—which he calls sound—and points to the fact that Congress had yet to adopt any of the commission's proposals.

Furthermore, Roosevelt comments on grazing practices in places such as the as-yet underdeveloped West Coast. In these locations, cattle farmers were fencing off public lands for their own private grazing, leading to overuse and destruction of these pastures through soil erosion and depletion. It was the responsibility of the federal government, Roosevelt says, to expand its oversight to protect and sustain these lands.

It was also incumbent upon the federal government to continue its efforts to protect the nation's forests, Roosevelt adds. Americans mistakenly believed that their natural resources were limitless, he says—the government needed to play a role in reversing that attitude. He, therefore, proposes continuing his policy of acquiring the forests of the White Mountains and the Appalachian Mountains. Such land acquisitions would conserve two vital timber regions as well as the waterways that came from them. The presence of government-sponsored lands in some of the country's most populated areas would help foster a new appreciation of America's natural resources, he says.

Essential Themes

The son of a cofounder of the American Museum of Natural History, Theodore Roosevelt was himself an avid outdoors and nature enthusiast. As one of the first presidents of the twentieth century, Roosevelt's presence in the White House has been considered fortuitous for the nation, therefore, as the country was on the verge of overusing its natural resources. Roosevelt's seventh annual address to Congress (and indeed the entire nation) provided a reminder of the need for sustainable natural resource use in the modern United States.

Roosevelt, who during his presidency was taking advantage of a trend in which the executive branch was enjoying an increasing amount of political power, had already expanded significantly the federal government's control over a large portion of open space in the nation. He used his seventh address to call for further federal acquisitions of forest areas in New England and the Mid-Atlantic area as well as swampland in the South. In it, he also makes a point to call for federal projects to improve the nation's irrigation and maritime systems. Such projects, he argues, would lessen dependence on the rails and bring much-needed economic development in the Midwest, the South, and the Northwest.

Roosevelt's speech has two main themes to accompany its proposals. The first is that the United States had for too long operated under the mistaken notion that its natural resources were too plentiful to exhaust. Roosevelt argues that it was time for a change in attitude. The country's timber and mineral resources—and even grazing land—were rapidly depleting and, without intervention, would continue to decrease.

Roosevelt's second main point is that the federal government had to be the entity to intervene. He says he has created agencies and commissions to increase oversight over the country's natural resources—these entities had already achieved success in increasing awareness of and protecting natural resources. However, Roosevelt stresses that in order to move into the next steps toward conservation and sustainable development, Congress must recognize and support his agenda.

—*Michael P. Auerbach, MA*

Bibliography and Additional Reading

Benson, W. Todd. *President Theodore Roosevelt's Conservation Legacy.* West Conshohocken: Infinity, 2003. Print.

Brinkley, Douglas. *The Wilderness Warrior: Theodore Roosevelt and the Crusade for America.* New York: HarperCollins, 2009. Print.

Morris, Edmund. *Theodore Rex.* New York: Random, 2002. Print.

Peters, Gerhard. "Seventh Annual Message." *American Presidency Project.* U of California Santa Barbara, 2014. Web. 28 Feb. 2014.

Peterson, Tarla Rai. *Green Talk in the White House: The Rhetorical Presidency Encounters Ecology.* College Station: Texas A&M UP, 2004. Print.

■ Declaration of the Conservation Conference

Date: May 15, 1908
Authors: Governors of the US states and territories
Genre: political tract; report

Summary Overview

President Theodore Roosevelt convened a national conference of governors at the White House in the spring of 1908. The participants fell into line with Roosevelt's thoughts: both that a more concerted effort was warranted in the protection of the nation's natural resources and that more sustainable development practices should be implemented. The governors also agreed that the federal and state governments should, in concert, play a major role in these policies and that the states should also take a leadership position on these issues.

Defining Moment

In the decades that followed the Civil War, the United States underwent a period of major economic growth. The East Coast saw significant industrial development, while other areas, such as those along the Mississippi River, started to grow as well. To support this growth, the United States relied on the increased exploitation of its natural resources, including its vast grazing land, forests, and mineral deposits. In the minds of environmental and conservation activists, such as John Muir (founder of the Sierra Club), the country's seemingly unchecked use of these natural resources would eventually destroy the environment and limit the future growth of the country.

A wildlife and outdoor enthusiast and influenced by the ideals espoused by Muir and his contemporaries, Roosevelt focused much of his domestic agenda on the nation's natural resources. Roosevelt had already established the federal Reclamation Service (now the Bureau of Reclamation) in 1902 and the Forest Service in 1905, and he spent much of his presidency placing open spaces, wetlands, and forests under the federal umbrella. Among the sites named as national parks and federal preserves were the Grand Canyon, the Florida Everglades, and Alaska's Tongass Forest. Toward the end of his presidency, Roosevelt had already made the case before Congress that greater attention should be paid to land reclamation, irrigation systems, and sustainable mining and agricultural practices.

Roosevelt's successes in this arena were largely based on the fact that the executive branch of the US government was enjoying an increased amount of authority relative to the other two branches. During the Civil War years, the president was heavily dependent on congressional action to proceed with the executive agenda. Toward the end of the nineteenth century, however, the executive branch started to reassert its authority over the federal government's operations. Roosevelt took this trend further than his predecessors. In 1905, for example, members of Congress, pressured by the timber industry, proposed a measure to limit Roosevelt's ability to reclaim forest acreage in the West. The measure was part of a larger agricultural bill that Roosevelt was under great pressure to, and ultimately did, sign— but only after first placing about 16 million acres of that same forestland under federal control.

Roosevelt was a dynamic, charismatic figure who enjoyed popular approval. At the end of his presidency, he drew upon this approval in calling a national conference on conservation. Held at the White House in May 1908, the Conservation Conference drew together governors, legislators, cabinet officials, conservationists, scientists, and other interested parties. The purpose of the event was to underscore the need to pay greater attention to what Roosevelt dubbed "the weightiest problem now before the nation": the depletion of the nation's forest and mineral resources. He also sought to create a National Conservation Commission and encouraged the governors gathered at the conference to do the same at the state level. Furthermore, Roosevelt needed the participants to prod Congress to support the president's agenda. At the close of the conference, the governors and other participants drafted a formal agreement on the optimal course of action with regard to the country's natural resources.

HISTORICAL DOCUMENT

We the Governors of the States and Territories of the United States of America, in Conference assembled, do hereby declare the conviction that the great prosperity of our country rests upon the abundant resources of the land chosen by our forefathers for their homes and where they laid the foundation of this great Nation.

We look upon these resources as a heritage to be made use of in establishing and promoting the comfort, prosperity, and happiness of the American People, but not to be wasted, deteriorated, or needlessly destroyed.

We agree that our country's future is involved in this; that the great natural resources supply the material basis on which our civilization must continue to depend, and on which the perpetuity of the Nation itself rests.

We agree, in the light of facts brought to our knowledge and from information received from sources which we can not doubt, that this material basis is threatened with exhaustion. Even as each succeeding generation from the birth of the Nation has performed its part in promoting the progress and development of the Republic, so do we in this generation recognize it as a high duty to perform our part; and this duty in large degree lies in the adoption of measures for the conservation of the natural wealth of the country.

We declare our firm conviction that this conservation of our natural resources is a subject of transcendent importance, which should engage unremittingly the attention of the Nation, the States, and the People in earnest cooperation. These natural resources include the land on which we live and which yields our food; the living waters which fertilize the soil, supply power, and form great avenues of commerce; the forests which yield the materials for our homes, prevent erosion of the soil, and conserve the navigation and other uses of our streams; and the minerals which form the basis of our industrial life, an supply us with heat, light, and power.

We agree that the land should be so used that erosion and soil-wash shall cease; that there should be reclamation of arid and semi-arid regions by means of irrigation, and of swamp and overflowed regions by means of drainage; that the waters should be so conserved and used as to promote navigation, to enable the arid regions to be reclaimed by irrigation, and to develop power in the interests of the People; that the forests which regulate our rivers, support our industries, and promote the fertility and productiveness of the soil should be preserved and perpetuated; that the minerals found so abundantly beneath the surface should be so used as to prolong their utility; that the beauty, healthfulness, and habitability of our country should be preserved and increased; that the sources of national wealth exist for the benefit of the People, and that monopoly thereof should not be tolerated.

We commend the wise forethought of the President in sounding the note of warning as to the waste and exhaustion of the natural resources of the country, and signify our high appreciation of his action in calling this Conference to consider the same and to seek remedies therefor through cooperation of the Nation and the States.

We agree that this cooperation should find expression in suitable action by the Congress within the limits of and coextensive with the national jurisdiction of the subject, and, complementary thereto, by the legislatures of the several States within the limits of and coextensive with their jurisdiction.

We declare the conviction that in the use of the natural resources our independent States are interdependent and bound together by ties of mutual benefits, responsibilities and duties.

We agree in the wisdom of future conferences between the President, Members of Congress, and the Governors of States on the conservation of our natural resources with a view of continued cooperation and action on the lines suggested; and to this end we advise that from to time, as in his judgment may seem wise, the President call the Governors of the States and Members of Congress and others into conference.

We agree that further action is advisable to ascertain

the present condition of our natural resources and to promote the conservation of the same; and to that end we recommend the appointment by each State of a Commission on the Conservation of Natural Resources, to cooperate with each other and with any similar commission of the Federal Government.

We urge the continuation and extension of forest policies adapted to secure the husbanding and renewal of our diminishing timber supply, the prevention of soil erosion, the protection of headwaters, and the maintenance of the purity and navigability of our streams. We recognize that the private ownership of forest lands entails responsibilities in the interests of all the People, and we favor the enactment of laws looking to the protection and replacement of privately owned forests.

We recognize in our waters a most valuable asset of the People of the United States, and we recommend the enactment of laws looking to the conservation of water resources for irrigation, water supply, power, and navigation, to the end that navigable and source streams may be brought under complete control and fully utilized for every purpose. We especially urge on the Federal Congress the immediate adoption of a wise, active, and thorough waterway policy, providing for the prompt improvement of our streams and the conservation of their watersheds required for the uses of commerce and the protection of the interests of our People.

We recommend the enactment of laws looking to the prevention of waste in the mining and extraction of coal, oil, gas, and other minerals with a view to their wise conservation for the use of the People, and to the protection of human life in the mines.

Let us conserve the foundations of our prosperity.

Document Analysis

The declaration issued by the Conservation Conference echoes the sentiments expressed by Roosevelt throughout his presidency. The participants first underscore the connection between the abundance of natural resources in the United States and the nation's continued development. Second, they argue that the United States is in danger of depleting its natural resources if it continues to consume them at an unsustainable rate. Third, the group agrees that it is critical that state legislatures, governors, the president, and Congress cooperate to develop and implement an effective natural-resource conservation policy.

The conference participants note that the economic and political profile of the United States is rising on the world stage, largely because the country has throughout its history enjoyed a vast array of abundant resources. Any continuation of US development is thus dependent upon sustaining the country's water, timber, mineral, and other natural resources. Even the soil, from which the nation's myriad agricultural products come, should be part of the "transcendent importance" ascribed to conservation, according to the conference participants.

The participants, therefore, declare that it is critical to launch a program of land reclamation. In the document, the group stresses that arid land areas need irrigation in order to foster fertility and swampland can be drained for the same purpose. Furthermore, the declaration states, it is vital to use resources, such as mineral deposits, in such a way that extraction occurs at a sustainable rate and the land and nation do not suffer from overuse. The country's natural resources should be available to all, the group agrees—no one party should have exclusive access to it.

The conference agrees that the president was correct to call the nation's attention to this issue. The participants, therefore, call for a collective national effort first to assess and then to protect and conserve the country's natural resources. To this end, the declaration recommends the creation of both federal and state-level conservation commissions. In the federal government, this commission is envisioned as being used to manage multijurisdictional sites and industries subject to federal oversight.

The conference participants further assert their support for Roosevelt's initiatives on irrigation (including deepening waterways to facilitate navigation, which would ease some of the pressure on the country's railways), sustainable development, and federal reclamation of forests and other open spaces. Additionally, the declaration expresses support for federal laws preventing wasteful and hazardous natural-resource extraction, including protections for mine workers. Thus, the conference adjourned with a show of unity behind the president's initiatives, taking some responsibility and deferring policy to Congress and Roosevelt with regard to the sustainable use of natural resources for the benefit of the entire country.

Essential Themes

The Conservation Conference convened by President Roosevelt resulted in a great show of support by the participants for the president's natural-resource protection agenda. It also demonstrated a commitment by the states to join the president and Congress in ensuring that the country's natural resources were being used both in a sustainable manner and by all Americans (as opposed to merely a small group of organizations).

The conference participants acknowledged that the nation's natural resources and open spaces were in danger of depletion and degradation unless action was taken. In the conference declaration, the participants argued that the country's waters, soil, forests, and other lands were being overused. It was time, the declaration suggests, to pay attention to this crisis.

The proper course of action, the participants agreed, was a collective and comprehensive approach to protecting the country's natural resources. This approach meant establishing conservation commissions on both the federal and state levels. It also meant assignment of certain forests, open spaces, and waterways as federal property, thereby protecting the resources contained therein.

Additionally, the conference called for support of the president's initiatives on irrigation, land reclamation, and waterway development. Roosevelt advocated these initiatives in his final address to Congress (he had actually put the onus on Congress to take action in support of his proposals), and the conference fell in line in support of his agenda. An important theme contained in this document is one that cites the need for collective action to ensure that the country's natural resources are available to all Americans. The nation had long relied on its natural resources for its success, the conference argued in this declaration. The link between development and natural resources is clear; therefore, sustainable natural-resource management practices were essential to the effective continuation of the country's forward progress.

—*Michael P. Auerbach, MA*

Bibliography and Additional Reading

Hays, Samuel P. *The American People and the National Forests*. Pittsburgh: U of Pittsburgh P, 2009. Print.

Judd, Richard William. *Common Lands, Common People: The Origins of Conservation in Northern New England*. Cambridge: Harvard UP, 1997. Print.

"Theodore Roosevelt and the Environment." *PBS*. WGBH Educational Foundation, n.d. Web. 22 Apr. 2014.

US National Conservation Commission. *Proceedings of the Joint Conservation Conference*, Washington, DC, Dec. 8, 9, 10, 1908. Washington: GPO, 1909. Print.

Wellock, Thomas R. *Preserving the Nation: The Conservation and Environmental Movements, 1870–2000*. Marblehead: Wiley, 2007. Print.

■ An Argument for Prohibition

Date: December 22, 1914
Author: Richmond P. Hobson
Genre: speech

Summary Overview

Richmond P. Hobson, a US representative from Alabama, spoke on the floor of the House of Representatives on December 22, 1914, to express his support for a proposed constitutional amendment to ban the sale of alcohol in the United States. In his speech, Hobson criticized his opponents for failing to support their positions with scientific facts. He also emphasized that the target of this amendment was not consumers, but those who sold liquor. Still, he made clear his belief that alcohol was an addictive "poison" that undermined every level of American society. Therefore, he argued, it was critical to destroy alcohol abuse by banning the sale of alcohol nationwide.

Defining Moment

The movement to limit alcohol use in the United States grew significantly during the early nineteenth century, as Protestant groups became increasingly active in social reform efforts. Concerned about the high rates of domestic violence, child neglect, illness, and unemployment that accompanied alcoholism, Protestant groups called for moderation or outright abstinence from alcohol consumption. These so-called teetotalers and affiliated organizations such as the Women's Christian Temperance Union (WCTU) appealed to Americans to limit their consumption of alcohol.

Following the Civil War, the explosive growth of America's urban centers, economy, and infrastructure coincided with an increase in the social ills that had inspired the early temperance movement in the 1830s and 1840s. Those who had urged moderation in alcohol use began calling for outright bans on all liquor sales. Instead of merely distributing pamphlets warning of the evils of alcohol in bars, prohibitionists began to take action against the liquor merchants themselves. They looked to defeat all components of the "liquor interests," including the distillers, distributors, and even the political leaders who aligned themselves with the industry. Some were considered moderates, looking to restrict local liquor sales and increase public awareness of the dangers of alcohol abuse. Others were more radical in their goals, calling for absolute teetotalism and seeking to implement state and even national laws banning the sale of alcohol.

By the late 1800s and early 1900s, the radical elements of the prohibition movement prevailed, finding support for the passage of legislation banning the sale of alcohol in several states. Much of the support was a by-product of the Progressive Era that occurred at the turn of the twentieth century. During this period, considerable focus was paid to America's social ills and political corruption. The crime and extreme poverty that were prevalent in the country's urban centers inspired a wide range of social reformers, including prohibition advocates, such as the Anti-Saloon League.

In the early 1900s, the Anti-Saloon League, one of the leading organizations in the prohibition movement, began to shift its strategy from state-level reforms to the national stage. In 1913, the League announced its intention to sponsor a constitutional amendment to ban the sale of alcohol nationwide. The WCTU joined forces with the League in this endeavor.

In 1914, Representative Hobson, a longtime supporter of the prohibition movement, introduced the Hobson-Sheppard Resolution to the House of Representatives, proposing the adoption of a constitutional amendment banning the sale of alcohol nationwide. It was a lofty goal, as a constitutional amendment requires the support of a two-thirds majority in Congress as well as ratification by three-quarters of the states. Then again, the complexity and length of the process also meant that if passed and ratified, the amendment would be extremely difficult to remove from the Constitution.

Author Biography

Richmond Pearson Hobson was born on August 17, 1870, in Greensboro, Alabama. He graduated from the United States Naval Academy in Annapolis, Maryland, in 1889. Hobson fought in the Spanish-American War and was a key figure in the Battle of Santiago de Cuba, where he was taken prisoner by the Cubans. He retired from the Navy in 1903 as a war hero. In 1907, he won election to the US House of Representatives, and he went on to win reelection three times. In Congress, he introduced a constitutional amendment to prohibit the sale of alcohol, earning him the nickname "the father of Prohibition." After losing the Democratic nomination for another term in 1916, he organized and held senior positions in a number of organizations dedicated to eradicating narcotics in the United States. In 1933, he received the Congressional Medal of Honor for his actions during the Battle of Santiago de Cuba and, in 1935, he was advanced to the position of rear admiral by an Act of Congress. He died on March 16, 1937, in New York City.

HISTORICAL DOCUMENT

What is the object of this resolution? It is to destroy the agency that debauches the youth of the land and thereby perpetuates its hold upon the Nation. How does the resolution propose to destroy this agent? In the simplest manner. It does not coerce any drinker. It simply says that barter and sale, matters that have been a public function from the semi-civilized days of society, shall not continue the debauching of the youth. Now, the Liquor Trust are wise enough to know that they can not perpetuate their sway by depending on debauching grown people, so they go to an organic method of teaching the young to drink. Now we apply exactly the same method to destroy them. We do not try to force old drinkers to stop drinking, but we do effectively put an end to the systematic, organized debauching of our youth through thousands and tens of thousands of agencies throughout the land. Men here may try to escape the simplicity of this problem. They can not. Some are trying to defend alcohol by saying that its abuse only is bad and that its temperate use is all right. Science absolutely denies it, and proclaims that drunkenness does not produce one-tenth part of the harm to society that the widespread, temperate, moderate drinking does. Some say it is adulteration that harms. Some are trying to say that it is only distilled liquors that do harm. Science comes in now and says that all alcohol does harm; that the malt and fermented liquors produce vastly more harm than distilled liquors, and that it is the general public use of such drinks that has entailed the gradual decline and degeneracy of the nations of the past.

[The wets] have no foundation in scientific truth to stand upon, and so they resort to all kinds of devious methods.

Their favorite contention is that we can not reach the evil because of our institutions. This assumes that here is something very harmful and injurious to the public health and morals, that imperils our very institutions themselves and the perpetuity of the Nation, but the Nation has not within itself, because of its peculiar organization, the power to bring about the public good and end a great public wrong. They invoke the principle of State rights. As a matter of fact, we are fighting more consistently for State rights than they ever dreamed of. We know the States have the right to settle this question, and furthermore our confidence in three-quarters of all the States to act wisely does not lead us to fear that if we submit the proposition to them they might establish an imperialistic empire. We believe that three-quarters of all the States have the wisdom as well as the right to settle the national prohibition question for this country.

Neither can they take refuge about any assumed question of individual liberty. We do not say that a man shall not drink. We ask for no sumptuary action. We do not say that a man shall not have or make liquor in his own home for his own use. Nothing of that sort is involved in this resolution. We only touch the sale. A man may feel he has a right to drink, but he certainly has no inherent right to sell liquor. A man's liberties are absolutely secure in this resolution. The liberties and sanctity of the home are protected. The liberties of the community are secure, the liberties of the county are secure, and the liberties of the State are secure.

Let no one imagine that a State to-day has the real power and right to be wet of its own volition. Under the taxing power of the Federal Government by act of Congress, Congress could make every State in the country dry. They need not think it is an inherent right for a State to be wet; it is not; but there is an inherent right in every State and every county and every township to be dry, and these rights are now trampled upon, and this monster prides himself in trampling upon them.

Why, here to-day Member after Member has proclaimed that prohibition does not prohibit, and I have heard them actually tell us that prohibition could not prohibit. They tell us that this interstate liquor power is greater than the National Government....

I say now, as I said before, I will meet this foe on a hundred battlefields. If the Sixty-third Congress does not grant this plain right of the people for this referendum to change their organic law, to meet this mighty evil, the Sixty-fourth Congress will be likewise invoked. I do not say that we are going to get a two-thirds majority here tonight ... because we have not yet had a chance to appeal to Caesar: but I do say that the day is coming when we shall have that referendum sent to the States, nor is that day as far distant as some may imagine. Unless this question has been made a State matter, as we are asking now for it to be so made by being removed from national politics, and referred to the States—if this is not done by the intervening Congresses, I here announce to you the determination of the great moral, the great spiritual, the great temperance and prohibition forces of this whole Nation to make this question the paramount issue in 1916, not only to gain a two-thirds majority in the Houses of Congress, but to have an administration that neither in the open nor under cover will fight this reform, so that in the spring of 1917 with an extraordinary session of the Sixty-fifth Congress we will have a command from the masters of men and of Congress to grant this right to the people. My appeal is to each one of you now—be a man when the vote is taken and do your duty. [Applause.]

A Habit-Forming Drug

Alcohol has the property of chloroform and ether of penetrating actually into the nerve fibers themselves, putting the tissues under an anesthetic which prevents pain at first, but when the anesthetic effect is over discomfort follows throughout the tissues of the whole body, particularly the nervous system, which causes a craving for relief by recourse to the very substance that produced the disturbance. This craving grows directly with the amount and regularity of the drinking.

Undermines the Will Power

The poisoning attack of alcohol is specially severe in the cortex cerebrum—the top part of the brain—where resides the center of inhibition, or of will power, causing partial paralysis, which liberates lower activities otherwise held in control, causing a man to be more of a brute, but to imagine that he has been stimulated, when he is really partially paralyzed. This center of inhibition is the seat of the will power, which of necessity declines a little in strength every time partial paralysis takes place.

Little Less of a Man After Each Drink

Thus a man is little less of a man after each drink he takes. In this way continued drinking causes a progressive weakening of the will and a progressive growing of the craving, so that after a time, if persisted in, there must come a point where the will power can not control the craving and the victim is in the grip of the habit.

Slaves in Shackles

When the drinking begins young the power of the habit becomes overwhelming, and the victim might as well have shackles. It is estimated that there are 5,000,000 heavy drinkers and drunkards in America, and these men might as well have a ball and chain on their ankles, for they are more abject slaves than those black men who were driven by slave drivers.

Present-day Slave Owners

These victims are driven imperatively to procure their liquor, no matter at what cost. A few thousand brewers and distillers, making up the organizations composing the great Liquor Trust, have a monopoly of the supply, and they therefore own these 5,000,000 slaves and through them they are able to collect two and one-half billions of dollars cash from the American people every year.

Liquor Degenerates the Character

The first finding of science that alcohol is a protoplasmic poison and the second finding that it is an insidious, habit-forming drug, though of great importance, are as unimportant when compared with the third finding, that alcohol degenerates the character of men and tears down their spiritual nature. Like the other members of the group of oxide derivatives of hydrocarbons, alcohol is not only a general poison, but it has a chemical affinity or deadly appetite for certain particular tissues. Strychnine tears down the spinal cord. Alcohol tears down the top part of the brain in a man, attacks certain tissues in an animal, certain cells in a flower. It has been established that whatever the line of a creature's evolution alcohol will attack that line. Every type and every species is evolving in building from generation to generation along some particular line. Man is evolving in the top part of the brain, the seat of the will power, the seat of the moral senses, and of the spiritual nature, the recognition of right and wrong, the consciousness of God and of duty and of brotherly love and of self-sacrifice.

Reverses the Life Principle of the Universe

All life in the universe is founded upon the principle of evolution. Alcohol directly reverses that principle. Man has risen from the savage up through successive steps to the level of the semisavage, the semicivilized, and the highly civilized.

Liquor and the Red Man

Liquor promptly degenerates the red man, throws him back into savagery. It will promptly put a tribe on the war path.

Liquor and the Black Man

Liquor will actually make a brute out of a negro, causing him to commit unnatural crimes.

Liquor and the White Man

The effect is the same on the white man, though the white man being further evolved it takes longer time to reduce him to the same level. Starting young, however, it does not take a very long time to speedily cause a man in the forefront of civilization to pass through the successive stages and become semicivilized, semisavage, savage, and, at last, below the brute.

The Great Tragedy

The spiritual nature of man gives dignity to his life above the life of the brute. It is this spiritual nature of man that makes him in the image of his Maker, so that the Bible referred to man as being a little lower than the angels. It is a tragedy to blight the physical life. No measure can be made of blighting the spiritual life.

The Blight Degeneracy

Nature does not tolerate reversing its evolutionary principle, and proceeds automatically to exterminate any creature, any animal, any race, any species that degenerates. Nature adopts two methods of extermination—one to shorten the life, the other to blight the offspring.

The Verdict

Science has thus demonstrated that alcohol is a protoplasmic poison, poisoning all living things; that alcohol is a habit-forming drug that shackles millions of our citizens and maintains slavery in our midst; that it lowers in a fearful way the standard of efficiency of the Nation, reducing enormously the national wealth, entailing startling burdens of taxation, encumbering the public with the care of crime, pauperism, and insanity; that it corrupts politics and public servants, corrupts the Government, corrupts the public morals, lowers terrifically the average standard of character of the citizenship, and undermines the liberties and institutions of the Nation; that it undermines and blights the home and the family, checks education, attacks the young when they are entitled to protection, undermines the public health, slaughtering, killing, and wounding our citizens many fold times more than war, pestilence, and famine combined; that it blights the progeny of the Nation, flooding the land with a horde of degenerates; that it strikes deadly blows at the life of the Nation itself and at the very life of the race, reversing the great evolutionary principles of nature and the purposes of the Almighty.

There can be but one verdict, and that is this great

destroyer must be destroyed. The time is ripe for fulfill-ment. The present generation, the generation to which we belong, must cut this millstone of degeneracy from the neck of humanity....

The Final Conclusion

To cure this organic disease we must have recourse to the organic law. The people themselves must act upon this question. A generation must be prevailed upon to place prohibition in their own constitutional law, and such a generation could be counted upon to keep it in the Constitution during its lifetime. The Liquor Trust of necessity would disintegrate. The youth would grow up sober. The final, scientific conclusion is that we must have constitutional prohibition, prohibiting only the sale, the manufacture for sale, and everything that pertains to the sale, and invoke the power of both Federal and State Governments for enforcement. The resolution is drawn to fill these requirements.

GLOSSARY

oxide derivatives…: likely a reference to compounds such as ether and morphine

protoplasmic: of or relating to cell matter

strychnine: a poison (used as a pesticide)

sumptuary action: a law regulating or the imposition of a tax on a consumer good

wets: supporters of drinking (as opposed to "the dries," who denounce it)

Document Analysis

In Hobson's speech from the floor of the House of Representatives, he makes two general arguments. First, he emphasizes that the purpose of the amendment is not to make the consumption of alcohol illegal but rather to ban the sale of alcohol in order to destroy the liquor industry that enables and encourages alcohol abuse. Second, he looks to debunk the arguments made by liquor-industry advocates (whom he refers to as the "Liquor Trust" or the "wets") using "scientific" evidence.

Hobson claims that the purpose of his proposal is to defeat the alcohol industry itself rather than to target individual Americans who drink. Liquor merchants and businesses ("agents") were, in Hobson's estimation, encouraging alcohol abuse and the "organized debauching of our youth." To be sure, he declares, Americans could continue to make and consume their own liquor in the privacy of their homes, if they so desired. Hobson insists, however, that the sale of alcohol is a social evil that he aims to "destroy."

Hobson takes aim at the arguments of the "wets," which he claims have no basis in fact. For example, he challenges the Liquor Trust's claim that a ban on liquor sales is a matter of state and not federal law. By proposing an amendment to the US Constitution, Hobson says he is demonstrating his confidence that more than three-quarters of the states would ratify the proposed amendment. The House might not give Hobson's bill the two-third majority it needed to pass today, he said, but the day would soon come when the constitutional referendum would go to the states for approval. Hobson dismisses the argument that each state has the right to determine whether to be a "wet" state, insisting instead that "there is an inherent right in every State . . . to be dry, and these rights are now being trampled upon" by the liquor industry in its quest for profits.

Hobson also provides "scientific" evidence of the "debauchery" alcohol is causing in the United States. Liquor, he said, had addictive properties that immediately affect the willpower and character of the individual who consumes it. These addictive properties turn people into slaves to the liquor industry. Meanwhile, he claims that alcohol reverses evolution, turning men into savages. Hobson employs extremely racist arguments to claim that African Americans and American Indians are even more susceptible to the dangers of alcohol because they are not as "evolved" as white people and would be further hurtled back into a state of regression by alcohol use. Furthermore, Hobson claims "it is [the] spiritual nature of man that makes him in the image of his Maker," arguing that alcohol turns men into savage animals and strips them of their spirituality and godliness.

The only recourse, Hobson says, is for the matter of prohibition to be brought straight to the people. The Constitution, he argues, provides an "organic" legal vehicle for the public to use to advance their welfare. According to Hobson, American politicians have been corrupted by the liquor industry, and the matter must be turned over to the states for ratification. Hobson concludes with the hope that the passage of his proposed resolution would lead to both a generation of Americans growing up sober and the disintegration of the corrupt Liquor Trust.

Essential Themes
Hobson was an ardent prohibitionist, and he used this speech to assail the main arguments of his opponents, whom he refers to as the Liquor Trust. Opponents of prohibition claimed that a national ban on the sale of alcohol represented a violation of states' rights and the destruction of property owned by the manufacturers and distributors of liquor. In his speech before the House of Representatives, Hobson countered these arguments by painting the liquor industry as a corrupting force that undermined not only individual well-being but also the entire US political system. Because the Liquor Trust was so financially powerful and politically connected, he urged his fellow representatives to vote for and advance his resolution in order to destroy the liquor industry for the benefit of the American people. In making his arguments in favor of nationwide prohibition, Hobson relied on incendiary rhetoric that he claimed to be scientific fact. Namely, he invoked Social Darwinist principles that were in vogue at the time to claim that alcohol had a degenerating effect that reversed evolution, particularly for nonwhite drinkers. By appealing to his listeners' religious beliefs and racial fears, Hobson hoped to advance his resolution and ban the sale of alcohol nationwide.

Although the Hobson-Sheppard Resolution received majority support in the House, it failed to garner the two-thirds majority needed to advance. Nevertheless, on August 1, 1917, the Senate passed the prohibition amendment with the necessary two-thirds majority, and the measure passed the House later that year. Within thirteen months, three-fourths of state legislatures voted to adopt the proposed amendment, and the Eighteenth Amendment was ratified on January 16, 1919, and took effect on January 17, 1920. Ironically, Hobson's goal of curtailing corruption and crime by banning the sale of alcohol was not borne out. The Eighteenth Amendment was ultimately repealed in 1933 by the Twenty-First Amendment after thirteen years of prohibition saw rising rates of crime and corruption related to the unregulated black market sale of alcohol.

—*Michael P. Auerbach, MA*

Bibliography and Additional Reading
Graham, Amy. *A Look at the Eighteenth and Twenty-First Amendments: The Prohibition and Sale of Intoxicating Liquors*. Berkeley Heights: Enslow, 2007. Print.
Okrent, Daniel. *Last Call: The Rise and Fall of Prohibition*. New York: Scribner, 2011. Print.
Slavicek, Louis Chipley. **The Prohibition Era: Temperance in the United States**. New York: Chelsea, 2008. Print.
Szymanski, Ann-Marie E. *Pathways to Prohibition: Radicals, Moderates, and Social Movement Outcomes*. Durham: Duke UP, 2003. Print.
Timberlake, James H. *Prohibition and the Progressive Movement, 1900–1920*. Cambridge: Harvard UP, 1966. Print.

A TECHNOLOGICAL BREAKTHROUGH

Included in this last section is a single document from 1903, an entry from Orville Wright's diary describing his and his brother Wilbur's successful attempt at powered air flight at Kitty Hawk, North Carolina. The Wright brothers' achievement may be said to epitomize the emergence of modern America. American aviation would come to dominate the scene. Other technological innovations giving rise to the modern era were likewise American: the light bulb and electrification, the telephone, motion pictures, the automobile (at least the mass-produced automobile), and the assembly line. A little over a decade after the Wright brothers' first controlled flight, the world would become witness to a massive convergence of global technological power and destruction (including effective air divisions) in World War I.

■ The Wright Brothers' First Powered Flight

Date: December 17, 1903
Author: Orville Wright
Genre: diary

Summary Overview

Humans had longed dreamed of mastering the ability to travel aloft, and during the late eighteenth century, inventors began experimenting with machines to bring this dream to life. Beginning in the late 1800s, the Wright brothers refined existing ideas about controlled flight. After a series of experiments, they added an engine to provide power in 1903. Using this machine, the brothers took turns making a series of brief, but controlled, flights on the windy sand dunes of Kitty Hawk, North Carolina, in December of that year. Orville Wright, who piloted the inaugural flight, recorded the details of these first successful heavier-than-air flights in his diary, noting information about the weather conditions, flight speeds, distances covered, and time elapsed airborne. Wright's primary-source retelling of these seminal events in scientific history provides a close look at the brothers' innovative techniques and monumental achievement.

Defining Moment

Although human history suggests a long and multicultural fascination with the ability of individuals to fly, the first true practical steps toward doing so did not occur until the eighteenth century. Recognizing that one key to flight was developing a machine lighter than the surrounding air, inventors began experimenting with balloons propelled upward by heated air. In 1783, two French brothers named Jacques-Étienne and Joseph-Michel Montgolfier successfully launched a large paper-and-fabric balloon, and an era of fascination with the possibilities of the hot air balloon commenced in earnest, mostly around the city of Paris. Over the next several months, experimentation led to a process of using hydrogen gas to propel such balloons. Following a pattern that would be repeated nearly two centuries

later with space flight, scientists first sent animals into the air using the new devices before attempting the first manned hot air balloon flight in late 1783. By 1785, the hot air balloon had become reliable enough that Jean Pierre Blanchard and John Jeffries were able to cross the English Channel using one.

Experiments with hot air balloons continued into the nineteenth century, even as inventors pursued another possibility—winged flight. Drawing on existing contraptions, such as the kite and the pinwheel, French and English thinkers developed rudimentary flying devices, such as gliders and small machines that resembled miniature modern helicopters. One version of these helicopters, produced as toys in the 1870s, was capable of traveling many feet into the air and remaining in flight for nearly thirty seconds. These miniature flying models soon inspired burgeoning aeronautics enthusiasts to attempt to construct larger machines capable of carrying humans in heavier-than-air flight.

Among this group of experimenters were two young Ohioans, Orville and Wilbur Wright. As boys in the 1870s, the two enjoyed playing with the popular flying toy helicopters of the day. As they grew up, they developed practical technical skills through the operation of printing presses, and, later, through the construction and repair of bicycles. By 1901, the Wright brothers identified three key challenges that had to be overcome to achieve and sustain machine-powered flight: the construction of useful wings to lift the aircraft, the powering of the machine to move it forward, and the control of the aircraft through a steering device. The pair looked to existing technology to inform their own designs, combining the concepts of glider wings and automobile engines.

The Wright brothers began conducting experimental flights in the open fields near their hometown of

Dayton, Ohio, and traveled to the windier, loftier dunes near Kitty Hawk, North Carolina, to take advantage of the favorable conditions there. They developed advanced gliders in 1901 and 1902, which allowed them to perfect a rudder system that addressed the problem of steering. By late 1903, they were prepared to experiment with a true, engine-powered airplane.

Author Biography

Orville Wright, along with his brother Wilbur (1867–1912), became world renowned as a pioneering aviator after the pair made the first successful heavier-than-air powered flights in Kitty Hawk, North Carolina, on December 17,1903. A native of Dayton, Ohio, Wright was born in 1871 and worked with his older brother as a printer and bicycle-shop owner before turning to aviation. The skills the brothers developed in constructing and repairing bicycles proved helpful as they began designing flying machines around the turn of the century. After achieving flight, the pair continued to refine their designs and, in 1908, began to market the device commercially and to the US military. They also began to vigorously defend the patent rights to their inventions in court. Orville Wright continued to operate the firm that the brothers founded for only a few years after his brother's death, but he maintained a presence in aviation until his own death in 1948.

HISTORICAL DOCUMENT

When we got up, a wind of between 20 and 25 miles was blowing from the north.

We got the machine out early and put out the signal for the men at the station. Before we were quite ready, John T. Daniels, W. S. Dough, A. D. Etheridge, W. C. Brinkley of Manteo, and Johnny Moore of Nags Head arrived.

After running the engine and propellers a few minutes to get them in working order, I got on the machine at 10:35 for the first trial. The wind, according to our anemometers at this time, was blowing a little over 27 miles according to the Government anemometer at Kitty Hawk. On slipping the rope the machine started off increasing in speed to probably 7 or 8 miles. The machine lifted from the truck just as it was entering on the fourth rail. Mr. Daniels took a picture just as it left the tracks.

I found the control of the front rudder quite difficult on account of its being balanced too near the center and thus had a tendency to turn itself when started so that the rudder was turned too far on one side and then too far on the other. As a result the machine would rise suddenly to about 10 ft. and then as suddenly, on turning the rudder, dart for the ground. A sudden dart when out about 100 feet from the end of the tracks ended the flight. Time about 12 seconds (not known exactly as watch was not promptly stopped). The lever for throwing off the engine was broken, and the skid under the rudder cracked. After repairs, at 20 min. after 11 o'clock Will made the second trial.

The course was about like mine, up and down but a little longer over the ground though about the same in time. Dist. not measured but about 175 ft. Wind speed not quite so strong.

With the aid of the station men present, we picked the machine up and carried it back to the starting ways. At about 20 minutes till 12 o'clock I made the third trial. When out about the same distance as Will's, I met with a strong gust from the left which raised the left wing and sidled the machine off to the right in a lively manner. I immediately turned the rudder to bring the machine down and then worked the end control. Much to our surprise, on reaching the ground the left wing struck first, showing the lateral control of this machine much more effective than on any of our former ones. At the time of its sidling it had raised to a height of probably 12 to 14 feet.

At just 12 o'clock Will started on the fourth and last trip. The machine started off with its ups and downs as it had before, but by the time he had gone over three or four hundred feet he had it under much better control, and was traveling on a fairly even course. It proceeded in this manner till it reached a small hummock out about 800 feet from the starting ways, when it began its pitching again and suddenly darted into the ground.

The front rudder frame was badly broken up, but the main frame suffered none at all. The distance over the ground was 852 feet in 59 seconds. The engine turns was 1071, but this included several seconds while on the starting ways and probably about a half second after landing. The jar of landing had set the watch on machine back so that we have no exact record for the 1071 turns. Will took a picture of my third flight just before the gust struck the machine.

The machine left the ways successfully at every trial, and the tail was never caught by the truck as we had feared.

After removing the front rudder, we carried the machine back to camp. We set the machine down a few feet west of the building, and while standing about dis-cussing the last flight, a sudden gust of wind struck the machine and started to turn it over. All rushed to stop it. Will who was near one end ran to the front, but too late to do any good. Mr. Daniels and myself seized spars at the rear, but to no purpose. The machine gradually turned over on us. Mr. Daniels, having had no experience in handling a machine of this kind, hung on to it from the inside, and as a result was knocked down and turned over and over with it as it went. His escape was miracu-lous, as he was in with the engine and chains. The engine legs were all broken off, the chain guides badly bent, a number of uprights, and nearly all the rear ends of the ribs were broken. One spar only was broken.

After dinner we went to Kitty Hawk to send off tele-gram to M.W. While there we called on Capt. and Mrs. Hobbs, Dr. Cogswell and the station men.

Document Analysis

Orville Wright's account of the Wright brothers' first flights at Kitty Hawk shows the main events, chal-lenges, and successes of the day. In doing so, it reveals how the Wright brothers managed to address the three impediments to powered, controlled flight that they had previously identified—lift, propulsion, and control. Their achievements drew on a wing design that cap-tured wind to create lift; a specially designed engine to produce power to move the aircraft forward; and a tem-peramental, but ultimately effective, rudder to provide control through manual steering.

Climatic conditions are immediately shown to be a factor that the brothers monitored closely. Wright opens his account with a measurement of wind speed and direction, and gives readings from the anemom-eter, an instrument that measures wind speed, and other commentary on the prevailing winds throughout his account—wind being the key to the wings' ability to pull the plane upward. Wright also reports that wind af-fected control of the airplane, noting that "a strong gust from the left" forced the machine to move off course. This event, however, allowed the brothers to develop a favorable opinion of the changes that they had made to the aircraft's control system, as Wright's movement of the rudder revealed the success of the steering and wing control modifications that the brothers had made to this version of the aircraft.

Wright also describes some of the technical chal-lenges that the brothers encountered in their flights, particularly in regard to the tricky problem of control. He especially struggled with the front rudder on the first flight, resulting in an aircraft that was hard to han-dle and "would rise suddenly . . . and then as suddenly, on turning the rudder, dart for the ground." The risk of crashing the aircraft from even the low altitudes at which the planes flew was, therefore, quite great, and, indeed, it was a drop in altitude from this problem that brought the inaugural flight to an end.

Although the airplane succeeded, its design, Wright reveals, was less than ideally suited for ground storage. Wright announces that the airplane "left the ways suc-cessfully at every trial," avoiding even damage to the tail that the brothers had expected. Yet the same wind that had helped carry the airplane above the ground proved to be the machine's undoing. A gust caught the aircraft while the Wrights and the observers who had spent the day at Kitty Hawk were talking over the day's events, forcing it to roll over repeatedly, heavily damaging the plane, and nearly killing one of the men.

Essential Themes

Although the achievements that Wright describes in this diary entry attracted little immediate attention, over the next several years, the development of flight sped up. The first airplane flight in Europe took place in 1906, and in only a few years, airplane design had advanced to allow for long-distance flights over the English Channel (1909) and the American continent (1911). Inventors had taken more than a century to progress from balloon flight to controlled flight in a manned airplane, but the advances that the Wrights made in preparing for their first flights allowed for such rapid technological change that Charles Lindbergh was able to make his famous first nonstop solo trip across the Atlantic Ocean only a quarter-century later. Unsurprisingly, the Wrights' achievement in flight made them household names and scientific legends of the highest order, and their work and later aircraft are still displayed and studied by US and aeronautic historians.

Wright's account of the first powered flight also provides an intriguing glimpse at what historians have acknowledged as one of the most important historical events of the twentieth century. The effects of the flight revolution have been immense. Just a decade after the Wrights launched the first, fragile, powered airplane at Kitty Hawk, European military planes flew missions in World War I, and aircraft became a key part of war and national defense thereafter. Airplanes began replacing railroads and ships as preferred methods of long-distance passenger and cargo transportation, contributing to the development of the modern globalized economy.

The perfection of the airplane, which took place in the period after the first flight, set the stage for innovation in space flight as scientists built satellites and spacecraft capable of reaching Earth's orbit and beyond during the 1950s and 1960s. These developments, in turn, allowed for technological innovations ranging from the cell phone to medical devices to the cordless power drill. Without the first halting flights that carried Orville and Wilbur Wright into the air for seconds at a time in 1903, modern life and technology would likely function very differently, even in fields not directly related to flight or transport.

—*Vanessa E. Vaughn, MA*

Bibliography and Additional Reading

Crouch, Tom D. *The Bishop's Boys: A Life of Wilbur and Orville Wright*. New York: Norton, 1989. Print.

_____. Wings: *A History of Aviation from Kites to the Space Age*. New York: Norton, 2003. Print.

Goldstone, Lawrence. *Birdmen: The Wright Brothers, Glenn Curtiss, and the Battle to Control the Skies*. New York: Ballantine, 2014. Digital file.

Roach, Edward J. *The Wright Company: From Invention to Industry*. Athens: Ohio UP, 2014. Digital file.

Wright, Orville. *How We Invented the Airplane: An Illustrated History*. New York: McKay, 1953. Print.

APPENDIXES

Chronological List

Web Resources

boundless.com/u-s-history/the-gilded-age-1870-1900

An interlinked set of learning materials relating to the Gilded Age, including coverage of populism and the populist movement.

http://www.dcte.udel.edu/hlp2/resources/summer09/progressive_era_media.pdf

A helpful list of websites and films concerning topics, people, and movements associated with the Progressive Era through the 1920s.

digitalhistory.uh.edu

Offers an online history textbook, Hypertext History, which chronicles the story of America, along with interactive timelines. This online source also contains handouts, lesson plans, e-lectures, movies, games, biographies, glossaries, maps, music, and much more.

docsouth.unc.edu

A digital publishing project that reflects the southern perspective of American history and culture. It offers a wide collection of titles that students, teachers, and researchers of all levels can utilize.

docsteach.org

Centered on teaching through the use of primary source documents. This online resource provides activities for many different historical eras dating to the American Revolution as well as thousands of primary source documents.

edsitement.neh.gov

An online resource for teachers, students, and parents seeking to further their understanding of the humanities. This site offers lesson plan searches, student resources, and interactive activities.

gilderlehrman.org

Offers many options in relation to the history of America. The History by Era section provides detailed explanations of specific time periods while the primary sources present firsthand accounts from a historical perspective.

havefunwithhistory.com

An online, interactive resource for students, teachers, and anybody who has an interest in American history.

history.com/topics/american-history

Tells the story of America through topics of interest such as the Declaration of Independence, major wars, and notable Americans. Features videos from The History Channel and other resources.

historymatters.gmu.edu

An online resource from George Mason University that provides links, teaching materials, primary documents, and guides for evaluating historical records.

http://memory.loc.gov/ammem/index.html

Covers the various eras and ages of American history in detail, including resources such as readings, interactive activities, multimedia, and more.

nwhm.org/online-exhibits/progressiveera/introprogressive.html

A useful collection of photographs and descriptions concerning women and reform in the Progressive Era.

pbs.org/wgbh/americanexperience

Offers an array of source materials linked to topics featured in the award winning *American Experience* history series.

publichistory.org/reviews/view_issue.asp?IssueNumber=9

A diverse collection of online resources relating to the people. places, politics, and social movements of the Progressive Era.

si.edu/encyclopedia_si/nmah/timeline.htm

Details the course of American history chronologically. Important dates and significant events link to other pages within the Smithsonian site that offer more details.

smithsonianeducation.org

An online resource for educators, families, and students offering lesson plans, interactive activities, and more.

teachingamericanhistory.org

Allows visitors to learn more about American history through original source documents detailing the broad spectrum of American history. The site contains document libraries, audio lectures, lesson plans, and more.

teachinghistory.org

A project funded by the US Department of Education that aims to assist teachers of all levels to augment their efforts in teaching American history. It strives to amplify student achievement through improving the knowledge of teachers.

ushistory.org/us

Contains an outline that details the entire record of American history. This resource offers historical insight and stories that demonstrate what truly an American truly is from a historical perspective.

Bibliography

"About Jacob Riis." *Victorian Richmond Hill*. New York: Richmond Hill Chapter, Queens Hist. Soc., 1980. Web. 8 Apr. 2014.

Addams, Jane. *Twenty Years at Hull House*. London: Penguin, 1910. Print.

Addams, Jane. *Twenty Years at Hull House*. London: Penguin, 1910. Print.

"American President: Theodore Roosevelt (1858–1919)." *Miller Center*. U of Virginia, 2013. Web. 8 Apr. 2014.

Anbinder, Tyler. *Five Points: The 19th-Century New York City Neighborhood That Invented Tap Dance, Stole Elections, and Became the World's Most Notorious Slum*. New York: Simon, 2001. Print.

Anbinder, Tyler. Five Points: *The Nineteenth Century New York City Neighborhood that Invented Tap Dance, Stole Elections, and Became the World's Most Notorious Slum*. New York: Simon, 2001. Print.

Ashbury, John W. *Frederick County Characters: Innovators, Pioneers and Patriots of Western Maryland*. Gloucestershire: History, 2013. Print.

Avrich, Paul. *The Haymarket Tragedy*. Princeton: Princeton UP, 1984. Print.

Baba, Mary. "Irish Immigrant Families in Mid-Late Nineteenth Century America." *Yale-New Haven Teachers Institute*. Yale-New Haven Teachers Inst., 1990. Web. 8 Apr. 2014.

Barbuto, Domenica M. *American Settlement Houses and Progressive Social Reform: An Encyclopedia of the American Settlement Movement*. Westport: Greenwood, 1999. Print.

Barkhorn, Eleanor. "'Vote No on Women's Suffrage': Bizarre Reasons for Not Letting Women Vote." *Atlantic*. Atlantic Monthly Group, 6 Nov. 2012. Web. 23 Apr. 2014.

Barrett, James R. *Work and Community in the Jungle: Chicago's Packinghouse Workers, 1894–1922*. Champaign: U of Illinois P, 1990. Print.

Barry, Kathleen. *Susan B. Anthony: A Biography of a Singular Feminist*. New York: NYUP, 1988. Print.

Bausum, Ann. *With Courage and Cloth: Winning the Fight for a Woman's Right to Vote*. Washington, DC: Natl. Geographic, 2004. Print.

Bechtel, Ali. "Building Is Tribute to Prominent Berks Attorney Who Once Battled Clarence Darrow." *Berks Barrister* (Spring 2013): 10–13. Web. 17 Feb. 2014.

Bell, Daniel. *Marxian Socialism in the United States*. Rev. ed. Ithaca: Cornell UP, 1995. Print.

Benjamin, Anne M. G. *A History of the Anti-Suffrage Movement in the United States from 1895 to 1920: Women against Equality*. Lewiston: Mellen, 1991. Print.

Benjamin, Thomas. *La Revolucion: Mexico's Great Revolution as Memory, Myth & History*. Austin: University of Texas Press, 2000.

Benson, W. Todd. *President Theodore Roosevelt's Conservation Legacy*. West Conshohocken: Infinity, 2003. Print.

Blackburn, Marc "Pancho Villa, General Pershing and the U.S. Army Truck." *The Ultimate History Project*. 2014. Web. 22 May 2014.

Blatz, Perry K. *Democratic Miners: Work and Labor Relations in the Anthracite Coal Industry, 1875–1925*. Albany: State U of New York P, 1994. Print.

Bordin, Ruth. *Frances Willard: A Biography*. Chapel Hill: U of North Carolina P, 1986. Print.

Brinkley, Douglas. *The Wilderness Warrior: Theodore Roosevelt and the Crusade for America*. New York: HarperCollins, 2009. Print.

Brody, David. *Steelworkers in America: The Nonunion Era*. New York: Harper, 1969, Print.

Burgan, Michael. *The Pullman Strike of 1894*. North Mankato: Compass Point, 2007. Print.

Burgess, Larry E. *The Lake Mohonk Conference of the Friends of the Indian: Guide to the Annual Reports*. New York: Clearwater, 1975. Print.

Burgoyne, Arthur G. *The Homestead Strike of 1892*. Pittsburgh: U of Pittsburgh P, 1979. Print.

Burgoyne, Arthur G. *The Homestead Strike of 1892*. Pittsburgh: U of Pittsburgh P, 1979. Print.

Calhoun, Charles W., ed. The Gilded Age: Essays on the Origins of Modern America, 2d ed. Lanham, MD: Rowman & Littlefield, 2006.

Calvert, Karin. "Children in the House: 1890 to 1930." *American Home Life, 1880–1930: A Social History of Spaces and Services*. Ed. Jessica H. Foy and Thomas J. Schlereth. Knoxville: U of Tennessee P, 1997. 75–93. Print.

Campbell, James, ed. *Selected Writings of James Hayden Tufts*. Carbondale: Southern Illinois UP, 1992. Print.

Cashman, Sean Dennis. America in the Gilded Age: From the Death of Lincoln to the Rise of Theodore

Roosevelt. New York: Oxford University Press, 1993.

"Childhood Lost: Child Labor during the Industrial Revolution." *Eastern Illinois University*. Eastern Illinois University, n.d. Web. 16 Apr. 2014.

"Childhood Lost: Child Labor during the Industrial Revolution." *Teaching with Primary Sources*. Eastern Illinois University, n.d. Web. 10 Apr. 2014.

Cholmeley, Robert Francis. *The Women's Anti-Suffrage Movement*. London: Natl. Union of Women's Suffrage Soc., 1908. Print.

Churchill, Bernardita Reyes. "The Philippine-American War (1899–1902)." *NCCA*. Philippines National Commission for Culture and the Arts, 2011. Web. 18 Apr. 2014.

Connelly, Scott. "The Greatest Strike Ever." *Pennsylvania Center for the Book*. Pennsylvania State U, Spring 2010. Web. 17 Feb. 2014.

Cornell, Robert J. *The Anthracite Coal Strike of 1902*. Washington: Catholic U of Amer., 1957. Print.

Crawford, Elizabeth. *The Women's Suffrage Movement: A Reference Guide, 1866–1928*. London: Routledge, 2001. Print.

Cronon, William. "Turner's First Stand: The Significance of Significance in American History." *Writing Western History: Essays on Major Western Historians*. Ed. R. W. Etulain. Albuquerque: U of New Mexico P, 1991. 73–101. Print.

Crouch, Tom D. *The Bishop's Boys: A Life of Wilbur and Orville Wright*. New York: Norton, 1989. Print.

Curtis, Bruce. *William Graham Sumner*. Boston: Twayne, 1981. Print.

Dalton, Kathleen. *Theodore Roosevelt: A Strenuous Life*. New York: Random, 2007. Print.

David, Henry. *The History of the Haymarket Affair: A Study in the American Social-Revolutionary and Labor Movements*. New York: Russell, 1958. Print.

Dawley, Alan. Struggles for Justice: Social Responsibility and the Liberal State. Cambridge, MA: Belknap Press, 1993.

Dean, Edward Ayers, and Hugh P. Kelley. *The Promise of the New South: Life after Reconstruction*. Oxford: Oxford UP, 2007. Print.

Demarest, David. *"The River Ran Red": Homestead 1892*. Pittsburgh: U of Pittsburgh P, 1992. Print.

Dewey, John, and John J. McDermott. *The Philosophy of John Dewey*. New York: Putnam, 1981. Print.

Diner, Steven J. A Very Different Age: Americans of the Progressive Era. New York: Hill & Wang, 1998.

Dolan, Edward F. *The Spanish-American War*. Minneapolis: Twenty-First Century, 2001. Print.

Dorsey, Leroy G. "Managing Women's Equality: Theodore Roosevelt, the Frontier Myth, and the Modern Woman." *Rhetoric and Public Affairs* 16.3 (2013): 423–56. Print.

Dublin, Thomas, and Walter Light. *The Face of Decline: The Pennsylvania Anthracite Region in the Twentieth Century*. Ithaca: Cornell UP, 2005. Print.

Edwards, Rebecca. "Mary E. Lease." 1896: *The Presidential Campaign*. Vassar College, 2000. Web. 24 Apr. 2014.

Edwards, Rebecca. "The Populist Party." 1896: *The Presidential Campaign*. Vassar College, 2000. Web. 24 Apr. 2014.

Eisenhower, John S.D. *Intervention: the United States and the Mexican Revolution, 1913–1917*. New York: W.W. Norton, 1993.

Feffer, Andrew. *The Chicago Pragmatists and American Progressivism*. Ithaca: Cornell UP, 1993. Print.

Fishkin, Shelly Fisher. *A Historical Guide to Mark Twain*. New York: Oxford UP, 2002. Print.

Fletcher, Holly Berkley. *Gender and the American Temperance Movement of the Nineteenth Century*. London: Routledge, 2008. Print.

Fradin, Dennis Brindell, and Judith Bloom Fradin. *Fight On! Mary Church Terrell's Battle for Integration*. New York: Clarion, 2005. Print.

"Frances Elizabeth Caroline Willard (1839–1898)." *National Women's History Museum*. National Women's History Museum, n.d. Web. 25 Feb. 2014.

Franzen, Trisha. Anna Howard Shaw: *The Work of Woman Suffrage*. Champaign: U of Illinois P, 2014. Print.

Freeman, Jo. *A Room at a Time: How Women Entered Party Politics*. Lanham: Rowman, 2002. Print.

Friedman, Michael, and Brett Friedman. *Settlement Houses: Improving the Social Welfare of America's Immigrants*. London: Rosen, 2006. Print.

Frost-Knappman, Elizabeth, and Kathryn Cullen-DuPont. *Women's Suffrage in America: An Eyewitness History*. New York: Facts on File, 1992. Print.

Gable, John. Interview. *PBS.org*. WGBH Educational Foundation, 2013. Web. 8 Apr. 2014.

Garcia, Mario T. Desert *Immigrants: The Mexicans of El Paso, 1880–1920*. New Haven: Yale UP, 1981. Print.

Gentzinger, Donna. *The Triangle Shirtwaist Factory Fire*. Greensboro: Reynolds, 2008. Print.

Gibson, Arrell M. Oklahoma: *A History of Five Centuries*. 2nd ed. Norman: U of Oklahoma P, 2010. Print.

Gifford, Carolyn De Swarte, and Amy R. Slagell, eds. *Let Something Good Be Said: Speeches and Writings of Frances E. Willard*. Urbana: U of Illinois P, 2007. Print.

Gifford, Carolyn De Swarte, ed. *Writing Out My Heart: Selections from the Journal of Frances E. Willard, 1855–96*. Urbana: U of Illinois P, 1995. Print.

Ginger, Ray. *The Bending Cross: A Biography of Eugene Victor Debs*. Chicago: Haymarket, 2007 Print.

Goldstone, Lawrence. *Birdmen: The Wright Brothers, Glenn Curtiss, and the Battle to Control the Skies*. New York: Ballantine, 2014. Digital file.

Goodier, Susan. *No Votes for Women: The New York State Anti-Suffrage Movement*. Urbana: U of Illinois P, 2013. Print.

Goodwyn, Lawrence. *Democratic Promise: The Populist Moment in America*. New York: Oxford UP, 1976. Print.

Goodwyn, Lawrence. The Populist Moment: *A Short History of the Agrarian Revolt in America*. New York: Oxford UP, 1978. Print.

Gordon, Ann D., ed. *The Selected Papers of Elizabeth Cady Stanton and Susan B. Anthony*. 6 Vols. New Brunswick: Rutgers UP, 1997–2013. Print.

Graham, Amy. *A Look at the Eighteenth and Twenty-First Amendments: The Prohibition and Sale of Intoxicating Liquors*. Berkeley Heights: Enslow, 2007. Print.

Graham, George Edward. *Schley and Santiago*. Ann Arbor: U of Michigan, 1902. Print.

Green, Dan S., and Edwin D. Driver, eds. *W. E. B. Du Bois on Sociology and the Black Community*. Chicago: U of Chicago P, 1978. Print.

Green, James. *Death in the Haymarket: A Story of Chicago, the First Labor Movement and the Bombing that Divided Gilded Age America*. New York: Pantheon, 2006. Print.

Gressley, Gene M. "The Turner Thesis: A Problem in Historiography." *Agricultural History* 32.4 (1958): 227–49. Print.

Grier, Katherine C. *Culture and Comfort: Parlor Making and Middle-Class Identity, 1850–1930*. Washington: Smithsonian Inst. P, 1997. Print.

Grossman, Jonathan. "The Coal Strike of 1902—Turning Point in U.S. Policy." *U.S. Dept. of Labor*. U.S. Dept. of Labor, n.d. Web. 15 Apr. 2014.

Gusfield, Joseph R. *Symbolic Crusade: Status Politics and the American Temperance Movement*. Champaign: U of Illinois P, 1986. Print.

Gyory, Andrew. *Closing the Gate: Race, Politics, and the Chinese Exclusion Act*. Chapel Hill: U of North Carolina P, 1998. Print.

Halpern, Rick. *Down on the Killing Floor: Black and White Workers in Chicago's Packinghouses, 1904–1954*. Urbana: U of Illinois P, 1997. Print.

Halstead, Murat. *The Story of the Philippines and Our New Possessions: Including the Ladrones, Hawaii, Cuba and Porto Rico the Eldorado of the Orient*. 1898. Alexandria: Library of Alexandria, 2006. Print.

"Hawaii's Last Queen: The Program." *American Experience*. PBS Online, n.d. Web. 28 Apr. 2014.

"Hawaii's Last Queen: Timeline." *American Experience*. PBS Online, n.d. Web. 28 Apr. 2014.

Hays, Samuel P. *The American People and the National Forests*. Pittsburgh: U of Pittsburgh P, 2009. Print.

Hays, Samuel P. *The Response to Industrialism: 1885–1914*. 2nd ed. Chicago: U of Chicago P, 1995. Print.

Hendrickson, Kenneth E. *The Spanish-American War*. Westport: Greenwood, 2003. Print.

Hernandez, Roger E. *The Spanish-American War*. New York: Marshall Cavendish, 2009. Print.

Herring, George C. *From Colony to Superpower: U.S. Foreign Relations since 1776*. New York: Oxford UP, 2008. Print.

Hindman, Hugh D. *Child Labor: An American History*. Armonk: Sharpe, 2002. Print.

Hoffer, William James Hull. Plessy v. Ferguson: *Race and Inequality in Jim Crow America*. Lawrence: UP of Kansas, 2012. Print.

Hofstadter, Richard. *Social Darwinism in American Thought*. Boston: Beacon, 1992. Print.

Hofstadter, Richard. *The Age of Reform: From Bryan to F.D.R.* New York: Vintage, 1955. Print.

Hogarty, Richard A. *Massachusetts Political and Public Policy: Studies in Power and Leadership*. Amherst: U of Massachusetts P, 2002. Print.

Hoig, Stan. *The Oklahoma Land Rush of 1889*. Oklahoma City: Oklahoma Hist. Soc., 1989. Print.

Holland, Antonio Frederick. Nathan B. *Young and the Struggle over Black Higher Education*. Columbia: U of Missouri P, 2006. Print.

Holland, Jesse J. *Black Men Built the Capitol: Discovering African-American History in and around Washington*. Guilford: Globe Pequot, 2007. Print.

Howarth, Stephen. *To Shining Sea: A History of the United States Navy, 1775–1998*. Norman: U of Oklahoma P, 1999. Print.

Hull, N. E. H. *The Woman Who Dared to Vote*. Lawrence: U of Kansas P, 2012. Digital file.

Hurst, James W. *Pancho Villa and Black Jack Pershing: the Punitive Expedition in Mexico*. Westport CT: Praeger, 2008.

Ignacio, Abe, et al. *The Forbidden Book: The Philippine-American War in Cartoons*. San Francisco: T'Boli, 2004. Print.

"Jane Addams—Biographical." *NobelPrize.org*. Nobel Media, 2014. Web. 28 Feb. 2014.

"John Sherman's Life and Career (1823–1900)." *Shermanhouse.org*. John Sherman House, n.d. PDF file.

Jones, Gavin. "'Whose Line Is It Anyway?' W. E. B. Du Bois and the Language of the Color-Line." *Race Consciousness: African-American Studies for the New Century*. Eds. Judith Jackson Fossett and Jeffrey A. Tucker. New York: NYUP, 1997. 19–34. Print.

Josephson, Matthew. *The Robber Barons: The Great American Capitalists, 1861–1901*. New Brunswick: Transaction, 2011. Print.

Joslin, Katherine. *Jane Addams: A Writer's Life*. Champaign: U of Illinois P, 2004. Print.

Judd, Richard William. *Common Lands, Common People: The Origins of Conservation in Northern New England*. Cambridge: Harvard UP, 1997. Print.

Kahan, Paul. *The Homestead Strike: Labor, Violence, and American Industry*. New York: Routledge, 2014. Print.

Kahan, Paul. *The Homestead Strike: Labor, Violence, and American Industry*. New York: Routledge, 2014. Print.

Katzman, David M., and William M. Tuttle, Jr. *Plain Folk: The Life Stories of Undistinguished Americans*. Champaign: U of Illinois P, 1982. Print.

Kazin, Michael. *The Populist Persuasion: An American History*. Rev. ed. Ithaca: Cornell UP, 1998. Print.

Kazin, Michael. The Populist Persuasion: An American History, rev. ed. Ithaca, NY: Cornell UP, 1998.

Kelly, Blair L. M. *Right to Ride: Streetcar Boycotts and African American Citizenship in the Era of Plessy v. Ferguson*. Chapel Hill: U of North Carolina P, 2010. Print.

Kloppenberg, James T. *Uncertain Victory: Social Democracy and Progressivism in European and American Thought, 1870–1920*. New York: Oxford UP, 1988. Print.

Krause, Paul. *The Battle for Homestead, 1880–1892: Politics, Culture, and Steel*. Pittsburgh: U of Pittsburgh P, 1992. Print.

Lagemann, Ellen Condliff. *The Politics of Knowledge: The Carnegie Corporation, Philanthropy, and Public Policy*. Chicago: U of Chicago P, 1989. Print.

Lambert, Frank. *The Battle of Ole Miss: Civil Rights v. States Rights*. Oxford: Oxford UP, 2009. Print.

Lee, Erika. *At America's Gates: Chinese Immigration During the Exclusion Era, 1882–1943*. Chapel Hill: U of North Carolina P, 2007. Print.

Lewis, David Levering. *W. E. B. Du Bois, 1868–1919: Biography of a Race*. New York: Holt, 1993. Print.

Lewis, David Levering. *W. E. B. Du Bois, 1868–1919: Biography of a Race*. New York: Holt, 1993. Print.

Lightman, David. "Racial Barriers Fell Slowly in Capital." *Journal Sentinel* [Milwaukee]. Journal Sentinel, 16 Jan. 2009. Web. 28 Apr. 2014.

Limerick, Patricia Nelson, Clyde A. Milner II, and Charles E. Rankin, eds. *Trails: Toward a New Western History*. Lawrence: UP of Kansas, 1991. Print.

Lindermuth, John R. *Digging Dusky Diamonds: A History of the Pennsylvania Coal Region*. Mechanicsburg: Sunbury, 2013. Print.

Lindsey, Almont. *The Pullman Strike: The Story of a Unique Experiment and of a Great Labor Upheaval*. Chicago: U of Chicago P, 1964. Print.

Link, William A., and Susannah J. Link. *The Gilded Age and Progressive Era: A Documentary Reader*. Malden: Wiley, 2012. Print.

Linn, James Weber. *Jane Addams: A Biography*. Champaign: U of Illinois P, 1935. Print.

Linn, James Weber. *Jane Addams: A Biography*. Champaign: U of Illinois P, 1935. Print.

Lipset, Seymour Martin, and Gary Marks. *It Didn't Happen Here: Why Socialism Failed in the United States*. New York: Norton, 2000. Print.

Lorey, David E. *The U.S.–Mexican Border in the Twentieth Century: A History of Economic and Social Transformation*. Lanham: Rowman, 1999. Print.

Lubove, Roy. *The Progressives and the Slums: Tenement House Reform in New York City, 1890–1917*. Pittsburgh: U of Pittsburgh P, 1963. Print.

Lubove, Roy. *The Progressives and the Slums: Tenement House Reform in New York City, 1890–1917*. Pittsburgh: U of Pittsburgh P, 1963. Print.

MacKay, James. *Andrew Carnegie: Little Boss*. New York: Random, 2012. Print.

Markel, Howard. *Quarantine! East European Jewish Immigrants and the New York City Epidemics of 1892*. Baltimore: Johns Hopkins UP, 1999. Print.

Markel, Howard. *Quarantine! East European Jewish Immigrants and the New York City Epidemics of 1892*. Baltimore: Johns Hopkins UP, 1999. Print.

"Mary van Kleeck Papers, 1849–1998: Biographical Note." *Sophia Smith Collection*. Smith College, n.d. Web. 10 Apr. 2014.

"Massachusetts Governor William Eustis Russell." *Former Governors' Bios*. National Governors Assoc., 2014. Web. 25 Apr. 2014.

McCloskey, Robert Green. *American Conservatism in the Age of Enterprise 1865–1910: A Study of William Graham Sumner, Stephen J. Field, and Andrew Carnegie*. New York: Harper, 1964. Print.

McDonough, Jack. *The Fire Down Below: The Great Anthracite Strike of 1902 and the People Who Made the Decisions*. Scranton: Avocado, 2002. Print.

McGerr, Michael. A Fierce Discontent: The Rise and Fall of the Progressive Movement in America, 1870-1920. New York: NYU Press, 2005.

McMath, Robert C. American Populism: A Social History, 1877-1898. New York: Hill & Wang, 1993.

McPherson, James M. *The Abolitionist Legacy: From Reconstruction to the NAACP*. Princeton: Princeton UP, 1975. Print.

Medley, Keith. *We as Freemen:* Plessy v. Ferguson. Gretna: Pelican, 2012. Print.

Menand, Louis. *Pragmatism: A Reader*. New York: Vintage, 1997. Print.

Merry, Sally Engle. *Colonizing Hawaii: The Cultural Power of Law*. Princeton: Princeton UP, 2000. Print.

Mills, Charles. *The Chinese Exclusion Act and American Labor*. Alexandria: Apple Cheeks, 2009. Print.

Mintz, Steven, ed. *Mexican American Voices: A Documentary Reader*. Malden: Wiley, 2009. Print.

Morgan, Howard Wayne. *William McKinley and His America*. Rev. ed. Kent: Kent State UP, 2003. Print.

Morris, Edmund. *Theodore Rex*. New York: Random, 2001. Print.

Morris, Edmund. *Theodore Rex*. New York: Random, 2002. Print.

Muhammad, Khalil Gibran. *The Condemnation of Blackness: Race, Crime, and the Making of Modern Urban America*. Cambridge: Harvard UP, 2010. Print.

Nardinelli, Clark. *Child Labor and the Industrial Revolution*. Bloomington: Indiana UP, 1990. Print.

Nasaw, David. *Andrew Carnegie*. New York: Penguin, 2007. Print.

Nasaw, David. *Andrew Carnegie*. New York: Penguin, 2007. Print.

New York (State) Factory Investigating Commission. *Preliminary Report of the Factory Investigating Commission*. 3 vols. Albany: Argus, 1912. Print.

Nugent, Walter. *The Tolerant Populists: Kansas Populism and Nativism*. 2d ed. Chicago: The U of Chicago P, 2013. Print.

Okker, Patricia. *Our Sister Editors: Sarah J. Hale and the Tradition of Nineteenth-Century American Women Editors*. Athens: U of Georgia P, 1995. Print.

Okrent, Daniel. *Last Call: The Rise and Fall of Prohibition*. New York: Scribner, 2011. Print.

Outlaw, Lucius T. "W. E. B. Du Bois on the Study of Social Problems." *Annals of the American Academy of Political and Social Science* 568.1 (2000): 281–97. Print.

Pafford, John M. *The Forgotten Conservative: Rediscovering Grover Cleveland*. Washington: Regenery History, 2013. Print.

Painter, Nell Irvin. *Standing at Armageddon: A Grassroots History of the Progressive Era*. New York: Norton, 1987. Print.

Painter, Nell Irvin. Standing at Armageddon: A Grassroots History of the Progressive Era. New York: W.W. Norton, 2013.

"Panic of 1893." *The Life and Times of Florence Kelley in Chicago 1891–1899*. Northwestern Univ. School of Law, 2008. Web. 25 Apr. 2014.

Papke, David Ray. *The Pullman Case: The Clash of Labor and Capital in Industrial America*. Lawrence: UP of Kansas, 1999. Print.

Parker, James. *Rear-Admirals Schley, Sampson and Cervera: A Review of the Naval Campaign of 1898*. New York: Neale, 1910. Print.

Peters, Gerhard. "Seventh Annual Message." *American Presidency Project*. U of California Santa Barbara, 2014. Web. 28 Feb. 2014.

Peterson, Tarla Rai. *Green Talk in the White House: The Rhetorical Presidency Encounters Ecology*. College Station: Texas A&M UP, 2004. Print.

Phipps, William E. *Mark Twain's Religion*. Macon: Mercer UP, 2003. Print.

Prucha, Francis Paul. The Great Father: *The United States Government and the American Indian*. 2 vols. Lincoln: U of Nebraska P, 1984.

Prucha, Francis Paul. *The Great Father: The United States Government and the American Indians*. 2 vols. Lincoln: U of Nebraska P, 1984. Print.

"Public Opinion: Part of Life in the Cumberland Valley." *Public Opinion*. Chambersburg Public Opinion, 2014. Web. 15 Apr. 2014.

Reed, Lawrence W. *A Lesson from the Past: The Silver*

Panic of 1893. Irvington: Foundation for Economic Educ., 1993. Print.

Reed, Lawrence W. *A Lesson from the Past: The Silver Panic of 1893.* Irvington: Foundation for Economic Education, 1993. Print.

Ricard, Serge. *A Companion to Theodore Roosevelt.* Hoboken: Wiley, 2011. Print.

Roach, Edward J. *The Wright Company: From Invention to Industry.* Athens: Ohio UP, 2014. Digital file.

Rodgers, Daniel T. Atlantic Crossings: Social Politics in a Progressive Era. Cambridge, MA: Harvard UP, 1998.

Rosenberg, Chaim M. *Child Labor in America: A History.* Jefferson: McFarland, 2013. Print.

Rushing, Kittrell. "The Case of the Haymarket Riot (1886)." *The Press on Trial: Crimes and Trials as Media Events.* Ed. Lloyd Chiasson. Westport: Greenwood, 1997. Print.

Ruthsdotter, Mary. "Years of Hope, Years of Struggle." *University of Maryland—Maryland Institute for Technology in the Humanities.* Natl. Women's Hist. Project, 2014. Web. 23 Apr. 2014.

Salvatore, Nick. *Eugene V. Debs: Citizen and Socialist.* 2nd ed. Urbana: U of Illinois P, 2007. Print.

Sansing, David. "James Kimble Vardaman: Thirty-Sixth Governor of Mississippi: 1904–1908." *Mississippi History Now.* Mississippi Historical Society, Jan. 2004. Web. 16 Apr. 2014.

Satter, Beryl. *Each Mind a Kingdom: American Women, Sexual Purity, and the New Thought Movement, 1875–1920.* Berkeley: U of California P, 2001. Print.

Schlereth, Thomas J. *Victorian America: Transformation in Everyday Life, 1876–1915.* New York: Harper, 1991. Print.

Schneirov, Richard, Shelton Stromquist, and Nick Salvatore, eds. *The Pullman Strike and the Crisis of the 1890s: Essays on Labor and Politics.* Champaign: U of Illinois P, 1999. Print.

Seymour, Richard. *American Insurgents: A Brief History of American Anti-Imperialism.* Chicago: Haymarket, 2012. Print.

Shaw, Anna Howard. *The Story of a Pioneer.* Teddington: Echo Lib., 2006. Print.

"Sherman, John, (1823–1900)." *Biographical Directory of the United States Congress.* Office of the Hist., n.d. Web. 24 Apr. 2014.

Sherr, Lynn. *Failure Is Impossible: Susan B. Anthony in Her Own Words.* New York: Times Books, 1995. Print.

Sibley, David J. *A War of Frontier and Empire: The Philippine-American War, 1899–1902.* New York: Hill, 2007. Print.

Skrabec, Quentin R., Jr. *Henry Clay Frick: The Life of the Perfect Capitalist.* Jefferson: McFarland, 2010. Print.

Slavicek, Louis Chipley. **The Prohibition Era: Temperance in the United States.** New York: Chelsea, 2008. Print.

Smith, Carl. *The Dramas of Haymarket.* Chicago Historical Soc. and Northwestern U. Web. 28 Mar. 2014.

Smith-Rosenberg, Carroll. *Disorderly Conduct: Visions of Gender in Victorian America.* New York: Knopf, 1985. Print.

Soennichsen, John. *The Chinese Exclusion Act of 1882.* Westport: Greenwood, 2011. Print.

Standiford, Les. *Meet You in Hell: Andrew Carnegie, Henry Clay Frick, and the Bitter Partnership that Changed America.* New York: Broadway, 2006. Print.

Stanton, Elizabeth Cady, and Susan Brownell Anthony. *The Elizabeth Cady Stanton–Susan B. Anthony Reader: Correspondence, Writings, Speeches.* Ed. Ellen Carol DuBois. Boston: Northeastern UP, 1992. Print.

Steeples, Douglas, and David O. Whitten. *Democracy in Desperation: The Depression of 1893.* Westport: Greenwood, 1998. Print.

Steeples, Douglas W., and David O. Whitten. *Democracy in Desperation: The Depression of 1893.* Westport: Praeger, 1998. Print.

Stein, Leon. *The Triangle Fire.* Centennial ed. Ithaca: Cornell UP, 2011. Print.

Stock, Catherine McNicol. *Rural Radicals: Righteous Rage in the American Grain.* Ithaca: Cornell UP, 1996. Print.

Stromquist, Shelton, and Marvin Bergman. *Unionizing the Jungles: Labor and Community in the Twentieth-Century Meatpacking Industry.* Iowa City: U of Iowa P, 1997. Print.

Sumner, William Graham. *On Liberty, Society and Politics: The Essential Essays of William Graham Sumner.* Ed. Robert C. Bannister. Indianapolis: Liberty Fund, 1992. Print.

Synnestvedt, Sig. *The White Response to Black Emancipation.* New York: Macmillan, 1972. Print.

Szymanski, Ann-Marie E. *Pathways to Prohibition: Radicals, Moderates, and Social Movement Outcomes.* Durham: Duke UP, 2003. Print.

"The New York Factory Investigating Commission."

United States Department of Labor, 2014. Web. 28 Feb. 2014.

"Theodore Roosevelt and the Environment." *PBS.* WGBH Educational Foundation, n.d. Web. 22 Apr. 2014.

_____. *The Trial of Susan B. Anthony.* Washington, DC: Federal Judicial Center, 2005. Digital file.

Thomas, Brook, and Waldo E. Martin. *Brown v. Board and Plessy v. Ferguson: A Brief History with Documents.* New York: Bedford, 1999. Print.

Tian, Kelly. "The Chinese Exclusion Act of 1882 and Its Impact on North American Society." *Undergraduate Research Journal for the Human Sciences* 9 (2010): n. pag. Web. 16 Jan. 2014.

Timberlake, James H. *Prohibition and the Progressive Movement, 1900–1920.* Cambridge: Harvard UP, 1966. Print.

Trachtenberg, Alan. The Incorporation of America: Culture and Society in the Gilded Age, 25th Anniversary ed. New York: Hill & Wang, 2007.

Turner, Frederick Jackson. *The Frontier in American History.* Rev. ed. Tucson: U of Arizona P, 1994. Print

Twain, Mark. *Following the Equator and Anti-Imperialist Essays.* Ed. Shelley Fisher Fishkin. Vol. 20. New York: Oxford UP, 1996. Print.

Twain, Mark. *Mark Twain's Weapons of Satire: Anti-Imperialist Writings on the Philippine-American War.* Ed. Jim Zwick. Syracuse: Syracuse UP, 1992. Print.

United States Anthracite Coal Strike Commission. *Report to the President on the Anthracite Coal Strike of May–October, 1902.* Washington: GPO, 1903. Print.

U.S. Department of State. "Punitive Expedition in Mexico, 1916–1917." U.S. Department of State Archive. 2001–2009. Web. 22 May 2014.

US National Conservation Commission. *Proceedings of the Joint Conservation Conference, Washington, DC, Dec. 8, 9, 10, 1908.* Washington: GPO, 1909. Print.

Von Drehle, David. *Triangle: The Fire That Changed America.* New York: Grove, 2004. Print.

Warren, Wilson J. *Tied to the Great Packing Machine: The Midwest and Meatpacking.* Iowa City: U of Iowa P, 2007. Print.

Weber, David J., ed. *Foreigners in Their Native Land: Historical Roots of the Mexican Americans.* Albuquerque: U of New Mexico P, 2003. Print.

Welch, Richard E., Jr. *George Frisbie Hoar and the Half-Breed Republicans.* Cambridge: Harvard UP, 1971. Print.

Welch, Richard E., Jr. *Response to Imperialism: The United States and the Philippine-American War, 1899–1902.* Chapel Hill: U of North Carolina P, 1979. Print.

_____. "'We'll Discuss It at Mohonk.'" *Quaker History* 40 (1971): 14–28. Print.

Wellock, Thomas R. *Preserving the Nation: The Conservation and Environmental Movements, 1870–2000.* Marblehead: Wiley, 2007. Print.

Wells, Merle W. *Gold Camps and Silver Cities.* Moscow: U of Idaho P, 2002. Print.

Wenger, Beth S. *The Jewish Americans: Three Centuries of Jewish Voices in America.* New York: Random, 2007. Print.

White, Anna R. *Youth's Educator for Home and Society.* Chicago: Monarch, 1896. Print.

Willard Frances E. *How I Learned to Ride the Bicycle: Reflections of an Influential 19th Century Woman.* Sunnyvale: Fair Oaks, 1991. Print.

Willard, Frances E. *Let Something Good Be Said: Speeches and Writings of Frances E. Willard.* Champaign: U of Illinois P, 2007. Print.

"William Eustis Russell." *Mass.gov.* Commonwealth of Massachusetts, 2014. Web. 25 Apr. 2014.

_____. Wings: *A History of Aviation from Kites to the Space Age.* New York: Norton, 2003. Print.

Woestman, Kelly A. "Mary Elizabeth Lease: Populist Reformer." *Gilder Lehrman Institute of American History*: History by Era. Gilder Lehrman Institute of American History, 2014. Web. 12 Apr. 2014.

Woodward, C. Vann. *The Strange Career of Jim Crow.* New York: Oxford UP, 1955. Print.

Wright, Orville. *How We Invented the Airplane: An Illustrated History.* New York: McKay, 1953. Print.

Zamir, Shamoon. Dark Voices: *W. E. B. Du Bois and American Thought, 1888–1903.* Chicago: U of Chicago P, 1995. Print.

Zehr, Martin. "The Psychologies of Mark Twain." *Monitor on Psychology* 41.4 (2010): 28. Print.

Zinn, Howard. *A People's History of the United States: 1492 to Present.* New York: Harper, 2005. Print.

Zinn, Howard. *A People's History of the United States: 1492 to Present.* New York: Harper, 2005. Print.

Zolberg, Aristide R. *A Nation by Design: Immigration Policy in the Fashioning of America.* Cambridge: Harvard UP, 2009. Print.

Index